WRITING THE FRONTIER

Writing the Frontier

*Anthony Trollope between
Britain and Ireland*

JOHN McCOURT

OXFORD
UNIVERSITY PRESS

OXFORD

UNIVERSITY PRESS

Great Clarendon Street, Oxford, OX2 6DP,
United Kingdom

Oxford University Press is a department of the University of Oxford.
It furthers the University's objective of excellence in research, scholarship,
and education by publishing worldwide. Oxford is a registered trade mark of
Oxford University Press in the UK and in certain other countries

Published in the United States of America by Oxford University Press
198 Madison Avenue, New York, NY 10016, United States of America

British Library Cataloguing in Publication Data
Data available

Library of Congress Control Number: 2014954509

ISBN 978–0–19–872960–0

Printed and bound by
CPI Group (UK) Ltd, Croydon, CR0 4YY

Links to third party websites are provided by Oxford in good faith and
for information only. Oxford disclaims any responsibility for the materials
contained in any third party website referenced in this work.

To Liam and Eoin

Acknowledgements

I would like to thank the following people for reading and helpfully commenting on various sections of this work: Elizabeth Bonapfel, Elisabetta d'Erme, Maria Kager, John Lonergan, Katherine Mullin, Francis O'Gorman, Cormac Ó Gráda, and Laura Pelaschiar. I would like to acknowledge the support of the Dipartimento di Letterature Comparate and later the Dipartimento di Lingue, Letterature e Culture Straniere at the Università Roma Tre, and particularly of Franca Ruggieri. Early versions of some of the material in this volume have already appeared in *Études Irlandaises*, *Quaderno di Dipartimento di Letterature comparate*, *Rivista di Studi Vittoriani*, and *Variants—The Journal of the European Society for Textual Scholarship*. I am grateful to Priscilla Hungerford and the Trollope Society for the invitation to give the twentieth Annual Trollope Society Lecture at the Liberal Club in London in 2007 (later published in *Trollopiana, the Journal of the Trollope Society*). Invitations from Nicholas Allen and Ondřej Pilný to lecture on Trollope at the Moore Institute, NUI Galway (2010) and at the Centre for Irish Studies at the Charles University in Prague (2012) offered helpful moments of focus and reflection. I would like to express my deep gratitude to Jean-Michel Rabaté (and James English) for the opportunity to spend a term teaching at the English Department at the University of Pennsylvania at an early stage in this project. My time spent there, teaching the Irish nineteenth-century novel to graduate students and doing research at the Van Pelt library was very important for the genesis of this book. I am also grateful for the useful time spent at the National Library of Ireland, the Harry Ransom Center at the University of Texas at Austin (thanks to a Mellon Fellowship), and at the Firestone Library, Princeton University. Gratitude also to both SilviaDe Rosa and Elizabeth Bonapfel for occasional but vital assistance in tracking down obscure articles and references at key moments.

At Oxford University Press I wish to thank Jacqueline Baker for her continuous support and encouragement. I am also grateful to Rachel Platt, Megan Wakely, Lucy McClune, and Emma Turner, all of OUP, for their expertise and help. Many thanks to Shwetha Panduranganath, Penelope Isaac, and Nathan Fisher for their important work during the production phase of this book. Important encouragement came from Roy Foster at various moments, and in particular from Laura Marcus, a consistent supporter of this project. Finally, a word of thanks to Laura, Liam, and Eoin, for putting up with my ten-year absorption in this project and the absences it necessitated.

Contents

Abbreviations for Trollope editions used in this text (these editions are not re-listed in the bibliography)

Trollope works

Auto	*An Autobiography*, 1883. Oxford: Oxford University Press, 1999.
Bertrams	*The Bertrams*, 1859. London: Chapman & Hall, 1859.
BJR	*The Struggles of Brown, Jones and Robinson*, 1862. London Penguin, 1993.
BT	*Barchester Towers*, 1857. London: Penguin, 1994.
Clarissa	'Clarissa', *Saint Pauls Magazine*, November 1868, 163–72.
CR	*Castle Richmond*, 1859. Oxford: Oxford University Press, 1989.
CSF	Julian Thompson, ed. *The Complete Shorter Fiction*. New York: Carroll & Graf Publishers, 1992.
CYFH	*Can You Forgive Her?*, 1864. Oxford: Oxford University Press, 1999.
Duke's Children	*The Duke's Children*, 1880. Oxford: Oxford University Press, 2011.
Eustace Diamonds	*The Eustace Diamonds*, 1873. London: Penguin, 1986.
Examiner	Helen Garlinghouse King, ed. 'Trollope's Letters to the *Examiner*', *The Princeton University Library Chronicle*, 26/2 (Winter 1965), 71–101.
EYE	*An Eye for An Eye*, 1879. London: The Folio Society, 1993.
Harry Heathcote	*Harry Heathcote of Gangoil*, 1874. Oxford: Oxford University Press, 2005.
Irish Church	'The Irish Church'. *Fortnightly Review*, 15 August 1865, reprinted in Michael Y. Mason, intro., *Anthony Trollope, Miscellaneous Essays and Reviews*. New York: Arno Press, 1981, 82–90.
Kellys	*The Kellys and the O'Kellys*, 1848. London: The Folio Society, 1992.
Last Chronicle	*The Last Chronicle of Barset*, 1867. London: Penguin, 2002.
Letters I	N. John Hall, ed. *The Letters of Anthony Trollope, 1871–1882*, vol. I. Stanford: Stanford University Press, 1983.

Letters II	N. John Hall, ed. *The Letters of Anthony Trollope, 1871–1882*, vol. II. Stanford: Stanford University Press, 1983.
LL	*The Landleaguers*, 1883. London: Trollope Society, 1995.
Macdermots	*The Macdermots of Ballycloran*, 1847. Oxford: Oxford University Press, 1989.
Miss Mack	*Miss Mackenzie*, 1865. London: Chapman & Hall, 1868.
NA	*North America*, 1862. New York: Harper & Brothers, 1862.
Palmerston	*Lord Palmerston*, 1882. London: Isbister, 1882.
PF	*Phineas Finn, The Irish Member*, 1869. London: Penguin, 1972.
PM	*The Prime Minister*, 1876. London: Penguin, 1994.
PR	*Phineas Redux*, 1873. Oxford: Oxford University Press, 2011.
Scarborough	*Mr. Scarborough's Family*, 1883. Hamburg: Karl Gradener & J. F. Ricter, 1883.
South Africa	*South Africa,* 1879. London: Chapman & Hall, 1879.
Thackeray	*Thackeray*, 1879. London: Macmillan, 1879.
Three Clerks.	*The Three Clerks*, 1858. New York: Dover, 1981.
Warden	*The Warden*, 1855. Oxford: Oxford University Press, 2009.
West Indies	*West Indies and the Spanish Main*, 1862. New York: Carroll and Graf Publishers, 1999.
WWLN	*The Way We Live Now*, 1875. Oxford: Oxford University Press, 2009.

(Other editions of Trollope's works are listed in the bibliography only if their introductions have been quoted.)

1

Introduction

Anthony Trollope between Britain and Ireland

I. BECOMING TROLLOPE IN IRELAND

'All Irishmen should respect this author [Trollope], who always showed the finer traits of the Irishman.'[1]

'It has often seemed to me', wrote Anthony Trollope in *Phineas Finn*, 'that men in Parliament know less about Ireland than they do of the interior of Africa' (*PF*, 549). He was echoing Sir Robert Peel, who had claimed that an 'honest Englishman' knew as much about Ireland as he did about the state of 'Kamchatka',[2] but also one of Peel's predecessors as Chief Secretary for Ireland, Henry Goulburn, who had compared the country to what he considered the dark and primitive continent of Africa.[3] But the English were not alone in fearing that the Irish were as unmanageable and ungovernable as they considered the Africans to be. William Carleton, in his Famine novel, *The Black Prophet*, described 'whole masses' of Irish driven by hunger and the 'insanity of desolation', and warned that there is 'no beast, however, in the deepest jungle of Africa itself, so wild, savage and ferocious, as a human mob, when left to its own blind and headlong impulses.'[4]

In his Irish novels, Anthony Trollope avoids such analogies, and stretches beyond preconceptions in the hope of communicating a better understanding of the country and its people. In so doing he treads a tricky

---

[1] Unsigned review entitled 'Mr Le Fanu's Irish Stories', *New York Times*, 24 December 1893. http://query.nytimes.com/mem/archive-free/pdf?res=9B07E5D9173EEF33A25757 C2A9649D94629ED7CF.

[2] Peel is quoted in Brian Jenkins, *Irish Nationalism and the British State: From Repeal to Revolutionary Nationalism* (Montréal: McGill-Queen's Press, 2006), 20.

[3] Quoted in Jenkins, *Irish Nationalism*, 21.

[4] William Carleton, *The Black Prophet. A Tale of Irish Famine* (London: Simms and M'Intyre, 1847), 251.

course along the established borders between Ireland and England and between nineteenth-century Irish and English narrative forms. While Irish novelists struggled to represent an Irish reality dominated by fragmentation, disjunction, instability, poverty, land agitation, and Famine to a paltry native audience or to a largely disinterested English one, their English counterparts had an easier task, writing for a growing reading public within the structures and strictures of a well-established form, against the backdrop of a solid nation, a burgeoning class-based industrial economy, and a sense of progress and stability. In becoming a published writer with novels about Ireland, and after settling in the country where he would remain for the greater part of twenty years, Trollope made life harder for himself than it otherwise might have been. His first two Irish novels failed to find an adequate critical or popular audience, not because they were good or bad, but because they were Irish, because they were full of Irish ingredients that were of little interest to the middle-class English reader, who wished, above all else, to be entertained rather than challenged by unsettling images of the unruly, often dishevelled island that made up the smaller part of the United Kingdom.

Trollope's capacity to portray English Victorian life has been at the centre of critical appraisals of the writer. Up to the present day, most critics have concurred with Richard Holt Hutton's assertion that 'no historian' would attempt 'to delineate English society in the third quarter of the present century' without possessing 'a familiar knowledge' of Trollope's novels. Trollope's name would endure because of his capacity to 'picture the society of our day with a fidelity with which society has never been pictured before.'[5] And yet, it should not be forgotten that Trollope was a writer whose English roots were unusually loose. When faced with great financial difficulties at home, his mother, Rose, famously took up a successful new life in the United States, while his own decision to go to Ireland (like that of his older brother, Thomas, to move to Florence) was partly fuelled by frustration at his unpromising situation in London. Like his mother, Trollope was remarkably mobile; he had little difficulty making his home in Ireland and, later, in journeying, relentlessly, around the globe on Post Office business. Although critics, such as Simon Gikandi, have argued with effect that 'it is in the contrastive space afforded to it by its colonies that English identity consolidates itself',[6] this present work will argue that the contrastive space of Ireland, so familiar and yet so

[5] R. H. Hutton, *Spectator*, 55 (9 December 1882), 1574, quoted in Donald Smalley, ed., *Anthony Trollope: The Critical Heritage* (London: Routledge and Kegan Paul, 1969), 508.

[6] Simon Gikandi, *Maps of Englishness: Writing Identity in the Culture of Colonialism* (New York: Columbia University Press, 1996), 46.

different to Trollope's England, is the key element for a new understanding of Trollope, man and writer.

In 1926, while acknowledging that Trollope was as 'English as John Bull', Stephen Gwynn stigmatized the common belief that his Irish output could be overlooked. Prefacing his remarks with the strident comment that 'an Englishman's observations about Ireland must be taken with such allowance as should be made for those of a German on Poland',[7] Gwynn stressed the importance of Trollope's Irish novels, and this present work will follow a similar path, arguing that Trollope's Irish writings are vital to any understanding of his overall output, and that Ireland, as Corbett put it, is the 'great lost domain of Trollope's mental landscape.'[8] It will show that Trollope's Irish works constitute both a vital and distinct group of works, add significantly to our overall vision of the writer, and represent a rich and underestimated contribution to the canon of the nineteenth-century Irish novel *tout court*, complicating the sometimes arbitrary divisions that are drawn between the English and the Irish traditions. Trollope felt that he was in a unique position as a cultural mediator between Ireland and England, with both the advantages of living for so long in Ireland and the moral obligations that this sojourn imposed upon him, to attempt to give narrative shape to the complexities of a country whose voice—feeble in mid-century—was none too willingly heard in Britain. Trollope's Irish novels need to be distinguished from those of other English writers who turned an occasional eye across the water to Ireland. As Dudley Edwards points out: 'Every one of them saw Ireland as outsiders. Trollope did not. His view of Ireland from first to last was that of a participant: Ireland made him.'[9]

Trollope found his English voice during his long encounter with the alternative world that was Ireland and did his utmost to impose English order on this Irish space, both in his Post Office duties and in his fiction. In choosing to live in an Ireland that was anything but a comfort zone, Trollope rapidly took on a role as a cultural mediator between the two worlds by sending home to London urgent but often unread dispatches—private and public letters, novels, short stories, reviews, and Post Office reports—reminding his readers across the water of the situation as he found it (and no one, certainly no Englishman, as he often reminded his readers, was better equipped to do so). But Ireland also gave him the frame

---

[7] Stephen Gwynn, 'Trollope and Ireland', *Contemporary Review*, 129 (Jan./June 1926), 72.

[8] Mary Jean Corbett, *Allegories of Union in Irish and English Writing* (Cambridge: Cambridge University Press, 2000), 134.

[9] Owen Dudley Edwards, 'Anthony Trollope, Irish Writer', *Nineteenth-Century Fiction*, 38/1 (June 1983), 1.

and the space within which he came to understand his Englishness for the first time. It was in Ireland that Trollope belatedly identified his talents for rationality, industry, and order, in contrast to what he saw as Irish passivity and emotivity. Thus, as Sadleir wrote, Trollope became 'an ambassador of England, living in disputatious amity with one of the most race-conscious nations in the world. And from this sense of being—however humbly—an envoy of his country, his literary ambition and his politics grew rapidly and side by side.'[10] But Trollope also became—and not so humbly because humility was not a quality that distinguished him, despite or perhaps because of his lingering social and intellectual insecurity—an envoy of his second country, Ireland, and lived in what was at times at equally disputatious amity with his English interlocuters when discussing the country and its needs.

Known today as one of the great Victorian novelists, noted for his pragmatic conservativism, it is easy to forget Trollope's shaky beginnings. Perhaps because he had grown up as an outsider at home, school, and in his early working career, Trollope contributed to the view that he and his writings were all-too-comfortably mainstream when, in his *Autobiography*, he approvingly quoted Nathaniel Hawthorne's view that his quintessentially English novels were written on the 'strength of beef and through the inspiration of ale . . . these books are just as English as a beef-steak' (*Auto*, 144). It was a description that stuck, and still today Trollope is generally seen as embodying Victorian England, and as being, as George Levine put it, 'a conventional artist . . . who unquestioningly accepted the conventions he inherited.'[11] Similarly, Catherine Hall has described him, rather patronisingly, as 'safe and English . . . riveted by the daily round of politics without being political, producing happy endings for his novels, believing in church, family and nation in ways which confirmed complacency rather than producing unsettled states of mind.'[12] I will argue that Trollope became the classic English Victorian writer by leaving England and by finding himself in Ireland, but I will also suggest that Ireland turned him, unexpectedly, into an Irish writer embroiled in all the great issues to affect the country during and after his long sojourn there. The attempt to reconcile these English and Irish versions of Trollope provides much of the creative energy behind his novels.

---

[10] Michael Sadleir, *Trollope: A Commentary* (Oxford: Oxford University Press, 1961), 140–1.

[11] George Levine, 'Can You Forgive Him? Trollope's *Can You Forgive Her?* and the Myth of Realism', *Victorian Studies*, 18 (1974), 5–30.

[12] Catherine Hall, *Civilising Subjects: Metropole and Colony in the English Imagination, 1830–1867* (Chicago: University of Chicago Press, 2002), 210–11.

Perhaps because of the overt moralizing aim of his fiction, there is a widespread but mistaken belief that Trollope ignored unexplored subject territories and 'acquiesced rather too easily in the conventions of mid-Victorian realism, and therefore in the social and moral assumptions those conventions express.'[13] He is criticised for having accepted what Henry James calls 'all the common restrictions, and found that even within the barriers there was plenty of material.'[14] Hillis Miller's words are indicative of how this general belief about Trollope has persisted:

> For the most part, the narrator of Trollope's novels and Trollope himself. . . cheerfully reaffirms the main values endorsed by high Victorian ideology. This includes the racist ideology of British imperialism. A good place to see the latter is Trollope's books on South Africa, the West Indies, North America, Australia, and New Zealand. If you want to know what Victorian ideology was, or at least one strong version of it, read Trollope.[15]

This view fails to credit Trollope for the often deeply embedded counter-narratives in his novels, for his deep ambivalence towards British colonialism, for his sympathy for those who get squeezed by or are at odds with the systems of power which he, at the same time, minutely describes and substantially endorses. This ambivalence and sympathy grows out of Trollope's initial position as an outsider who knew what it meant to live on the fringe of 'gentlemanly' society and only began to feel a sense of belonging and acceptance by belatedly establishing himself in Ireland. A growing number of critics have begun to take greater account of the attempts to interrogate rather than simply endorse the political and social status quo in Britain and also to explore the formal experimentation in which he engaged, with mixed success, throughout his career. John Hagan hits the mark when noting how Trollope's 'instinctive or emotional conservatism constantly clashes with what he felt was the more rational, utilitarian, and liberal bent of his temperament; and, these two opposing forces never being reconciled, there is often engendered in vital areas of his fiction uncertainty and ambiguity to a very high degree.'[16] This ambiguity plays an important role in keeping Trollope's fiction fresh today, in giving it an often-denied edge and in showing that it has an enduring power to

---

[13] Robin Gilmour, 'A Lesser Thackeray? Trollope and the Victorian Novel', in Tony Bareham, ed., *Anthony Trollope* (London: Vision Press, 1980), 182.

[14] Henry James, 'Anthony Trollope', in Donald Smalley, ed., *Trollope: The Critical Heritage* (London: Routledge and Kegan Paul, 1969), 540.

[15] J. Hillis Miller, *Boustrophedonic Reading. Cultural Memory in the Present* (Stanford: Stanford University Press, 1999), 229–30.

[16] John Hagan, 'The Divided Mind of Anthony Trollope', *Nineteenth-Century Fiction*, 13/1 (1959), 2.

ask questions of the society it portrays and for the most part endorses. Overton points to the 'dichotomy between the "official" face of Trollope, the civil servant and Establishment man, and the private, careful, intensive artist who shaped his fiction from 'unofficial standpoints.'[17] Glendinning concurs, when citing criticism of the character of La Signora Neroni in *Barchester Towers* ('a great blot on the work', according to Calvin, who read it for the first publisher), to point out that such 'strictures belie any conventional supposition that Anthony Trollope was always in tune with his times, or that he deliberately tailored his work to the acceptable standard. His off-key, or off-colour, sense of humour reflects how little opportunity he had had to become conditioned by the assumptions of the "polite" English world—which in artistic terms, was to his advantage and ours.'[18] More recently, Denenholz Morse, among others, has challenged the established views of Trollope as an un-conflicted imperialist and has done so in terms that also reveal his sometimes unconventional take on gender issues.[19]

It is chiefly in his Irish novels that the unconventional Trollope emerges, a conflicted and sometimes almost subversive figure, caught between his 'official' and 'unofficial' opinions as he vacillated between endorsing standard English views about Ireland and offering his own alternative, sometimes awkward, counter-readings. In the earlier Irish novels, the liberal (rather than the later, increasingly conservative) Trollope dominates and his pet characters, including Phineas, the Duke of Omnium, and Mr Monk, are all cast within this frame, all working for slow, patient change.

Trollope sets out his cautiously progressive liberal position in his *Autobiography*, hoping politics can bolster 'a tendency towards equality' and progress, seeing the Conservatives as a reactionary party while at the same time viewing the conservative brake as a means for steering and controlling change. As a 'Conservative-Liberal' (*Auto*, 293–4), Trollope's position was close to that of his fictional favourite, Plantagenet Palliser, who sees England's 'exquisite combination of conservatism and progress' as her 'present strength and best security for the future' (*CYFH?*, 267). Ireland is one of the areas in which Trollope worked for 'slow but definite change'. As a lifelong believer in the Union, which he held could work to

---

[17] Bill Overton, *The Unofficial Trollope* (Sussex/New York: Harvester Press/Barnes & Noble, 1982), xxi.

[18] Victoria Glendinning, *Trollope* (London: Hutchinson, 1992), 218.

[19] Deborah Denenholz Morse, ' "Some Girls Who Come From the Tropics": Gender, Race, and Imperialism in Anthony Trollope's *He Knew He Was Right*', in Margaret Markwick, Deborah Denenholz Morse, and Regenia Gagnier, eds., *The Politics of Gender in Anthony Trollope's Novels* (London: Ashgate, 2009), 80.

the benefit of both partners, he felt that the country could and should be improved and that it was the duty of the English and the Irish together to make this happen. At the same time, in his Irish works, Trollope also attempts to see the world from the Irish point of view, to the chagrin, at times, of his fellow Englishmen. Dudley Edwards synthesizes Trollope's Irish-English intersections well, writing of how he

> went to the frontier, for in a linguistic, religious, political, social and economic sense Ireland was one.... learned his literary trade on the frontier. He discovered that frontier-made goods were not good selling material... He began to build his literary achievement in forms acceptable to England and apparently English. But the tools and perceptions were Irish in the initial instance, and much of the workmanship after his return to England was still based on the rough designs he had initially executed on Irish soil, with Irish themes, about Irish characters, and with Irish insights.[20]

By accident rather than design he became a border crosser, one who would have to accept that, following his initiation as a successful public servant and writer in Ireland, he would always be betwixt and between, caught by sometimes conflicting loyalties to both cultures. This would, initially at least, prove to be a creatively liberating situation for Trollope, even if he would gradually rein in his sympathy for the Irish point of view and retreat to a more defensive and exclusively mainstream, 'English' position.

II. LIFE IN IRELAND

On 15 September 1841, the twenty-six-year-old Anthony Trollope landed in Dublin and began his almost twenty-year career as a 'clerk to an Irish surveyor, in Connaught, with a salary of £100 a year' (*Auto*, 61). His choice to go to Ireland, whose postal system had been amalgamated with the English one in 1830, was unusual. None of his colleagues at the General Post Office at St-Martins-le-Grand would have willingly accepted such a posting and agreed to leave London, a city rapidly assuming the grandeur of an imperial metropolis. Few mourned his departure. He travelled armed with a poor reference from the secretary, Colonel Maberly, but on arrival he was relieved to be told he would be judged on his own merits. Finally he had the chance to put his life on a new, more positive footing. Sykes Davies, following Trollope's own retrospective mythologizing of his Irish life, describes the change:

---

[20] Edwards, 'Anthony Trollope, Irish Writer', 41–2.

Ireland accomplished a transformation in him hardly less dramatic than that which characterizes the life-cycles of insects. Hitherto, his state had been dark and larval, or chrysalid at best, and his days had been spent in obscurity and lonely poverty.... The essence of the Irish magic was that for the first time he found himself among people who liked him, who did not regard him as a shameful and useless encumbrance.[21]

Trollope quickly became a figure of substance in Ireland, a valued public servant. He never failed to underline his contentment there: 'My life in England for twenty-six years from the time of my birth to the day on which I left it, had been wretched. I had been poor, friendless, and joyless' (*Auto*, 132). The optimism, the belief in the possibility of individual and collective improvement and progress that drove Britain onward and upward in the nineteenth century, had not, up to then, caught Trollope in its current. It would be in Ireland that Trollope would realize the Victorian dream of individual success by following the classic values of the time—self-reliance, personal responsibility, thrift, and, most of all, hard work—and in doing so he would gain a sense of his own personal worth. In Ireland, Trollope became the quintessential Victorian by belatedly adopting those sound principles so often urged upon young men and laid out by William Cobbett (1763–1835) in his *Advice to Young Men* (1829), a staple of middle-class reading in Britain:

There must be something more than *genius*: there must be industry: there must be perseverance: there must be, before the eyes of the nation, proofs of extraordinary exertion... These are the things, and *not genius*, which have caused my labours to be so incessant and so successful: and, though I do not affect to believe, that *every young man*, who shall read this work, will become able to perform labours of equal magnitude and importance, I do pretend, that *every* young man, who will attend to my advice, will become able to perform a great deal more than men generally do perform, whatever may be his situation in life...[22]

In making him, Ireland proved herself in his eyes to be an integral part of his United Kingdom, a part that had plenty to offer and that deserved the larger island's respect and commitment. In Ireland, Trollope's life was transformed by his coming to understand the rectitude of perseverance and solid work habits. When, at the end of his career, Trollope wrote his

[21] Hugh Sykes Davies, *Trollope* (London: Longmans Green, 1960), 7–8.

[22] William Cobbett, *Cobbett's Advice to Young Men, and (Incidentally) to Young Women, in the Middle and Higher Ranks of Life. In a series of letters, addressed to a youth, a bachelor, a lover, a husband, a father, a citizen, or a subject* (London: Henry Frowde, 1906), Intro., para. 6.

affectionate biography of Lord Palmerston, he praised the statesman for his energy and steady commitment, noting that he was

> by no means a man of genius, possessed of not more than ordinary gifts of talent, with no startling oratory, and, above all, with no specially strong liberal opinions.... He was a man who from the first was determined to do the best he could with himself; and he did it with a healthy energy, never despairing, never expecting too much, never being in a hurry, but always ready to seize the good thing when it came (*Palmerston*, 9).

This description is also a self-portrait of Trollope at career's end looking back and concluding: 'Hard work was to him the first necessity of his existence' (*Palmerston*, 213). In Ireland, Trollope became a self-made man, gained a modicum of wealth and considerable respectability, and thus, for very personal reasons, he felt he owed a debt to his adopted country which would be repaid in his fiction. Thus he persisted in intermittingly setting novels in Ireland and in giving them Irish themes and characters, despite the protests of his publishers. Trollope later recalled in his biography that Henry Colburn had written after the publication of *The Kellys and the O'Kellys* to tell him that it was 'evident that readers do not like novels on Irish subjects as well as others' (*Auto*, 78). Trollope seems to have felt almost morally compelled to return to matters Irish, even when he knew it was financially foolhardy to do so (and he was rarely one to underestimate the importance of making money from his fiction, as his *Autobiography* damagingly revealed).

Prior to going to Ireland, his opinions of the country were superficial and stereotypical. He saw it as a place in which he could attempt to make a new start and which also happened to be 'a land flowing with fun and whisky, in which irregularity was the rule of life, and where broken heads were looked upon as honourable badges' (*Auto*, 62). Once he had established himself there, however, Ireland proved itself a pleasant place and his salary and expenses allowed him a much-improved tenor of life compared to that to which he was accustomed:

> The Irish people did not murder me, nor did they even break my head. I soon found them to be good-humoured, clever—the working classes very much more intelligent than those of England—oeconomical and hospitable. We hear much of their spendthrift nature; but extravagance is not the nature of an Irishman. He will count the shillings in a pound much more accurately than an Englishman, and will with much more certainty get twelve pennyworth from each. But they are perverse, irrational and but little bound by the love of truth. I lived for many years among them—not finally leaving the country until 1859, and I had the means of studying their character (*Auto*, 65).

Initially Trollope's annual salary was £100, but this was supplemented by travel expenses; these can be traced in his carefully annotated travel account books, which show a net income of £313 4s. 2d. for his first year in Ireland.[23] Trollope immersed himself in Irish life with enthusiasm and, although he continually gravitated back towards London, he was not the 'insular Englishman whose early sympathies and antipathies were unmodified by reason or by observation',[24] whom early critics describe. However, an Englishman he remained, carrying with him an innate sense of superiority, which he described in *South Africa*:

> Let an Englishman be where he may about the surface of the globe, he always thinks himself superior to other men around him. . . . He,—and the American who in this respect is the same as an English,—always consumes the wheat while others put up with the rye. . . . He expects to be 'boss' while others work under him (*South Africa*, 17).

This certainly was not intended as a self-portrait. However, in attempting to impose an 'English' system of management on the Irish postal system, Trollope was engaged in what was a colonial or imperial enterprise. The assumption that lies at the heart of most of Trollope's work in Ireland (and in his Irish writings) is one of a superiority built on the paternalistic belief that he, being sympathetic to the plight of the Irish, knew what was best for them. In *Castle Richmond*, he expresses the belief that the Irish were happy to be led by their 'betters' but, at the same time, questions what he considers their natural subservience: 'Pat is a happy man when he can address his landlord as "Sir Patrick"' (*CR*, 348). Like many of his compatriots, he was fully convinced that he knew better than those working under his charge, yet, it would be more appropriate to read his Irish work (both postal and literary) as an expression of his Unionist beliefs. In a letter to the Liverpool *Mercury* in 1874, Trollope shows that he was a reluctant colonialist, maintaining 'that Great Britain possesses enough of the world . . . and that new territorial possessions must be regarded rather as increased burdens than increased strength.'[25] Rather than look on Ireland as a colonial burden, he saw it instead as an integral part of the United Kingdom, believed the country (unlike the colonies) could be modernized and improved by being made more like England, and felt that this process would strengthen the Union and could only be of benefit to England's own security and wealth.

---

[23] The travel account books are kept in the Parrish Collection, Firestone Library, Princeton University.

[24] Lucy Poate Stebbins and Richard Poate Stebbins, *The Trollopes: The Chronicle of a Writing Family* (New York: Columbia University Press, 1945), 321.

[25] Patrick Brantlinger, *Rule of Darkness: British Literature and Imperialism, 1830–1914* (Ithaca: Cornell University Press, 1988), 6.

Trollope's initial posting was in Banagher, an outpost on the river Shannon, some sixty miles from Dublin in the King's County (today County Offaly). With a population of 2,500, the contrast with London was total. Banagher was a trading town with a corn market, a distillery, a brewery, a malt house, and tan yards. It was linked by the Shannon with Limerick and by the Grand Canal with Athlone, Ballinasloe, and Dublin. In *The Kellys and the O'Kellys*, Trollope would later describe a *Heart of Darkness*-like 'horrid voyage' for Martin Kelly from Portobello in Dublin to Ballinasloe, 'a twenty hours' sojourn in one of these floating prisons', to be followed by a further trip, 'by Bianconi's car, as far as Tuam, and when there he went at once to the hotel, to get a hack car to take him home to Dunmore' (*Kellys*, 77). This would have been very similar to his own odyssey down to Banagher, a town known for its eighteen-arch bridge, built by Roderick O'Connor, which united the province of Leinster with 'the ominous lands of Connaught'[26] (and which was being replaced during Trollope's time there). It was also home to an infantry barracks, Catholic and Protestant churches and schools, a dispensary, and a Reading Room.[27] Charlotte Brontë's husband, Arthur Bell Nicholls, had been brought up in Banagher at Cuba Court, home to the Royal School, which was run by his uncle, Dr Alan Bell (William Wilde figures among the school's most illustrious alumni). Arthur and Charlotte enjoyed part of their honeymoon there and he eventually moved back to Banagher following her death.

Trollope settled into this small world quickly and began to lead 'a very jolly life' (*Auto*, 65), getting involved in the local hunts (the Galway Blazers hunted nearby). This provided him with the chance to begin to enjoy what became a lifelong sporting passion, and a recurring if not always indispensable element in his fiction. It was also in Banagher that Trollope hired Barney MacIntyre as his groom. Barney would remain with him for the rest of his life and become his general factotum, being remembered chiefly for his waking the author at five every morning with coffee so that he could write before going to his 'real' job at the Post Office. Trollope was prone to admitting that he owed more to Barney than to anyone else for all the success he enjoyed.

Trollope took the postal service work very seriously and found his new role energizing, even if he was less than impressed by his new superior, James Drought, the Surveyor for the West of Ireland (one of just three surveyors for the entire country). Thomas, the author's brother, later attributed his success in Ireland to his being able to win Drought's

---

[26] James Pope-Hennessy, *Anthony Trollope* (London: Phoenix Press, 1971), 73.
[27] Samuel Lewis, *Topographical Dictionary of Ireland* (London: Lewis and Co., 1837).

'good graces by virtue of simply having taken the whole work and affairs of the postal district on his shoulders.'[28] He would later use his name for the doughty old Tory, Sir Orlando Drought, in *Phineas Redux* and *The Prime Minister*. In the latter novel Drought makes a thorough nuisance of himself and helps to bring down the coalition government led by the Duke of Omnium, a liberal whose ideas closely correspond to Trollope's own.

Over the coming years, Trollope lived in more substantial cities and towns, such as Cork (September 1844–February 1845), Clonmel (1845–8), and Mallow, where he had a house for a time at 159 Bank Place and later on High Street from 1848 to 1853. His years working as an overseer in Mallow were good ones, in which he continued to hunt at the Duhallow Hunt Club (the oldest club in Ireland, having been founded in 1745). He also lived for long spells in the cities of Belfast and Dublin, where he set up a considerable home in Donnybrook at 5 Seaview Terrace from May 1855 until the end of the decade. He took holidays in fashionable coastal resorts, such as Killarney and Glengariff, and in smaller towns, such as Milltown Malbay. In *Castle Richmond*, in tones more befitting a guide book than a Famine novel, he warmly praised Cork and Kerry as 'the most interesting, and certainly the most beautiful part of Ireland', singling out 'Killarney, Glengarriffe, Bantry, and Inchigeela', and concluding warmly: 'I know not where is to be found a land more rich in all that constitutes the loveliness of scenery' (*CR*, 2).

Thus he gained intimate first-hand knowledge of both rural and urban Ireland and was not backward about letting his correspondents know his opinions on the various places he explored. Mostly they were positive, but he does seem to have taken a particular dislike to Belfast, where he lived for about a year when employed as Acting Surveyor and subsequently Surveyor for the Northern District of Ireland. In a letter to his close friend, John Lewis Merivale, he described it as 'a filthy, disagreeable, unwholesome, uninteresting town, with bad water and worse inhabitants and nothing on earth to recommend it unless a man knows how to make linen: I don't.'[29] It was in Belfast that he began to write his Barchester novels, and in doing so it was almost as if he was compensating for the inhospitable nature of what was Ireland's only industrial city by idealizing the rural English world of Barchester, which he created out of the West

---

[28] Thomas Adolphus Trollope, *What I Remember*, II (London: Richard Bentley, 1887), 328.

[29] This statement is taken from an unpublished letter, part of which was printed in 'Trollope letters fetch €48,000', *Irish Independent*, 23 November 2002: http://www.independent.ie/irish-news/trollope-letters-fetch-48000-26028358.html.

Country he had come to know during a short posting there. Fortunately, he looked more kindly on the rest of the country and was pleasantly amused, several years later in 1854, to note that his son Harry had picked up 'such a Cork brogue' (*Letters I*, 35).

Trollope lost little time in making friends and also became quite a 'catch' for young ladies, which was not surprising as unattached men, 'especially if they would dance, were gold dust in the country-house world of rural Ireland.'[30] For a couple of years, Trollope danced almost as much as he hunted, and in all probability enjoyed more than a few romances— his own personal experience would prove useful for many of his dashing young male characters, such as Phineas Finn or Frank Greystock, who have a knack for falling in love many times over and of being in love with different women simultaneously. Gradually he also came to know a range of illustrious figures, including his old acquaintance from earlier, unhappier times at Harrow, Sir William Gregory, who welcomed him to his home at Coole Park in County Galway, a place that was, as Escott colourfully described:

a hotbed of social varieties, and in the heart of a district literally overflowing with the local colour, incidents, and personages...The earliest year of Trollope's Irish residence saw him an habitué of the place, and introduced him to the home life, not only of the local magnates, but of the surrounding peasantry, then generally in the clutches of the 'gombeen man,' sometimes a peasant himself, sometimes a shopkeeper or fifth-rate solicitor, who, at usurious rates of interest, used to advance the tenants money to make up their rent.[31]

Although two years Trollope's junior, Gregory was already an MP for Dublin and had been sponsored by Sir Robert Peel, the Prime Minister, for early promotion (shades here of the rapid rise of Phineas Finn). He would make many useful introductions for Trollope, although history would remember him chiefly for the infamous 'Gregory clause', an amendment to the Irish Poor Law Act of 1847, which exempted from relief anybody who owned more than a quarter of an acre of land. This clause was responsible for endless hardship and thousands of evictions. But that was some years ahead, and in the meantime, Trollope enjoyed his visits to Coole and listened 'to the social and political gossip', hearing stories

[30] Glendinning, *Trollope*, 124–5.
[31] T. H. S. Escott, *Anthony Trollope. His Work, Associates and Literary Originals* (London: Bodley Head, 1913), 49–50.

about the doings and the personalities of famous men and of people in public life long before he ever met such people himself. It was the best possible fodder for a novelist. He was also buying and keeping political pamphlets of all kinds. It was the politics and the sexual scandals of the 1840's, when he knew almost no one, which were to be the starting points for his fiction long after he left Ireland.[32]

At Coole he encountered the former British ambassador to Russia and future Postmaster General, the influential Galway landlord, Lord Clanricarde, a man he thought 'good-natured' and 'amenable' (he was the model for Lord Brittleback in *Framley Parsonage*). Clanricarde would later welcome Trollope to his home in Carlton Terrace in London (an address that would later be an important location in the Palliser novels). He also got to know Charles Lever (1806–72), who had recently given up his medical practice and was editor of the *Dublin University Magazine* as well as the successful author of *The Confessions of Harry Lorrequer* (1839) and *Charles O'Malley: the Irish Dragoon* (1841). Lever had mixed feelings about Trollope and his novels, telling John Blackwood later in a letter: 'I don't think Trollope *pleasant*, though he has a certain hard common-sense about him and coarse shrewdness that prevents him being dull or tiresome. His books are not of a high order, but still I am always surprised that he could write them. He is a good fellow, I believe, *au fond*, and has few jealousies and no rancours; and for a writer, is not that saying much?'[33] Trollope, on the other hand, published Lever's *Paul Gosslett's Confessions* in *Saint Pauls Magazine* and remembered him as 'an intimate friend... whom I very dearly loved... Of all the clever men I have known, his wit was the readiest. In conversation he was the quickest goer and the best stager I ever knew.' He keenly observed the evolution of Lever's career, noting: 'In literature it was peculiar to him to have altogether changed his manner and tone, from the time of *Harry Lorrequer* to that of *Tony Butler*, and to have been quite at home and quite successful in each.... His was a kind friendly nature, prone to cake and ale, and resolved to make the best of life when, as you no doubt know, things were often very sad with him.'[34]

Trollope's social rise in Ireland was also facilitated by his joining the Freemasons. The archives of the Grand Masonic Lodge in Dublin show that he was proposed for membership on 11 October 1841 by Brothers Bird and Harrington. 'Being an official and ordered on duty', he was

---

[32] Escott, *Trollope*, 152.

[33] Quoted in Edmund Downey, *Charles Lever: His Life in His Letters*, 2 vols (Edinburgh and London: Blackwood, 1906), II, 227.

[34] Fitzpatrick quotes Trollope's letter of 24 March 1879 to him about Lever in William J. Fitzpatrick, *The Life of Charles Lever* (London, 1873), 269–70.

initiated in an emergency meeting of Lodge 306, held in Banagher on 8 November. In December of the same year he was raised to the degree of Master Mason. His final autograph signature in the attendance book is dated 5 August 1844, which suggests he was an active member for three full years. Later, in writing *The Small House at Allington*, Trollope would include material about the Freemasons' rituals that he must have gathered during this time.

More importantly, Ireland also provided Trollope with a wife—even if she was English. In 1842, he met Rose Heseltine at Kingstown and they married on 11 June 1844. Trollope recounted that when he brought his English Rose to Banagher, he was made to feel that he had 'behaved badly' towards Ireland by not finding an Irish bride (*Auto*, 72). Perhaps he had looked a little too keenly among the Irish before meeting Rose. An echo of this may be heard in *The Three Clerks*, where the story of Charley Tudor's 'squalid love' is said to be based on events in Trollope's own life. As the Stebbinses write: 'The young hero, Charley Tudor, was the boy Anthony supposed himself to have been, and much of the book was autobiographical, even to the entanglement and the fear of a breach of promise suit.'[35] Thus there is some reason to believe that Charley's 'barmaid houri, his Norah Geraghty, to whom he had sworn all manner of undying love, and for whom in some sort of fashion he really had an affection' (*Three Clerks*, 176) has roots in Trollope's own experiences. Charley is attracted by Norah but soon discovers that she is not 'as easy to lay down as to pick up' and realizes that he is at risk of being caught in marriage with her:

He ought to have been happy enough, for he had his charmer in his arms; but he showed very little of the ecstatic joy of a favoured lover. There he sat with Norah in his arms, and as we have said, Norah was a handsome girl; but he would much sooner have been copying the Kennett and Avon canal lock entries in Mr. Snape's room at the Internal Navigation (*Three Clerks*, 206).

In any case, Norah sees that she is overreaching in hoping to marry Charley and instead weds Mr Peppermint, a safe catch, although a widower with three children. Charley's behaviour is a comic version of the tragic behaviour of Captain Ussher in *The Macdermots of Ballycloran* and Fred Neville in *An Eye for an Eye*.

Trollope was probably pleased to be transferred away from any recriminations to Clonmel in 1844. The Tipperary town was the birthplace, among other things, of Lady Blessington (1789–1849), who, according to Thackeray, was one of the 'untalented scribblers' belonging to the Silver Fork school of fiction, but also one of the most popular Irish novelists of

[35] Stebbins and Stebbins, *The Trollopes*, 150.

the 1830s, along with Mrs Hall and William Carleton. It was in this pretty town on the river Suir that he and Rose settled for three years from March 1844. Here Rose gave birth, in 1846, to their first child, Henry, who was christened in St Mary's Church by the Rev. J. B. Gordon and, the following year, to Frederick. With a population of 13,000, Clonmel offered the young couple much more than Banagher ever could, although Trollope, with mounting work and heavier domestic commitments, had less time to enjoy the town and the local countryside and to pursue his hunting. This was a pity, because the town was home to the Tipperary foxhounds and boasted a club for the 'Gentlemen of the County'. The river furnished it with a gateway to the sea and it was a busy and prosperous centre, located on the eastern side of the Golden Vale. The local aristocracy was made up of the de Burgo family, although the lordship had passed to the Fitzgeralds (the earls of Desmond). All of these names would echo in Trollope's fiction (particularly in the principal family names in *Castle Richmond*, but also in Burgo Fitzgerald in *Can You Forgive Her?*). Trollope also appropriated the name of Palliser's Castle, a nearby rock formation (he would also have been familiar with the Palliser family of Comeragh House, who owned over three and a half thousand acres of land in the county) for the central family in his parliamentary novels.

Mention is made of Tipperary in *The Eustace Diamonds* in one of those scenes in which Trollope has a cut at English prejudice towards all things Irish. In the novel, Lord Fawn suffers because 'unfortunately he . . . was an Irish landlord' (*Eustace Diamonds*, 114), an absentee who believes that Tipperary is 'not at all a desirable country to live in' (*Eustace Diamonds*, 109) and has never set foot in the country. From this English nobleman's point of view, nothing could have been worse than to have had to actually live on his Irish estate, a choice his sister suggests to him as a way to escape Lizzie Eustace's grasp. As one of Trollope's most negatively cast noblemen, Fawn's hostility towards Ireland is a black mark against him.

It was during his time in Clonmel that Trollope came to know the prominent Catholic businessman, Charles Bianconi. He was already well known for having established the first comprehensive transport system in Ireland, and served two terms as Mayor of Clonmel in 1845 and 1846 during Trollope's time there. Bianconi also enjoyed a close friendship with Daniel O'Connell (his daughter married a nephew of the Liberator). He had been banished to Ireland from Italy by his father following a scandal, and had worked his way to the top by dint of hard labour and sound business sense; a lesson, this, that was surely not lost on Trollope, who paid him fulsome tribute in his history of the Irish Post Office: 'Mr. Bianconi has done good service. By birth he is well known to be Italian; but he is now naturalised, and England, as well as Ireland, should be ready to acknowledge his merits. It may perhaps be said that no living man has worked more than he has for the benefit of the sister kingdom'.[36] The most direct help that the industrious Italian gave Trollope was in assisting him in designing cost-effective postal travel routes. But perhaps Bianconi's coachguards were of even more assistance in providing Trollope with information about the country that would be just as useful for building the postal service as it would be for constructing his novels. One such guard was a certain M'Cluskie, who is remembered as a great storyteller in Bianconi's biography (which carries the name of Bianconi's daughter as author but was ghostwritten by Trollope's son): 'Most famous of all guards was M'Cluskie, whom I recognised in one of Mr. Anthony Trollope's novels *The Macdermots of Ballycloran*, and from him I got the following letter about the old guard'. In the cited letter, Trollope remembers M'Cluskie as the 'guard on the Dublin and Boyle coach. I did not know that he had ever been one of your father's folk. But he and I were great friends':

> 'A fellow-feeling makes us wondrous kind,' he said to me once on the top of the coach, when I had been vindicating the character of donkeys. One day I was going down the streets of Lucan, and I was proselytizing him, telling him how wrong were the Papists and how right were the Protestants! We were then passing just between the church and the chapel. 'Yes,' said he, 'I see it all. While we raise on high the blessed emblem of our redemption, you believe in the cock.' There was an old-fashioned weathercock on the spire of the church.[37]

M'Cluskie's significance is also signalled by Trollope's borrowing of his surname for Lady Glencora in *Can You Forgive Her?*. He is just one example of the broad spectrum of Irish people that Trollope met during the course of his work which allowed him to become acquainted with the entire island, with

> the surface of the roads, not only where Dunmore was, but what it looked like, and what the hotel was like; not only the situation of Galway and Mayo, Roscommon and Leitrim, but the country on the borders of Galway and Mayo, and the borders of Roscommon and Leitrim, and the bit of Roscommon that runs between Galway and Mayo. Few Dubliners know as much.[38]

---

[36] Trollope is quoted in Mrs Morgan John O'Connell, *Charles Bianconi: A Biography* (London: Chapman and Hall, 1878), 73. After Bianconi's death, his daughter, Mrs O'Connell, consulted Trollope for advice before writing his biography: 'I turned to my good friend Mr. Anthony Trollope for council [sic], the only man equally versed in books and in coaches to whom I could appeal', 45.

[37] O'Connell, *Bianconi*, 138.

[38] Christine Longford, 'Trollope in Ireland', *The Bell*, 5/3 (December 1942), 185.

He boasted of having visited every parish and was capable of Ordnance Survey-style descriptions of the most remote places in the country. The detailed *incipit* of *The Macdermots of Ballycloran* is evidence of this, and seems more the work of a precise topographer—with all the controlling tendencies of that profession—than a budding novelist:

> In the autumn, 184–, business took me into the West of Ireland, and, amongst other places, to the quiet little village of Drumsna, which is in the province of Connaught, County of Leitrim, about 72 miles W.N.W. of Dublin, on the Mail Coach Road to Sligo (*Macdermots*, 1).

Trollope was instrumental in improving the Irish postal service, and in lowering costs to a level below that in England and Scotland, often going beyond the call of duty to identify those who, in his view, were not pulling their weight. In Tralee, by using a marked sovereign, he caught out an assistant postmistress called Mary O'Reilly, whom he suspected of stealing from the mails. Her trial at the Kerry summer assizes in 1849 became the occasion for Trollope to be cross-examined by the prominent young lawyer and future founder of the Home Rule League, Isaac Butt, who went so far as to quote from the court scenes in *The Macdermots of Ballycloran*. Although Trollope proved to be the match of his questioner, Miss O'Reilly got off.[39] Her relief was brief, however, as he soon found a way to dismiss her.

Normally, the issues at stake were run of the mill as Trollope attempted to cajole underpaid and overstretched staff and placate customers unhappy at the services provided. The following letter, sent to Trollope in 1857 by May Hill, Postmistress of Dromara, describes well a postmistress's lot and is probably typical of the kind of disgruntled correspondence to which he replied on a regular basis. She complains that her salary is too low:

> The sum allowed—£6 a year, with £4 to a letter carrier for the village—is too small a remuneration for the duties I have to perform. The duties are these: When the mail arrives from Dromore I rise every morning at the unseasonable hour of four o'clock and prepare and send off the bags for Ballinahinch, Saintfield and Comber. At half-past seven I despatch the mail bags to Kinallen and Ballykeel by the foot messenger, and at half-past eight o'clock send the messenger round the village with the letters. During the day I attend the office for the delivery of the country letters and try to get them sent safely to those addressed, which is attended with very considerable trouble, indeed. In the evening the walking postman arrives with the letters from Ballykeel, when I assort them and the letters posted here during the day until the arrival of the mail car at nine o'clock p.m., when I despatch them to Dromore.

---

[39] Justin Huntly McCarthy, *Reminiscences* (New York: Harper, 1899), 369–72.

These are the duties I perform for £6 annually; and as the number of letters has increased greatly during the last few years (which you will see by kindly looking into your books), the trouble has increased in proportion and I hope, therefore, you will not consider me too presuming in asking for an increase of salary. Praying you to take this matter into your favourable consideration, I am, sir, your obedient, humble servant, May Hill, Postmistress.[40]

As the postal service was partly still being constructed during Trollope's years in Ireland, he dealt with numerous requests for new Post Offices, always displaying sound business sense and refusing to give concessions, regardless of who was seeking them. Another of his tasks was to deal with a steady stream of complaints:

> On one visit he drove up in his jaunting car through a snow-storm to a squire's house in Country Cavan. The man had written several irate letters complaining of bad postal service. When the postal official appeared the Irishman turned on all his charm and sent his butler for brandy and hot water. Then he insisted that his guest must dine and spend the night. It was only after breakfast the next morning that the squire agreed to discuss business and admitted that he had no real complaint. He amused himself in his lonely abode by writing outraged letters to various government departments.[41]

Slowly but surely, by dint of hard graft, and despite having little support from his superiors in Dublin or London, Trollope established himself as the Post Office's key man in Ireland, firstly, from October 1854, as Surveyor for the Northern District, and later as Surveyor to the General Post Office in Dublin. His initial salary of £100 was substantially supplemented by travel allowances, which he noted with great care in his account books, and rose rapidly to the more princely sum of £700 in 1854. This was a considerable figure, put in perspective, on the one hand, by May Hill's '£6 a year', and on the other, by the £1,200 annual salary Charles Lever received for editing the *Dublin University Magazine* in the early 1840s. Trollope's name was regularly in the newspapers, usually when he advertised for applications for mail conveyances in various districts of the country. The notices were written with a linguistic economy not always to be found in his fiction:

TENDERS FOR CONVEYANCE OF THE MAILS to and from CAVAN and AVRA through Crossdoney and Ballinagh, in a suitable two wheeled

---

[40] This letter was sent to Trollope in 1857 and published in the *Irish Times* on 15 July 1932, 4.

[41] Richard Mullen, *Anthony Trollope: A Victorian in his World* (Savannah: Frederic D. Beil, 1990), 121.

CAR, drawn by one horse, will be received by me at the Post Office, Dublin at or before Twelve o'clock, on the 1st day of JUNE, 1857, with a Certificate of competency to perform the service from two respectable persons. A. Trollope, General Post Office.[42]

As a highly effective Post Office chief in Ireland, Trollope was not afraid to exercise his authority in gruff, peremptory tones. As Pope-Hennessy describes it, his 'manner to his underlings was aggressive and offhand, nor can the western Irish, famous then as now for their kindness and enduring charm, have relished what Trollope's friends used to call his "abrupt bow-wow way" of addressing them.'[43] James Russell Lowell reported meeting Trollope years later in Boston and described him as 'a big, redfaced, rather underbred Englishman of the bald-with-spectacles type. A good roaring positive fellow who deafened me... till I thought of Dante's Cerberus.'[44] Coral Lansbury puts it even less diplomatically, describing Trollope terrorizing those working under his charge, a man suffering from intermittent depression and indulging in 'glowering rages that tested the few friends he owned'.[45]

At times, he believed that this was the best way to address the Irish, whom he felt were 'naturally courteous as well as obedient. Let a well-dressed stranger desire of an Irish peasant the performance of some small behest, and the man immediately sets about the task, without asking or even thinking by what right he is so commanded' (*Examiner*, 98). To some extent, the well-dressed stranger that was Trollope corresponded to Charles Lever's description in *Sir Brook Fossbrooke* of rude English officials in Ireland:

> English officials have a manner specially assumed for Ireland and the Irish— a thing like the fur cloak a man wears in Russia, or the snowshoes he puts on in Lapland not intended for other latitudes, but admirably adapted for the locality it is made for.... I do not say it is a bad manner—a presuming manner—a manner of deprecation towards those it is used to, or a manner indicative of indifference in him who uses it. I simply say that they who employ it keep it as especially for Ireland as they keep their Macintosh capes for wet weather, and would no more think of displaying it in England than they would go to her Majesty's levee in a shooting-jacket.[46]

Trollope would not have been unduly worried about coming across brusquely, so intent was he in his role in modernizing the country's postal

---

[42] *Anglo Celt*, 14 May 1857.   [43] Pope-Hennessy, *Trollope*, 81.

[44] Horace Elisha Scudder, *James Russell Lowell: A Biography*, 2 vols (Boston: Houghton Mifflin, 1901), II, 82.

[45] Coral Lansbury, *The Reasonable Man: Trollope's Legal Fiction* (Princeton: Princeton University Press, 1981), 41.

[46] Charles Lever, *Sir Brook Fossbrooke* (Boston: Little, Brown & Co., 1917), 343.

system, convinced that in doing so he was doing his duty; a duty too few, he believed, carried out with sufficient zeal. In 1856, he was called as 'chief witness' before the Select Committee on Postal Arrangements in Ireland, which was investigating the case for making greater use of railways in the carriage of mail. He was reportedly 'cantankerous in his insistence' on speaking at length, 'even when the questioner seemed eager to move on',[47] and told the committee: 'I do not think any other officer has local knowledge of the whole district except myself; I have local knowledge over the whole of Ireland.' He argued that cars were sometimes more efficient than railways and suggested that 'petitions for railways had been contrived by the railway companies.'[48] His old friend, Bianconi, would have agreed.

Speculation connected with the development of the Irish railway network would become a minor theme in *The Three Clerks*, which sees the villainous parasite Undy Scott and the overreaching Alaric Tudor make a short-term speculative investment in the Great West Cork line. The 'momentous question', treated with irony by Trollope, was whether the remote town of Ballydehob should be included on the line which was to run from Skibbereen to Bantry:

> If Undy could carry the West Cork and Ballydehob branch entire, he would make a pretty thing of it; but if, as there was too much reason to fear, his Irish foes should prevail, and leave . . . the unfortunate agricultural and commercial interest of Ballydehob steeped in Cimmerian darkness, the chances were that poor Undy would be well nigh ruined.[49]

As it turned out, the railway did not reach Ballydehob until 1886.

Trollope's career moved considerably faster. By the second half of the 1850s his reputation had consolidated not only in the Post Office, but also on the literary front. Following the modest success of *The Warden*, *Barchester Towers* was published to unanimous praise, and from that point on he was able to demand significant advances for new novels. At the Post Office, he continued to oversee (from Dublin), the Northern District, but was frequently called to work in England and had gained a reputation, as Hall puts it, as a 'troubleshooter', to be sent to sort out difficult postal problems around the globe (he was dispatched to Egypt, Scotland, and the West Indies in 1858 alone). When he was in the West Indies, his novel *The Bertrams* was published and the list of the locations in

---

[47] R. H. Super, *The Chronicler of Barsetshire: A Life of Anthony Trollope* (Ann Arbor: University of Michigan Press, 1988), 62.

[48] See N. John Hall, *Trollope: A Biography* (Oxford: Oxford University Press, 1993), 141.

[49] Anthony Trollope, *The Three Clerks* (New York: Dover, 1981), 253. The line in question was begun in 1851 and completed in 1893.

which it was written is testimony to the frenetic working life of the Victorian age's most travelled writer: 'Alexandria, Malta, Gibraltar, London, Glasgow, Dublin, Belfast, Coleraine, Derry, and Kingston, and aboard ship on four separate sea voyages.'[50]

His reward for his unflagging efforts finally came in the summer of 1859 when he was offered the surveyorship of the Eastern District in England. He would always look with pride on his role in modernizing the mail service in Ireland, writing, in his history of the Irish postal service, that

> in no part of the United Kingdom has more been done for the welfare of the people by the use of railways for carrying mails and by the penny postage system than in Ireland. What was the state of the service in 1784 has been shown. There were then posts six days a week on only four lines of road; letters to all other places being conveyed only twice or thrice a week. Now there are daily posts to almost every village; and I know of but one important town that has not two daily mails both with London and Dublin.[51]

In deciding to live in London, Trollope was of the belief that his literary career would be better served by his presence there. Being in the capital meant being at the heart of the action. He quickly established a connection with the *Cornhill*, and this became 'the means of introducing me very quickly to that literary world from which I had hitherto been severed by the fact of my residence in Ireland' (*Auto*, 146). He later reflected 'that a man who could write books ought not to live in Ireland,—ought to live within reach of the publishers, the clubs, and the dinner parties of the metropolis' (*Auto*, 132), but this was a revisionary view and during his years in Ireland he never gave the impression that his literary career was being held back by his being there. In any case, long after resettling in England, his affection for and sense of belonging in Ireland remained. As he put it in *North America*:

> It has been my fate to have so close an intimacy with Ireland, that when I meet an Irishman abroad I always recognize in him more of a kinsman than I do in your Englishman. I never ask an Englishman from what county he comes, or what was his town. To Irishmen I usually put such a question, and I am generally familiar with the old haunts which they name (*NA*, 599).

---

[50] Hall, *Trollope*, 182.
[51] Anthony Trollope, House of Commons, *Sessional Papers*, 4 (1857), 354–60, 360.

III. TROLLOPE'S IRELAND

Unlike many Englishmen who 'headed the Executive [in Dublin and] tended to view Ireland more as a imperial possession than as an integral region of the United Kingdom',[52] Trollope saw the country as a sister nation and believed that the Union could be beneficial to both, even if Ireland was to be considered the junior partner in drastic need of English discipline. In his 1865 article entitled 'The Irish Church', he argues that the 'Act of Union has been very good to Ireland, has been and is beneficent', and should be reinforced (*Irish Church*, 85). The Ireland that Trollope first encountered in 1843 was feeling the effects of a decade of Whig rule, during which the country had been 'improved', despite the innate conservatism of most members of Parliament and despite O'Connell's 'ambivalence with respect to social legislation.'[53] Under Lord Melbourne the police had been reformed, the tithe modified, Protestant privilege checked, and many Orangemen purged from office to be replaced with Catholics who were also increasingly being favoured as judges. The Irish Poor Law, extending to Ireland the privileges of the New Poor Law, was passed in 1838, and commutation of tithes finally brought to an end the forced payment by Irish Catholics in support of the Anglican Church. As Brian Jenkins writes:

> The power of the Protestant Ascendancy, at least in the person of the landlord, had evidently been weakened as a result both of Catholic agitation and administrative reform. The dispensaries established shortly after union to provide free medical attention to the poor had by 1840 increased in number to six hundred, and together with country infirmaries, fever hospitals, and regional mental hospitals, they offered the rudiments of a health service. A new board of works throughout the 1830s sponsored a variety of constructive projects, improving communications and promoting land reclamation. Religious discrimination was now less egregious; the country had a generally sound and honest administration; the national schools were steadily increasing literacy in English, which by mid-century was the boast of more than half the population; and legislation with respect to the Church Establishment, the tithe, municipal corporations, and the Poor Law confirmed the willingness of the British to address serious Irish problems.[54]

The Whigs believed, by 1840, that they had made significant progress in reversing centuries of misgovernment of Ireland and expected gratitude

[52] Timothy J. White, 'Modeling the Origins and Evolution of Postcolonial Politics: The Case of Ireland', *Postcolonial Text*, 3/3 (2007), 10.
[53] Jenkins, *Irish Nationalism*, 40.   [54] Jenkins, *Irish Nationalism*, 39.

from the Catholic Irish. Instead they got agitation, and demands for repeal of the Union. Despite progress, this era of reform had failed to reconcile Irish opponents of the Union and many serious problems remained, none more so than the Irish Poor Law, which was 'a ticking human time bomb, having put in place an English system of relief ill-suited to the island's problems and needs.'[55] In addition, O'Connell had been leading a formidable campaign for repeal of the Union from the early 1830s on. Even his arrest and trial in 1843–4 (which is prominent in *The Kellys and the O'Kellys*) did not halt the movement for repeal, which was also sustained by the Young Ireland Party.

The Loyal National Repeal Association pledged allegiance to the Queen while at the same time demanding repeal of the Union. Catholic influence over the association was powerful, and O'Connell promised the hierarchy that his Ireland would not simply be Catholic, but would also be ultramontane. A truly Irish parliament would be 'devoted to Religion, to Catholic truth in doctrine, discipline and submission to authority, with an undeviating attachment to the authority of the Holy See.'[56] While beating the repeal drum, O'Connell also continued to press for ameliorative measures: religious equality, better balance on land between landlords and tenants, a more representative Irish presence in Parliament, municipal reform, and the fiscal punishment of absentee landowners. O'Connell's task was not made any easier by the concessions that the Whigs had granted to Ireland. Thus he was forced to turn to increasingly demagogic denunciations of the 'English Parliament' and its six hundred 'scoundrels'. O'Connell adopted a language of blame that was the counterpart of anti-Irish English hostility towards his country, and by so doing was 'heightening ethnic consciousness, if not inflaming racial antipathies ... erecting a formidable barrier to Ireland's political integration into the British state.'[57]

In this climate, in London there was genuine worry about what was considered an explosive Irish situation. Although Trollope understood the motivations of those seeking repeal, he had little time for those on either side of the Irish Sea whom he believed obstructed rather than facilitated the Union. Despite Ireland's incomplete integration into the United Kingdom and its consequentially fragile and patchy economy, Trollope continued to argue in favour of the Union long after it had grown unpopular to do so, sure in his conviction that it offered the country the best opportunity for improvement. In a typical gesture, which aimed at denying the existence of any real political maturity in Ireland, Trollope

[55] Jenkins, *Irish Nationalism*, 40.   [56] Quoted in Jenkins, *Irish Nationalism*, 44.
[57] Jenkins, *Irish Nationalism*, 45.

asserted that the Irish did not want repeal but had been taken in by a cult of personality in the figure of O'Connell:

> No one who has known the people will deny that for many years the people were his people. Their hearts were in his hand, their wishes were governed by his will, and their political aspirations were the echo of his demands. That last demand was for the repeal of the Union, and in 1843 it was echoed with so loud a shout that the Government thought that Ireland was in earnest—so she was, but her earnest was the deification of a man, and not the performance of a right (*Examiner*, 99).

Trollope's view that O'Connell had become a monument to himself was shared by many who had earlier supported his campaign for Catholic Emancipation, including Sydney Owenson:

> The first flower of the earth, first gem of the sea O'Connell, wants back the days of Brian Boru, himself to be the king, with a crown of emerald shamrocks, a train of yellow velvet and mantel of Irish tabint, a sceptre in one hand and a cross in the other, and the people crying 'long live O'Connell'. This is the object of his views and ambitions.[58]

In mid-century, with the onset of the Famine, many English commentators and politicians began to believe that a looser rather than a more intimate Union might be better. Others felt that a stiffer hand was needed to keep the childlike Irish in check because they were incapable of ruling themselves, much less entering into a partnership of equals or semi-equals. Trollope's Irish life and writings resonate with the opinion that Ireland needed to be made more English, but also that Ireland had much to offer England and the Empire if only it were understood and better treated. A good working approximation of Trollope's position can be found in William Carleton's wish that his people 'through the influence of education, by the leadings of purer knowledge, and by the fosterings of a paternal government, [could become] the pride, the strength, and support of the British empire, instead of, as now, forming its weakness and its reproach.'[59] Ireland, in short, needed to be led by England and the English, being itself incapable of political action following the demise of O'Connell. The ever-conscientious Trollope put himself in the front line in trying to both bolster Ireland through his position in the Post Office and in attempting to articulate its needs and difficulties through his literary works.

---

[58] Lady Morgan quoted in M. Campbell, *Lady Morgan. The Life and Times of Sydney Owenson* (London: Pandora, 1988), 194.
[59] William Carleton, *Traits and Stories of the Irish Peasantry*, 2 vols (Dublin: Curry, 1834), I, viii.

IV. TROLLOPE'S IRISH OUTPUT AND RECEPTION

In repeatedly attempting to tackle the Irish question in his fiction, Trollope was writing against his own sometimes jaundiced feelings, an example, this, of his capacity to imagine himself into the motivations and beliefs of those with whom he might not naturally have empathized. He was also writing against more general prejudices towards the Irish to be found in British public discourse, both political and cultural. Members of the English political classes were often outspokenly negative about Ireland. Robert Peel, for instance, wrote of 'the wretched depravity and sanguinary disposition' of the Irish lower orders, who had 'a natural predilection for outrage and a lawless life', while Trollope's nemesis, Benjamin Disraeli, denounced this 'wild, reckless, indolent, uncertain and superstitious race' that has 'no sympathy with the English character.... Their history describes an unbroken circle of bigotry and blood.'[60] This was the era of the vaudeville Irishmen on the London stage. The Irish actor Tyrone Power led the way in performing Irish characters such as Murtoch Delany in *The Irishman in London*, Sir Patrick Plenipo in *The Irish Ambassador*, and Tim More, the travelling tailor in *The Irish Lion*. These, and other works, as Thackeray commented, 'led Cockneys to suppose . . . that Paddy was in a perpetual whirl of high spirits and whiskey; forever screeching and whooping mad songs and wild jokes.'[61] This was also the age of *Punch*'s cartoons depicting the Irish as a rowdy bunch of pig-faced anthropoids. Anti-Irish sentiment grew in mid-century as the Irish arrived en masse into Liverpool, Manchester, London, and other industrial cities as cheap, often starving and dishevelled, labour. Thomas Carlyle wrote about what he called 'that strange Ragged Tragedy of a Country',[62] and, in his 1848 essay, 'The Repeal of the Union', complained 'our lands [have become] overrun with hordes of hungry white savages, covered with dirt and rags full of noise, falsity and turbulence, . . . submerging our population into the depths of dirt, savagery, and degradation.'[63] While acknowledging

---

[60] Quoted in L. Perry Curtis, Jr., *Anglo-Saxons and Celts. A Study of Anti-Irish Prejudice in Victorian England*. (Bridgeport: University of Bridgeport Press, 1968), 51.

[61] William Makepeace Thackeray, *Critical Reviews, Tales, Various Essays, Letters, Sketches, Etc. with A Life of the Author* by Leslie Stephen and a Bibliography (New York and London: Harper & Brothers Publishers, 1899), 401.

[62] Thomas Carlyle, letter of 7 December 1856 to Margaret Callen, in Brent E. Kinser, ed., *The Carlyle Letters Online* (Baltimore: Duke University Press, 2007). http://carlyleletters.dukejournals.org/cgi/content/full/32/1/lt-18561207-TC-MACA-01.

[63] Thomas Carlyle, *Memoirs of the Life and Writings of Thomas Carlyle: With Personal Reminiscences and Selections from His Private Letters to Numerous Correspondents* (New York: Adegi Graphics LLC, 2001), 373.

that the 'Celt of Connemara' was 'white and not black', he insisted that 'it is not the colour of the skin that determines the savagery of a man.'[64] Robert Knox claimed that 'the source of all evil lies in the race, the Celtic race of Ireland', and felt the Irish were beyond help. The Union offered no hope for the future for an Ireland which was, in his view, nothing more than 'a country held by force of arms, like India; a country inhabited by another race.'[65]

Ireland only peripherally impinged upon the English nineteenth-century novel. That said, one might be forgiven of late, reading contemporary criticism, for thinking that Ireland was a core preoccupation of English fiction, with the 'little Caliban' that is Heathcliff, in effect, an Irish Famine refugee,[66] Gaskell's 'The Poor Clare', an allegorical comment on the Great Famine,[67] *Middlemarch*, 'a novel that is covertly about Ireland, with the marriage which ends it as a national marriage, symbolically enacting the reconciliation of Ireland and Britain',[68] and *Adam Bede*, a novel harbouring concern about Anglo-Irish relations, 'with a central female character's passivity before dominant men seen as being "in keeping with the commonplace stereotype of Ireland."'[69] For all the validity of these risky readings, which highlight aspects that appear to have gone unnoticed in contemporary criticism, in reality Irish issues occupied only a secondary place in the English literary imagination.

There were, however, writers who did look across the water with more than passing interest. Thackeray, for example, fills his *The Irish SketchBook* (1843) and *Barry Lyndon* with corrective rewritings of some of the stage or sham-Irish caricatures he saw in the London theatres or read in the early works of Lever and Lover, even if he makes clear that his intention in his picaresque Irish novel is to provide entertainment rather than offer any deep understanding of the country. Gaskell, who showed such sympathy for the English working classes in the 1840s, shows less concern, in *North and South* (1855), with the plight of the Irish immigrant workers, depicting them as barely civilized strike-breakers. This portrayal was representative of a more general sentiment, which identified the growing Irish

[64] Carlyle, *Memoirs*, 384.

[65] Robert Knox, *The Races of Men: A Philosophical Inquiry into the Influence of Race over the Destinies of Nations* (2nd edn, London: Henry Renshaw, 1862), 379, 375.

[66] Terry Eagleton, *Heathcliff and the Great Hunger: Studies in Irish Culture* (London and New York: Verso, 1995), 3.

[67] See Raphael Ingelbien, 'Elizabeth Gaskell's "The Poor Clare" and the Irish Famine', *Irish University Review*, 40/2 (2010), 1–19.

[68] James Murphy, *Irish Novelists & the Victorian Age* (Oxford: Oxford University Press, 2011), 2.

[69] Neil McCaw, 'Some mid-Victorian Irishness(es): Trollope, Thackeray, Eliot', in Neil McCaw, ed., *Writing Irishness in Nineteenth-Century British Culture* (Aldershot: Ashgate, 2004), 149.

population in Britain as a threat to the status quo, and saw the possibility of the poor Irish joining forces with the English working classes as a particular danger.

While Charles Kingsley was virulently anti-Irish in his private letters, where he wrote of being 'haunted by the human chimpanzees I saw along that hundred miles of horrible country',[70] his *Alton Locke* (1850) is one of few social problem novels to take the Irish into serious consideration. Kingsley provides a realistic portrayal of the Irish presence in working-class London, depicting, among others, the editor of the *Weekly Warwhoop*, Mr O'Flynn (a version of Irish Chartist leader, Feargus O'Connor), Kelly, a starving Irish tailor, and Jemmy Downe's Irish wife. Mostly, the Irish emerge negatively from the novel. Alton, for example, pitches the negative aspects of the Irish against 'the true English stuff . . . the stuff which has held Gibraltar and conquered at Waterloo—which has created a Birmingham and a Manchester, and colonized every quarter of the globe—that grim, earnest, stubborn energy, which, since the days of the old Romans, the English possess alone of all the nations of the earth.'[71]

The majority of English novelists and historians apportioned blame to the Irish themselves for the disastrous economic and political situation 'across the water' while at the same time fearing that the Irish would export disorder into England. The sense of superiority was, however, variegated and often paradoxical. Kingsley advocated intermarriage with the quicksilver Celt in order to alleviate Saxon dullness,[72] thus echoing Edmund Burke's belief, as summarized by Declan Kiberd, that 'the Irish and the English taken together had the makings of a whole person',[73] and anticipating Matthew Arnold's view of the Irish as 'a complement or antidote to the English.'[74] *Punch* sometimes portrayed Hibernia as a classic Greek beauty, even if its Irish coverage became increasingly negative during and after the Famine, which it portrayed as a tragic if necessary step towards putting the country on a more stable footing (this, too, was Trollope's line). Many sympathetic articles about the Irish plight did appear in English newspapers, such as the *Illustrated London News*, which consistently attempted to convey the extent of Irish Famine

---

[70] Charles Kingsley, *His Letters and Memories of His Life*, Edited By His Wife, 2 vols (London: C. Kegan Paul, 1877), II, 107.

[71] Charles Kingsley, *Alton Locke, Tailor and Poet*, ed. Elizabeth A. Cripps (Oxford and New York: Oxford University Press, 1983), 132.

[72] R. F. Foster, *Paddy & Mr Punch. Connections in Irish and English History* (London: Penguin, 1995), 287.

[73] Declan Kiberd, *Inventing Ireland, the Literature of the Modern Nation* (London: Vintage, 1996), 20.

[74] Peter Mandler, *The English National Character* (New Haven and London: Yale, 2006), 99.

suffering, most notably in 1847 when it commissioned and published James Mahoney's shocking 'Sketches in the West of Ireland'.

Given the English exhaustion with the Irish situation in the middle decades of the century, it is no real surprise that Irish writers found it increasingly hard to find an audience for novels about their country. Charles Lever, once enormously popular, now complained to Maria Edgeworth 'that anything Irish is an ungracious theme to English ears just now',[75] and Harriet Martineau concurred in 1853, noting that 'the world', and especially 'the English reading world', is 'weary of the subject of Ireland':

> The mere name brings up images of men in long coats and women in long cloaks; of mud cabins and potatoes; the conacre, the middleman, and the priest; the faction fight, and the funeral howl. The sadness of the subject has of late years increased the weariness.[76]

As Mary Hamer put it: 'Ireland had become a most painful and unmanageable topic for the British reading public by 1847. Nightmare reports in parliament and the press of mass starvation, destitution, disease and violence forced a new perception of Ireland and raised questions of moral and material responsibility that could not readily be answered.'[77] Increasingly, blame for the Irish situation was apportioned to the Anglo-Irish landlord class. The radical English MP George Poulett Scrope accused the Anglo-Irish Ascendancy of driving tenants to emigrate or starve to death because of their high rents. Radicals were not alone in taking this line. According to *The Times*: 'the prime cause why the Irish peasantry have been reduced to their present level must be sought for in the neglect and unthrift of past generations of claret-drinking, writ-despising, landlords.'[78] Worse still, in Poulett Scrope's words, the Anglo-Irish perpetuated 'the system which has given to the character of the Celt some of the qualities peculiar to a slave population,'[79] and effectively blocked any possibility of change. The only possible way out of the impasse was to enact a new Poor Law that would force the Anglo-Irish to pay their way and support all of the country's poor. In so doing, expensive

---

[75] Quoted in Edmund Downey, *Charles Lever: His Life in His Letters*, 2 vols (Edinburgh: William Blackwood and Sons, 1906), 1, 257.

[76] Harriet Martineau, 'Condition and Prospects of Ireland', *Westminster Review*, 8 (January 1853), 25, quoted in McCaw, ed., *Writing Irishness*, 129.

[77] Mary Hamer, 'Introduction' to Anthony Trollope, *Castle Richmond* (Oxford: Oxford University Press, 1992), xii.

[78] *The Times*, 24 August 1847.

[79] George Poulett Scrope, *How to Make Ireland Self-Supporting; or, Irish Clearances, and Improvement of Waste Lands* (London: James Ridgway, 1848), 17.

English relief efforts could be trimmed back.[80] This thesis was vehemently opposed by the moderate Whig, Nassau Senior, who believed that such a policy would bring an already struggling landlord class to its knees, and bankrupt Ireland, leading to an even larger bill being laid at England's door. In any case, 1847 saw the passing of an Irish Poor Law Bill, which was implemented with disastrous results by Charles Trevelyan, and which put much of the responsibility for relief provision in the hands of the Anglo-Irish (Trollope, as we shall see, approved of this controversial measure).

Given the complexities of the Irish situation in the middle decades of the nineteenth century, to many the easiest response was to recoil and fall back on a deeply set anti-Irish feeling, which formed a predominant discourse of an age that saw the world in terms of binary hierarchies, with the English representing culture and civilization, and the Irish seen to embody anarchy, barbarity, and chaos. In this key, the Irish were everything that the English were not, and they provided a mirror image against which English identity could take shape. The Irish, on the other hand, while advocating greater help from Britain, often resented that assistance being offered on British terms and only in return for imposed political compromise.

This, in necessarily broad strokes, was the complex backdrop against which Trollope began to write his Irish works. His first two published novels were *The Macdermots of Ballycloran* (1847) and *The Kellys and the O'Kellys* (1848). Karen Faulkner's assertion that 'had Trollope written nothing but *The Macdermots of Ballycloran*, *The Kellys and the O'Kellys*, and *La Vendée*, he would not have earned mention as even a minor novelist of the nineteenth century',[81] is both hasty and unfair. He would have earned at least honourable mention, and arguably would have occupied a more prominent place in the Irish canon. As it turned out, his interest in Ireland persisted and his career was brought to a close with the unfinished *The Landleaguers* (1883). He also penned a handful of Irish short stories as well as the Famine novel *Castle Richmond* (1860), which he prefaced, saying: 'I fear that Irish character is in these days considered as unattractive as historical incident but nevertheless I will make the attempt' (*CR*, 2). The second and fourth Palliser novels, *Phineas Finn, The Irish Member* (1869) and *Phineas Redux* (1874), have as their hero the Irishman, Phineas Finn, and the entire series can be seen 'as an attempt to challenge Irish stereotypes in general, while offering a distinctive

---

[80] George Poulett Scrope, *How is Ireland to be Governed?* (London: James Ridgway, 1846), 36–9.

[81] Karen Faulkner, 'Anthony Trollope's Apprenticeship', *Nineteenth-Century Literature*, 38/2 (Sept. 1983), 161–88.

treatment of two of the most common images of Irishness: the Stage Irishman and the presentation of Ireland as a feminized victim';[82] all this as part of the more general thrust of the series to describe the decades-long marital history of Plantagenet Palliser and his wife, Lady Glencora, and to enact a dissection of British parliamentary politics as a refraction of the workings of society. A final Irish novel, *An Eye for an Eye* (1879), deserves to take its place among the series of his courageous if flawed attempts to contain the matter of Ireland in novelistic form.

Trollope also wrote a significant number of short stories set in Ireland ('The O'Conors of Castle Conor' and 'Father Giles of Ballymoy'), or with significant Irish content or characters, such as Mr Molloy in 'The Turkish Bath' and Mrs Greene in 'The Man Who Kept His Money in a Box'. Conscious of the popularity of Irish guidebooks, such as Anna Maria and Samuel Carter Hall's three volume *Ireland: Its Scenery, Character, etc.* (1841–3) and their *A Week at Killarney* (1843), Trollope made one additional attempt in 1850 to 'get' Ireland between covers, seeking to interest the publisher John Murray in 'a handbook for Ireland'. As he recalled: 'I "did" the city of Dublin, and the county of Kerry, in which lies the lake scenery of Killarney; and I "did" the route from Dublin to Killarney, altogether completing nearly a quarter of the proposed volume' (*Auto*, 87). He sent the manuscript off to Albemarle Street where, to his great annoyance, it was not even opened, not to mention published. A flavour of the prose Trollope might have written is to be found in one of the chapters he cut from the 1860 revised edition of *The Macdermots of Ballycloran*, which describes Father John Magrath's journey from Leitrim to Dublin. Trollope's keen topographical eye misses nothing:

> The first idea that strikes a stranger on passing through this portion of Ireland is astonishment that Erin should have had the epithet green applied to it—for certainly in most of the central counties, it is, generally speaking, as brown a country as ever the eye rested on.... They passed by Rooskey, then a quiet little village, with an old bridge over the Shannon, but now bustling with Shannon commissioners and their servants—young engineers, carpenters, bricklayers, busy at their work, disturbing the sleeping river with their piles, coffer dams and masonry—through Newtown Forbes, with its beautiful and deserted demesne—by the Longford Artillery barracks—and at last the horses stopped at their well-known appointed spot before Sutcliff's hotel (*Macdermots*, 637–8).

[82] Patrick Lonergan, 'Anthony Trollope's Palliser Novels and Anti-Irish Prejudice', *New Hibernia Review/ Iris Éireannach Nua*, 11/2 (Summer 2007), 116.

Considerable attention is given to describing the improving 'metropolis' of Dublin, seen as an imperial city, resplendent with public monuments commemorating great English military leaders. Trollope even notes William of Orange on horseback (this statue was blown up by republicans in the 1930s):

> So he returned along Leinster-street and Nassau-street—not the Nassau-street of the present day since it has been thrown open to the gardens of Trinity College, and made one of the handsomest streets in Europe—but the Nassau-street of ten years since, when it was as narrow, dirty, crowded and disagreeable as any large and thronged thoroughfare need be, through the bottom of Grafton-street, between the gates of Trinity and the famous statue of *pious, glorious and immortal* Willy—under the splendid portico of the bank, by far the finest building in Ireland—down Westmoreland street, over Carlisle Bridge, and up Sackville-street till he reached the foot of the splendid pillar, with which Ireland has testified her admiration of England's naval hero. The taste which has been displayed in erecting the pillar in this magnificent street to Nelson's honor, must, it is presumed, be taken in atonement for the atrocious pile of gigantic stones with which the Duke of Wellington had been disgraced in the Phoenix Park (*Macdermots*, 651–2).

Interesting as this material is—and it would have fitted better in a guidebook than in Trollope's novel—he should have known better than to propose such as project at a time when the country was only beginning a fragile recovery from the Famine and offered little allure as a holiday destination. Murray eventually published an anonymous Irish handbook—not Trollope's—in 1864.

Trollope also includes many Irish characters in his non-Irish fiction and sometimes even in his travel writing. A case in point is that of the O'Gorman Mahon (Charles James Patrick Mahon, 1800–91), whom he met in 1859 in Costa Rica along with Don Juan Rafael Mora, President of the Republic of Costa Rica, and Prince Polignac; all were gathered to discuss the building of a canal in Costa Rica and Nicaragua. Although Trollope differed politically with the O'Gorman Mahon, who had played a key role in the campaign for Catholic Emancipation and who would later support Parnell, he clearly enjoyed the company of this larger-than-life Irish character:

> On entering the public sitting-room a melodiously rich Irish brogue at once greeted my ears, and I saw seated at the table, joyous in a semi-military uniform, The O'Gorman Mahon, great as in bygone unemancipated days, when with head erect and stentorian voice he would make himself audible to half the County Clare. The head was still as erect, and the brogue as unexceptionable (*West Indies*, 250).

The sight of the three luminaries makes Trollope think of 'the heterogeneous heroes of "The Groves of Blarney"', which he presumably found in one of Father Prout's satirical versions of Richard Alfred Milliken's poem. Trollope quotes from memory but, by his own admission, erroneously:

> There were Nicodemus, and Polyphemus,
> Oliver Cromwell and Leslie Foster.
> 'And now, boys, ate a bit of what's going, and take a dhrop of dhrink,' said The O'Gorman, patting us on the shoulders with kind patronage. We did as we were bid, ate and drank, paid the bill, and went our way rejoicing (*West Indies*, 251).

Trollope later revealed his familiarity with the figure of Father Prout in his biography of Thackeray, when he recalls that both he and Father Prout appeared in the first number of the *Cornhill Magazine* (*Thackeray*, 53).

Among the generous sprinkling of fictional Irish characters, or characters with conspicuous Irish ancestry in his 'non-Irish' novels, we find Mistress Morony in *The Struggles of Brown, Jones and Robinson*. An Irish virago, she plays a cameo in this short novel, which was published in the *Cornhill* from August 1861 to March 1862, with a second-hand title borrowed from Richard Doyle's *The Foreign Tour of Messrs. Brown, Jones and Robinson* (1855). Trollope intended this work as a satire on trade and on the growing role of advertising at the expense of quality. The deeply unpleasant Mistress Morony is 'a full-sized lady, not without a certain amount of good looks', of about fifty. 'Her face was florid, if not red, her arms were thick and powerful, her eyes were bright, but, as seen by Brown, Jones, and Robinson, not pleasant to the view, and she always carried with her an air of undaunted resolution' (*BJR*, 143). She is correct in her demands that she be given a pelisse displayed in the shop window rather than an inferior alternative from behind the counter. She causes such an immense stir over the pelisse that police intervention is needed, and the fracas becomes the subject of a damaging article in the *Daily Jupiter*. Although she tells 'the magistrates in Worship Street' that she 'had lived in the very highest circles in Limerick', her Irishness adds little more than a layer of colour to this amusing chapter at the centre of Trollope's rather loose satire.

The more sinister figure of Captain Patrick Carroll is to be found in *Mr Scarborough's Family*, a posthumous work that represents Trollope's gathering impatience with Ireland and the Irish in his latter years. His name echoes with that of 'Pat Carroll and all the little Patlings must now be fed', evoked contemptuously in Trollope's fourth *Examiner* letter (*Examiner*, 90), and with Pat Carroll, the agrarian agitator in *The Landleaguers* (1883), who leads the boycott against his landlord, intimidates his young son, Florian, and embodies all the causes of Trollope's dismay with the country he so long looked to with great affection but no longer understood. Captain Carroll in *Mr Scarborough's Family* is the most negatively drawn of Trollope's Irish leeches. 'An improvident, worthless, drunken Irishman' with six daughters, he lives off his brother-in-law, the decent English lawyer, John Grey, who had incautiously promised Carroll that he 'would never see his sister want' (*Scarborough*, 193). Trollope dedicates an entire chapter to describing this dysfunctional Irish family and the dread felt by the Greys on the news that 'Aunt Carroll' will be coming over with her daughters for dinner, as they know only too well that she will be pleading for yet another loan to pay off some of her husband's more urgent debts. Despite the objections of his own family, Mr Grey agrees to the request because he cannot bear arguing with his sister, even if he knows the money is being given to a lost cause. Given that Trollope saw Ireland as the sister-island, it is difficult not to read this relationship of craven dependence as his rather harsh metaphor for the connection between Britain and Ireland.

Less negative references to matters Irish pop up throughout the body of Trollope's fiction and range from Mrs Quiverful's 'Irish stew' for her 'fourteen young birds' in *Barchester Towers* (*BT*, 393) to the debate on Sir Abraham Haphazard's anti-Catholic 'Convent Custody Bill' in *The Warden* (1855), which so divides the Irish Parliamentary Party 'who had bound themselves together to force on the ministry a bill for compelling all men to drink Irish whiskey, and all women to wear Irish poplins' (*Warden*, 95). More instances of interest in Irishness occur in the smattering of Irish characters that includes Mickey O'Dowd, the sometimes homesick Irish boundary rider in *Harry Heathcote of Gangoil*, who believes 'the masther should be the masther, no doubt' (*Harry Heathcote*, 186), and the 'stout gentleman' in *The Last Chronicle of Barset* called 'Onesiphorus Dunn... actually called Siph by his intimate friends' (*Last Chronicle*, 546). Dunn is a likeable freeloader, 'an Irishman, living on the best of everything in the world, with apparently no fortune of his own, and certainly never earning anything.' Although a figure of almost no consequence, Trollope cannot resist affectionately fleshing out his Irish character:

> He did not borrow money, and he did not encroach. He did like being asked out to dinner, and he did think that they to whom he gave the light of his countenance in town owed him the return of a week's run in the country. He neither shot, nor hunted nor fished, nor read, and yet he was never in the way in any house. He did play billiards, and whist, and croquet—very badly. He was a good judge of wine, and would occasionally condescend to look after the bottling of it on behalf of some very intimate friend (*Last Chronicle*, 546).

Characters of more substance and with Irish ancestry include Dr Proudie in *Barchester Towers*, who is described as 'the nephew of an Irish baron by his mother's side' (*BT*, 21), and Augustus Melmotte in *The Way We Live Now* (1875). He appears to have an Irish background, even if his exact lineage is veiled in obscurity: In the novel it is believed that he is a European Jew and a 'great French swindler' (*WWLN*, 477), but 'the general opinion seemed to be that his father had been a noted coiner in New York, —an Irishman of the name of Melmody' (*WWLN*, 449). That Melmotte is Irish-American is important, since Trollope was increasingly irritated by what he felt was Irish-American political and financial interference in Irish affairs (strident testimony to this can be found in *The Landleaguers*). Unlike the loyal Irishman, Phineas Finn, men like Melmotte are a threat, in Trollope's view, to the very foundations of the state. Even if Melmotte's Irish lineage is a marginal issue, it is likely that his character (like that of Lever's Davenport Dunn) was inspired by John Sadleir, a man who would have been perfectly at home in Celtic Tiger Ireland, but who was in fact a junior Lord of the Treasury, but more importantly an embezzler, a swindler, and a forger, who brought down the Irish Tipperary Bank in 1856, and, in doing so, 'ruined half Ireland' before committing suicide by taking prussic acid. Melmotte too is a character who builds a property empire on spurious funds and eventually makes 'himself odious by his ruin to friends who had taken him up as a pillar of strength in regard to wealth'. Like Sadleir, he is 'found dead, with a bottle of prussic acid by his side' (*WWLN*, 356).

Trollope's Irish writings always received mixed reviews, although they often were praised among a restricted circle of Irish readers and critics. The conservative *Dublin Review* praised '[t]his Englishman, keenly observant . . . absolutely sincere and unprejudiced, [who] writes a story as true to the saddest and heaviest truths of Irish life, as racy of the soil, as rich with the peculiar humour, the moral features, the social oddities, the subtle individuality of the far west of Ireland as George Eliot's novels are true to the truths of English life.'[83] A quarter of a century later, Maurice Francis Egan commented in particular on Trollope's unusually accommodating treatment of Irish priests and of Irish Catholicism:

> Trollope's point of view was sympathetic, and, though he could not do what he did for the Anglican parson—that is, give us the best pictures of Protestant clerical life done in English . . . his Father John and his curate are much truer and kinder than might be expected from a man who had little

---

[83] *Dublin Review*, 71 (1872), 393.

knowledge of the inner life of priests. He was faithful to Irish life as he saw it.[84]

Trollope struggled on and off for decades with Ireland, trying to find a form adequate for the country's predicament and, at the same time, still capable of appealing to his English readership. This took him on a path which involved borrowing from many genres, including the comedy of manners, the social or thesis novel, the short story, the political novel, the National Tale, the Big-House novel, the gothic, the tragic, and sometimes uneasy combinations of all of these. No wonder then that Trollope's more conservative English critics would see his Irish novels as aberrations. Michael Sadleir, long his most influential critic in the early decades of the twentieth century (and also known for his 1940 novel, *Fanny by Gaslight*), sees 'Trollope's Irish fiction as something from which he was fortunate to escape into more congenial subjects which came to him when he fell "beneath the slow, wise, soothing spell of rural England."'[85] Sadleir continues:

> Ireland produced the man; but it was left to England to inspire the novelist.
> Indeed one may go further. Ireland, having by friendliness, sport and open air saved Trollope from himself, all but choked the very genius that she had vitalised by her insane absorption in her own wrongs and thwarted hopes.[86]

This makes for rather offensive reading, given that Ireland's 'insane absorption' shortly after Trollope arrived there was the Great Famine. Sadleir implies that Trollope should have followed the path of Maria Edgeworth who, following Catholic Emancipation in 1829, ceased writing about Ireland. In his *History of the Novel*, Ernest Baker insists that Trollope's Irish novels display nothing of the genuine Trollope, and he begins his main discussion of the author in the next section of his entry which is entitled 'The Novels that Count',[87] leaving the reader in no doubt as to the status of the early Irish work. For critics such as Sadleir and Baker, Trollope's error appears to have been to open a chink in the fictional frame which allows light to fall away from the comedy of manners and onto the harsh Irish realities of rural agitation, poverty, and Famine, which are the troubled and troubling backgrounds to his Irish novels, and for which the English reading public, 'the literary appreciation that knows no nationality', had, perhaps understandably, a limited appetite.

[84] Maurice Francis Egan, 'On Irish Novels', *Catholic University Bulletin*, 10/3 (1904), 31.
[85] John Cronin, 'Trollope and the Matter of Ireland', in Bareham, ed., *Trollope*, 24.
[86] Sadleir, *Trollope*, 143.
[87] Ernest A. Baker, *The History of the English Novel*, vol. 8 (1937; repr. New York: Barnes and Nobel, 1950), 116.

Some Irish critics were equally unimpressed. M. J. MacManus, for instance, believed that 'Trollope's Irish novels are easily his worst',[88] but not all reception was negative and Trollope's Irish works had their supporters. Shane Leslie railed against the blanket dismissal of the Irish novels:

> by the Irish, who cannot believe that an Englishman could write a good Irish novel, and by the English, who grudge one of their great novelists even for his apprenticeship on the Irish scene. He was the only Englishman who could write an Irish novel without a mistake. Dickens never dared describe an Irishman. His English characters were already more exaggerated than any stage Irishman. In *Pendennis* Thackeray drew his Captain Costigan and Charley Shandon, the latter only a caricature of Dr. Mainn, but his Irish folk were not like Trollope's as 'Irish as O'Hanlon's breech.'[89]

In the *Irish Times* in 1943, Seán Ó Faoláin praised Trollope's treatment of matters Irish as evidence that he 'dearly loved our people',[90] while Lennox Robinson took issue with Sadleir's reading and described Trollope as 'a very honest writer, but he couldn't always tell the whole truth: no Victorian novelist could'. In Robinson's evaluation

> Ireland made him write. . . . it seems almost incredible that an Englishman after a couple of years in Ireland could write of a foreign country with such understanding and without sentiment. I can only compare these books with 'The Real Charlotte,' and I think them better. They are tragic. The description of the kitchen and the upstairs room in the Dunmore Inn ('The Kellys') can be put beside Balzac. . . . he never got nearer tragedy than in those two early Irish novels.[91]

V. TROLLOPE'S IRISH INFLUENCES

In his Irish novels Trollope finds a space as an in-between writer, working beyond the conventional geographical frontiers of the Victorian English novel in a borderland of encounter between Britain and Ireland. The Irish novel provided him with a rather precarious paradigm to follow. While Victorian England was awash with novelists (a minority of them Irish, such as the hugely popular Charlotte Riddell, writing 'English' novels, and

---

[88] MacManus is cited in Longford, 'Trollope in Ireland', 185.
[89] Shane Leslie, 'Introduction' to Anthony Trollope, *The Kellys and the O'Kellys*, ed. Shane Leslie (New York, Random House, 1937), vii.
[90] Seán Ó Faoláin, 'An Autobiography for Authors', *Irish Times* (13 November 1943), 3.
[91] Lennox Robinson, 'Trollope in Ireland: An Open Letter to Winifred Letts', *Irish Times* (17 February 1945), 2.

so largely invisible in today's canon of the Irish novel), Ireland, particularly in the middle of the century, could muster far fewer, although not as few as critics long led us to believe.[92] For even if the Irish nineteenth century failed to produce a 'great' novelist akin to Scott in Scotland (although it might be argued that Scott himself saw Maria Edgeworth filling this role), or a great *Ulysses*-like novel that would embody or define the country or the century, it did produce a healthy body of mainly realistic novels as well as a strong flurry of 'Protestant Gothic' novels, which expressed, as Eagleton and others have argued, 'the political unconscious of Irish society.'[93]

Trollope read an ample selection of works by the canonical figures of Irish nineteenth-century fiction, such as Maria Edgeworth, Charles Maturin, Thomas Moore, Sydney Owenson, Mrs Hall, William Carleton, the Banim brothers, Gerald Griffin, Samuel Lover, and Charles Lever. His first source for these works was, in all probability, the Gregory library at Coole Park. The majority of the works fitted into a category of Irish novel described by MacDonagh as 'ample, discursive, domestic and generally, if quite innocently, sociological in content . . . as close, perhaps, as it is possible to get in literature to that of the historian.'[94] These works, many of which owed much to Sir Walter Scott's 'anthropolitical' works' which fudged 'distinctions between biography, fiction and history',[95] tended to have insistently rural settings, a focus on the community rather than the individual, an ongoing social concern, and a mediatory impulse towards an English audience rather than to a domestic one. The descriptive, discursive thrust of the Irish novel was propelled through narratives that presented the Irish at a considerable remove from an English readership which identified primarily with an intermediary narrator. Thus the Irish novel represented its subject matter, essentially Ireland and the Irish, from a distance: 'The destinatory vector towards an English audience is so strong that the author no longer identifies with the country which is represented, but becomes an intermediary, an exteriorised, detached observer.'[96] Trollope fits into the scheme by adopting the same mediatory

[92] See Rolf Loeber and Magda Stouthamer-Loeber, with Anne M. Burnham, *A Guide to Irish Fiction, 1650–1900* (Dublin: Four Courts Press, 2006).

[93] Eagleton, *Heathcliff*, 187.

[94] Oliver MacDonagh, 'The Nineteenth Century Novel and Irish Social History: Some Aspects', O'Donnell Lecture, National University of Ireland. Delivered at University College Cork on 21 April 1970, 3.

[95] K. D. M. Snell, 'The Regional Novel: Themes for Interdisciplinary Research', in K. D. M. Snell, *The Regional Novel in Britain and Ireland* (Cambridge: Cambridge University Press, 1998), 5.

[96] Joep Leerssen, *Remembrance and Imagination: Patterns in the Historical and Literary Representation of Ireland in the Nineteenth Century* (Cork: Cork University Press, 1996), 34.

technique, arguably, in his English case, with more justification, although he does alternate between detachment and empathy.

The sociological or historical content of the Irish novel was another distinguishing quality, but the need to explain Ireland's problems risked overwhelming more purely artistic aims. In 1919, Stephen Gwynn described 'literature in Ireland' as

> almost inextricably connected with consideration foreign to art; it is regarded as a means, not an end. During the nineteenth century the belief being general among all classes of Irish people that the English know nothing of Ireland, every book on an Irish subject was judged by the effect it was likely to have upon English opinion . . . Ireland, though she ought to count herself amply justified of her children, is still complaining that she is misunderstood among the nations; she is forever crying out for someone to give her keener sympathy, fuller appreciation, and exhibit herself and her grievances to the world in a true light. The result is that kind of insincerity and special pleading which has been the curse of Irish or Anglo-Irish literature.[97]

In short, the Irish novel laboured under a basic foundational burden of being asked to do too much. As Belanger puts it, 'the genre of the novel itself seemed to buckle under the weight of its polemical or explanatory functions for a readership often located outside of Ireland'.[98] On the one hand, it should arouse sympathy in Britain for the Irish plight; on the other, it was expected to respond to aesthetic imperatives that often must have seemed insignificant in the light of the country's troubled actuality. We need only consider the marriage plots of both Carleton's *The Black Prophet* and Trollope's *Castle Richmond*, which, although responding to formulaic aesthetic expectations of the time, are trivial in the extreme when juxtaposed with the Famine descriptions that compete for the readers' attention.

Castle Richmond, and Trollope's Irish writings more in general, exemplify both the strengths and weaknesses of what might be called the explanatory impulse in Irish fiction of the time. This partly explains why they are accused of suffering in aesthetic terms for being overly engaged in interpreting Ireland for the English reader and for being overburdened with sociological information. This is in marked contrast with most of his English novels, especially his Barsetshire chronicles, which describe a world arguably as foreign to Trollope as the Ireland that he struggled to fit into fiction but one which was more immediately recognizable to his readers. And yet, the very qualities that early English critics complained of

---

[97] Stephen Gwynn, *Irish Books and Irish People* (Dublin: Talbot Press, 1919), 8.

[98] Jacqueline Belanger, 'Introduction', in Jacqueline Belanger, ed., *The Irish Novel in the Nineteenth Century: Facts and Fictions* (Dublin: Four Courts Press, 2005), 13.

in Trollope's Irish novels—his concern with Irish 'background', socio-logical explanation, place, and context—are precisely what qualifies these works to be read as part of the canonical tradition of the Irish novel, a tradition which owes so much to its foundational National Tales, Edge-worth's *Castle Rackrent* (subtitled 'An Hibernian Tale, Taken from Facts, and from the Manners of the Irish Squires, Before the Year 1782') and Sydney Owenson's *The Wild Irish Girl* (1806). This genre wavers between the realist and the romantic, and strives to convey the illusion of fact, as a footnote to Owenson's novel announces: 'Neither the rencontre with, nor the character or story of Murtoch, partakes in the least degree of fiction'. The National Tale is distinguished by a 'thick evocation of place' and a desire to 'address questions of cultural distinctiveness, national policy, and political separatism.'[99]

The Irish national tale, so often a dialogic, multi-voiced text, is a ramshackle genre in which the imperative of a busy plot competes with the compelling necessity to address large, ideological questions, to explain why the country is the way it is, and to offer images pointing towards a hoped-for reconciliation both between the divided internal parts and a larger union with Britain. The cast of principal characters is used to illustrate the national dilemma, while a variety of distinctive voices compete for the readers' attention. Antiquarianism jostles with Irish-English dialogue and with a surfeit of analysis which is more usually to be found in a political pamphlet. Sometimes sentimental comedy is added to the mix and sits uncomfortably with depictions of agrarian crime, sensationalized cabin poverty, and lingering descriptions of Irish ruins, ancient castles, and their often decrepit inhabitants.

Ian Duncan defines Owenson's version of national fiction as 'bardic, sentimental, philo-Jacobin', in contrast to Edgeworth's 'satirical, reform-ist, liberal-conservative branch',[100] and these oppositional definitions serve to suggest why Edgeworth's ideology and style (rather than Owen-son's) appealed more to Trollope as he set about identifying a model to follow. Owenson, at least initially, stressed Irish cultural difference, while Edgeworth, particularly in the novels following *Castle Rackrent*, tended to assimilate Ireland within the Union. Trollope would have looked at how both writers wrote with a British audience in mind and how their Irish works were laden with sociological observations about the speech, cus-toms, and history of the various strata of Catholic Irish and Anglo-Irish

[99] Katie Trumpener, *Bardic Nationalism: The Romantic Novel and the British Empire* (Princeton, NJ: Princeton University Press, 1997), 131–2.
[100] Ian Duncan, *Scott's Shadow: The Novel in Romantic Edinburgh* (Princeton, NJ: Princeton University Press, 2007), 73.

society, and he would have been aware that not everyone approved of this approach. Gerald Griffin, for example, in his preface to *Tales of the Munster Festivals* (1827), criticized 'those writers, who professing to present faithful illustrations of the minds and hearts of our peasantry, greedily rake up the ... unhappy blemishes of our island ... to the eyes of a world that, unfortunately for us, is but too eager to seize every occasion for mockery and upbraiding against our forlorn and neglected country.'[101] Undoubtedly, there was a tricky path to be trod between expressing and exploiting the country, and this would be particularly so for such a markedly English writer, no matter how well intentioned Trollope was in his position as go-between.

Trollope regularly interlaces his Irish narratives with historical/socio-logical observations. In doing so, he looked to Edgeworth (who, in her preface to *Castle Rackrent*, announced that she would include notes 'For the information of the ignorant English reader') as his chief model. A fan of Scott, Trollope would surely have agreed with his evaluation of Edgeworth:

> Without being so presumptuous as to hope to emulate the rich humour, pathetic tenderness, and admirable tact, which pervade the works of my accomplished friend, I felt that something might be attempted for my own country with that which Miss Edgeworth so fortunately achieved for Ire-land—something which might introduce her natives to those of her sister kingdom in a more favourable light than they had been placed hitherto, and tend to procure sympathy for their virtue and indulgences for their foibles.[102]

Scott wrote of Edgeworth's Irish tales as the template for his own portrayal of Scotland on the big historical stage, claiming that she 'may be truly said to have done more towards completing the Union [of Ireland with Britain] than perhaps all the legislative enactments by which it has been followed up.'[103] It was very much in the spirit of analysing the problems in the Union in order ultimately to reinforce it that Trollope turned to Edgeworth as model and muse for his Irish works, although he struggled and ultimately found himself unable to offer the note of optimism that characterizes the endings of her three other Irish novels, *Ennui, The Absentee,* and *Ormond,* each of which concludes with expectations of well-run estates managed by reforming young landlords. These endings contrast with the note of doom that brings *Castle Rackrent* to a close, with

---

[101] Quoted in Eagleton, *Heathcliff,* 153.

[102] Sir Walter Scott, 'General Preface', in Sir Walter Scott, *Waverley; or, 'Tis Sixty Years Since,* ed. Claire Lamont (Oxford: Oxford World's Classics, 2008), 352–3.

[103] Scott, 'General Preface', 352.

its evocation of the Rackrent family's ruin and the purchase of their estate by Thady's own son, an Irish Catholic—the enactment, that is, of the worst nightmare of the anxious and often economically stretched Anglo-Irish landowning class.

Scott admired Edgeworth's ability to elicit understanding and sympathy for Ireland in her English readers. By sympathy, he would have intended the sense in which it is used by Adam Smith, that is, to mean fellow feeling which can be stimulated by affective appeal and which allows us, as Smith argued, not so much to feel 'what other men feel', but to conceive, through the imagination, 'what we ourselves should feel in the like situation.'[104] The ability to arouse sympathy for another—who is, however, always different, always 'Other'—to make a reader feel what it might be like to stand in someone else's shoes, is, of course, a central aim of the novel *tout court*, and Trollope's sensitive treatment of Thady Macdermot in *The Macdermots of Ballycloran* is a successful example of this, even if the Victorian concept of sympathy becomes more complex when applied to an Irish novel directed at an English audience. Irish novelists had to tread a perilous path so as not to offend either of their two very different constituencies of reader. Sometimes they directly draw attention to this dual readership: Lever, for example, in *Harry Lorrequer*, renders explicit for his English reader what he feels is implicit for the Irish one: 'How much reason Denis had to boast of imparting early information to the new secretary I leave my English readers to guess; my Irish ones I may trust to do him ample justice.'[105] The capacity to achieve a sense of fellow feeling in a non-Irish reader became a yardstick for the success of the Irish novel. It risked being a classist act, however, with one (usually well-educated) writer addressing an audience of fellow middle-class readers about a distant and often dismal Irish Catholic other world, often seen to be beyond redemption, even within the terms of fiction, not to mention those of reality. The danger of falling into stereotype by stressing weakness is constant, and the risk is that one is constantly appealing for charity rather than admitting difference and demanding equality. Yeats, in his slighting assessment of Lever, accused him of writing 'ever with one eye on London',[106] but it is hard to imagine how an Irish novelist at the time was to survive without doing so. Carleton also wrote expressly with an English audience in mind, hoping to arouse sympathy and help for his country in

[104] Adam Smith, *Theory of Moral Sentiments* (1759; repr. Indianapolis: Liberty Classics, 1982), 9.

[105] Charles Lever, *The Confessions of Harry Lorrequer* (Dublin: William Curry, 1839), 96.

[106] W.B. Yeats, *Uncollected Prose by W.B. Yeats*, vol. 1, ed. John P. Frayne (London: Macmillan, 1970), 162.

works such as *The Black Prophet*, which is scattered with asides about an absent but hoped-for English reader, such as, 'Alas! little do our English neighbours know or dream of the horrors which attend a year of severe famine in this unhappy country.'[107] This was a method adopted by Trollope and later, we might well say, by Yeats himself, for all his far more complex stances in negotiating an ongoing cultural and political exchange between the two countries.

Seamus Deane has written of the dangers inherent in writing novels in the Edgeworth manner, while at the same time praising her as 'the first Irish writer of the century' to make 'a serious attempt in fiction to analyse and recommend improvements for Irish society as it was.'[108] The downside of what she sought to achieve—'sympathy for her Irish Catholic subjects'—was that she 'tended to avail of the stereotyped view of the vivacious, endearingly child-like Irish.'[109] Whatever Deane's reservations, whatever the narratorial concessions necessary to render her Irish subjects palatable to an English public, there is little doubt that in the old Catholic family retainer, Thady Quirk, Edgeworth found the means to give voice to an 'authentic' Irish tale of family decline in a form so strikingly original as to be foundational.

Edgeworth subsequently shied away from the experimental early fiction of *Castle Rackrent*, writing more conventional, polished, and accessible but less Irish novels in the decades that followed. Having created a singular narrative space, voice, and form with which to give expression to various classes of the Irish, she thereafter opted for a more conservative style, which treated the matter of Ireland only from the limited point of view of the Big House, leaving the peasants, their voices, and troubles to become the stuff of other novelists, closer to the ground, such as Carleton. Particularly after Catholic Emancipation, Edgeworth felt alienated in a new reality in which the Protestant Ascendancy was losing its grip on the country and she eventually abandoned her writing about Ireland altogether, feeling that the 'realities are too strong, party passions too violent, to bear to see, or care to look at their faces in a looking glass. The people would only break the glass, and curse the fool who held the mirror up to nature—distorted nature, in a fever.'[110] Her own sympathy, it seems, had run out.

---

107 Carleton, *Black Prophet*, 256.
108 Seamus Deane, *A Short History of Irish Literature* (London: Hutchinson, 1986), 90.
109 Deane, *A Short History*, 93.
110 Quoted in Marilyn Butler, *Maria Edgeworth: A Literary Biography* (Oxford: Oxford University Press, 1972), 452–3.

Despite this, Edgeworth's Irish works left a deep mark and effectively opened up a territory that had lain silent. In setting up a tension between Thady and the editor of *Castle Rackrent*, Edgeworth was, *de facto*, authorizing Irish-English as against Standard English, opening the fictional door (that arguably she herself would attempt to re-close) to the Irish Catholic lower classes, who were now, for the first time, to be read in Protestant English drawing rooms. She was introducing into fiction a battle that would endure, between the impositions of a metropolitan voice and the claims of an emerging Irish voice that she was also keen to contain. With Edgeworth, the Irish novel became a buffer zone between its primarily English readership and its Irish subject matter. At the same time, she took much of the political edge off her writing by situating her novels as 'tales of other times'. This ploy would also be later adopted by practically every novelist (Trollope included) who sought to write about Ireland in the nineteenth century.

Trollope would probably have shared Thackeray's view of the Irish novel after Edgeworth: 'All Irish stories are sad, all humorous Irish stories are sad... there is never a burst of laughter excited by them but, as I fancy, tears are near at hand; and from *Castle Rackrent* downwards, every Hibernian tale I have ever read is sure to leave a woeful tender impression.'[111] This last phrase, once again, conjures up the idea of sympathy, a sympathy Trollope would strive to achieve in his first Irish novel. But Edgeworth's stance also reveals the limits of sympathy as a narrative strategy and as a means to change. What Edgeworth articulated, especially in the rather strained optimism of the Irish novels that followed *Castle Rackrent*, was a defence of the status quo based on the Anglo-Irish fear of the emergence of a Catholic middle class.

While remaining unconvinced by Trollope's hard-headed and indeed callous stance with regard to the Irish Famine in *Castle Richmond*, it could be argued that he mostly eschews achieving a rather easily obtained sympathy, nudges his readers towards a wider judgement, and endorses harsh practical 'solutions' offered by political economy. The easier route for him to have followed would have been to evoke fellow feeling for the suffering individual, which was such a hallmark of Victorian fiction in general and Dickens' early works in particular. Trollope's Irish works show the limits of the well-meaning individual response, avoid playing to the 'general heart' (he mocks Dickens, elsewhere, as 'Mr. Popular Sentiment'), and mostly refuse the sensational and the sentimental in

---

[111] Quoted in Robert A. Colby, *Thackeray's Canvass of Humanity: An Author and his Public* (Columbus: Ohio State University Press, 1979), 211.

order to suggest, through fiction, larger, practical solutions that will bring slow but always manageable economic, political, and social change.

Trollope also found fictional models to follow in the novels of Gerald Griffin (1803–40) and the Banim brothers, John (1798–1842) and Michael (1796–1874), who declared that the motivation for writing *The Tales by the O'Hara Family* was to 'insinuate through fiction the causes of Irish discontent, and to insinuate also, that if crime were consequent on discontent it was no great wonder; the conclusion to be arrived at by the reader, not by insisting on it on the part of the author, but from sympathy with the criminals.'[112] Griffin achieved a notable success with *The Collegians* (1829) but had long since shied away from the writing vocation, choosing instead the religious life. Even if his voice was but a fleeting one, Trollope was most impressed by *The Collegians* and once got himself into trouble for discussing it, as Henry Taylor recalled:

> A priest . . . whose name he did not know, was exhibiting to him the beauties of the lake, and Anthony Trollope, who was at that time fresh from the reading of the novel of 'The Collegians,' said, 'Ah, somewhere hereabouts poor Eily O'Connor was drowned; 'tis close upon this spot it must have been that the villain Hardress did that foulest of murders. What a scene! What passion, what character, what skill I find in that novel! What a frightful history it tells!' The priest remaining silent, Anthony Trollope thought that perhaps he did not know the story, and went on eagerly: 'Don't you know it? Isn't it a first-rate book? Isn't Eily O'Connor enchanting? Wasn't Hardress—.'
>
> 'Hardress?' said the priest . . . 'Hardress was my first cousin, and I stood on the steps of the scaffold when he was hung.'
>
> This was a painful moment for Anthony Trollope. However, the priest made no defence of his cousin, and only gave him some more hideous details concerning the crime: he told how not Danny Mann, but Hardress himself, held the unhappy woman's head down in the water till she was dead. It is well that Griffin altered this fact, which for a poetical work of fiction would have been too revolting.[113]

From this Trollope learnt how close to the ground an Irish novelist needed to be, the extent to which Irish fiction was fact-based, but also the inherent danger involved in transferring fact into fiction. What emerges from this anecdote is a sense of the novel as a communal concern, more the expression of a rural community, of stories told and retold, than it was

---

[112] Banim is quoted in Stephen James Meredith, *Ireland in Fiction: A Guide to Irish Novels, Tales, Romances, and Folk-Lore.* (new edn, New York: Burt Franklin, 1919 & 1970), 22.

[113] Quoted in a letter from Mrs Pollock to Henry Taylor, 1 July 1869 in *Correspondence of Henry Taylor*, ed. Edward Dowden (London: Longmans, 1888), 297–8.

the fruit of a single author's imagination. For this reason, it is somewhat misplaced to read the Irish novel as a deviation from its more 'standard' English model (as the individualistic form *par excellence*, both in terms of subject matter and authorship). When compared with Griffin, most practitioners of the Irish novel in the nineteenth century were at a remove from the mass of the peasantry by birth and circumstance. Those coming from the Anglo-Irish big houses were, by definition, at a remove, while others, however concerned they might have been with the problems of the peasantry, distanced themselves (Carleton, for example, by religious conversion). The very fact of writing primarily for an English audience alienated and insulated many Irish writers from their Irish subjects. At an even more basic level, distance was inevitable given that most novelists lived outside the country, especially from the 1840s onwards. Carleton complained that 'our literary men followed the example of our great landlords; they became absentees, and drained the country of its intellectual wealth precisely as the others exhausted it of its rents', and compared the reduced state of Irish literary production and publishing to a Famine: 'So it was with literature. Our men and women of genius uniformly carried their talents to the English market, whilst we laboured at home under all the dark privations of a literary famine.'[114]

Charles Lever joined the literary exodus in 1845, although he remained foremost among Trollope's influential Irish contemporaries. From Lever's early works Trollope would learn what best to avoid in writing an Irish comic novel; that is, undisciplined recourse to the incidental and the episodic, to comic moments that did not contribute to the work as a whole. Trollope would also resist his Irish contemporary's over-reliance on the picaresque, even if traces of this element can be read in Trollope's early Irish short stories. On a more positive note, Lever's early novel, *Charles O'Malley*, provided Trollope with a prototype for his own successful Irishman, Phineas Finn, even if O'Malley's success is military (at the Battle of Waterloo) while Finn's is political. Trollope would have learnt from Lever's later works about how to portray the Anglo-Irish and their incapacity to react to the challenges facing the country, and would have shared both his impatience with English misgovernance of Ireland and his tolerance of the Catholic population. Trollope also shared Lever's view of the Union as expressed in *The Knight of Gwynne, A Tale of the Time of the Union* (1847), as Ireland's betrayal by its own ruling class, even though he firmly believed in its importance for both countries. The focus of Lever's later works is a slow, increasingly intense indictment of the

[114] William Carleton, 'General Introduction', *Traits and Stories of the Irish Peasantry*, 2 vols (1842–3; repr. Gerrards Cross: Colin Smythe, 1990), 1, 1.

Protestant Ascendancy, which he portrayed as having given up what little power it had in return for paltry preferment. Although equally contemptuous of the methods that led Ireland to accept the Union, Trollope held firm to his belief that it was the best way forward for the country, but despaired at what the narrator of *The Knight of Gwynne* describes as 'a reckless indifference to the future ... in which little care was taken for the morrow, until, at last, thoughtless extravagance became a habit, and moneyed difficulties the lot of almost every family of Ireland.'[115]

From his assessment of Lever, it seems likely that Trollope did not read his last work, *Lord Kilgobbin*, which partly reverses the conservative, Unionist stance of the bulk of his writing, frets over the slow ebbing of the Protestant nation, and inches towards an endorsement of Home Rule. This was a move that would always be anathema to Trollope, even if he distinguished between early Home Rule campaigners who were 'loyal and patriotic' and 'simply desired to obtain for their country an increase of power in the management of their own affairs' (*LL*, 304) and those involved in the more radical campaigns of the 1870s and 1880s. Lever's career and life ended, as the reviewer of *Lord Kilgobbin* wrote in the *Dublin University Magazine*, haunted 'with a melancholy and over-true foreboding of great catastrophe',[116] and it might be said that similar apprehensions hang over Trollope's last Irish novels, *An Eye for an Eye* and the bleak and reactionary *The Landleaguers*. An Ireland entirely foreign to both men was in the early throes of its birth in the dying decades of the nineteenth century.

By reading Carleton, Trollope found access into the more sensational and less solid world of the romance, and into the oral culture represented by the folktale. Carleton's novels were a filter through which folk tradition passed into written form, and his *Willy Reilly and His Dear Colleen Bawn* is just one example of a novel that springs from an old folk ballad (Lover's *Rory O'More* has a similar genesis and indeed Walter Scott also used Scottish ballads as sources for his novels). The influence of the folk tradition is a sign of the generic fluidity that characterized the Irish novel, drawing as it did on non-realist popular and indeed oral culture. Trollope made passing nods towards these traditions through occasional references to pipers, songs, and the Irish language. In *The Macdermots*, he refers to a blind piper whom he calls 'Shamus na Pe'bria' (*Macdermots*,

---

[115] Charles Lever, *The Knight of Gwynne, A Tale of the Time of the Union* (Boston: Little, Brown, and Company, 1899), 1, 88.

[116] Review of *Lord Kilgobbin*, *Dublin University Magazine*, July 1872, quoted in A. Norman Jeffares, *Images of Invention. Essays on Irish Writing* (Gerrards Cross: Colin Smythe, 1996), 187.

107), and later, 'Shamuth of the pipes', who 'did the music about O'Connell all out of his own head'. In the big wedding scene, Trollope describes the piper's 'squeaking, and puffing', his playing the jig '"Paddy Carey" with full force and energy', and then shows another performer singing the 'Widow Machree' (*Macdermots*, 355).

The master of this material was Carleton, a figure that dominated a rather desolate Irish literary panorama into the mid-fifties, by which time he was considered 'a literary giant.'[117] In 1841, the *Dublin University Magazine* enthused that Carleton could 'vindicate his undisputed claim to the title of the novelist of Ireland. Whatever be his faults or his merits, he is alone.'[118] Trollope was an admirer of Carleton's stories of Irish peasant life, especially his *Tales of Ireland* (1834) and *Fardorougha the Miser* (1839), which offer a unique panorama of a lawless pre-Famine Ireland living in fear of groups such as the Whiteboys. Trollope cannot but have hoped to emulate Carleton's success in rendering the rhythms and sounds of Irish-English and the practices of Irish social life, not to mention his aspiration 'neither to distort his countrymen into demons, nor to enshrine them as suffering innocents and saints—but to exhibit them as they really are.'[119] But Carleton, born into a Tyrone family which for generations had cultivated the Gaelic oral tradition, was a difficult figure for an outsider to emulate. Carleton drew on what he heard at home, from his father, 'a perfect storehouse', unrivalled as 'a teller of old tales, legends, and historical anecdotes', fluent in Irish and English and acquainted with 'all kinds of charms, old ranns, or poems, old prophecies, religious superstitions, tales of pilgrims, miracles and tales of pilgrimages, anecdotes of blessed priests and friars, revelations from ghosts and fairies.'[120] His mother was also steeped in oral tradition and was famous for her ability as a keener, a singer, and as a reciter of poetry. While Carleton successfully rendered this inherited tradition, Trollope, no matter how sympathetic, was just too distant, even if, as we shall see, he did give his Irish contemporary a run for his money when it came to conveying Irish-English speech.

Carleton's testimony about his choice of subject matter, his historicizing aspiration, his desire to give voice to the Irish peasantry, 'a class unknown in literature', is instructive as to how it would have influenced Trollope:

---

[117] Melissa Fegan, *Literature and the Irish Famine, 1845–1919* (Oxford: Clarendon Press, 2002), 144.
[118] 'Our Portrait Gallery—no. xv. William Carleton', *Dublin University Magazine*, 17 (Jan. 1841), [66–72], 66.
[119] Carleton, *Traits and Stories* (1990), 1, viii–ix.
[120] Carleton, *Traits and Stories* (1990), 1, viii.

If I became the historian of their habits and manners, their feelings, their prejudices, their superstitions and their crimes; if I have attempted to delineate their moral, religious and physical state, it was because I saw no person willing to undertake a task which surely must be looked upon as an important one.[121]

Important as these individual Irish novelists were, they remain, with the exception of Edgeworth, somewhat problematic figures today. Indeed, the nineteenth-century Irish novel, with just a handful of exceptions, was, for a long time, seen as a failed entity, a problematic and occasional genre, devoid of the focus, scale, and ambition of its English counterpart. The perceived failure of the country to provide its own self-image in fiction has been attributed to diverse causes. The first is audience: in the absence of a stable, educated, middle-class Irish Catholic reading public, the writer sought to address a dual audience of the Irish themselves and a larger but largely disinterested English readership. Connected with this problem was the uneasy coexistence of Irish-English and standard English as the means for literary production, and what worked for one readership might well not work for the other. The second issue was the lack of a political and economic stability in Ireland. The absence of a solid material base or economic substructure, which caused James Joyce, as late as 1906, to refer to his 'poor impoverished country', meant that Ireland was, in O'Toole's words, 'too raw, too unformed, too impoverished to sustain a classical tradition of fiction.'[122] Nineteenth-century Ireland was caught in a liminal state of semi-permanent crisis and suffering, and was a reality too brittle and unformed to be able to sustain a form similar to that of the traditional English novel, which, as Kiberd has pointed out, in an apt but overly formulaic generalization, describes 'a land of stable gradations of made lives'. Irish writers, on the other hand, to be faithful to their world, were called on to depict an unstable society of 'lives in the making'.[123] To say it with Eagleton, the realist novel 'is the form *par excellence* of settlement and stability, gathering individual lives into an integrated whole; and social conditions in Ireland hardly lent themselves to any such sanguine reconciliation.'[124] Unlike its English counterpart, the Irish novel rarely describes a journey towards success, resolution, or marriage; rather, it is the site for presenting the unravelling of individual lives, of families, of whole communities, and ways

---

[121] Carleton, *Traits and Stories* (1834), 1, x.
[122] Fintan O'Toole, 'Writing the Boom', *Irish Times* (6 April 2002), 10.
[123] Declan Kiberd, 'The War against the Past,' in *The Uses of the Past: Essays on Irish Culture*, eds. Audrey S. Eyler and Robert Garrnatt (Newark, NJ: University of Delaware Press, 1988), 24–53.
[124] Eagleton, *Heathcliff*, 147.

of life. James Pope-Hennessy's criticism of Trollope's first novel as an
'inchoate work' that 'lacks discipline' could well be applied to his other
Irish novels and also, more broadly, sums up staple responses to the
nineteenth-century Irish novel *tout court*, as an inevitably undisciplined
genre precisely because 'it deals with a society in conditions of disruption—
that chronic Irish state of disruption which had always persisted through
the long centuries of British rule.'[125] The ruptured nature of Irish history
which tells of Ireland's perennial discontinuity and complexity—in Colm
Tóibín's words, 'the half-formed chaos of Ireland'[126]—made it difficult for
novelists to find adequate representational forms, and as a result the novels
of the nineteenth century reflect a variety of approaches, each grasping at
but often falling short of conjuring an entirely successful representation of
the country.

    To cite difficult material conditions is not, however, enough to explain
the supposed inadequacies of the Irish novel. Joyce emerged from what
was a difficult political, economic, and personal background, while from
further afield, the twentieth century saw a blossoming, for example, of
North African writers emerging from, at best, equally problematic conditions. Rather than talk of inadequacy or lack of discipline, it is more useful
today to describe what makes the Irish novel distinctively different, as
Margaret Kelleher has recently argued:

> The years 1830 to 1890 mark a period in which differentiations of 'English'
> and 'Irish' writing, whether in prose or drama, are not easily made. . . . Rather
> than being a sign of aesthetic inferiority . . . such cultural hybridity is instead
> where much of the richness of nineteenth-century Irish literature in English
> lies.[127]

These 'differentiations' might be described in terms of theme: distinctly
Irish political questions are either foregrounded or present by default
through their very absence; character: there is at least as strong a focus
on the community as on the individual (a habit Trollope makes his own
both in his Irish but also in his English novels, especially in the chronicles
of Barsetshire), and where there is a focus on the individual, his or her
private story becomes the vehicle for expressing national problems; setting:
while the English novel gradually takes to the city and is more often than

---

[125] Pope-Hennessy, *Trollope*, 107–8.
[126] Colm Tóibín, 'Introduction', *The Penguin Book of Irish Fiction* (London: Viking,
1999), ix.
[127] Margaret Kelleher, 'Prose Writing and Drama in English, 1830–1890: From Catholic Emancipation to the Fall of Parnell', in Margaret Kelleher and Philip O'Leary, eds., *The
Cambridge History of Irish Literature*, 2 vols (Cambridge: Cambridge University Press,
2006), 1, 450–1.

not set in the 'now', which is itself washed with a belief in progressive, evolutionary narratives, the Irish counterpart remains stubbornly rural, and this rurality, through gradients of remoteness or wildness, comes to signify layers of 'then', of the past, of backwardness and/or paralysis; form: the Irish novel contains a hybrid mixture of discourses and styles that make it a dialogic genre drawn from domestic written and oral culture and also from analogous forms imported from Britain and Europe; language: there is a constant negotiation between standard English and Irish-English, a dualism between the authoritative written form and the slippery oral form adopted to give voice, predominantly, to the peasantry; and audience: the Irish novel is a buffer zone in which the author is an in-between, an intermediary between two separate yet minutely intertwined cultures. Thus there is sometimes a second-hand quality to the writing, which is to some extent a more accessible rewriting of material considered native to one part of the readership and foreign to the other, as the author is constrained to both tell stories and simultaneously contextualize and interpret them for his English audience.

All of these elements suggest an instability in both the subject matter, in Kevin Whelan's words, a 'strident emphasis on national character and on the absolute particularity of the Irish as a people',[128] and in form, which interlaces fiction with extra-literary elements. The issue of audience, as seen in the Irish novels' insistence in making a case to the English public, synthesized in Carleton's desire 'to awaken those who legislate for us', helps to explain the genre's 'unstable tone', 'at once moralizing, apologetic, defensive and didactic'. If the Irish novel finally achieves greatness with Joyce, it is partly because he sets aside pleading to an external audience, does away with explaining, and, in a real sense, seeks *in primis* to engage native readers by being, in Patrick Kavanagh's terms, 'parochial' rather than 'provincial'. He ceases to worry about the judgement of the English metropolis and is fully convinced of 'the social and artistic validity of his parish.'[129]

In his attempts to portray Ireland in fiction, Trollope too often saw the country not in parochial terms, but as a province to be explained. He felt qualified to write about what he called the 'subject of Ireland; her undoubted grievances, her modern history, her recent sufferings, and her present actual state'; all issues, these, that 'are singularly misunderstood by

---

[128] Kevin Whelan, 'Writing Ireland: Reading England', in Leon Litvack and Glenn Hooper, eds., *Ireland in the Nineteenth Century: Regional Identity* (Dublin: Four Courts Press, 2000), 189.

[129] Patrick Kavanagh, quoted in the 'Introduction' in Peter Fallon and Derek Mahon, eds., *The Penguin Book of Contemporary Irish Poetry* (New York: Penguin, 1990), xviii.

the public in England' (*Examiner*, 77). He did so, always with an eye to London, feeling that he possessed a 'level of implicit knowledge' usually common only among the natural members of the culture and which usually 'evade the outside observer.'[130] With much justification, Michael Sadleir described him aptly as 'a compendium of facts relative to Ireland and her uneasy partnership with Britain',[131] and he sought to use his knowledge to posit himself as a messenger, a go-between for the two countries in both his postal and his literary work.

He was fully convinced that he had Ireland within his grasp, and said as much in his seven letters published in the *Examiner*, written in 1849 to counter Sidney Godolphin Osborne's criticism of the British administration of Ireland during the Famine in *The Times*:

> I have been eight years in the country, and have passed those years in continual journeys through its south, western, and midland portions. During this time I have been thrown among Irishmen of every class. I have seen them in their comparative prosperity, and their too positive adversity; I have watched the results of coercive and conciliatory measures—I have felt the overwhelming shock of agitation in 1843, and the galvanic convulsions of 1848; and I have observed, I will not say as an alien or a foreigner, but still as a stranger, the effects of the laws passed in those years with the object of ameliorating the condition of the people (*Examiner*, 73).

While deeply aware of Irish difference, he also attempted to portray similarities with the English experience, and there is little doubt that his time in Ireland made him aware, as Sadleir puts it, of 'his own Englishry. Listening to their persistent talk of Ireland's wrongs, and hearing— amused but argumentative—their comments on his own people, he was impelled—almost despite himself—to mental counter-comment from the English point of view.'[132] His Irish works suggest the extent to which the two countries and the two cultures were necessarily interpenetrated, related, similar. What could happen in Ireland could quite conceivably happen in England too. Thus we read that 'Castle Richmond might have been in Hampshire or Essex', or that 'Sir Thomas Fitzgerald might have been a Leicestershire baronet' (*CR*, 2–3). In this domesticating strategy, the hoped-for effect is to worry the reader to conscience in order to stimulate reasoned action, to elicit responses to the proposition that Ireland is England's double, and an—at times—chilling portent of what it too might become. The flipside which Trollope so heartily wishes to

[130] Bernice Martin, *A Sociology of Contemporary Cultural Change* (Oxford: Blackwell, 1981), 33.
[131] Sadleir, *Trollope*, 137.   [132] Sadleir, *Trollope*, 133.

assert as a firm believer in the Union is that what happens in England could, whatever the cultural differences, also happen in Ireland. He believed that he himself was material proof of this because he emerged from failure and anonymity to recognition and success in Ireland. Ireland too could be improved by interacting with England, by following the English example and English attitudes such as those he himself had followed and attempted to instil in others in his Post Office work. Although his later Irish novels carry a shrill note of hopelessness, anger, and despair, the bulk of Trollope's Irish writings perform the mediatory role he felt uniquely equipped to fill: that is, to describe and explain the country for the English reader with a steady hand and with a sense of fairness.

2

Questions of Justice in the Early Irish Novels

I. JUSTICE DENIED: *THE MACDERMOTS OF BALLYCLORAN*

The worst year of the Great Famine in Ireland, 1847, was also one of the best years, on the literary front, across the water in England. It saw the publication of Thackeray's *Vanity Fair*, and of an extraordinary trilogy, written by the three daughters of the partly Irish (on the father's side) Brontë family: Charlotte published *Jane Eyre*, Anne, *Agnes Grey*, and Emily, *Wuthering Heights*. It was also the year that Trollope published his first novel, an Irish work entitled *The Macdermots of Ballycloran*, which quietly inaugurated what was to develop into a mighty literary career but received scant popular or critical success before sinking into the dark recesses of the nineteenth-century English and Irish literary canons.

While the Brontës had to pose as men to be published, Trollope could count on being his mother's son, even if this was a choice which was not without its cost. Although he complained about his first publisher, Thomas Cautley Newby, in truth Trollope was comparatively well treated. Charlotte and Anne Brontë had to pay £50 each for the publication of *Wuthering Heights* and *Agnes Grey*, whereas Trollope was given a 'half profits' agreement from Newby, the first publisher he (or better, his mother) had contacted, and he was not obliged to make any payment. Newby grudgingly published only 250 (of 350 promised) copies of the first edition of *Agnes Grey*, and this only following the instant success of *Jane Eyre* (published, in the meantime, by Smith, Elder, and Company), but printed 400 copies of Trollope's novel. So, relatively speaking, Trollope's initiation as a published novelist was not as negative as he himself would retrospectively have us believe, even if the somewhat dodgy Newby did little or nothing to sell his book (which was republished in 1860 by Chapman and Hall in the shortened and slightly adapted version which is usually available today).

The Macdermots narrates the thwarted love of Captain Myles Ussher and Feemy Macdermot, two characters who come from impossibly different social and cultural realities. It is a dark, uncompromising work of tragic power, in which Trollope gives earnest voice to Ireland without making allowances for the tastes and expectations of the Victorian English reader. In the words of Christine Longford, it 'is a gloomy, violent story of poverty, drunkenness, insanity, seduction and terrorism, which might have been written by Liam O'Flaherty.'[1] The novel's grim end is foreshadowed in its desolate beginning and the whole work is born out of a genuine encounter with the harsh realities of Irish life, offering a broad social snapshot of the country in pre-Famine times. Here, Trollope comes closer than Thackeray ever came to honouring his own assertion that the Irish question should be 'a matter of historical research' and should never be treated 'as a romance.'[2] *The Macdermots* tells various stories, each of which is exemplary of the Ireland Trollope had just begun to know. It chronicles the fall of the family of Larry Macdermot, an impoverished survivor of the old Irish Catholic gentry, who represents a doubly marginalized reality, held at a distance by the Anglo-Irish, but also by the peasantry that resents his family's rank, even if they have fallen into abject poverty. He and his son Thady and daughter Feemy live in a dilapidated mansion of recent construction in County Leitrim, unable to pay the mortgage which is being enforced by the local builder made good, Joe Flannelly, who built the house for them many years earlier, and by his lawyer and son-in-law, Hyacinth Keegan. Flannelly attempted to have his daughter, Sally, marry into the Macdermot family, but was rebuffed and wishes to gain revenge by hounding the Macdermots out of their home. Larry regrets 'the slighted offers of Sally Flannelly's charms and cash' and that she is 'now Sally Keegan, the wife of Hyacinth Keegan' (*Macdermots*, 14). Larry's refusal is a wrong-headed, class-based decision to spurn the opportunity to make an alliance with the rising Catholic middle classes:

> Mr. Macdermot thus regarded his creditor as a vulgar, low-born bloodsucker, who, having by chicanery obtained an unwarrantable hold over him, was determined, if possible, to crush him. The builder, on the other hand, who had spent a long life of constant industry, but doubtful honesty, in scraping up a decent fortune, looked on his debtor as one who gave himself airs to which his poverty did not entitle him; and was determined to

[1] Christine Longford, 'Trollope in Ireland', *The Bell*, 5/3 (1942), 185–6.
[2] William Makepeace Thackeray, Review of Venedey's *Irland*, *Morning Chronicle*, 16 March 1844, reprinted in Gordon N. Ray, ed., *Thackeray, William, Makepeace. Contributions to the Morning Chronicle* (Urbana: University of Illinois Press, 1955).

make him feel that though he could not be the father, he could be the master of a 'rale gintleman' (*Macdermots*, 15).

Keegan wants to remove the Macdermots so that he can eventually possess the property through his father-in-law. He is aided and abetted to this end by the Macdermots' dishonest and deeply feared bailiff, Pat Brady, who realizes that 'the days of the Macdermots were over, and that it was necessary for him to ingratiate himself with Keegan, the probable future "masther;"'(*Macdermots*, 173). This element of the novel comes to a head when Larry angrily refuses Keegan's offensively low offer for the estate.

The greater part of the novel hinges around the disastrous relationship between Feemy, who walks 'as if all the blood of the old Irish princes was in her veins' (*Macdermots*, 11), and Captain Myles Ussher, 'a Protestant, from the County Antrim' and 'the illegitimate son of a gentleman of large property, who had procured him the situation which he held' (*Macdermots*, 27). Ussher represents a somewhat dingy, down-at-heel version of the Anglo-Irish Ascendancy. Much of the narrative is concerned with Thady's attempts to hold him to account on his sister's behalf. Although well intentioned, Thady fatally procrastinates and only confronts Ussher when he believes that he is going to abduct Feemy. His intervention is disastrous. He attempts to block Ussher by hitting him with a heavy stick and ends up killing him. In a single blow Thady mistakenly achieves what the local Ribbonmen have long been threatening to do (the Ribbonmen were members of a popular rural protest movement, at times willing to use violent means on behalf of the tenantry against their landlords). Thady subsequently flees and is given shelter in a hideout in the mountains where he is forced to take the Ribbon oath in return for refuge. Too honest to stay in hiding, Thady turns himself in and is tried and convicted of murder, wrongly convicted for having committed a political crime, an act of Ribbonism, when in fact he was trying to preserve his sister's honour and to prevent what he thought was her abduction. The pleas of the local priest on his behalf fall on deaf ears when the magistrates, following evidence given by Pat Brady, who perjures himself under threat from Keegan, implement an exemplary punishment against a tense backdrop of rural agitation which includes a brutal attack on Keegan by some local Ribbonmen, anxious to support Thady. Keegan wrongly attributes 'his horrible mutilation to the influence of the Macdermots' (*Macdermots*, 448) and, because of all these events, 'people in the country began to say that some severe example was necessary' (*Macdermots*, 450). Thus, Thady is condemned to death. The novel ends on a hopeless note with Thady's hanging, his father's madness, and with Feemy's death during the birth of Ussher's child; a detail, this, removed by Trollope from the 1860 edition.[3]

Even if the focus is on Thady, the novel conveys a drama involving a whole community through a complex development of the public and private plots as well as bigger choral scenes, such as the marriage of Feemy's servant, Mary Brady, to the local blacksmith, the Race Day, and Ussher's seizure of the illegal poteen still. Each of these scenes broadens the scope of the novel, allowing Trollope to paint an intricately interconnected social fabric stretching from the poorest peasants and Ribbonmen to the rising middle-class Catholic farming community and to the Anglo-Irish magistracy and landlords.

When staying in Drumsna in County Leitrim, Trollope stumbled upon the location of the novel—'the modern ruins of a country house . . . one of the most melancholy spots I ever visited':

> We wandered about the place, suggesting to each other causes for the misery we saw there, and while I was still among the ruined walls and decayed beams I fabricated the plot of *The Macdermots of Ballycloran* (*Auto*, 70).

Trollope believed that he had never come up with a better plot 'or, at any rate, one so susceptible of pathos' (*Auto*, 70), and was proud of the novel which had, he wrote in 1874, 'truth, freshness and a certain tragic earnestness.'[4] In the *Autobiography*, Trollope initiates the habit of reading this and his subsequent Irish novels more for their sociological content than for any literary quality, when he writes: '[it] is a good novel, and worth reading by anyone who wishes to understand what Irish life was before the potato disease, the Famine, and the Encumbered Estates Bill' (*Auto*, 71).

Critical reception was sparse, mixed, and initially connected the novel with those of Trollope's mother, Fanny. *Hewitt's Journal* opined that '[t]he son assuredly inherits a considerable portion of the mother's talent', while for the *Spectator* there was 'more mellowness in the composition of Mr. A. Trollope, and less of forced contrivance in the management of his story than the fluent lady ever achieved.'[5] *Douglas Jerrold's Shilling Magazine* proclaimed that 'the novel augured well for a successful career in

---

[3] Trollope was usually loath to make cuts to his completed manuscripts so it is noteworthy that he would choose to remove three full chapters from the original version of this novel. The only other examples of similar cutting are with regard to *The Duke's Children* and *The Three Clerks*.

[4] Bradford A. Booth, ed., *The Letters of Anthony Trollope* (Oxford: Oxford University Press, 1951), 540.

[5] *Hewitt's Journal of Literature and Popular Progress*, I (12 June 1847), 350; *Spectator, A Weekly Journal*, 20 (8 May 1847), 449.

fiction writing',[6] while Sir Patrick O'Brien, MP for the King's County (whom Trollope had probably met in Coole Park), declared it 'the best Irish story that has appeared for something like half a century',[7] thus effectively claiming that Trollope could be considered the successor to Maria Edgeworth. Twentieth-century readings were mixed. Hugh Walpole judged the novel to be 'almost in the first flight of Trollope' and saw Feemy as one of 'the finest of all of Trollope's heroines',[8] but Michael Sadleir dismissed the novel as 'a false dawn.'[9] Beatrice Curtis Brown felt it was 'not a great book, but it is the book of a man who may write great books later, the book, in fact, of an incipient great writer as distinct from a great novelist.'[10] Thomas Flanagan enthused that Trollope 'had not written a novel about Ireland; he had written an Irish novel',[11] while E. W. Wittig claimed it was 'Trollope's only Irish novel to succeed as a work of fiction. It does so because it presents a vision sensitive to the harsh and complex realities of Irish life.'[12]

The Macdermots begins at the end by focusing on what remains of the Macdermots' broken-down castle, one of so many such buildings strewn around the country, bleak reminders of Gaelic Ireland's lost nobility. In 1839, the Reverend Caesar Otway described a country full of similar ruins in *A Tour in Connaught*:

> Ireland is the land of ruins and memorials–of powers and people that have successively passed away. The ruined fortress–the devastated abbey–the lonely *dun*–the fairy-footed rath–the round tower that sends its slender shaft on high to assert that the almost imperishable simplicity of its form can survive human record, and even outlast man's tradition–these are what render Ireland a land interesting to the traveller[13]

Like many other writers before and after him, Trollope yielded to the poetic fascination of Connacht, Ireland's smallest, poorest province, but he had good reason to do so as it was, at that time, the part of the country with which he was best acquainted. In Trollope's novel, Ballycloran

[6] *Douglas Jerrold's Shilling Magazine*, 5 (Jan.–June 1847), 564.

[7] Quoted in T. H. S. Escott, *Anthony Trollope, His Work, Associates and Literary Originals* (London: John Lane/The Bodley Head, 1913), 61.

[8] Hugh Walpole, *Anthony Trollope* (London: Macmillan, 1928), 25, 27.

[9] Michael Sadleir, *Trollope: A Commentary* (London: Oxford University Press, 1961), 151.

[10] Beatrice Curtis Brown, *Anthony Trollope* (London: Arthur Barker, 1950), 35.

[11] Thomas Flanagan, *The Irish Novelists, 1800–1850* (New York: Columbia University Press, 1959), 230.

[12] E. W. Wittig, 'Trollope's Irish Fiction', *Éire-Ireland*, 9/3 (Fall 1974), 98.

[13] Caesar Otway, *A Tour in Connaught, Comprising Sketches of Clonmacnoise, Joyce Country and Achill* (Dublin: William Curry, 1839), 4–5.

Castle, 'a picture of misery, of useless expenditure, unfinished pretence, and premature decay', is home to Larry Macdermot, 'an extravagant landlord, reckless tenants, debt, embarrassment, despair, and ruin' (*Macdermots*, 3). The disrepair evokes a world that has run out of time. All that remains at the moment of writing is the skeletal structure of an abandoned ruin: 'the rest ready to fall, like the skeleton of a felon left to rot on an open gibbet' (*Macdermots*, 4), an image, this, which chillingly anticipates Thady's destiny. There is nothing abnormal about this dismal 'unnatural ruin'; rather, it is a 'characteristic specimen of Irish life' (*Macdermots*, 5), one to be found in many Irish national tales, starting with *The Wild Irish Girl*, where Sydney Owenson depicted similar relics as emblematic of the decaying Irish nobility.

Unlike the ruins of Owenson's novel, which are 'grand even in desolation and magnificent in decay',[14] Trollope's mausoleum shows no signs of either past or present magnificence, and is of recent construction. It is home to the last surviving generations of the Macdermot family, whose fate has already been determined by the excesses of the past. Although resident at the start of the story, Larry is effectively an absentee landlord, not in the tradition of the Anglo-Irish who watch their Irish holdings from the comfort and safety of Britain, but as a resident Irish Catholic landowner who has failed to nurture his modest inheritance and to manage his estate, and, as a result, has fallen prey to his scheming middle-man, Pat Brady. Larry suffers blow after economic blow before succumbing to an almost Beckettian apathy and despair in the knowledge that he will inevitably lose his property.

The Gaelic chieftain's traumatic separation from his castle is a common trope in the Irish nineteenth-century novel; for example, in Maturin's *The Milesian Chief* (1812), in which the castle is lost to the absentee Anglo-Irish landlord, Montclare. Contrarily, in Trollope's novel, the 'castle' is lost to a rising Catholic middle class; lost, not because of the effects of a colonial politics of appropriation, but because the family is incapable of managing its own affairs and falls victim to the grasping machinations of Flannelly and Keegan, who represent the Catholic 'speculator-class'.[15] When alluding to the Macdermots' 'noble' Milesian background, Trollope was both drawing on and challenging a tradition that had its most notable example in *The Wild Irish Girl*, where the Prince is depicted as a living relic of an older Catholic Ireland and he and his daughter speak

[14] Sydney Owenson, *The Wild Irish Girl, a National Tale*, ed. Kathryn Kirkpatrick (Oxford: Oxford University Press, 1999), 44.

[15] Margaret MacCurtain, 'Pre-Famine Peasantry in Ireland: Definition and Theme', *Irish University Review*, 4/2 (Autumn 1974), 194.

Irish, dress in an old Irish fashion, and keep a museum of antiquities. By clinging to the last vestiges of their Milesian nobility, they embody a form of resistance to the political status quo. Owenson's romanticized Prince has 'a form almost gigantic in stature, yet gently thrown forward by evident infirmity; limbs of Herculean mould, and a countenance rather furrowed by the inroads of vehement passions, than the deep trace of years'.[16] Robert Tracy sees Larry as a 'revised version of Lady Morgan's proud and reclusive Prince in his ruined castle', with the 'learned and accomplished Glorvina... revised into the slatternly "Princess" of Bally-cloran, Feemy Macdermot.'[17] Trollope writes against Owensen's romanticizing turn and allows for no ennoblement of Macdermot or his family. Only Thady is capable of offering token resistance to the forces that he faces, while his father, Larry, who is scarcely able to rise from his bed, has capitulated utterly to his fate, to a destiny long since sealed by the excesses of his own father, another Thady: 'About sixty years ago, a something Macdermot, true Milesian, pious Catholic, and descendant of king some-body, died somewhere, having managed to keep a comfortable little portion of his ancestors' royalties to console him for the loss of their sceptre' (*Macdermots*, 7).[18] Thady was the younger of his two sons, and, having inherited 'six hundred as bad acres as a gentleman might wish to call his own', insisted on having 'a gentleman's residence on his estate, and the house of Ballycloran was accordingly built' on a scale worthy of what 'he thought the descendant of a Connaught Prince might inhabit without disgrace'. This 'ill built, half finished' house was inherited along with 'long bills' and notions of grandeur by Larry Macdermot, and is the semi-ruin in which the novel is set in the 1830s.

The one thing that the Macdermots do possess is an important name, which suggests that Trollope may have wanted to make a link with the Milesians, and in particular with Cormac Macdermot (1218–1244), King of Moylurg, whose successors were hereditary marshals of Connaught. The name Feemy, at the time a common Irish abbreviation of Euphemia, also raises lofty expectation, as it means 'well spoken of' and refers to the fourth-century virgin martyr. With such a name it might have been expected that she would, like Glorvina in *The Wild Irish Girl*, be a paragon of 'chastely modest reserve'.[19] Initially she is shown to possess the nobility of a tragic heroine and the physical grace that 'old families have':

[16] Owenson, *Wild Irish Girl*, 47.

[17] Robert Tracy, '"The Unnatural Ruin": Trollope and Nineteenth-Century Irish Fiction', *Nineteenth-Century Fiction*, 37 (December 1982), 366.

[18] In mentioning 'sixty years ago', Trollope seems to be echoing Walter Scott's *Waverley: or, 'Tis Sixty Years Since*, a key text for all subsequent writers of historical novels.

[19] Owenson, *Wild Irish Girl*, 190.

she was a tall, dark girl, with that bold, upright, well-poised figure, which is so peculiarly Irish. . . . Feemy, also, had large, bright brown eyes, and long, soft, shining dark hair, which was divided behind, and fell over her shoulders, or was tied with ribands; and she had a well-formed nose, as all coming of old families have (*Macdermots*, 11).

However, in what would become a typical narrative ploy in his character descriptions, having given praise, Trollope instantly qualifies it. Thus, she has 'a bright olive complexion, only the olive was a little too brown, the skin a little too coarse', her mouth is 'half an inch too long; but her teeth were white and good, and her chin was well turned and short, with a dimple on it large enough for any finger Venus might put there'. In the end, she is 'a fine girl in the eyes of a man not too much accustomed to refinement' (*Macdermots*, 12). In a manner reminiscent of the masculine spectatorship so often to be found in the Restoration dressing room poems—at one point, the narrator announces, 'I will not further violate the mysteries of Feemy's wardrobe'—attention lingers on her 'morning dishevelment' (*Macdermots*, 105), her 'untidiness', 'her frock . . . all ripped and torn', her 'down at heel' shoes, and 'wofully dirty' stockings. All this becomes a partial justification for the narrator's voyeuristic invasion and for Ussher's subsequent mistreatment of her as a sexual object. Trollope goes as far as he can to suggest the sexual nature—the 'pleasure'—of their relationship by writing: 'Ussher followed Feemy into her own room, and here we will leave them', before adding 'that poor Feemy, though more than once she prepared to make her dreaded speech to her lover, each time hesitated and stopped, and at last made up her mind that it would be just as well to put off the evil hour till her pleasure was over' (*Macdermots*, 185). In so doing her fate is sealed. Feemy has broken the Victorian rules of sexual propriety and will fall in an instant from Madonna to Magdalene: her ruin will be complete. Where Victorian wives were not particularly thought to participate in sexual pleasure (that was more the man's domain), it is noteworthy that the narrator refers to 'her pleasure' rather than 'their pleasure' or 'his pleasure'. It is hard to read this as anything other than condemnatory, however much her naivety might mitigate blame. Feemy's desire for escape is so strong that it blinds her to the dangers of involvement with Ussher. Having lived her life in seclusion, Feemy can rely only on her romantic novels for guidance and these help her to construe her idea of the captain as a romantic hero:

he was handsome, he carried arms, was a man of danger, and talked of deeds of courage; he wore a uniform; he rode more gracefully, talked more fluently, and seemed a more mighty personage, than any other one whom Feemy usually met. Besides, he gloried in the title of Captain, and would not that be sufficient to engage the heart of any girl in Feemy's position? (*Macdermots*, 28).

It never occurs to her that Ussher will insist on a financial element in any possible marriage arrangement, that her family will be unable to provide it, and that she will inevitably be cast off as a fallen woman. Thady seeks to redress Ussher's violation of his sister by reprimanding her and attempting to convince him to do the right thing and marry her. But she will not bend to her brother's advice that she cast off the man she sees as her only hope of escape. Thady is less than clear about how to proceed against Ussher, 'a black ruffian and a Protestant... filling her head up with nonsense' (*Macdermots*, 56), and so heeds Father John's advice that the marriage would be no bad thing for a Catholic girl of some pretensions but no means. Ussher is never adequately challenged to assume his responsibilities and Feemy is portrayed as a victim reacting to what is happening around her. Her long wait in the hope that positive news will come from Ussher anticipates that of the equally penniless Lucy Morris in *The Eustace Diamonds*, except that Lucy's wait is finally rewarded. Like Lucy, Feemy will be farmed out for her wait, at the comfortable home of the McKeon's, a middle-class Catholic family and a Trollopian model of industry and improvement:

> Though Mr. McKeon had no property of his own, he was much better off than many around him that had. He had a large farm on a profitable lease; he underlet a good deal of land by con-acre, or corn-acre;—few of my English readers will understand the complicated misery to the poorest of the Irish which this accursed word embraces;—he took contracts for making and repairing roads and bridges; and, altogether, he contrived to live very well on his ways and means. He was honest in everything, barring horse-flesh; was a good Catholic (*Macdermots*, 253–4).

The McKeons display all the commonsense, middle-class qualities so lacking in the Macdermots, and Father John's hope is that the 'poor motherless, friendless' Feemy (*Macdermots*, 259) can find a friend and guide in Mrs McKeon.

The McKeon family is the single bright spot in the otherwise bleak panorama in the 'small country town' of Mohill, which is described in considerable detail, even if the detail runs somewhat contrary to what that town was actually like in those years. In fact Mohill seems to have been considerably larger than Trollope painted it, with some 17,918 inhabitants in the greater area according to the census of 1841 (rising to over 23,000 ten years later).[20] Samuel Lewis, in his 1837 *Topography of Ireland*, describes the town as 'neatly built', 'well supplied with grain and provisions', a market, a local dispensary, and several schools catering for the

---

[20] http://homepage.eircom.net/~tina/mohill/Mohill-Census.htm#1841.

local population.[21] Trollope, however, paints an 'impoverished town' that is 'destitute of anything to give it interest or prosperity—without business, without trade, and without society'. Why, the narrator wonders, would anyone choose to live in such a place? And yet, this 'is a question which proposes itself at the sight of many Irish towns; they look so poor, so destitute of advantage, so unfriended. Mohill is by no means the only town in the west of Ireland that strikes one as being there without a cause.' It is sparsely dotted with the odd 'slated house, but they are few and far between'; the rest is 'cabins—hovels without chimneys, windows, door, or signs of humanity' (*Macdermots*, 126). It is hard to believe that these mud hovels, these 'barren places', can be 'the habitation of any of the human race'. The reader is taken inside a cabin and brought face to face with the impossibly harsh economic realities endured by its inhabitants who 'defy description':

> A sickly woman, the entangled nature of whose insufficient garments would defy description, is sitting on a low stool before the fire, suckling a miserably dirty infant.... Two or three dim children—their number is lost in their obscurity—are cowering round the dull, dark fire, atop of one another; and on a miserable pallet beyond—a few rotten boards, propped upon equally infirm supports, and covered over with only one thin black quilt—is sitting the master of the mansion; his grizzly, unshorn beard, his lantern jaws and shaggy hair, are such as his home and family would lead one to expect. And now you have counted all that this man possesses; other furniture has he none—neither table nor chair, except that low stool on which his wife is sitting. Squatting on the ground—from off the ground, like pigs, only much more poorly fed—his children eat the scanty earnings of his continual labour.
> And yet for this abode the man pays rent (*Macdermots,* 126–7).

The narrator's focus lingers on the 'suburban misery' and 'lowest poverty' of the town, 'its squalidness and filth' and the 'miserable appearance of Irish peasants' (*Macdermots*, 127). The tone of indignation is heightened by the switch into the present tense, as if to assert that the novel is not only narrating past events, but also commenting, albeit indirectly, on current problems. At the same time, Trollope's description seems the fulfilment of Thackeray's claim that 'poverty and misery have... their *sublime,* and that sublime is to be found in Ireland.'[22] Blame for this situation is scornfully laid at the door of the absentee Anglo-Irish Lord Birmingham, 'a kind,

---

[21] For a description of Mohill see Samuel Lewis, *A Topographical Dictionary of Ireland* (London: Lewis and Co., 1837). http://www.libraryireland.com/topog/m2.php.
[22] Thackeray, Review of Venedey's *Irland.*

good man, a most charitable man!' who helps everyone except his own people:

> Is he not the presiding genius of the company for relieving the Poles? A vice-presiding genius for relieving destitute authors, destitute actors, destitute clergymen's widows, destitute half-pay officers' widows? Is he not patron of the Mendicity Society, patron of the Lying-in, Small Pox, Lock, and Fever Hospitals? Is his name not down for large amounts in aid of funds of every description for lessening human wants and pangs?... In short, is not every one aware that Lord Birmingham has spent a long and brilliant life in acts of public and private philanthropy? 'Tis true he lives in England, was rarely in his life in Ireland, never in Mohill. Could he be blamed for this? Could he live in two countries at once? (*Macdermots*, 128).

The tone and content of Trollope's description take much from Edgeworth's biting portrayals in *Ennui* (1809) and *The Absentee* (1812), and have much in common with Lever's mocking depiction of Owen Leslie in *St Patrick's Eve* (1845), an absentee landlord who, 'of his Irish estates... knew nothing, save through the half-yearly accounts of his agent.'[23] Lord Birmingham is presented as an unworthy absentee landlord and is based on successive Earls of Leitrim. Trollope had in mind Nathaniel Clements, the second Earl (1768–1854), who held the Barony of Mohill but preferred to live in Dublin, London (Portman Square), or at his main residence in Kildare. His son Robert Bermingham Clements did mostly live in Mohill until his early death in 1839, and his name perhaps provides the link. He was succeeded as Earl by his brother, William Sydney Clements, a notoriously cruel and unpopular landlord (who was assassinated by locals in 1878).

The Widow Mulready's—the key location of local Ribbonism—is located in the shadow of Lord Birmingham's 'big house'. It is here that the Ribbonmen, led by Joe Reynolds, whose brother has been wrongfully arrested, toast what they hope will be the imminent death of Captain Ussher. By juxtaposing Big House and shebeen, Trollope locates cause and effect, reading Irish agitation as the inevitable consequence of English and Anglo-Irish absence and neglect. This will be a keynote in all of Trollope's Irish writings: an underlining of the failures of the Anglo-Irish who have, since 'the treachery of the Union' (*Auto*, 72), continued to sell the country short and refused to assume the responsibilities of a ruling class. Trollope writes to awaken the Anglo-Irish to responsibility and to urge the English reader to a better understanding—the first step towards a better administration—of Ireland. The alternative, his novels warn, will be

---

[23] Charles Lever, *St Patrick's Eve* (London: Chapman and Hall, 1845), 70.

Irish wretchedness spilling into agitation and violence, which sooner or later will spread across the water.

Trollope has the narrator relate a 'true' story, heard from a local source; a device, this, borrowed straight from Edgeworth. His choice of a reliable, local voice, a coach-driver bearing the name 'McC' (short for Bianconi's aforementioned coachman, M'Cluskie) serves to assert the authenticity of the story and makes the link with Edgeworth explicit, even if the Irish-English voice is not always perfectly sustained. The initial 'I' used by the coach-driver soon morphs into the more detached authorial 'I' of the English narrator, who proceeds almost as if he were a barrister pleading on Thady's behalf. This strategy of advocacy would be used again, many times over, in Trollope's subsequent novels. Trollope's way of making Thady's case is akin to that enunciated by the narrator of Henry Grattan Curran's *Confessions of a Whitefoot* (1844): ' "Brand the murderer as you will," said he, "but to do justice to society, as well as to the accused, extend your inquisition to the dead—put the victim of violence upon his trial, and scrutinize the conduct by which he may have drawn down the blow".'[24] Trollope's narrator scrutinizes, motivates, and explains Thady's actions (his victim is far more of a villain than Thady will ever be) before a mixed court of readers invited to come to their own conclusions regardless of the legal resolution staged in the novel.

Trollope seeks to render justice by illustrating both underlying causes, such as hunger, impoverishment, ongoing landlord-tenant issues, and persistent reactions such as Ribbonism and other forms of agrarian agitation. Similarly, in his *Examiner* letters, he argues that, although 'it is impossible to palliate the horrid deeds of blood which were so rife in Limerick, Clare, and Tipperary, it still should be remarked that tenant-farmers have in those counties received a harsher usage than in others; that there has been there less of a kindly feeling from the gentry towards their dependants [sic]; and that the fell spirit of revenge which has been exhibited has not been without its cause' (*Examiner*, 101).

Legal rights and wrongs are one of the dominant thematic preoccupations of the novel, which asks what justice should mean and how it might be effectively applied in Ireland. The question of justice, particularly for the powerless and the disenfranchised, is explored by Trollope both with regard to individuals and to the ramshackle social institutions existing in Ireland. How far, Trollope asks, is the justice system of the State to go in making concessions with regard to lawbreaking that is at least partially caused by appalling social conditions? What acts are to be considered

---

[24] Henry Grattan Curran, *Confessions of a Whitefoot* (London: Bentley, 1846), 15–16.

criminal in a country awash with, on the one hand, exploitation, rack-renting (making tenants pay extortionate rents), and neglect, and, on the other, agrarian revolt and secret organizations? What methods can legitimately be used to investigate crime and unmask men who are effectively terrorists? These are questions that would exercise Trollope to varying degrees in all of his Irish novels, but never again would he show such empathy with those at the lowest end of the social scale who, almost inevitably, find themselves on the wrong side of the law.

These questions are explored within the key contextual background of Ribbonism, which was a prominent component of the wave of rural agitation which swept through nineteenth-century Ireland. The country was, in Tom Garvin's words: 'in a state of what might best be described as a slow-moving and low-intensity guerrilla warfare'. The main causes of agrarian agitation were 'unrestricted landlordism, unrestricted subletting and a rapid population increase putting increasing pressure on a limited supply of land.'[25] Yet Ribbonism was mostly a means to self-preservation by Catholic peasants, who could hope for no satisfaction from the legal system and who ignored both the Church ban on membership and denunciations by mainstream political leaders, such as O'Connell, who charged Ribbonism and Whiteboyism with increasing 'misery and oppression' rather than producing 'relief or mitigation of the suffering of the people.'[26]

It was also opposed by the magistrates and the police, often through the use of informers. Nevertheless, the movement continued to thrive, and O'Connell was not above drawing indirectly on its force to bolster his own campaigns. Even if some memberships were forced by fear rather than inspired by belief in its aims, being part of the Ribbon movement offered a sense of belonging and community, as well as a means to fight against eviction and in favour of rent reductions and the abolition of tithes. Sometimes, it was little different to a protection organization, and used scare tactics, including 'the arms raid, the threatening letter, the disguised visit at midnight, the mutilation of animals as well as people' in the hope of enforcing 'a crude land law on landlord, farmer and peasant alike.'[27] Acts of 'extreme brutality' were carried out by local groups, formed into a 'Parochial Tribunal' that adjudicated in all cases of complaint, and imposed a form of rough justice that included intimidation, beatings,

---

[25] Tom Garvin, *The Evolution of Irish Nationalist Politics* (Dublin: Gill and Macmillan, 2005), 39.

[26] Daniel O'Connell; Richard Lalor Sheil, *A collection of speeches spoken by Daniel O'Connell, esq. and Richard Sheil, esq. on subjects connected with the Catholic question* (Dublin: John Cumming, 1828), 205.

[27] Garvin, *Irish Nationalist Politics*, 39.

and the occasional murder. These practices were nowhere more prevalent than in Trollope's base in Leitrim. Writing in 1846, Sir Robert Peel claimed that while much of Ireland 'may be considered tolerably peaceable ... in the wild part of Leitrim and Roscommon and their adjacent districts'

> Ribbonism is still in force; intimidation by means of threatening notices and visits from armed and disguised 'Molly Maguires' is persevered in; waylaying, assaults, and robberies of arms and money take place; and all these arising, for the most part, from what is termed agrarian causes.[28]

In addition to finding himself in a hotbed of Ribbonism, Trollope was also able to look at much recent fiction about agrarian agitation, such as Charlotte Elizabeth Tonna's *The Rockite* (1829), which describes Whiteboy agitation as a cancerous evil eating at the heart of the country, and Harriet Martineau's *Ireland: A Tale* (1832), in which the Whiteboys are seen as an inevitable consequence of British misrule. He might also have read Matthew Archdeacon's *Everard: An Irish Tale of 19th Century* (1835), a denunciation of Ribbonism in Connacht during the Tithe War of the 1830s, as seen through the story of a young man whose family has fallen on hard times and who is convinced to join the Ribbonmen. The novel equally condemns 'those vampire absentee landlords, who, provided they can drain the lifeblood from the land, to minister to their luxuries in happier climes, leave, with unparalleled heartlessness, its wretched inhabitants without food, without raiment, and without hope, to wrestle with a lot far more abject than that of ancient slave, or modern negro—or fly to midnight crime for redress or vengeance.'[29] Other notable works on the subject included Michael Banim's 'Crohoore of the Billhook' (1825) and Mrs Hall's *The Whiteboy* (1845), a dark work set against the backdrop of agrarian agitation in 1822 and portraying a people with 'no hope beyond hunger, revolt and death.'[30] In Henry Grattan Curran's *Confessions of a Whitefoot*, Trollope would have found useful analysis of the social and economic causes of agrarian agitation: 'passionate retaliation', Curran writes in the preface, 'is more explicable than justifiable', especially when the 'sordid and merciless oppressors are Irish landlords'. Lever, too, had turned to the subject in *St Patrick's Eve*, writing that '[f]rom no man's life, perhaps, is hope more rigidly excluded than from that of the

---

[28] Sir Robert Peel, *Memoirs by the Right Honourable Sir Robert Peel*. Pt II–III (London: Adamant Media Corporation, 2005 [a reprint of the edition published in 1857 by John Murray]), 303.

[29] Matthew Archdeacon, *Everard: An Irish Tale of the Nineteenth Century. By the Author of Connaught: A Tale of 1798. In Two Volumes* (Dublin: Taaffe, 1835), 74.

[30] Anna Maria Hall, *The Whiteboy*, 1845, 2 vols (New York: Garland Press, 1979) 2, 8.

Irish peasant', and describing the devastation that could be wreaked on the peasantry by a ruthless land agent such as the one running the absentee Leslie estate, where the 'misery of the people was a thing to shudder at.'[31] Like many of these writers, Trollope would show that Ribbon violence arose from an instinct for self-preservation on the part of peasants who were being mistreated and whose very survival was at risk.

Carleton's take was unique because he wrote about the Ribbonmen from the point of view of a former insider, having been initiated into the movement in Monaghan in 1813, following his family's eviction. 'Wild-goose Lodge' was first published in the *Dublin Literary Gazette* in 1830 as 'Confessions of a Reformed Ribbonman' and describes the brutal killing of a farmer and his family by a group of 'malignant and reckless' Ribbonmen. The novel, in MacCurtain's words, 'carries a dreadful note of warning':

> In Irish peasant society, respect for any form of law could not develop because the laws seemed devised to operate against the peasant, and so a private code of law came into operation through the agrarian secret societies. But the rage which was an expression of frustration was capable of turning savagely against itself. It was the violence of the peasant struggling to liberate himself from the sub-human mentality engendered by oppression, debarred from articulating his grievances through an equitable machinery of law, and tragically brutalising the community he was trying to emancipate. In 'Wild-goose Lodge', the Ribbonmen viciously murder the members of a household who informed on the cousins of Ribbonmen for a heinous crime they had committed.[32]

Fardorougha the Miser is also set against a background of 1830s Ribbonism, while *Rody the rover, or, The Ribbonman* (1845), an equally forceful warning of the dangers of this movement, depicts the Ribbon leaders as treacherous men who enrol acquaintances only to later inform on them. The novel describes Rody's recruiting of a young man, Tom M'Mahon, into the Ribbon organization, which he says works for the freedom of the country and of Catholics. M'Mahon takes the oath and swears never to reveal Rody's name. He is also made an Article Bearer (so he can administer the oath to others) and is given the power to lead local recruits. However, he is unable to control his men, who get involved in acts of violence, and finds himself accused of a murder which he did everything in his power to prevent. He is betrayed by Rody, and other Ribbonmen who provide false evidence against him, and is arrested, tried, found guilty, and executed.

---

[31] Curran, *Whitefoot*, 6, 9; Lever, *St Patrick's Eve*, 71.
[32] Margaret MacCurtain, 'Pre-Famine Peasantry in Ireland: Definition and Theme', *Irish University Review*, 4/2 (Autumn 1974), 197.

The novel is a relentless exposé of the treachery that Carleton believes lies at the heart of the Ribbon movement, but also an attack on the government system of employing informers. As a result of his criticism of informing, Carleton was accused of disloyalty, a charge he rebuffed by claiming that 'his warnings and exposures' had led to 'the dispersal of six hundred Ribbon lodges.'[33]

All these Ribbon issues—violence, informing, betrayal, miscarriages of justice, and secret practices on the part of both the government forces and the Ribbon movement—are live topics within Trollope's first novel, which paints a picture of a country where the law is misused for personal gain, law-enforcers are revealed to be dishonest and corrupt, and law-breakers are shown to be in such desperate situations as to be almost justified in their deeds. Captain Ussher's name carries a cheeky echo of the very illustrious James Ussher, seventeenth-century Church of Ireland Archbishop of Armagh, but he belongs, more pertinently, to a well-established literary tradition of cruel and repressive law-enforcers, including Major Hempenshagh, magistrate and captain-general of the police in Eyre Evans Crowe's novella, *The Carders* (1825), and Lever's Major Barton in *Tom Burke of 'Ours'* (1843). Ussher believes that the use of informers is the only way to bring order to a 'lawless' country in which 'illicit distillation was carried to a great extent' and many 'tenants refused to pay either rent, tithes, or county cesses till compelled to do so' (*Macdermots*, 16). He enforces the law with reckless disregard for his own safely and shows scant interest in the context of suffering in which he works, believing the poor too 'cowed and frightened' to 'have the spirit to rise up against him' (*Macdermots*, 218).

The narrator insists on the non-political nature of Ussher's manslaughter and underlines that it is not connected with Ribbonism. Matters come to a head when Ussher tells Feemy that he is to be transferred to Cashel. She asks him about what she presumes is their forthcoming marriage but he fends her off with excuses that he cannot marry before his imminent departure: 'If we are to be married at all, it can't be here.' (*Macdermots*, 284). With the use of 'if' rather than 'when', Feemy finally realizes that he will desert her. He rebuts her with lies, telling her he cannot marry her because Thady has mistreated him and because it would prevent his rising in the ranks; 'they won't promote a married man. You see I couldn't marry till after I was settled at Cashel' (*Macdermots*, 285). 'Feemy', the

---

[33] Quoted in David J. O'Donoghue, *The Life of William Carleton: being his autobiography and letters, and an account of his life and writings, from the point at which the autobiography breaks off*...with an introduction by Mrs Cashel Hoey, 2 vols (London: Downey & Co., 1896), I, 81.

narrator notes, 'received the lie with which Ussher's brain had at the moment furnished him, without a doubt' (*Macdermots*, 285). The reference to Ussher's brain suggests a disconnection between his reasoning mind and his sentimental and sexual feelings. He can rationally justify his actions to himself by denying the cold fact that he will destroy her if he does not marry her. Eventually, he manages to convince her to leave with him 'without her father's blessing, or the priest's—to go with him in a manner which she knew would disgrace herself, her name, and her family, and to trust to him afterwards to give her what reparation a tardy marriage could afford' (*Macdermots*, 285–6). It is precisely when Feemy is waiting outside to flee with Ussher that Thady turns up and strikes him dead.

Thady has acted in good faith, but on the basis of unverifiable information given in secret. His self-awareness throughout the spiral of events that lead to his hanging makes him a truly tragic figure:

> Though Thady had never known the refinements of a gentleman, or the comforts of good society, still he felt that the fall, even from his present station to that in which he was going to place himself, would be dreadful. But it was not the privations which he might suffer, but the disgrace, the additional disgrace which he would bring on his family, which afflicted him (*Macdermots*, 269).

However, Trollope depoliticizes Ussher's clash with the locals by casting him as an Ulsterman rather than an Englishman, even if he still represents the Forces of the Crown. Furthermore, his death will not be a consequence of his trying to impose the law, but of his failure to honour the unwritten moral laws of decency with regard to Feemy. In depoliticizing the murder into a domestic squabble, Trollope was following Carleton, who offers an explanation for the violence in *Fardorougha the Miser* in the 'savage principle of personal vengeance', rather than in any political or economic grievance.[34] However, the other acts of violence in Trollope's novel have motivations that are entirely political. Hyacinth Keegan, for example, is mutilated by Ribbonmen precisely because he is intent on driving the Macdermots and their tenants out of Ballycloran. They want to repay Thady for having done 'the good service of ridding the country of Ussher'

---

[34] Margaret Kelleher, 'Prose Writing and Drama in English, 1830–1890: From Catholic Emancipation to the Fall of Parnell', in Margaret Kelleher and Philip O'Leary, eds., *The Cambridge History of Irish Literature*, 2 vols (Cambridge: Cambridge University Press, 2006), 1, 457. Thomas Tracy gives a different political reading of Thady's actions, arguing that 'Thady's perception of theft or abduction accurately reflects the reaction of a significant portion of Ireland's population, from varying political backgrounds, to the "treachery" of Union'. Thomas Tracy, *Irishness and Womanhood in Nineteenth-Century British Writing* (London: Ashgate, 2009), 128.

by punishing Keegan, whom they believe is 'robbing Thady of his right and his property' (*Macdermots*, 445).

Throughout the novel, Thady, who has 'something manly in his original disposition', suffers because he cannot adequately oppose Keegan or Ussher. He would like to 'avenge himself like a man', but instead finds himself 'leaguing with others to commit murder in the dark, like a coward and a felon'. His courage puts him in contrast with Ussher, who fails in his duty as a man in an age in which manly values were stressed. Thady feels powerless before Keegan, this 'gentleman [who] had long looked forward to the day when he should be able to describe himself as Hyacinth Keegan, Esq., of Ballycloran', and who, on 'his father-in-law's death', will inherit the property (*Macdermots*, 171). Possession of Ballycloran will allow Keegan 'admission into the more decent society of Carrick-on-Shannon' and permit him to seek the 'sub-shrievalty of the county'. In one sense, given that both he and the police make systematic use of informers, he is well qualified to become sheriff. However, the general practice of informing, 'a most iniquitous system of espionage' (*Macdermots*, 174), is roundly condemned, and the 'worst villain, the informer', is, in Christine Longford's words, described by Trollope 'with passionate hatred and missionary zeal':[35]

> those who have observed the working of the system must admit that the treachery which it creates—the feeling of suspicion which it generates—but, above all, the villanies to which it gives and has given rise, in allowing informers, by the prospect of blood-money, to give false informations, and to entrap the unwary into crimes—are by no means atoned for by the occasional detection and punishment of a criminal (*Macdermots*, 174).

Trollope particularizes his condemnation of informing by studying how it is used by a range of characters, especially Ussher, Keegan, and Pat Brady, but he shies away from pursuing the larger political ramifications of informing by exonerating the British government from wrongdoing (unlike Carleton) while, at the same time, claiming, contradictorily, that the use of informers significantly raises crime levels:

> I cannot but think the system of secret informers—to which those in positions of inferior authority too often have recourse—has greatly increased crime in many districts of Ireland. I by no means intend to assert that this system is patronised or even recognised by Government. I believe the contrary most fully (*Macdermots*, 175).

---

[35] Longford, 'Trollope in Ireland', 187.

Trollope would later change his mind on informing in *The Landleaguers*, by which time he had come to the belief that the state of unrest in Ireland justified its use.

The issue of the giving and withholding of information is vital to the structure of the novel and links the private and the public plots. The law is shown to hang on words, uttered or unuttered by those on whom judgement must be passed. Thady's destiny is determined by an informer's false words, by his sister's refusal to speak, and by his own loose, incautious words. While an informer provides evidence to justify the arrest of illicit poteen makers and Pat Brady's selective use of information allows him to exercise control over both Thady and the tenants, it is precisely Feemy's refusal to convey the vital information regarding her aborted flight with Ussher that condemns Thady to death by hanging. Similarly, Thady's failure to give straight answers to Father McGrath deprives the priest of the means to stop his dangerous involvement with Ribbonism. Father John implores Thady not to mix with the Ribbonmen and to disregard whatever oath he may have taken, and, in return, promises absolute secrecy. Thady, however, is evasive in his answers, claims that he does not 'belong to any society' (*Macdermots*, 294), and finally swears 'most solemnly, on the sacred volume, that he would do as the priest directed him respecting these men' (*Macdermots*, 296). Thady will not live up to his word and will pay the price for having put himself 'in the power of Brady and Joe Reynolds—as though he could not escape from them' (*Macdermots*, 298).

The theme of information and secrecy is nowhere worked through more prominently than in the character of Pat Brady, who is depicted with contempt in the narrative which, unusually for Trollope, draws on stereotypically anti-Irish tropes to describe him. Thus Brady's nose is 'all but flattened on to his face', and he is a 'bow-legged' 'appendage' who gains control of Ballycloran by gathering 'secret knowledge' about the tenants' affairs (*Macdermots*, 16–17), so as to keep them in check. This knowledge of everyone else's business is what gives him power over Thady, whom he gradually lures into the Ribbon movement by always appearing, Iago-like, at the right moment to play on Thady's weaknesses. Such a moment comes immediately after Thady has been verbally and physically humiliated by Keegan and left 'like a dog cowed by a blow' (*Macdermots*, 169). Brady knows how to exploit this moment by challenging him not to accept what Keegan has done 'paceable an' in quiet', and promising him that 'Keegan shall never harum you or yours, if you'll be one of us—one of us heart and sowl . . . an' dearly he'll pay for the blow he strike you' (*Macdermots*, 227). Thady is reassured by Brady's assurances that 'when you're one of us, it's not much longer he [Ussher] shall throuble you' (*Macdermots*, 228). Thus he falls victim to Brady's pressure, not realizing that his agent is now firmly in Keegan's pay.

Keegan uses Brady as his chief source of information about the Macdermots and about those suspected of committing crimes in the county, and is an example for Trollope of how the instruments of the law can be used not to obtain justice, but to enact personal retribution through blackmail. This misuse of the law is suggested in the coinage 'lawcraft', which is applied to Keegan's means of operating. His whole way of life is devoid of moral scruple, built on illicitly obtaining information and threatening to use it so as to build his personal power. Brady is little better and, having foreseen 'that the days of the Macdermots were over', works to 'ingratiate himself with the probable future "masther"', believing that 'great worldly advantages...might accrue from being chief informer' (*Macdermots*, 173). Brady is on a par with another of the novel's informers, Cogan, who provides Ussher with information that leads to the arrest of the men accused of making poteen, including Joe Reynold's innocent brother, Tim, who does not have the means to defend himself except by threatening physical Ribbon retaliation. The narration of these arrests is followed by a description of a discussion about this event at Mulready's whiskey shop, the headquarters of local Ribbonism. The focus is on Joe Reynolds, who 'presides', and on Pat Brady, who manipulates him. Violent threats are made against Ussher, 'as Joe Reynolds expressed it, "we'll hole him till there ar'nt a bit left in him to hole"' (*Macdermots*, 37). The narrator provides a detailed sociological interpolation describing Ribbonism in Mohill, and showing how the Ribbonmen are united in attempting to protect themselves against rent increases. They tell Brady that they wish to align themselves with 'the good ould blood that's in it now' (the Catholic Macdermot family) against all outside threats, and especially against Ussher and 'the likes of Flannelly and Keegan' who wish to be 'masthers in Ballycloran' (*Macdermots*, 38). They side with the Macdermots because they represent the lesser evil, and instruct Brady to tell Thady to stay away from Ussher so that they can guarantee that he'll be protected. Throughout all this, Brady makes cynical use of Joe Reynolds, allowing him to believe that he is the leader of the group when he is actually manipulating him. Trollope's narrator finds some excuse for the drunken Reynolds's verbal violence and his belonging to the Ribbon movement, which is born of desperation, but he is far less forgiving of the double-dealing (and sober) Brady, who 'enjoyed comparative comfort' and does not need to be involved in crime. Given Brady's duplicitous ways, it is not surprising that Thady is both reassured by the promise of Ribbon support and fearful that his association with them will be used against him. He cannot forget a trial at Carrick in which a man was hanged on evidence from an informer, 'an ill-featured, sullen-looking fellow', who had been a 'friend and assistant of the murderer . . . the sharer and promoter of all his plans—the man who had led him on to the murder—his sworn friend. . . . Yet this man had come forward to hang his friend!—and Thady shuddered coldly as he thought how likely it might be that his associates would betray him' (*Macdermots*, 270–1). All this recalls Carleton's Ribbon depictions.

Although Thady fears that Brady will testify against him, he fails to break fully with the Ribbonmen, and, following the murder, feels he has no choice but to turn to them for help. He is taken to a remote hideout called Aughacashel, having promised that he will join the movement. He is now in the hands of Joe Reynolds, who agrees to help him because he has 'an idea of justice', even though 'it was contrary to their regulations to bring a stranger to the haunts where his companions carried on their illegal trade' (*Macdermots*, 407). The narrative lingers on the poverty and misery of Aughacashel, and its few inhabitants who live in 'miserably poor cabins'. The 'barren soil' allows them to obtain only 'wretchedly poor crops of potatoes', and so, to make ends meet, they engage in 'the more profitable but hazardous business of making potheen'. These impossible material conditions are the principal reason that the inhabitants are 'a lawless, reckless set of people—paying, some little, and others no rent, and living without the common blessings or restraints of civilization' (*Macdermots*, 407). Thady is given refuge in one of two cabins occupied

> by a very old man and his daughter . . . and the other belonged to another partner in the [potheen] business. . . . This man's name was Daniel Kennedy, and to the reckless, desperate contempt of authority and hatred of those who exercised it, which characterized Reynolds, he added a cruelty of disposition, and a love of wickedness, from which the other was much more free (*Macdermots*, 408).

The description of this lawless, mountainous country follows a familiar trope in Irish fiction, to be found, for example, in Lady Morgan's 'Mount Sackville' (1833), set in a Sligo full of 'wild disorder and outraged peasantry, where the mountain districts were filled with outlaws' driven there by evictions and a unsympathetic magistracy.[36] More than disorder and outrage, however, the residents of Aughnacashel seem to incarnate paralysis, and Thady wonders 'how the old man got through the tedium of

---

[36] Lady Morgan, 'Mount Sackville', in *Dramatic Scenes from Real Life* (1833; repr. New York: Garland, 1979), 53–5. The name also echoes with that of the Ribbon stronghold of Aughnaglass, described in Matthew Archdeacon's *Legends of Connaught* (Dublin: J. Cumming, 1829).

his miserable existence . . . Why did he sit there so quiet, doing nothing—saying nothing—looking at nothing—and apparently thinking of nothing? It was as sitting with a dead body or a ghost—that sitting there with that lifeless but yet breathing creature' (*Macdermots*, 422). Thady is safe here, at a remove from the outside world and, more specifically, from the English forces of authority: 'should anyone be axing about you, they'll niver 'peach, or give the word to the police, or anyone else' (*Macdermots*, 416). He has little choice but to take the Ribbon oath and bind himself to secrecy about the hideout, to a commitment to help his fellow Ribbonmen 'against any who attempted to molest them, but especially against all Revenue officers and their men' (*Macdermots*, 425–6). He soon realizes, however, that he cannot remain hidden, and makes a second escape in order to give himself up. He takes refuge with Father John, who hopes a jury will see that Thady 'had only been actuated by the praiseworthy purpose of defending his sister from disgrace and violence', that his 'presence on the scene at the moment was accidental, and that the attack could not have been premeditated' (*Macdermots*, 434).

Thady's cause is fatally compromised when Joe Reynolds and his associates enforce brutal Ribbon justice of their own against Keegan by severing his foot with an axe, in a scene described with chilling effect:

> the first blow only cut his trousers and his boot, and bruised him sorely,—for his boots protected him; the second cut the flesh, and grated against the bone; in vain he struggled violently, and with all the force of a man struggling for his life; a third, and a fourth, and a fifth descended, crushing the bone, dividing the marrow, and ultimately severing the foot from the leg (*Macdermots*, 446).

There is much evidence of similar criminal acts of vengeance taking place in Leitrim in the 1840s, usually carried out by peasants 'who feared that their way of life was under threat from outside forces.'[37] This is essentially the motivation which drives the Ribbonmen to mutilate Keegan. The preservation of the status quo is specifically requested in the barely literate letter to 'Captin Furster', Ussher's replacement:

> This is to giv' notis, Captin Furster, av you'll live and let live, and be quite an' pacable—divil a rason is there, why you need be afeard—but av you go on among the Leatrim boys—as that bloody thundhering ruffin Ussher, by the etarnal blessed Glory, you wul soon be stretched as he war—for the Leatrim boys isn't thim as wul put up with it (*Macdermots*, 449).

---

[37] Jennifer Kelly, 'A study of Ribbonism in County Leitrim in 1841', in Joost Augusteijn and Mary Ann Lyons, eds., *Irish History: A Research Yearbook 2* (Dublin: Four Courts Press, 2003), 46.

But these are motivations and character nuances that the reader rather than the system of justice can come to know, and the description of the three presiding judges in the trial scene at the Assizes in Carrick-on-Shannon leaves the reader with little hope on Thady's behalf. The first judge, Jonas Brown, is an 'irritable, overbearing magistrate, a greedy landlord, and an unprincipled father', whose entailed estate is rack-rented to such an extent that 'there would be little to leave to a younger son' (*Macdermots*, 333–4). His family is a mirror image of the Macdermots: they are just a generation away from the ruin suffered by the older Catholic family. Brown insists that Ussher has 'been murdered in cold blood by a known Ribbonman' (*Macdermots*, 453) and is supported in this belief by the ineffectual Sir Michael Gibson. Only Counsellor Webb, 'a kind-hearted landlord—ever anxious to ameliorate the condition of the poor', takes Thady's side. Pat Brady's false testimony that Thady had acted on behalf of the Ribbon movement proves crucial, and Thady is condemned. Counsellor Webb travels to Dublin to plead his case with the Lord Lieutenant, but to no avail. An example is to be made of Thady.

Despite the legal refusal to accept the defence made on Thady's behalf, the narrator understands, defends, and ennobles him as a selfless if weak victim of circumstances: 'Patient under poverty—industrious under accumulated sufferings—he has led a life which would not have disgraced a priest; he has been ever found sincere in his thoughts, moral in his conduct, and most unselfish in his actions' (*Macdermots*, 571). By the end of the novel, however, his crisis has become existential: 'Could he be but once quiet in his grave, and have done with it all—be rid of the care, turmoil, and uneasiness, he would have been content' (*Macdermots*, 530–1). In the plangent final scenes, Trollope shows how an entire Irish community unites in grief and points to a system of justice which, by condemning Thady, far from dispensing a fair sentence, effectively plays into the hands of the Ribbonmen. The reader is left with a rather contradictory conclusion: on the one hand, the narrative suggests that justice must be done and be seen to be done; on the other, what passes for justice at the conclusion of the novel is exposed as its very opposite. Thady is shown to have done the right thing, to have ultimately rejected violence and rebellion, and to have yielded to the state system of justice. His return to the Assizes from the most peripheral geographical location in the novel—its historical backwardness and pastness stressed by its geographical remoteness—symbolises his re-assimilation into society, even if he is then dispatched to his death by his betrayers and by an inadequate system of justice. It is important to remember that Thady's prosecution is conducted by the British government—a decision confirmed at the very top of the political pyramid in Dublin by the Lord Lieutenant. The legal system is used in the case of Thady to send out a precise message—to intimidate the Irish into renouncing violence—but the result is an immediate show of restraint and solidarity for the condemned man and an inevitable rise in future disaffection.

The product of the son of a failed chancery lawyer, Trollope's first Irish novel places the law centre stage, even if it concludes despondently with the sense that no justice is possible for its Irish protagonist (and, by extension, for the inarticulate Ireland that he embodies). This novel inaugurates a thematic preoccupation with questions of justice, with private and public legal matters that would play a central role in the author's future works. It also offers an early instance of his enduring sense of the limits and inadequacies of the law, and his idea that a legal truth might be quite different from the truth expressed through a work of fiction. The novel, in Trollope's terms, can aspire to a more complete truth than the law: 'They say that novels are false;—meaning that they are untrue in the broadest sense, because they are fictions . . . but fiction may be as true as fact.'[38]

II. A POSSIBLE JUSTICE: *THE KELLYS*
AND THE O'KELLYS

Trollope's second novel, *The Kellys and the O'Kellys*, revisits many of the legal issues raised in *The Macdermots* and would attempt to marry the judgements offered by the enactment of a local, rather homemade system of justice with the wider vision of equity suggested through this fictional work. The novel offers a significant treatment of matters legal, in both the domestic and the larger political spheres, which is of relevance not only within the context of his Irish output, but within the panorama of his fiction as a whole, and within the Victorian novel's near obsession with the law. Trollope shows how the words, spoken or unspoken, by those on whom the law is called to pass judgement, determine their fate. If, in *The Macdermots*, Thady's destiny is determined by an informer's false words, his sister's refusal to speak, and by his own loose, incautious words, in *The Kellys and the O'Kellys*, Barry Lynch's reckless and violent words, rather than his actual deeds, will be what brings about his undoing. Lynch's improvised punishment (unlike that of Thady) is thoroughly deserved

---

[38] Anthony Trollope, 'On English Prose Fiction as a Rational Amusement' (1870), in Morris L. Parrish, intro. and ed., *Four Lectures* (London: Constable, 1938), 108–9.

and carries the narrator's endorsement, even if it rides roughshod over legal niceties.

Given that *The Kellys and the O'Kellys* was written in 1847, it offers a stubbornly optimistic vision of its Irish setting: food and drink seem to be in abundant supply as we read, for example, of a minor character who 'indulged in tea almost to stupefaction' (*Kellys*, 173), while the doctor insists that the ailing Anty be fed 'a mutton chop and a glass of sherry every day at one o'clock' (*Kellys*, 361). Perhaps Trollope was resigned to the fact that his English readers would only stomach so much Famine suffering and rural agitation, or perhaps he was alluding to the fact that Famine left the small Irish middle class relatively unharmed. However, the work, which is laced with biting but mostly affectionate satire aimed at its Irish protagonists, enjoyed less initial critical and popular success than its predecessor, with the first edition recording a net loss of some £60. *The Times* was dismissive:

> Of *The Kellys and the O'Kellys* we may say what the master said to his footman, when the man complained of the constant supply of mutton on the kitchen table. 'Well, John, legs of mutton are good substantial food,' and we may say also what John replied, 'Substantial, sir; yes, sir, they are substantial, but a little coarse' (*Auto*, 77–8).

Colburn, Trollope's disappointed publisher, declared 'that readers do not like novels on Irish subjects as well as on others' and warned him that it was 'impossible for me to give you any encouragement to proceed in novel-writing' (*Auto*, 78). And yet, the commonplace view that the novel failed can be challenged by the fact of five separate editions appearing before the end of the nineteenth century, with the slightly amended 1859 edition—Trollope changed the chapter divisions—running to ten impressions. At least a dozen editions have been published in the twentieth century.

Michael Sadleir was predictably negative in describing the work as being, like its predecessor, 'a pamphlet in fictional guise' and 'equally a product of Trollope's absorption in the Irish question',[39] but other early twentieth-century reviews disagreed. Arnold Bennett called the novel 'consistently excellent', while Hugh Walpole felt it was on a level with what are today far more acclaimed works such as *The Warden*, *Barchester Towers*, and *The Way We Live Now*.[40] It was precisely the novel's engagement with Irish issues that caused Shane Leslie to compare it with Edgeworth's *Castle Rackrent*, Lever's *Charles O'Malley*, and Carleton's *Valentine McClutchy*, to praise its 'wealth of allusion and accuracy of names' that

---

[39] Sadleir, *Trollope*, 145.   [40] Walpole, *Anthony Trollope*, 25.

'could hardly be reproduced by a historian grubbing today amongst the documents of the past', and to claim that 'no other piece of English literature describes [the epoch of O'Connell] so intimately as Trollope's novel, except John Mitchel's *Jail Journal*'. While Lever and Carleton tended to add 'an over-spice of Celtic distortion. This Trollope never did. He saw Irish life steadily and he saw it whole.'[41] More recently, William Trevor described the novel as the site

> where Ireland and England meet in the 1840s. Touched with English manners and culture, the gilded families seem as secure in their haven as those which have retained the Irish idiom are in theirs—but the great Daniel O'Connell hovers in the background, and the Famine which was to change the course of Irish history in a sense hovers also. Early as its place is in Trollope's canon, this novel is one of the best he ever wrote.[42]

If the plot construction is, as *The Times* suggested, a little coarse and dominated by an inordinate quantity of dialogue (most of which is, however, lively and to the point), the work is a more entertaining reading experience than the earnest but sometimes plodding *Macdermots*, and it offers a more complete panorama of an entire rural community; a feature, this, which Trollope would brilliantly translate into his English settings. The book exemplifies what Trollope later had in mind when he challenged the idea that novels could be broken into two distinct classes, 'the sensational school' and 'the realistic, or life-like school'. In his view, 'a novel is bound to be both sensational and realistic. And I think that if a novel fail in either particular it is, so far, a failure in Art'. In Trollope's view,

> No novel is anything, for purposes either of tragedy or of comedy, unless the reader can sympathise with the characters whose names he finds upon the page. Let an author so tell his tale as to touch your heart and draw your tears, and he has so far done his work well. Truth let there be;—truth of description, truth of character, human truth as to men and women. If there be such truth I do not know that a novel can be too sensational.[43]

The Kellys and the O'Kellys combines careful attention to detail with 'sensational' scenes such as the one in which Barry Lynch physically attacks his sister, Anty, and a combination of narrative effects designed to win the readers' sympathy for the characters and their plights. It also contains many of the quintessential Trollopian themes and techniques

---

[41] Shane Leslie, 'Introduction' to Anthony Trollope, *The Kellys and the O'Kellys*, ed. Shane Leslie (New York: Random House, 1937), vi, xiii.

[42] William Trevor, 'Introduction' to Anthony Trollope, *The Kellys and the* O'Kellys, ed. W. J. McCormack (New York: Oxford University Press, 1982), xiii.

[43] Trollope, 'On English Prose Fiction', in Parrish, *Four Lectures*, 123–4.

that would come to dominate his English novels: the double romantic plot, as much based on financial issues as love, the difficult relationships between noble (but once-profligate) fathers and their wasteful sons, and the plight of women with regard to the laws of succession. As Dudley Edwards noted, the novel is awash with colourful and convincing characterizations of its Irish protagonists, often cast in satirical terms, which are analogous to those to be found in his later comedies:

> It is here, not in the first book, that we can see the kind of character types he would polish, mature, subject to cunning variations, and learn to delay in their full revelation or push forward to the ideal moment of discovery as he increasingly mastered the economics of movement within the novel.[44]

Frank O'Kelly or Lord Ballindine, for example, is a very convincing first version of a type that would reappear in Trollope's fiction: the likeable young gentleman who is warm, sensitive, and good-hearted, but also a somewhat immature rogue. In a similar light, the widow Kelly has been seen as 'an avatar of Trollope's long line of female politicans.'[45] At once self-calculating and kind, she is a resolute character who has made her way in a male-dominated world through ceaseless work and a razor-sharp tongue. The novel also boasts Trollope's first fictional account of what it describes as the country's 'national sport' (*Kellys*, 225), that is, fox hunting, used, in this case, to great effect, to transmit not only a sense of Lord Ballindine's county Mayo community, but also as a means of focusing on key characters who show their true colours once on horseback.

The Kelly and O'Kelly surnames that give the book its title signal that we are dealing with 'a cleverly counterpointed study of marital and financial politics at two social levels of Irish life', with Trollope spotting 'that "O'Kelly" could be, in Irish terms, a grander name than "Kelly."'[46] It seems likely that Trollope had at least passing knowledge of the O'Kellys of Uí Maine (an area covering parts of Galway and Roscommon), a family that dated back to the ninth century and whose chief was popularly recognized as 'The O'Kelly'. The *Annals of the Four Masters* offer accounts of the family, although Trollope's source is likely to have been John O'Donovan's 1843 *The Tribes and Customs of Hy-Many, commonly called*

[44] Owen Dudley Edwards, 'Anthony Trollope, Irish Writer', *Nineteenth-Century Fiction*, 38/1 (June 1983), 9.
[45] R. F. Foster, *Paddy & Mr Punch: Connections in Irish and English History* (London: Penguin, 1995), 144.
[46] R. F. Foster, *The Irish Story: Telling Tales and Making It Up in Ireland* (London: Penguin, 2001), 132.

O'Kelly's Country.[47] Here he would have read about the landowning O'Kellys in Mayo and Roscommon who were also 'the hereditary treasurers to the Kings of Connaught.'[48] All this is suggested in Trollope's history of the family:

> The head of the family had for many years back been styled 'The O'Kelly', and had enjoyed much more local influence under that denomination than their descendants had possessed, since they had obtained a more substantial though not a more respected title. The O'Kellys had possessed large tracts of not very good land, chiefly in County Roscommon, but partly in Mayo and Galway. Their property had extended from Dunmore nearly to Roscommon, and again on the other side to Castlerea and Ballyhaunis. But this had been in their palmy days, long, long ago. When the government, in consideration of past services, in the year 1800, converted 'the O'Kelly' into Viscount Ballindine, the family property consisted of the greater portion of the land lying between the villages of Dunmore and Ballindine. Their old residence, which the peer still kept up, was called Kelly's Court, and is situated in that corner of County Roscommnon which runs up between Mayo and Galway (*Kellys*, 15).

In titling his novel as he did, Trollope was showing his familiarity with his Irish context: apart from the title names and the flash through history, the other surnames chosen, including Daly, Blake, and Dillon, correspond to popular West of Ireland names, while the Ballindine name presumably refers to the small county Mayo village of the same name. The novel's subtitle, *Landlords and Tenants*, however, is slightly misleading, since it raises expectations that will be disappointed of a close, sociological reading of the issues at stake between these two classes, much in the way *The Macdermots* examined Ribbonism.

The Kellys and the O'Kellys is most concerned with achieving a rewriting of the negative conclusions of the first novel. If, in *The Macdermots*, a successful marriage plot was impossible and a once noble family is seen to be beyond redemption, here marriage and financial salvation become possible, twice over. If, in the first novel, the imposition of justice, which concludes with Thady's hanging, runs contrary to the broader idea of justice

---

[47] John O'Donovan, *The Tribes and Customs of Hy-Many, commonly called O'Kelly's Country*, first published from the Book of Lecan, a manuscript in the library of the Royal Irish Academy, with a translation and notes, and a map of Hy-many (Dublin: Irish Archaeological Society, 1843).

[48] O'Donovan notes that 'Tadhg, or Teige Mor O'Kelly, was prince of Hy-Many for thirteen years, when he fell in the battle of Clontarf, fighting on the side of Brian Boru, monarch of Ireland, AD 1014' (John O'Donovan, *The Tribes and Customs of Hy-Many*, 126), which is perhaps referenced by Trollope's naming of Frank's beloved horse as Brian Boru.

enunciated by the novel itself, here justice is seen to be achieved, not through customary legal avenues, but through the banishment of two villains, which clears the way for the successful conclusion of the parallel marriage plots. These romantic plots and the connected domestic legal land issues dominate this work, which is an early embodiment of Trollope's belief in the centrality of the love plot as the engine of the novel:

> Taking the general character of novels as our guide, we may say that the love stories are their mainstay and the staff of their existence. . . . They have other attractions, and deal with every phase of life; but the other attractions hang round and depend on the love story as the planets depend upon the sun. The love story is the thing. . . . No social question has been so important to us as that of the great bond of matrimony.[49]

The novel foregrounds the story of Martin Kelly's path towards marriage with Anastasia (Anty) Lynch, the sister of the villainous Barry Lynch, and juxtaposes it with the more aristocratic plot featuring his landlord and distant relative Frank O'Kelly (Lord Ballindine), and his eventual betrothed, Fanny Wyndham. Barry does his utmost to prevent Anty's marriage in the hope that he can gain sole possession of the family farm. Fanny Wyndham's suit is also obstructed for financial reasons by her guardian, Lord Cashel, who attempts to push her into marriage with his own dissolute son, Lord Kilcullen, so that he can appropriate her greater-than-expected fortune and rescue his son from ruin. These marriages will eventually bring a necessary equilibrium to both Martin's and Lord Ballindine's financial situations, but they will not come about before the protagonists win their struggles against Barry Lynch and Lord Cashel, respectively. Even if these marriages are founded on financial gain and neither suitor can be said to have set out with purely romantic intentions, both men discover in adversity a depth of genuine love for their future spouses.

Lord Cashel and his family are cast in negative terms from the outset. He and his daughter Selina are the constant targets of Trollope's satire and can be compared to Sir Walter Elliot and his daughter, Elizabeth, in Jane Austen's *Persuasion*. Indeed, the influence of Austen on Trollope was considerable and can be seen for the first time in this novel, which is, at least in its treatment of the aristocratic romance, a novel of manners and a social satire, penned, very distinctly, in the Austen mode, despite its Irish setting and despite equally strong Edgeworthian echoes. We can hear this in the ironic descriptions of the proud and self-centred Lady Selina Grey, who

---

[49] Trollope, 'On English Prose Fiction', in Parrish, *Four Lectures*, 108–9.

truly loved her family, and tried hard to love her neighbours, in which she might have succeeded but for the immeasurable height from which she looked down on them. She listened, complacently, to all those serious cautions against pride, which her religion taught her, and considered that she was obeying its warnings, when she spoke condescendingly to those around her. She thought that condescension was humility, and that her self-exaltation was not pride, but a proper feeling of her own and her family's dignity (*Kellys*, 116).

Similarly, his portrait of her mother, 'a very good-natured old woman, who slept the greatest portion of her time, and knitted through the rest of her existence', and of Lord Cashel, 'so sedate, and so slow, and so dull' (*Kellys*, 101), is testimony to what he learned from Austen and worthy of any of the satire to be found in his later novels. Lord Cashel's home, the aptly named 'Grey Abbey', is 'like a huge, square, Dutch old lady, and the two wings might be taken for her two equally fat, square, Dutch daughters'. It embodies the 'qualities' of its owner, located, as it is, 'in a flat, uninteresting, and not very fertile country' (*Kellys*, 105–6). Lord Cashel is seen in his bookroom: 'There, like a god, Lord Cashel sat alone, throned amid clouds of awful dulness, ruling the world of nothingness around by the silent solemnity of his inertia' (*Kellys*, 290). His ancestors have squandered an enormous property 'obtained in the reign of Henry II' and including 'immense tracts of land, stretching through Wicklow, Kildare, and the Queen's and King's Counties', and 'have been unable to retain ... anything like an eighth of what the family once pretended to claim', even if the current Earl still 'has enough left to enable him to consider himself a very great man' (*Kellys*, 106).

More than a mere embodiment of the Anglo-Irish landlord class, Cashel is a living indictment of its failings, which can be summed up in an inability to manage, maintain, and nurture what they have inherited. He stands indicted in the narrative for the cynical and unscrupulous manner in which he attempts to cheat Ballindine out of marriage to Fanny so as to favour his son, Kilcullen. While criticising Lord Ballindine for his 'dissipation', for not giving up his interest in horseracing and using this as an excuse to block his marriage to Fanny, Lord Cashel is, at the same time, indulgent in forgiving his own son's disastrously wasteful ways:

> It was true that Lord Kilcullen was a heartless roué, whereas Lord Ballindine was only a thoughtless rake; but then, Lord Kilcullen would be an earl, and a peer of parliament, and Lord Ballindine was only an Irish viscount. It was true that, in spite of her present anger, Fanny dearly loved Lord Ballindine, and was dearly loved by him; and that Lord Kilcullen was not a man to love or be loved; but then, the Kelly's Court rents—what were they to the Grey Abbey rents? Not a twentieth part of them! And, above all, Lord Kilcullen's

vices were filtered through the cleansing medium of his father's partiality, and Lord Ballindine's faults were magnified by the cautious scruples of Fanny's guardian (*Kellys*, 115).

His prejudiced views against Ballindine are given added ballast by the news that Fanny has, through the death of her brother, become far richer than was ever expected. Thus Cashel has even more reason to plot her marriage to his undeserving son, regardless of her own actual desires or Kilcullen's suitability to enter such a match. Cashel realizes that Kilcullen's only hope for a financial rescue lies with Fanny, whose father 'had held a governorship, or some golden appointment in the golden days of India, and consequently had died rich', leaving 'eighty thousand pounds to his son', now deceased, that will all pass to Fanny (*Kellys*, 111). In return for his son's agreement to play the highly convenient marriage card with Fanny, Lord Cashel agrees to settle his sprawling debts.

Fanny's coming into wealth through her father functions as an example of how the Irish can reap the benefits of participating in the Empire, a constant mantra, this, of Trollope's. The income from service abroad will, as was the case for Captain Wentworth and Anne Elliot in *Persuasion*, ultimately become the means through which Ballindine and Fanny can construct their future. In this sense, Trollope's vision of Ireland as a partner in the Union and a participant in Empire rather than another colony is further reinforced. This view was shared by many in Ireland, as Jennifer Ridden has shown: 'Many Irish Catholic people saw the empire in positive terms' and, 'between 1815 and 1910 about one-third of the population of white settlers in the British empire were Irish . . . this figure does not include those Irish people who were active in the empire as missionaries, soldiers, or who were in temporary colonial postings.'[50]

Lord Ballindine initially has no idea that he is being jilted to enable Fanny to marry her guardian's son but believes that she has been talked out of a marriage to him because of his own relative poverty, her new-found wealth, and his ongoing involvement with 'the turf'. In his view, the 'sordid earl considers that he can now be sure of a higher match for his niece, and Fanny has allowed herself . . . to be talked into the belief that it was her duty to give up a poor man like me' (*Kellys*, 144). Ballindine initially resists the necessary first step Cashel demands if he is to win Fanny's hand, that is, to give up his horses, the 'three Milesians' (*Kellys*, 162), 'Brian Boru, Granuell, and Finn M'Coul' (*Kellys*, 169), but

---

[50] Jennifer Ridden, 'Britishness as an imperial and diasporic identity: Irish elite perspectives, c.1820–1870s', in Peter Gray, ed. *Victoria's Ireland? Irishness and Britishness, 1837–1901* (Dublin: Four Courts Press, 2004), 88.

eventually he comes to an agreement with the conniving Dot Blake which relieves him of public ownership of his horses and guarantees him ready capital to deal with his immediate debts. All is not lost, however: he keeps a part ownership of Brian Boru and the horse goes on to fulfil its destiny and 'give the Saxons a dressing at Epsom, and put no one knows how many thousands into his owner's hands, by winning the Derby' (*Kellys*, 94). In other words, Ballindine assumes some responsibility, while Kilcullen's situation spirals out of control and 'claims of all kinds, bills, duns, remonstrances and threats, poured in not only upon the son but also upon the father' (*Kellys*, 287). Despite this, Cashel continues to make allowances for his son. As the novel unfolds, Lord Cashel is revealed as just as much of a villain as his son, and is shown to have failed as a father and to fail as a guardian when dishonestly trying 'to persuade himself that it was for Fanny's advantage that he was going to make her Lady Kilcullen' (*Kellys*, 289). What he does not take into consideration is Fanny's independence, an independence bolstered by her newly found financial security: 'Fanny Wyndham had much too strong a mind—much too marked a character of her own, to be made Lady Anything by Lord Anybody' (*Kellys*, 289). Fanny shows rare resolve in insisting on the importance of her relationship with Lord Ballindine and in knocking her cousin, Selina, off her 'lofty pedestal' (*Kellys*, 291) and telling her that she thinks more of her 'position as an earl's daughter—an aristocrat' than of her nature 'as a woman!' (*Kellys*, 295). Fanny makes a winning defence of the importance of love against Selina's barren insistence on duty and refutes the accusation that she is 'forgetting' or, indeed, disgracing herself.

Although Cashel knows well that Fanny is still very much in love with Ballindine, he insists that his son pursue her in order to rescue himself from ruin. Kilcullen, desperate because he knows his arrest is imminent, agrees to propose to her and adds, 'if she refuses me, your lordship will perhaps be able to persuade her to a measure so evidently beneficial to all parties.' Kilcullen has more self-awareness than his father, but he does try to win Fanny's hand and finds himself momentarily falling for her, to the extent that he begins 'to speculate whether it were absolutely within the verge of possibility that he should marry her—retrieve his circumstances—treat her well, and live happily for the rest of his life as a respectable nobleman' (*Kellys*, 330–1). But Kilcullen knows himself better:

> For two or three minutes the illusion remained, till it was banished by retrospection. It was certainly possible that he should marry her: it was his full intention to do so: but as to retrieving his circumstances and treating her well! The first was absolutely impossible the other nearly so; and as to his living happily at Grey Abbey as a family man, he yawned as he felt how

impossible it would be that he should spend a month in such a way, let alone a life (*Kellys*, 331).

Before long, Fanny tells Kilcullen of her love for Ballindine, declaring that she loves him with 'as true and devoted a love as woman ever felt for a man' (*Kellys*, 344). Despite his defeat, Kilcullen agrees to support her in her hopes of marrying Ballindine, and, surprisingly, Selina also makes her case with her father. By now it is clear that Kilcullen has run out of options and so, having obtained a final £500 from Lord Cashel, he leaves, never to return.

Ballindine has no knowledge of all these events. What is clear to him, however, is that he loves Fanny and that he has been duped by Lord Cashel. Knowing he cannot go to Grey Abbey himself, he asks his local clergyman, the reliable, decent, Protestant parson, Mr Armstrong, to go on his behalf. Armstrong travels to Grey Abbey, where he is welcomed far more warmly than he could have imagined, and soon it becomes evident that the path has been cleared for the marriage between Frank and Fanny.

Even if the fortunes at stake are far more modest, the path towards the second marriage in the novel, that between Anty and Martin Kelly, is lined with every bit as much danger. If Trollope had begun to imagine in his first novel, through the McKeon family, a possible Catholic Irish middle class that might eventually form the backbone of the country, he further encourages this idea through his description of Martin and his family and his presentation of Martin's sensible marriage to Anty, which, not inconsequentially, is mixed: Simeon Lynch was Protestant, while his wife was Catholic, with Barry following his father's religion and Anty her mother's. This means that a substantial Protestant-owned property will pass into Martin Kelly's Catholic hands following his marriage to Anty and her brother's removal from the scene. Thus the marriage which concludes the novel allows Trollope to follow Edgeworth's lead and to illustrate a process that was taking place in the country as the Protestant gentry diminished and a rising Catholic middle class consolidated its position through the acquisition of land which made their farms more viable, through financially sensible marriages, and through the kind of hard work in which the widow Kelly engages. It is thanks to her labours that the Kellys have managed to rise socially and to consolidate their position economically (to the extent that Lord Ballindine will come to Martin look for a short-term loan), and their rise will be cemented through this marriage.

Martin, 'a young farmer, of the better class, from the County Mayo, where he held three or four hundred wretchedly bad acres under Lord Ballindine' (*Kellys*, 4), although a comically hesitant wooer, is sketched as a sensible, hardworking young man, 'with that mixture of cunning and

frankness in his bright eye' and no illusions of grandeur. Somewhat fortuitously, as the youngest of three brothers, he has come to inherit the family
farm because his elder brother works as a gauger in Northern Ireland, while
the other is an attorney's clerk in Dublin. Trollope is at pains to stress the
necessity of getting Catholics off the land and into respectable jobs. Only by
so doing can the Catholic middle class be reinforced and can the land
become a viable source of income for those who remain to work it.

Trollope stresses the solidity of Martin's family, and the good sense of
the Widow Kelly, who keeps a small but profitable inn in Dunmore and
who, after the death of her husband, 'had put her shoulders to the wheel,
and had earned comfortably, by sheer industry' (*Kellys*, 4). The respectability she has earned in the community is seen in the fact that the 'people
of most influence...were Mrs Kelly...and her two sworn friends, the
parish priest and his curate'. Although aware, like Larry Macdermot, that
she comes from a once-important family (she recalls 'the Kellys of ould'),
she lives in the present and has no delusions of grandeur. Her initial
reaction to her son's involvement with Anty Lynch is to fear that he has
overstepped himself and will upset the financial and familial equilibrium
she has laboured so hard to achieve. The narrator shares her doubts,
worrying that Anty belongs to 'a rank somewhat higher than that in
which Martin Kelly might be supposed to look, with propriety, for his
bride' (*Kellys*, 6). The narrator's conservative views with regard to social or
class improvement are very much in harmony with those of Trollope, who
stresses, again and again, the importance of knowing one's place. Change,
and upward mobility, should only come slowly. Thus the narrator approvingly notes that before taking any steps, Martin will seek 'his landlord's
sanction' (*Kellys*, 6); a sign, this, of Martin's acceptance of the social status
quo and the entitlements that come with higher station. In a similar vein,
the widow eschews any easy participation in social climbing and does
not consider herself to be 'fit company for people who lived in grand
houses, . . . she had always lived where money was to be made, and she
didn't see the sense of going, in her old age, to a place where the only work
would be how to spend it. Some folks would find it was a dail asier to
scatther it than it wor to put it together' (*Kellys*, 423).

The widow is a complex character whose mixed motivations—she
wavers between genuinely wanting to help Anty and resenting the efforts,
financial and otherwise, that she and her family are called upon to make
during her convalescence. She constantly denounces 'schaming' and
roundly rejects any suggestion that her family are acting improperly,
while at the same time never forgetting how much they are set to gain
from her son's marriage. Martin's good fortune is that in Anty he finds a
wife who comes to possess at least one quality akin to those of his mother,

that of independence. She learns the value of her own independence during her convalescence and finds the strength to oppose her brother's desires and to take control of her own destiny. Although she has a 'humble, unpresuming disposition', she is able to defend herself and is 'careful enough to put her name to nothing that could injure her rights'. The narrator praises her for being 'honest, humble, and true', as well as largely disinterested in money, 'unelated by her newly acquired wealth'. Her characterization (along with that of Fanny Wyndham) is also testimony to Trollope's empathy for women who are at the mercy of the men with whom they live, often treated as servants or as marriageable material without rights by their own fathers, guardians, or brothers. In marked contrast to Feemy, Anty has no romantic flights, but is practical and aware of her limitations and seeks and accepts help in order to protect herself from her brother. As she faces what she thinks is certain death, she finds the strength to confront her brother, who has subjected her to physical attacks, bullying, and intimidation.

He is an entirely negative character whose initial error is to have notions amply above his station. He is an early study in the overreaching that later becomes one of the predominant themes in Trollope's fiction, present from *The Macdermots* right up to Augustus Melmotte in *The Way We Live Now*. The overreaching ambitions bred into Barry by his father began when he was foolishly sent 'to Eton,—merely because young O'Kelly was also there, and he was determined to show, that he was as rich and ambitious as the lord's family, whom he had done so much to ruin' (*Kellys*, 17). Barry continues his father's ambitious habits. In order to participate in Lord Ballindine's hunts, he 'supplied himself with all the fashionable requisites for the field,—not because he was fond of hunting, for he was not,—but in order to prove himself as much a gentleman as other people' (*Kellys*, 230). But no amount of sartorial elegance can buy him the place he covets in society and Barry's entire life is compromised by his father's disagreements with Lord Ballindine's family (the O'Kellys). He seeks to present himself as 'an independent country gentleman', but is only a grasping social climber devoid of gentlemanly qualities. The essential difference between Martin Kelly and Barry Lynch is that Martin accepts his place in the social hierarchy while Barry fails to do so. At the hunt, Martin 'was dressed just as usual, except that he had on a pair of spurs, but Barry was armed cap-a-pie' (*Kellys*, 230). The community ostracizes him, mostly because it is known that whatever wealth his family possesses is ill-gotten:

> He had been out twice this year, but had felt very miserable, for no one spoke to him, and he had gone home, on both occasions, early in the day; but he

had now made up his mind that he would show himself to his old school-fellow in his new character as an independent country gentleman; and what was more, he was determined that Lord Ballindine should not cut him (*Kellys*, 230).

Even if Trollope musters a little sympathy in the reader for the social pariah, it soon evaporates when we see Barry's roughness and cruelty in the hunt, where he breaks all the rules, mistreats his horse, and fatally injures the dog 'Goneaway'. That he is utterly out of place is not merely a class issue. While Martin shows that he knows how to behave in such a public arena, even if his family comes from a more humble background, Barry, 'a low, vulgar, paltry scoundrel', in the words of a bystander, has 'as much business here as a cow in a drawing-room' (*Kellys*, 237). Barry can never overcome the stigma of being the son of a man who gained his land through dishonest means, having been nominated to look after the estate for Lord Ballindine's grandfather:

> When large tracts of land fell out of lease, Sim had represented that tenants could not be found—that the land was not worth cultivating—that the country was in a state which prevented the possibility of letting; and, ultimately put himself into possession, with a lease for ever, at a rent varying from half a crown to five shillings an acre' (*Kellys*, 16).

Whatever the legal permutations of what Simeon has done, morally it is contemptible, and its portrayal owes much to Edgeworth's depiction of the Rackrents being bought out by their steward's son.

The O'Kellys of former generations are also guilty of not responsibly running their own affairs. They erred gravely in leaving everything in the hands of Simeon Lynch while seeking meaningless royal appointments in London (overreaching is common not only in the Irish Catholic classes, but also among the Ascendancy). As a result, their estate is compromised by absenteeism and mismanagement (the original Lord Ballindine is also guilty of having accepted his peerage in exchange for his acceptance of the Act of Union). The story of Simeon Lynch's brief rise and his son's rapid fall largely corresponds to Trollope's later description of the ills of Irish estate management in *Castle Richmond*: 'It was not the absence of the absentees that did the damage, but the presence of those they left behind them on the soil' (*CR*, 65).

As a result of the original Lord Ballindine's inattention, his son, Captain Kelly, was left to belatedly try to sort out the mess he inherited: 'Simeon Lynch was dismissed, and proceedings at common law were taken against him, to break such of the leases as were thought, by clever attorneys, to have the ghost of a flaw in them. Money was borrowed from a Dublin house, for the purpose of carrying on the suit, paying off debts, and making Kelly's Court habitable; and the estate was put into their hands' (*Kellys*, 17). The practical Captain Kelly is depicted as a model landlord: 'He planted, tilled, manured, and improved; he imported rose-trees and strawberry-plants, and civilised Kelly's Court a little' (*Kellys*, 17). Unfortunately, he was to die prematurely, leaving 'a widow and two daughters in Ireland; a son at school at Eton; and an expensive lawsuit, with numerous ramifications, all unsettled' (*Kellys*, 17). Eventually, 'the lawsuits were dropped, both parties having seriously injured their resources, without either of them obtaining any benefit' (*Kellys*, 17).

Barry Lynch attempts to cling onto some of the expectations created for him by his father but does not have the income to do so. To add insult to injury, instead of inheriting his father's estate and the 'miserable grandeur of Dunmore House', he must share it with his despised Catholic sister, Anty. Barry's limit is to see everything as his birthright and he is not willing to do any work to merit what should come to him (again, although drawn from a rather lowly Irish background, this trait would be one to afflict many of Trollope's young male heirs, both in Ireland and across the water). Barry's sense of entitlement contrasts with Martin Lynch's embarrassment at coming, at the novel's end, to own, with Anty, the Lynch estate: 'Martin felt rather ashamed of his grandeur. . . . and, when going up to the house, always felt an inclination to shirk in at the back-way' (*Kellys*, 421).

His path towards winning Anty's hand is not easy because Barry attempts, with what Trollope, in his novel *He Knew He Was Right*, calls 'malice prepense', not only to stop her from marrying, but also to seize her rightful share of the estate. In the ironically entitled chapter 'A Loving Brother', Trollope shows Barry's rage at coming to hear that Anty intends to marry Martin Kelly. Having fortified himself with punch, he verbally and physically abuses his sister, orders her to agree in writing never to marry without his consent, and threatens to have her locked up 'as an idiot as you are' in the 'Ballinasloe mad-house' (*Kellys*, 52). She makes 'one rush to escape from him' but, as she does, 'he raised his fist, and struck her on the face, with all his force. The blow fell upon her hands, as they were crossed over her face; but the force of the blow knocked her down, and she fell upon the floor, senseless, striking the back of her head against the table' (*Kellys*, 52). Eventually, she escapes to her bedroom and he returns to drinking before deciding to give her one final warning. He forces his way into her bedroom and tells her 'in a thick, harsh, hurried, drunken voice . . . "If you marry that man, I'll have your life!"' (*Kellys*, 54). She is rescued the following morning by the Widow Kelly, who responds to the appeal made on her behalf by her servant and takes her to stay at the inn, out of harm's way.

Much of the novel is subsequently taken up with Barry's attempts to have his sister return home, and with his efforts to rob her of her share in the family property. He enlists the help of a shady Tuam attorney, Mr Daly, who is, in Barry's correct view, 'a sharp fellow' who 'wanted practice' (*Kellys*, 69). Barry complains that his sister has been left 'half the land, half the cash, half the house, half everything, except the debts! and those were contracted in my name, and I must pay them all' (*Kellys*, 87), and asks Daly to attempt to break his father's will, which has so unexpectedly divided the estate. But Daly warns him that it 'would cost an immense sum of money... and the chances are ten to one you'd be beat' (*Kellys*, 86). This would be a restaging of the useless legal feud in which Barry's father engaged against the O'Kellys. Daly suggests that Anty might be convinced to pay her half of the debts, but Barry insists that 'she's cracked, poor thing, and quite unable to judge for herself, in money-matters... I'm afraid now, unless she's well managed, she'd end her life in the Ballinasloe Asylum' (*Kellys*, 88). Barry explains that he will not sit and 'see that young blackguard Kelly, run off with what ought to be my own' (*Kellys*, 91), and is insistent that the solution is to have her locked up. Daly, initially shocked, decides that 'if he didn't do the job, another would' and calms his 'qualms of conscience with the idea that, though employed by the brother, he might also... protect the sister' (*Kellys*, 92). He serves legal notice on the widow, telling her that he will indict her for conspiracy for having 'enticed' Anty away from her own home 'for the purpose of obtaining possession of her property, she being of weak mind, and not able properly to manage her own affairs' (*Kellys*, 92). Barry further attempts to buy the lawyer's support by promising him the agency for the estate and the use of Dunmore House if he was successful on his behalf. Although Daly agrees to follow Barry's affairs, he is horrified by his 'selfishness, and utter brutal want of feeling, conscience, and principle' (*Kellys*, 93). Nonetheless, he pursues the cause by helping Brady write a letter asking Anty to return home. When this comes to nought, Brady has Daly convince the agent, Moylan, an 'ill-made, ugly, stumpy man, about fifty; with a blotched face' (*Kellys*, 188), to testify that Martin had plotted against him in order to defraud him of his property by marrying Anty. Brady convinces Moylan by offering him 'the agency of the whole property... about a thousand a-year' (*Kellys*, 185). Moylan, another example of the conniving and amoral Irish middle-man, accepts. His false testimony allows Barry and his attorney to charge the Kellys 'with conspiracy to get possession of your [Anty's] fortune' (*Kellys*, 199). That Daly agrees to be part of this is to his discredit because he knows it is based on lies. He attempts to persuade himself that it is 'a wrong thing for Martin Kelly to marry such a woman as Anty Lynch, and that Barry has some show of justice on his side', but knows only too well that Martin is an 'honourable fellow' who will make Anty happy in marriage, while Barry is 'a ruffian of the deepest die', whose 'sole object' is to rob his sister (*Kellys*, 192). Despite all this, he proceeds, in the hope of frightening Anty and Mrs Kelly. Even if Anty is totally overcome by the legal threats and falls ill, the widow is more than a match for Daly, who soon finds himself working towards a deal between the warring parties, suggesting that Barry allow Martin Kelly to become his tenant at Dunmore so that he can then live off the rents he will receive.

Barry is tempted by the prospective 'rent of five-hundred a year; and . . . three hundred pounds for the furniture and stock' in return for his 'consent to the match' and 'a laise of three lives'. He likes the idea of 'future, idle, uncontrolled enjoyment', but cannot bear to be 'vanquished by his own sister', having already been 'brow-beaten by the widow, insulted by young Kelly, cowed and silenced by the attorney' (*Kellys*, 212). He cannot abide the idea of being cheated out of his land by his social inferiors, of 'giving away . . . my own property to a young shop-keeper . . . a low-born huxtering blackguard' (*Kellys*, 214).

Accordingly, the news of Anty's serious illness is a source of joy and hope for him, and he hopes that her death will cancel all risk of his losing half of his estate. On what she thinks is her death-bed, Anty insists on seeing her brother and attempts to convince him to reform, arguing that he has been turned to evil by materialistic desire: 'The money has done me no good, but the loss of it has blackened your heart, and turned your blood to gall against me' (*Kellys*, 251). Although initially moved, he does not mend his ways, and soon he is alarmed to hear that 'the fever has left her and there certainly is hope.' His impatience grows until he eventually tells Dr Colligan that 'Anty must never come out of that bed alive' (*Kellys*, 284). Colligan realizes the level of pure evil to which Barry has descended and, having physically attacked him, vows: 'if you're to be found in Connaught to-morrow, or in Ireland the next day, I'll hang you!' (*Kellys*, 286).

Colligan turns for help to Lord Ballindine, who is also the local magistrate. Fortuitously, the parson, Mr Armstrong, is also present, and on hearing Colligan's report, he argues that they should confront Barry directly in order to 'give him the optin to stand his trial or quit the country' (*Kellys*, 368). Enactment of justice comes about because these local authority figures come together to provide a home-grown version of rough justice. Lord Ballindine, Mr Armstrong, and Doctor Colligan tell Barry 'of the charge which was brought against him, and give him his option of standing his trial, or of leaving the country, under a written promise that he would never return to it'. They also demand his written consent to his sister's marriage and that he 'execute some deed by which all control over the property should be taken out of his own hands; and that he should agree to receive his income, whatever it might be, through the hands of an agent' (*Kellys*, 369). Armstrong is the driving force, motivated by a fear that no justice will be effected if they don't take action.

Lynch's protests that there has been 'a conspiracy against him', and his appeals to Lord Ballindine on the grounds that '[w]e were at school together, weren't we?' (*Kellys*, 378) fail, as do his attempts to discredit Colligan's testimony on religious grounds:

> I suppose my word's as good as Colligan's, gentlemen? I suppose my character as a Protestant gentleman stands higher than his—a dirty Papist apothecary. He tells one story; I tell another... I suppose, gentlemen, I'm not to be condemned on the word of such a man as that?... Ain't I a Protestant, Mr Armstrong, and ain't you a Protestant clergyman? Don't you know that such men as he will tell any lie; will do any dirty job (*Kellys*, 376–7).

He eventually agrees to leave, telling them: 'I don't want to live in the country... the country's nothing to me' (*Kellys*, 380). Justice will be done through his banishment. The narrator concludes by merging the fictional world of the novel with the real world he shares with the reader by announcing that Barry will be exiled from both: 'He went, however, as I have before said, and troubled the people of Dunmore no longer, nor shall he again trouble us' (*Kellys*, 382).

A community justice of sorts has been enacted, which is also—in a very real way—natural justice, in so far as the three who effect the punishment do so in the belief that they have followed their duty to act fairly for the common good (the Rev. Armstrong's centrality is interesting because, this episode apart, he is the incarnation of what Trollope called the 'absurd uselessness' of the Irish Anglican Church).[51] Here the fictional solution overrides what the actual system of justice would have been able to effect, but the reader is left in no doubt that Barry's elimination is the only just course. The self-appointed leaders in the community have done their duty, and in so doing they guarantee their own reinforcement. Thus the novel becomes an evolutionary tale of the survival of the fittest (in anticipation of Darwin and Spenser). Written as the famine was beginning to bite, Trollope was of the belief that the land could only support so many; therefore two potential protagonists—Barry and Lord Kilcullen— are literally written out of existence, banished. There is not enough land or wealth to go round, so only the more deserving survive. Similarly, Anty

---

[51] Quoted in Lance O Tingay, 'Trollope and the Beverley Election', *Nineteenth-Century Fiction*, 5 (1950), 27.

recovers from the inevitable death to which Feemy before her had succumbed. It is worth noting that Anty's illness is described in terms such as
'dreadfully emaciated', 'worn out, there was so little vitality left in her'
(*Kellys*, 275), that allow it to become a metaphor for the Famine that
Trollope was ignoring in the novel.

The legal thread is the key element in *The Kellys and the O'Kellys* and is
underlined by the opening, which features Daniel O'Connell's trial for
conspiracy in Dublin as witnessed by Martin Kelly. This provides the
prism through which to read the country, as Trollope offers a bird's-eye
view of the scene at Dublin's crowded Four Courts. Trollope does not
limit himself to the supposedly neutral description of an omniscient
narrator, but wades into the contemporary argument about O'Connell
by declaring that the later decision to free him was the right one because it
was the beginning of his political end. The fact that Trollope, writing in
1847, moves out of the moment in which the O'Connell trial was taking
place in Dublin, by anticipating the 1844 Law Lords reversal of the
original verdict reached by the packed Dublin jury, also has the effect of
undermining the political import of the O'Connell references. This giving
away of the conclusion—a frequent ploy in Trollope's fiction—is revelatory of the author's hostility towards O'Connell, and anticipates the
playing with temporal perspectives that will become a distinctive feature
of *Castle Richmond*, where the 'now' of the narrative clashes with later
moments evoked by the narrator.

Whatever about Trollope's own beliefs with regard to O'Connell, they
did not preclude him from sympathetically portraying Martin Kelly as a
representative of a consolidating Catholic farmer class, as well as 'a staunch
Repealer', who 'had gone as far as Galway, and Athlone, to be present at
the Monster Repeal Meetings' (*Kellys*, 6), and who showed 'patriotism by
paying a year's subscription in advance to the *Nation* newspaper' (*Kellys*,
37). However, the issue of repeal returns only sporadically in the novel and
is not nearly as important as the theme of Ribbonism in *The Macdermots*.
This is because Trollope had some sympathy for the motives that lay
behind the demands for land reform but none whatsoever for the calls for
Repeal. The subsequent comments about the O'Connell trial are rendered
somewhat toothless by the fact that the conclusion has been given away
and by the fact that Trollope's imagined community of Protestant landlord and Catholic tenant working in harmony effectively removes many of
the motives for complaint that lie at the heart of the Repeal demands and
of O'Connell's entire career.

The effect of giving away the final decision on O'Connell depoliticizes
the subsequent references to him to little more than comic colour. These
include Martin's reporting that Father Geoghegan tells the congregation

in his sermon 'to pray that the liberathor might be got out of his throubles' (*Kellys*, 178), as well as the heated exchange between Ballindine, Dot Blake, 'a little Connaught member of Parliament, named Morris' (*Kellys*, 145), and 'the fat, good-humoured, ready-witted Mat Tierney' who, we are told, believes (like Trollope) that 'if they imprison the whole set . . . and keep them in prison for twelve months, every Catholic in Ireland will be a Repealer by the end of that time' (*Kellys*, 147).

If *The Macdermots* closed on a hopeless note (describing a country blighted with violence, informing, distrust, and injustice), in his second novel Trollope turns this depiction on its head; offering, instead, an imagined, wished-for Ireland, reversing the negative conclusions to offer a vision of a place where the industrious are rewarded, where landlord and tenants can cooperate, where social progress and a modicum of justice is possible, and where the community knows how to deal with those who do not play to the rules. It is a country with no room for conspirators or conspiracy, on a national or a familial scale.

3

Trollope and the Famine

'We shall be equally blamed for keeping the Irish alive or letting them die and we have only to select between the Economists or the Philanthropists—which do you prefer?' (Lord Clarendon, August 1847, House of Commons)

Anthony Trollope's controversial ninth novel, *Castle Richmond*, written between August 1859 and March 1860, and published in three volumes on 10 May 1860, masquerades as a love story, but what remains with the reader is the insistence with which the harsh realities of Famine Ireland seethe beneath the surface of the narrative and erupt more than occasionally to overshadow the main romantic plot. The novel, written over a decade after the Famine, is a brave but flawed and sometimes wrong-headed attempt by an increasingly conservative author to contain the uncontainable, to convey the horrors of the catastrophic Irish Famine within the inadequate form of a romantic comedy while at the same time trying to play down the scale of the devastation and the extent of the failure to provide an adequate public or private response to it. Despite its evident limits, however, the novel is a fascinating document by one of the very few authors to attempt to directly recount the catastrophe through fiction.[1]

The novel's convoluted plot is punctuated with Famine vignettes that are perhaps not adequately worked into the overall structure of a work that falls short of what Trollope achieved in *The Macdermots of Ballycloran* in successfully giving voice to a composite local Irish community. Upon publication, the *Saturday Review* complained that Trollope mixed up a 'common form story' with comments on the Famine: 'the milk and water should really be served in separate pails. Pastry and roast beef should not

---

[1] Carleton writes about the famine in *Castle Squander* and Yorkshire-born novelist Annie Keary also attempts to capture the tragedy in her novel, *Castle Daly: The Story of An Irish Home Thirty Years Ago* (1875), which is, however, a second-hand version based on the Famine stories told to her by her Galway-born father. Also notable is Margaret Brew's *The Chronicles of Castle Cloyne: Or, Pictures of the Munster People* (1885).

be served on the same plate.' Although the reviewer insisted that Trollope should have left 'the love of the mother, daughter, and two cousins unrecorded, to tell the world what [he] saw of Ireland in 1847, and afterwards when pestilence and emigration had concluded that purgation of the country which Famine began', he also contradicted this view with the perhaps more realistic assertion that the 'topic of the Famine cannot be transformed into a fictional situation.'[2] Other reviews were grateful that Trollope limited the amount of Famine material. The *Spectator*, for example, conveys a prevalent English impatience with Ireland and is relieved that Trollope does not say all he must have had 'to say about the terrible event of which he was so close an observer.'[3] Later criticism was also mixed. Hugh Walpole branded the novel a 'complete failure'[4] but Stephen Gwynn praised the authenticity of its descriptions of Famine hunger, which had

> the stamp not of invention but of dreadful reminiscence. Trollope had evidently seen that ravenous glare somewhere in his comings and goings.... *Castle Richmond* is the *locus classicus* in literature for description of the Irish famine; for it renders not only the facts of destitution but the state of mind among those who were not destitute, reproduced with a simplicity that makes one rub one's eyes.[5]

Sadleir, on the other hand, was of the opinion that the novel was an aberration, that it was 'not in the classic sense Trollope at all' but notable only for its 'Irishisms'. It was to be read, if at all, as 'a document, not a work of art; its appeal is to nationalist enthusiasm, not to the literary appreciation that knows no nationality'.[6] This view suggests that Sadleir never actually read this book, which is as far from being a nationalist tract as is possible to imagine. If anything it enacts a form of literary unionism. But Sadleir can rest at ease: the fact that Trollope includes harrowing material does not erase the fact that he struggles and fails to find an adequate representational mode for Famine Ireland; in a word, starvation and silk do not sit easily together as the chapter entitled 'The Last Stage' reveals. Polhemus's description of Herbert, the priggish hero's moment of truth, is telling in this regard:

---

[2] 'Castle Richmond', *Saturday Review*, 9 (19 May 1860), 643.

[3] 'Castle Richmond', *Spectator*, 33 (19 May 1860), 477.

[4] Hugh Walpole, *Anthony Trollope* (London: Macmillan, 1928), 123.

[5] Stephen Gwynn, 'Trollope and Ireland', *Contemporary Review*, 129 (Jan./June 1926), 77.

[6] Michael Sadleir, *Trollope: A Commentary* (London: Oxford University Press, 1961), 387.

Taking shelter from the rain, he enters a peasant cottage where a young woman is slowly starving to death. He sees a baby lying near the woman on the ground, and when he goes over to look at it, he finds that the baby is dead. All his grandiose schemes for Ireland end in the hopeless gesture of covering the little corpse with a silk handkerchief, and he learns the reality of suffering.[7]

Cronin's assertion that 'Trollope's combination of the thesis novel with a novel of manners makes for an uneasy work'[8] is all too correct. From the work's formal unease with its own content, and from the presence of a variety of material that does not fit harmoniously together, one gets a sense of what Eagleton has in mind when commenting on the fragmentary and ruptured nature of much nineteenth-century Irish fiction, and marking a 'hiatus between the experience it has to record, and the conventions available for articulating it.'[9] Despite admiring his own plot, Trollope did not have a terribly high opinion of the novel ('a weak production'), which is a sometimes an unhappy mélange of romantic fiction and Famine 'faction': 'The characters do not excite sympathy. The heroine has two lovers, one of whom is a scamp and the other a prig. . . . The dialogue is often lively, and some of the incidents are well told; but the story as a whole was a failure' (*Auto*, 157). Revealingly, he does not dwell on its limits as an account of the Famine but focuses, instead, on its failure as a love story.

As was almost invariably the case, Trollope sold his work short. While far from being a fully successful novel, it is a fascinating one which introduced themes and preoccupations—such as marriage, bigamy, sexual attraction between people of different ages, and extreme Protestantism—that he explored in more detail elsewhere. Along with novels like *Dr Thorne* (1858) and *The Belton Estate* (1866), to name but two, *Castle Richmond* also offers a telling exploration of the legal, social, and emotional consequences of illicit liaisons. It also enjoyed the distinction of being rapidly translated 'into five different languages—Dutch, Danish, French, German, and Russian. No other Trollope novel was so honored.'[10]

Trollope drives his narrative forward relentlessly in the hope of convincing his reader that this will be fictional business as usual, but neither he

---

[7] Robert M. Polhemus, *The Changing World of Anthony Trollope* (Berkeley and Los Angeles: University of California Press, 1968), 65.

[8] John Cronin, 'Trollope and the Matter of Ireland', in Tony Bareham, ed., *Anthony Trollope*, (Plymouth and London: Vision, 1980), 29.

[9] Terry Eagleton, *Heathcliff and the Great Hunger: Studies in Irish Culture* (London and New York: Verso, 1995), 224.

[10] Bradford A. Booth, *Anthony Trollope: Aspects of his Life and Art* (London: Edward Hulton, 1958), 243n.

nor the reader can adequately come to terms with the suffering, starvation, and death happening in the slipstream. What remains in the mind is not so much the humdrum plot, which affirms that familiar Victorian realist novel's belief in history as progress, but the disturbing counter-images of Famine, of what Thackeray described as the 'livid ghastly face...of... popular starvation'.[11] The novel initially offers little or no anticipation of being set in a country devastated by crop failure, hunger, disease, emigration, and death.[12] What is stressed from the outset is the breezy 'normality' of the Irish setting, as Trollope seeks to convince a reluctant English readership, whom he addresses as his 'good-natured, middle-aged reader' (*CR*, 19), to engage with a novel about Ireland. The work is riddled with contradictions, which reveal what Yvonne Siddle sees positively as evidence of Trollope's 'capacity to reach beyond his position as a privileged Englishman' and which give a sense of 'a man battling conflicting emotions and motivations'. Ultimately, however, he retreats 'behind the party line to the comforting territory governed by political economy and providentialism',[13] and yet it is still hard not to be impressed with Trollope's stubborn insistence with Ireland, despite widespread disinterest and indeed exhaustion with the country and its troubles:

> I wonder whether the novel-reading world—that part of it, at least, which may honour my pages—will be offended if I lay the plot of this story in Ireland! That there is a strong feeling against things Irish it is impossible to deny. Irish servants need not apply; Irish acquaintances are treated with limited confidence; Irish cousins are regarded as being decidedly dangerous; and Irish stories are not popular with the booksellers (*CR*, 1).

Trollope stigmatizes British anti-Irish prejudice but at the same time feels the need to apologize for his insistence on the Famine within the narrative. At one point, he brings a section in 'The Famine Year' chapter to a brusque close with the words: 'But seeing that this book of mine is a novel, I have perhaps already written more on a dry subject than many will read' (*CR*, 68). Even if his choice of the term 'dry' to describe the Famine is ill-chosen and disingenuous, Trollope was well aware that English lack of interest in the Famine was often little more than a cover for the genuine

---

[11] W. M. Thackeray, *The Irish Sketch Book*, 1842 (New York: Scribner, 1911), 111.

[12] The past ten years or so has seen the publication of much valuable material on the Famine. A magnificent general overview is available in John Crowley, William J. Smyth, and Mike Murphy, eds., *Atlas of the Great Irish Famine* (Cork: Cork University Press, 2012). Equally convincing is Ciaran Ó Murchadha, *The Great Famine: Ireland's Agony, 1845–1852* (London: Continuum, 2011).

[13] Yvonne Siddle, 'Anthony Trollope's Representation of the Great Famine', in Peter Gray, ed., *Victoria's Ireland? Irishness and Britishness, 1837–1901* (Dublin: Four Courts Press, 2004), 145.

preoccupation that what was happening in Ireland could spread across the water. Thomas Carlyle gave voice to this fear of contamination in a letter to Charles Gavan Duffy:

> The aspect of Ireland is beyond words at present! The most thoughtless here is struck into momentary *silence* in looking at it; the wisest among us cannot guess what the end of these things is to be. For it is not Ireland alone: starving Ireland will become starving Scotland and starving England in a little while.[14]

Carlyle saw the Irish as a contagion that risked infecting the English working classes, particularly with the rise in Irish emigration to the British mainland in the dark years of mid-century.[15] 'Some 500,000 Irish entered Liverpool during the desperate year of 1847' and, even if up to 300,000 later left for the United States, those who remained were 'the abjectly poor who lacked the wherewithal to leave.'[16] Not surprisingly, then, the Irish were, as Swift and Gilley have written, 'the outcasts of Victorian society . . . the largest unassimilable section of society . . . a people set apart and everywhere rejected and despised.'[17] Even more sympathetic figures, such as the economist George Poulett Scrope, partly agreed, and feared that Britain would be mortally weakened by 'the gangrene of Irish poverty, Irish disaffection, and the deadly paralysis of industry that necessarily attends upon these elements of evil.'[18] Trollope acknowledged such opinions and shared the tendency to see Ireland's plight as a sickness in the series of letters on the Famine that he published in the *Examiner*, but he also felt that the albeit devastating effects of the Famine would ultimately, through measures like the New Poor Law, provide a remedy to Ireland's ills by having the country's gentry class finally pay its way:

> Ireland is looked on as an incurable sore inextricably attached to the otherwise healthy body of England, of which if England could get quit of either by the knife or caustic it would be well; but which in the despair of so dangerous an operation England must endure. There doubtless has been and is disease, ill-treatment or rather no treatment has almost made this chronic;

---

[14] Letter of 1 March 1847 from Thomas Carlyle to Charles Gavan Duffy. http://carlyleletters.dukejournals.org/cgi/content/long/21/1/lt-18470301-TC-CGD-01.

[15] For a detailed description on life for Irish emigrants to Britain during the 1840s, see Frank Neal, *Black '47: Britain and the Famine Irish* (London: Macmillan, 1998).

[16] Donald M. MacRaild, *The Irish Diaspora in Britain, 1750–1939* (London: Palgrave Macmillan, 2010), 4.

[17] Roger Swift and Sheridan Gilley, eds., *The Irish in the Victorian City* (London: Routledge, Kegan & Paul, 1985), 8–9.

[18] George Poulett Scrope, *How to Make Ireland Self-Supporting; or, Irish Clearances, and Improvement of Waste Lands* (London: James Ridgway, 1848), 28.

but now, now that a remedy has been applied, the salutary effects of which are already apparent, for heaven's sake let us beg the surgeon not to withdraw his hand because the patient cries out that he is in pain (*Examiner*, 77).

Trollope mostly refused the fear-mongering behind the more offensively stereotypical readings of Ireland and protested against blanket refusals and/or condemnation of all things Irish. He attempted to explain, from his point of view, the reasons for the Irish crisis, which he summarized in the *Examiner* letters:

Political agitation, the animosity of parties, and religious differences have doubtless deeply affected the people, and any one seeking to unravel the mystery of Irish misery must not overlook the strong traces which they have left; but it is not to O'Connell, nor to the Orange lodges, nor yet to the somewhat rampant animosity of priests and parsons, that we are to look for the generating cause of the universal distress (*Examiner*, 79).

Instead, he cited the system of land use and land tenure as being largely responsible for the country's distress and sought to illustrate this both in his journalistic letters and his novels. Thus his decision to persist with Ireland as a location for fiction should not be dismissed as unimportant or simply wrong-headed. Ultimately, it was well meant if, at times, patronizing. In arguing for the similarity between Irish and English settings for a novel, he, perhaps inadvertently, reinforces the idea that contagion could spread and thus renders the reading and the understanding of Ireland a more impellent necessity:

The readability of a story should depend, one would say, on its intrinsic merit rather than on the site of its adventures. No one will think that Hampshire is better for such a purpose than Cumberland, or Essex than Leicestershire. What abstract objection can there then be to the county Cork? (*CR*, 2).

In his aim of encouraging the English reader, he highlights the most beautiful parts of Cork in what is, given the year in which the novel is set, a rather preposterous rendering of the county in terms of its attractiveness for tourists. This flimsy description of a beautiful, almost 'English' Ireland clashes with the counter-images of poverty, starvation, and death that the novel will later illustrate. And yet, we should be slow to simply condemn it. As Joel Mokyr has argued, the 'real problem' underlying endemic Irish poverty and the Famine 'was that Ireland was considered by Britain an alien and even hostile country.'[19] Trollope, in writing of the

---

[19] Joel Mokyr, *Why Ireland Starved: A Quantitative and Analytical History of the Irish Economy, 1800–1850* (London: George Allen and Unwin, 1985), 291.

country's similarities to Britain, was attempting to recuperate the country for English eyes, render it a little less threatening, a little more 'fixable':

> Within this district, but hardly within that portion of it which is most attractive to tourists, is situated the house and domain of Castle Richmond. The river Blackwater rises in the county Kerry, and running from west to east through the northern part of the county Cork, enters the county Waterford beyond Fermoy. In its course it passes near the little town of Kanturk, and through the town of Mallow: Castle Richmond stands close upon its banks, within the barony of Desmond, and in that Kanturk region through which the Mallow and Killarney railway now passes, but which some thirteen years since knew nothing of the navvy's spade, or even of the engineer's theodolite (*CR*, 2).

With this, Trollope is being careful, from the outset, to foreshadow an optimistic conclusion, to stress that the county and the country have changed since the times in which the novel is set, that they have benefited from progress and improvements that were initiated in Famine times and are now cemented in the establishment of the railway, a material icon of progress and development. All this to justify the government Famine policies, which were almost universally criticized for compounding the crisis. John Stuart Mill, for instance, said that the government's relief efforts could not have been 'more imbecile; more devoid of plan, of purpose, of ideas, of practical resource'.[20] Criticism grew in the wake of the Famine when the disastrous limits of Liberal policies became ever more apparent—even to Liberals.[21] But Trollope insisted on seeing things differently, and chose to interpret the Famine as a necessary evil that pushed a reluctant country towards modernity. Thus, the property which gives the novel its title is portrayed so that it can exemplify the improvements that Trollope believed had their roots in the Famine. Castle Richmond is, like its owner, devoid of 'any of those interesting picturesque faults which are so generally attributed to Irish landlords, and Irish castles. . . . It was a good, substantial, modern family residence, built not more than thirty years since by the late baronet, with a lawn sloping down to the river, with kitchen gardens and walls for fruit, with ample stables, and a clock over the entrance to the stable yard' (*CR*, 3). All this thanks to the shrewd management of Sir Thomas Fitzgerald who, while treating his

---

[20] Ann and John Robson, eds., *John Stuart Mill, Collected Works*, vol. 25. *Newspaper Writings, Dec. 1847–June 1873* (Toronto: University of Toronto Press, 1986), 1098.

[21] I am indebted to Cormac Ó Gráda's *Ireland Before and After the Famine* (2nd edn, Manchester: Manchester University Press, 1993); *Ireland: A New Economic History, 1780–1939* (Oxford: Clarendon Press, 1994); and *Black '47 and Beyond: The Great Irish Famine in History, Economy, and Memory* (Princeton, NJ: Princeton University Press, 1999).

tenants well, managed to develop his estate to the extent that 'Castle Richmond might have been in Hampshire or Essex, and as regards his property, Sir Thomas Fitzgerald might have been a Leicestershire baronet' (*CR*, 3). The estate appears so well run, in short, that it might have been English, and indeed it has a strong English flavour down to its very name. Lady Fitzgerald behaves as a model Englishwoman in Ireland, positively influencing all those in her family circle, and is singled out as 'an excellent wife, a kind and careful mother, a loving neighbour to the poor, and courteous neighbour to the rich, all the county Cork admitted. She had lived down envy by her gentleness and soft humility, and every one spoke of her and her retiring habits with sympathy and reverence' (*CR*, 51).

Castle Richmond contrasts with the other great house in the novel, Desmond Court, which is in every way a bleak house, 'huge, ungainly, and uselessly extensive' and 'with hardly a scrap around it which courtesy can call a lawn'. Its occupiers, 'Clara, Countess of Desmond, widow of Patrick, once Earl of Desmond, and father of Patrick, now Earl of Desmond', along with Clara's daughter, who is also called Clara, are all, predictably, and, in the narrator's opinion, deservedly, in financial difficulties, although we also note that the 'Desmonds had once been mighty men in their country, ruling the people around them as serfs, and ruling them with hot iron rods' (*CR*, 4). The Desmonds, although owners of much land in what was 'a bleak, unadorned region, almost among the mountains' (*CR*, 5), failed to nurture their wealth, sought costly preference in England, damaged their property through 'bad management, lack of outlay, and rack-renting' (*CR*, 5), and now, in the narrator's view, deservedly have little to live on but their name. The 'beautiful, proud, and clever' (*CR*, 9) countess is a negative counterpart to Lady Fitzgerald. She is 'English to the backbone' and has never integrated in Ireland because she 'had not the means, nor perhaps the will, to fill the huge old house with parties of her Irish neighbours'. She feels the 'crushing evil' (*CR*, 122) of poverty and sees marriage, especially for her daughter Clara, as the only way to overcome it. The narrator makes clear his disdain by describing Lady Desmond as 'a woman of a mercenary spirit . . . two facts were strong against her that she had sold herself for a title, and had been willing to sell her daughter for a fortune' (*CR*, 279). She is depicted as an angry, grasping woman, condemned to a poverty that is not her own fault, but whose attitude to the world is entirely negative: 'I have been driven to hate those around me who have been rich, because I have been poor. I have been utterly friendless because I have been poor . . . Poverty and rank together have made me wretched—have left me without employment, without society, and without love' (*CR*, 318). Given the dire and genuine poverty in the country at the time, and the fact that her son is able to indulge in a

Grand Tour and study at Oxford, and that she continues to live in the great family home with its many material comforts, Lady Desmond's constant protestations about poverty cannot but grate.

The Desmonds exemplify all that mainstream British opinion felt was wrong with the Ascendancy in Ireland:

> Both before and during the Famine, in official British discourse as well as in the press, in literature, and elsewhere, the main line of explanation for Irish poverty and starvation emphasized how land in Ireland had been subdivided and rack-rented into ever smaller units, leaving the poor at the mercy both of the potato and of the farmers and middle-men above them, with the landlords often absent, as in Edgeworth's novels. During the Famine, this critique was shared by Chartist leaders, by Young Irelanders such as John Mitchel and Gavin Duffy, by Marx and Engels, and by John Stuart Mill.[22]

The detached Irish landlord class, exemplified by the Desmonds, are shown to have neglected their Irish holding, and, as a result, have put their own privileged lives at peril. And yet, as the novel tells it, with more than a hint of sarcasm:

> the Desmonds were great people, and owned a great name. They had been kings once over those wild mountains; and would be still, some said, if everyone had his own. Their grandeur was shown by the prevalence of their name. The barony in which they lived was the barony of Desmond. The river which gave water to their cattle was the river Desmond. The wretched, ragged, poverty-stricken village near their own dismantled gate was the town of Desmond. The earl was Earl of Desmond—not Earl Desmond, mark you; and the family name was Desmond. The grandfather of the present earl, who had repaired his fortune by selling himself at the time of the Union, had been Desmond Desmond, Earl of Desmond (*CR*, 5).

A final property, Hap House, completes a highly evocative triangle of residences. This more modest but nonetheless comfortably large house has recently been inherited by the twenty-two-year-old Owen Fitzgerald, a cousin of the Castle Richmond Fitzgeralds. Owen is described by the young Earl of Desmond as 'a small squire with a small income', while Hap House was a pleasant, comfortable residence, too large no doubt for such a property, as is so often the case in Ireland; surrounded by pleasant grounds and pleasant gardens, with a gorse fox covert belonging to the place within a mile of it, with a slated lodge, and a pretty drive along the river (*CR*, 6).

Although trained as a barrister in Dublin, the 'fine, high-spirited, handsome' Owen chooses to live on the property, but does not work

---

[22] Patrick Brantlinger, 'The Famine', *Victorian Literature and Culture*, 32/1 (March 2004), 196.

sufficiently hard to maintain it, preferring instead to hunt, play cards, and indulge his eye 'for a pretty girl' (*CR*, 7). The narrator hovers between indulgence and disapproval, but acknowledges Owen's Byronic charm:

> He was a very handsome man—tall, being somewhat over six feet in height—athletic, almost more than in proportion—with short, light, chestnut-tinted hair, blue eyes, and a mouth perfect as that of Phoebus. He was clever, too, though perhaps not educated as carefully as might have been: his speech was usually rapid, hearty, and short, and not seldom caustic and pointed (*CR*, 8).

Although the descriptions of the three houses and their occupants, whose names suggest Norman stock deeply integrated into Ireland, sketch out three very different economic realities, what interests Trollope more are the potential love connections that are prefigured within them. Owen is sought after by the 'beautiful, proud, and clever' English widow, the Countess of Desmond, while he unwisely declares his love for her sixteen-year-old daughter, Lady Clara, who is left speechless at his declaration. However, he takes her silence as assent. On being asked to be true to him she manages 'almost audibly' to say yes (*CR*, 27). Her mother immediately opposes what she considers an impossible match between her poverty-stricken but noble daughter and this struggling Cork squire. The somewhat unreal nature of these narrated events is compounded by the fact that characters seem at times more to be playing superficial stock roles than to be living real lives. Even Clara seems to be caught up more in a novelistic drama than a real-life situation as she attempts to come to terms with her mother's insistence that she abandon Owen: 'It was not that she had ceased to love him, but she had high ideas of truth and honour, and would not break her word. Perhaps she was sustained in her misery by the remembrance that heroines are always miserable' (*CR*, 43). Slowly Clara falls for the less dashing Herbert Fitzgerald, who is in a better financial situation to live up to her mother's aspirations for her.

The tussle for Clara's affections between Owen and Herbert is a central thread of the novel, with the English-educated, reliable but somewhat anaemic Herbert finally defeating his more passionate, dashing, and 'Irish' rival. Trollope probably enjoyed the fact that both of them have names that echo that of the 'rebel Earl', Gerald FitzGerald, 15th Earl of Desmond, an Irish nobleman and leader of the Desmond Rebellion against Queen Elizabeth I in 1579. Even the narrator seems to favour the full-blooded and romantic Owen, placing Herbert in the role of 'hero' only with reluctance: 'It is impossible that these volumes should be graced by any hero, for the story does not admit of one. But if there were to be a hero, Herbert Fitzgerald would be the man' (*CR*, 45). Hardly a ringing authorial endorsement. His chief quality, in the narrator's view, 'was no doubt his sturdy common sense' (*CR*, 333). But in Trollope's view of things, Herbert and Owen come to respectively embody English ways of doing things as against Irish. As Corbett asserts: 'Owen's story allegorizes an older and persistent narrative trope of Irish resistance to English conquest'.[23] But for the author it is a vain resistance, with Owen hopelessly making a claim on Clara long after she has declared a preference for Herbert. In the end, the novel's 'romantic allegory... supports Ireland's union with England',[24] and thus overwrites any objections there might have been to English (mis)management of the country during the Famine.

Clara's decision to opt for Herbert is couched in terms that stress the importance of duty and reason over the claims of passion. Herbert's

> soft words, and pleasant smiles, and sweet honeyed compliments... had never given her so strong a thrill of strange delight as had those few words from Owen. Her very heart's core had been affected by the vigour of his affection. There had been in it a mysterious grandeur which had half charmed and half frightened her. It had made her feel that he, were it fated that she should belong to him, would indeed be her lord and ruler; that his was a spirit before which hers would bend and feel itself subdued.... But could it be the same with him to whom she was now positively affianced, with him to whom she knew that she did now owe all her duty? She feared that it was not the same (*CR*, 182).

But the narrator makes her choice an ideological one, with Herbert pictured as 'a conqueror who has mastered half a continent by his own strategy' (*CR*, 126). Just as Clara ultimately rejects Owen, her mother is turned down by him and condemned to a life of parsimonious solitude in the conclusion of this novel, which is a successful rendering of an enduring thematic preoccupation of Trollope's, that is, the love triangle. In this case, the triangles are those involving Owen, Herbert, and Clara; Lady Desmond, Clara, and Owen; and, more suprisingly, Clara, Owen, and her younger brother Patrick, who is shown to be terribly disappointed at his family's losing Owen. As Kate Flint has argued, the novel offers a passing but significant glance at the attraction Patrick feels for Owen, as seen in his attempts to convince him to renew his courtship with Clara:

> It is clear that for Patrick, this is less a way of snagging a husband worthy of Clara than a means of trying to claim Owen for himself: the strength of the

---

[23] Mary Jean Corbett, *Allegories of Union in Irish and English Writing* (Cambridge: Cambridge University Press, 2000), 142.

[24] Bridget Matthews-Kane, 'Love's Labor Lost: Romantic Allegory in Trollope's *Castle Richmond*', *Victorian Literature and Culture*, 32 (2004), 117.

attraction between them is unmissable when Owen throws his arm over the earl's shoulder, presses him 'with something almost like an embrace,' and Patrick 'squeezed Owen's arm with strong boyish love,' and a little later throws himself on his breast in 'a passion of tears'—Owen's eyes are full of tears, too.[25]

Castle Richmond anticipates some elements of the plot mechanics of Trollope's later novels, especially the Pallisers, the first of which, *Can You Forgive Her?* was published in 1864. Clara, in giving up Owen for Herbert, anticipates Lady Glencora, who breaks her engagement to Burgo Fitzgerald, an infinitely more exciting and passionate partner than her future husband will ever be: 'When I went to him at the altar, I knew that I did not love the man that was to be my husband. But him,—Burgo,—I love him with all my heart and soul. I could stoop at his feet and clean his shoes for him, and think it no disgrace!' (*CYFH*, 305). Furthermore, we are told that when Palliser kisses her 'it was the embrace of a brother rather than a lover or a husband' (*CYFH*, 354). In Robert Tracy's terms, Lady Glencora and a host of other female characters in the Palliser series must choose between the 'wild man' and the 'worthy man',[26] and this is a dilemma which is initially formulated in *Castle Richmond*.

A counter-narrative, based on pet Victorian themes of property, legitimacy, and inheritance, forms when it is revealed that Sir Thomas's model English wife was briefly married previously to a Mr Talbot, long believed to have died in Paris. A sinister Englishman called Matthew Mollett appears and greatly upsets the domestic harmony by claiming that he was Lady Fitzgerald's first husband, and that her marriage to Sir Thomas is therefore null. It emerges that he has been blackmailing Sir Thomas for some time, threatening an exposure that would make their three children illegitimate and gift the estate to Owen. The utterly reprehensible Mollett is pushed by his even more despicable son, Abraham, into further pressurising Sir Thomas. Trollope plays with stereotypes by having as the novel's villains two depraved *English* alcoholics. As is so often the case in Trollope's narratives, physical appearance and dress proclaim the nature of the man:

Mr. Abraham Mollett was … a very smart man, with a profusion of dark, much-oiled hair, with dark, copious mustachoes—and mustachoes being then not common as they are now, added to his otherwise rakish, vulgar appearance—with various rings on his not well-washed hands, with a frilled

[25] Kate Flint, 'Queer Trollope', in Carolyn Dever and Lisa Niles, eds., *The Cambridge Companion to Anthony Trollope* (Cambridge: Cambridge University Press, 2011), 107.
[26] Robert Tracy, 'Trollope Redux: the Later Novels', in *Cambridge Companion to Anthony Trollope*, 64.

front to his not lately washed shirt, with a velvet collar to his coat, and patent-leather boots upon his feet. Free living had told more upon him, young as he was, than upon his father. His face was not yet pimply, but it was red and bloated; his eyes were bloodshot and protruding; his hand on a morning was unsteady; and his passion for brandy was stronger than that for beefsteaks; whereas his father's appetite for solid food had never flagged (*CR*, 57–8).

Not only does Trollope reverse expectations by making the criminal extortionists English, but he also is careful to locate them in and associate them with the Kanturk Hotel in Cork, a setting noted for its filth, 'a small, dingy house of three stories, the front door of which was always open, and the passage strewed with damp, dirty straw … The floor was uncarpeted, nearly black with dirt, and usually half covered with fragments of damp straw brought into it by the feet of customers' (*CR*, 54). This evocation of dirt immediately puts the reader on guard as dirt is, as Cohen has argued, that 'which instantly repudiates a threatening thing, person, or idea by ascribing alterity to it … filth is frequently so disturbing that it endangers the subjective integrity of the one who confronts it.'[27] Trollope reverses the common English identification of dirt with the Irish by illustrating how the filth associated with the Molletts has such a devastating effect on the decent Anglo-Irish Fitzgerald family. Having paid out substantial monies to buy the insatiable Molletts' silence, Sir Thomas finally decides to consult Mr Prendergast, the family lawyer in London, for advice on how to put a stop to the blackmail. Prendergast can see no way out but to acknowledge that the Mollett marriage is legitimate. Broken-hearted, Sir Thomas accepts this advice, falls into desperation, and dies while his family prepare to leave their beautiful home. The intended marriage of Herbert and Clara no longer has the necessary financial foundation to proceed, and Clara's mother hopes that Owen, now Sir Owen, new inheritor of Castle Richmond, can be enticed back into the picture. Owen declares himself happy to allow Herbert and his family to retain their home, but only on the grounds that he can marry Clara. Herbert is unwilling to permit this, and Clara too is by now firmly set against it.

All is not lost, however. Prendergast discovers that Mollett had been married before he met Mary Fitzgerald (née Wainwright) and that their marriage was in fact illegitimate. This means that her subsequent marriage to Sir Thomas was legal after all. Thus the family can remain *in situ*, Herbert can succeed to the estate and marry Lady Clara after his rival in love, Owen, has obligingly taken himself out of the picture by leaving

---

[27] William A. Cohen and Ryan Johnson, eds., *Filth: Dirt, Disgust, and Modern Life* (Minneapolis and London: University of Minnesota Press, 2005), ix.

the country to seek a life in the colonies: '"To Africa in the first instance," said he; "there seems to be some good hunting there, and I think that I shall try it."' (*CR*, 476). Although this is a singularly contrived solution, in giving Owen the chance of a new start in the colonies, Trollope was pointing to what he and many others considered a world of opportunity for the Irish; he believed, with some justification, that many Irish thrived abroad.[28]

> The Irishman when he expatriates himself to one of those American States loses much of that affectionate, confiding, master-worshipping nature which makes him so good a fellow when at home. But he becomes more of a man. He assumes a dignity which he never has known before. He learns to regard his labor as his own property. That which he earns he takes without thanks, but he desires to take no more than he earns. To me personally, he has, perhaps, become less pleasant than he was;—but to himself! It seems to me that such a man must feel himself half a god, if he has the power of comparing what he is with what he was (*NA*, 600).

What emerges most clearly from *Castle Richmond* is not so much the contorted plot structure, but that Trollope's real interest was the Famine, which he frustratingly shies away from because of his belief that his English reader will not engage with the subject. In a similar vein, writing about earlier Famine in *The Black Prophet*, Carleton also worried that the main concern of the novel should not be 'so gloomy a topic as famine' but 'the workings of those passions and feelings which usually agitate human life, and constitute the character of those who act in it.'[29] Trollope's response to the Famine was emphatically informed by the economists whose views he sought to support initially in his letters to the *Examiner* and, later, with the benefit of considerable hindsight, in this novel. He saw the well-meaning philanthropists, referred to in *Castle Richmond* as 'irrational' (*CR*, 346), as essentially slowing the possibility for change and improvement in the country, and he sought to illustrate this through his fiction. At the same time, he acknowledged the terrible suffering and the vast death caused by the Famine in passages such as: 'But very frightful are the flames as they rush through the chambers of the poor, and very frightful was the course of that violent remedy which brought Ireland out

---

[28] As Jennifer Ridden has commented: 'one of the main positive aspects of the Union between Britain and Ireland was that it widened Irish access to imperial opportunities in the nineteenth century, for the Protestant elite and also for Irish Catholics'. Jennifer Ridden, 'Britishness as an imperial and diasporic identity: Irish elite perspectives, c.1820–1870s', in Peter Gray, ed., *Victoria's Ireland? Irishness and Britishness, 1837–1901* (Dublin: Four Courts Press, 2004), 90.

[29] William Carleton, *The Black Prophet. A Tale of Irish Famine* (London: Simms and M'Intyre, 1847), vii.

of its misfortunes. Those who saw its course, and watched its victims, will not readily forget what they saw' (*CR*, 69). And yet, Trollope remained of the opinion that British intervention had done as much as possible to contain and alleviate the hardship. The novel offers a strict defence of government policy, which is described as 'prompt, wise, and beneficent', while most other neutral observers were increasingly willing to acknowledge mistakes and worse.

Trollope staged this defence of British policy initially in his letters to the *Examiner*, which were written in response to letters to *The Times*, penned by Sidney Godolphin Osborne (1908–1889), a brother of the Duke of Leeds, an Oxford graduate, and rector of Durweston in Dorset, normally known as a journalist under the initials 'S.G.O.' A 'favoured correspondent' of *The Times*, Lord Melbourne called him 'a popularity-hunting parson',[30] and Trollope would have concurred. In 1849, Osborne visited Famine Ireland and wrote four letters denouncing with 'utter disgust' what he had seen. He described the appearance of the starving, the inadequate attempts made to provide aid, and commented on the state of workhouses. He complained that land stood idle—'thousands of acres lie untilled'—while men were forced to labour on largely useless public works: 'I saw armies of men employed in breaking stones for road material at wages on which they starve.'[31]

Having read three of Osborne's letters, Trollope decided to respond forcefully in the liberal London newspaper, the *Examiner*, as he later recalled:

> In 1847 and 1848 there had come upon Ireland the desolation and destruction, first of the famine, and then of the pestilence which succeeded the famine. It was my duty at that time to be travelling constantly in those parts of Ireland in which the misery and troubles thence arising were, perhaps, at their worst. The western parts of Cork, Kerry, and Clare were pre-eminently unfortunate. The efforts—I may say the successful efforts—made by the Government to stay the hands of death will still be in the remembrance of many:—how Sir Robert Peel was instigated to repeal the Corn Laws; and how, subsequently, Lord John Russell took measures for employing the people, and supplying the country with Indian corn. The expediency of these latter measures was questioned by many. The people themselves wished of course to be fed without working; and the gentry, who were mainly responsible for the rates, were disposed to think that the management of affairs was taken too much out of their own hands. My mind at the time

[30] Quoted in Arnold White, ed., *The Letters of S.G.O.*; a series of letters on public affairs written by the Rev. Lord Sidney Godolphin Osborne and published in *The Times* 1844–1888 (London: 1890), I, xvii.

[31] Sidney Godolphin Osborne, *The Times*, 5 July 1849, 5.

was busy with the matter, and, thinking that the Government was right, I was inclined to defend them as far as my small powers went. S.G.O. (Lord Sidney Godolphin Osborne) was at that time denouncing the Irish scheme of the Administration in the *Times*, using very strong language,—as those who remember his style will know (*Auto*, 81).

Trollope was correct in many of his comments. The effects of the Famine varied, as historians have pointed out, from place to place. In Ó Gráda's words: 'the famine's impact was very uneven', while the extent of relief was large although insufficient: 'the numbers who received relief of one kind or another also underline the scope of the disaster: nearly one in twelve of the population on the public works at their peak in the spring of 1847; more than one in three on daily soup rations at their peak in July 1847; and over 140,000 in the workhouses and another 800,000 on outdoor relief a year later.'[32]

Despite the scale of the disaster, Trollope continued to believe that it had been exaggerated by the Irish press and criticized British newspapers for believing all the dispatches that arrived from across the water:

> you will remember that the Irish newspapers of the time teemed with the recital of such horrors,—that the air was said to be polluted by unburied corpses; that descriptions were given of streets and lanes in which bodies lay for days on the spots where the starved wretched had last sunk; and that districts were named in which the cabins were fabled to contain more dead than living tenants. The Irish press is not proverbial for a strict adherence to unadorned truth; and, under the circumstances, it was perhaps not surprising that writers habituated to disdain facts should exaggerate and compose novels; but those horrid novels were copied into the English papers, and were then believed by English readers (*Examiner*, 83).

He strains in this passage to hold this line, which actually contradicts what he said in his first letter, where he merely complains of the lack of originality in S.G.O.'s depictions of suffering: 'S.G.O. gives fearfully graphic pictures of the woes to be met with in a Famine and plague-stricken country. Heaven knows that he can describe no worse than I have witnessed. The same descriptions have been given and repeated by almost every class of people able to narrate what they have seen, till such pictures are awfully familiar to the eyes of all men' (*Examiner*, 74). In his subsequent letters, Trollope appears to be increasingly in denial of the scale of the Famine. Later again, he would undermine these opinions in the 'horrid vignettes' which punctuate *Castle Richmond* and echo the very descriptions he complained about in his letters. In the novel, he also undermines his own argument against the Irish press by putting a version of it into the mouth of the always ironically viewed and much vilified character, Mrs Townsend:

> And then there was a little general conversation about the potato, for no one came in for a quarter of an hour or so. The priest said that they were as badly off in Limerick and Clare as we are here. 'Now, I don't believe that; and when I asked him how he knew, he quoted the "Freeman."'
> 'The "Freeman," indeed! Just like him. I wonder it wasn't the "Nation."'

In Mrs Townsend's estimation, the parish priest was much to blame because he did not draw his public information from some newspaper specially addicted to the support of the Protestant cause (*CR*, 109).

In his *Examiner* letters, Trollope argues that 'the severity of the circum-stances' was 'ordained by Providence' and that it is wrong to attack the 'incompetence of the government in dealing with those circumstances' (*Examiner*, 75). Peel is exonerated and his government praised for acting, during the early years of the Famine, with 'wisdom and humanity: the evil was not within the scope of such a remedy; and although some of the acknowledged laws of political economy were violated, it appeared that the circumstances warranted such a deviation' (*Examiner*, 79). If anything, moved by pity, government was almost too generous in dispensing char-ity. Trollope believes, as Foster has written, that the 'state of Ireland had been misrepresented by sentimentalists', and sought to put that right.[33] Similarly, he seeks to contradict and dismiss the Irish 'verdict of man-slaughter against Lord John Russell' (*Examiner*, 81) and strongly opposes the idea that mere government could stop what God had set in motion:

> Famines there have been before, though I remember to have heard of none since the days of Joseph, in which the food of a stricken country seems to have been so absolutely removed; but never before has there been such an assured expectation that the severity of Providence was to be arrested by the exertions of a Government' (*Examiner*, 82).

Trollope makes clear that the does not doubt 'the statistical facts given by S.G.O.' and insists that he merely seeks to 'deny his deductions' (*Exam-iner*, 73), before claiming that 'Government has never yet got credit for the good their measures did' (*Examiner*, 76). Trollope simply will not admit the scale of the tragedy and is disingenuous in downplaying it, when, for example, he argues in favour of the public works schemes,

---

[33] R. F. Foster, *The Irish Story: Telling Tales and Making It Up in Ireland* (London: Penguin, 2001), 134.

claiming that 'the poor, instead of dying by hundreds, would truly have died in thousands, till the deaths might have been counted in millions. This desolation was prevented; and the useless barrows, the uneasy road, the insulated arch, and even the additional habits of idleness engendered among the people, deeply as they are to be regretted, have been much more than atoned for' (*Examiner*, 76). This understatement of death and overstatement of aid provided does little service to the fact that the work schemes did actually help many people survive, and it is offensive towards the multitude that died. Trollope is similarly in denial when refusing to admit to the material evidence of the Famine (which he elsewhere acknowledges): 'I never saw a dead body lying exposed in the open air, either in a town or in the country: I moreover never saw a dead body within a cabin which had not been laid out in some sort of rough manner' (*Examiner*, 83). This statement is negated by the presence of harrowing vignettes, describing the dying and the dead, in *Castle Richmond*.

One of Trollope's central arguments is that the Irish—this 'passive, long-suffering people personally indifferent to those principles to which the English attach so much importance'—need English guidance if they are to resurface from the calamity. Because of their innate passivity, they are 'more inclined to follow implicitly the guidance of a master, and to submit in all things to his command' (*Examiner*, 98). Now that the worst has passed, 'the doctor must take care that the patient does not cling to his bed till he dies of inanition'. To ward off this danger, Trollope hopes the English will take a more active interest in the island so as to fight against 'habitual sloth, and almost habitual despair', and against 'the prevailing feeling among Irishmen' that 'ruin and desolation are imminent':

> To combat this feeling should be the effort of every friend of Ireland; to encourage the industry, the hitherto feeble industry of the country; to do battle with habitual sloth, and almost habitual despair; to awake a manly feeling of inward confidence and a reliance on the justice of Heaven, should now be the work of Government, of Parliament, and of every individual who has an interest in the country. The man who takes a farm in Ireland and lives on it is Ireland's best friend (*Examiner*, 101).

Later, in *Castle Richmond*, the narrator returns to the material of these letters and in the novel seems to be more concerned with defending and in some cases denying British mis-administration of the country and its resources than with articulating adequately the suffering the Famine brought. He complains more about the criticism of the government effort than about the limits of their actions, and ignores the fact that people starved while large quantities of food left the country. He makes direct connections between the novel and his earlier letters, thus reinforcing the idea that both are written for similar, political ends:

> Much abuse at the time was thrown upon the government; and they who took upon themselves the management of the relief of the poor in the south-west were taken most severely to task. I was in the country, travelling always through it, during the whole period, and I have to say—as I did say at the time with a voice that was not very audible—that in my opinion the measures of the government were prompt, wise, and beneficent; and I have to say also that the efforts of those who managed the poor were, as a rule, unremitting, honest, impartial, and successful (*CR*, 69).

In the narrator's view, 'It is in such emergencies as these that the watching and the wisdom of a government are necessary; and I shall always think—as I did think then—that the wisdom of its action and the wisdom of its abstinence from action were very good' (*CR*, 346). The choice of the word 'abstinence', meaning voluntary restraint from indulging in something (usually alcohol or sex), suggests that to have offered more assistance would have been to indulge the Irish and reinforce their bad habits. He asserts that the government did what it could and points to the logistical challenges involved: 'The feeding of four million starving people with food, to be brought from foreign lands, is not an easy job. No government could bring the food itself; but by striving to do so it might effectually prevent such bringing on the part of others. Nor when the food was there, on the quays, was it easy to put it, in due proportions, into the four million mouths. Some mouths, and they, alas! the weaker ones, would remain unfed' (*CR*, 69).

In Trollope's lasting opinion, Famine death was regrettable but unavoidable, and no more could have been done to stave off starving and death. He regrets the terrible loss of life but rebuts criticism by pointing to the sheer scale of the disaster and the ease with which the reaction could be criticised, in his view, self-indulgently: 'This left space for the philanthropists to unfairly attack: But the opportunity was a good one for slashing philanthropical censure; and then the business of the slashing, censorious philanthropist is so easy, so exciting, and so pleasant!' (*CR*, 69). Trollope is having none of it, and reiterates what he said in his letters, that is, that Russell's government did all that could have been done, limited the damage, kept 'life and soul' (*CR*, 346) together, and established the basis for the country to change direction and pick itself up after the disaster. This was an unusual view and clashed with, among many others, that of William Carleton who, in dedicating *The Black Prophet* to Russell, laid blame squarely at his door: 'I cannot help thinking that the man who, in his Ministerial capacity, must be looked upon as a public exponent of those principles of Government which have brought our country to her present calamitous condition'.[34]

As Christine Kinealy has shown, with the worsening of the Famine in Ireland, British officials began to view the calamity as 'an opportunity to facilitate various long-desired changes within Ireland',[35] and clearly Trollope shared this opinion:

> It is in such emergencies as these that the watching and the wisdom of a government are necessary; and I shall always think—as I did think then—that the wisdom of its action and the wisdom of its abstinence from action were very good. And now again the fields in Ireland are green, and the markets are busy, and money is chucked to and fro like a weathercock which the players do not wish to have abiding with them; and the tardy speculator going over to look for a bit of land comes back muttering angrily that fancy prices are demanded. 'They'll run you up to thirty-three years' purchase,' says the tardy speculator, thinking, as it seems, that he is specially ill used. Agricultural wages have been nearly doubled in Ireland during the last fifteen years (*CR*, 346–7).

In order to try to read the Famine as a providential bump upon the road of progress, the chapter entitled 'The Famine year' insists that the famine 'was God's doing' and was not an example of his wrath but of his goodness. Nothing elsewhere in Trollope's fiction quite prepares the reader for this invocation of providence, even if he does insist in his *Autobiography* that:

> We do not understand the operations of Almighty wisdom, and are, therefore, unable to tell the causes of the terrible inequalities that we see—why some, why so many, should have so little to make life enjoyable, so much to make it painful, while a few others, not through their own merit, have had gifts poured out to them from a full hand. We acknowledge the hand of God and His wisdom, but still we are struck with awe and horror at the misery of many of our brethren (*Auto*, 291–2).

Nothing in the light providentialism that pervades the Barsetshire novels— and which is suggested in the marriage plots that, despite circuitous complications, eventually reach their predestined, and sometimes pre-announced, conclusions—could prepare the reader for the heavy-handed providentialist imprint that Trollope employs to retrospectively read the Famine. In *Can You Forgive Her?*, the reader finds a classic aside that gives voice to the providentialist thread holding the novel together when

---

[34] Carleton, 'Dedication', *Black Prophet*.
[35] Christine Kinealy, *This Great Calamity. The Irish Famine, 1845–1852* (Dublin: Gill and Macmillan, 1994), 353.

the narrator claims that he is 'inclined to believe that most men and women take their lots as they find them, marrying as the birds do by force of nature, and going on with their mates with a general, though not perhaps an undisturbed satisfaction, feeling inwardly assured that Providence, if it have not done the very best for them, has done for them as well as they could for themselves with all the thought in the world' (*CYFH?*, 109). Similarly, in the early Irish novel, *The Kellys and the O'Kellys*, the widow Kelly comments on Anty's illness and her chances of a recovery in providentialist terms: '"And good news it'll be for him," said Mrs Kelly; "the best he heard since the ould man died. Av he had his will of her, she'd niver rise from the bed where she's stretched. But, glory be to God, there's a providence over all, and maybe she'll live yet to give him the go-by"' (*Kellys*, 241).

But this is all harmless when compared to the bald providentialist reading of the Famine in *Castle Richmond*, where the narrator boldly declares that 'the destruction of the potato was the work of God' and the Famine itself an 'exhibition of his mercy' (*CR*, 66). Elsewhere, Trollope was even more forthright:

> But such punishments [secession in the United States, Famine in Ireland] come generally upon nations as great mercies. Ireland's Famine was the punishment of her imprudence and idleness, but it has given to her prosperity and progress (*NA*, 585).

Even if statements like this today are hard to stomach, they were rather commonplace among commentators of the time. Particularly widespread was the belief that the Famine was an act of God, and voices from State and Church united in hammering home this message, fortified by Malthus's 'Essay on Population', which suggested that Ireland was a country whose poverty and lack of food were the self-inducing outcome of a surplus population, and that the Famine disaster was a natural way to restore a better balance between supply and demand.[36] Thomas Carlyle spoke for many in expressing the hope that the continuing failure of the potato would force things to change for the better in Ireland:

> if this despicable root will but *continue* dead, we may at least all say that we have changed our sordid chronic pestilential atrophy into a swift fierce crisis of death or the beginning of cure; and all 'revolutions' are but small to this,—if the Potatoe will but *stay* away! Your Irish Governing Class are now actually brought to the bar; arraigned before Heaven and Earth or *mis*-governing this Ireland; and no Lord John Russell or 'Irish Party' in

---

[36] For more on Malthus, see Christopher Morash, *Writing the Irish Famine* (Oxford: Clarendon Press, 1995), 2–51.

Palaceyard, and no man or combination of men can save them from their sentence, To govern it better or to disappear and die.[37]

The Reverend Charles Parsons Reichel pronounced that the Famine was a 'national sin and we may expect accordingly will be punished in the present world by the righteous Governor.'[38] Effectively, this Anglican churchman was blaming the Irish themselves for the fact that they were starving to death. Charles Trevelyan, the man charged with directing British government relief to the victims of the Irish Famine in the 1840s, held a slightly less extreme view, one which, in Foster's words, 'epitomizes the Whig view of economic theory',[39] and which was shared by most members of Russell's government. He declared that the 'judgment of God sent the calamity to teach the Irish a lesson, that calamity must not be too much mitigated.... The real evil with which we have to contend is not the physical evil of the Famine, but the moral evil of the selfish, perverse and turbulent character of the people.'[40] Trevelyan (who would be portrayed as Sir Gregory Hardlines in *The Three Clerks*) justified his government's belief in minimal intervention, aimed at encouraging Irish self-reliance, by claiming that 'Supreme Wisdom has educed permanent good out of transient evil'[41] and, in Eagleton's words, 'held that the effects of Famine should not be too thoroughly mitigated by British aid, so that its improvident victims might learn their lesson.'[42]

Many Protestants saw the Famine as 'punishment for the prevalence of popery', and as a means to 'rescue the people from the darkness of popery and priestcraft and to bring them to the pure light of the gospel'.[43] For some Protestant proselytizers it was more important that Ireland be provided with 'the word of God' than with immediate material assistance to offset the mass starvation which was attributed to divine judgement. They offered food, clothes, and shoes to the poorest Catholics, hoping to win them over in what the Anglican Archbishop of Dublin, Richard Whately, condemned as 'a bribe for conversion',[44] and which Trollope repeatedly denounced in his novels. The providentialist reading

---

[37] Letter of 1 March 1847 from Thomas Carlyle to Charles Gavan Duffy. http://carlyleletters.dukejournals.org/cgi/content/long/21/1/lt-18470301-TC-CGD-01.

[38] Reichel is quoted in Morash, *Writing the Famine*, 92.

[39] R. F. Foster, *Modern Ireland, 1600–1972* (New York and London: Penguin, 1988), 326. For more on British political reaction to the Famine, see Peter Gray and Sarah Burns, *Famine, Land, and Politics: British Government and Irish Society, 1843–50* (Dublin: Irish Academic Press, 1999).

[40] Quoted in Cecil Woodham Smith, *The Great Hunger* (London: Penguin, 1991), 156.

[41] Quoted in Eagleton, *Heathcliff*, 15–16.   [42] Eagleton, *Heathcliff*, 16.

[43] D. A. Kerr, *A Nation of Beggars: Priests, People & Politics in Famine Ireland, 1846–1852* (Oxford: Clarendon Press, 1994), 207.

[44] Whately is quoted in Kerr, *Nation of Beggars*, 213.

exonerated all but the victims of the suffering for what was happening.
Some, particularly among Presbyterians, believed that the Famine was an
instance of 'divine vengeance' against both Irish Catholics and those
English politicians who had 'indulged' them with 'sins', such as the
granting of Catholic emancipation and the endowment of Maynooth
College.[45] Many Catholics held oddly analogous opinions, believing
that 'God was extracting a penance for the Irish people accepting money
from the British government to finance Maynooth College.'[46]

William Carleton, a leading member of the Protestant community in
Connaught, in 1847 also subscribed to the belief that the Famine was sent
from God. The starving in *The Black Prophet* are described as 'creatures
changed from their very humanity by some judicial plague that had been
sent down from heaven to punish and desolate the land',[47] while *Castle
Squander* closes with the assertion that the Famine 'came upon us, not
from Lord John Russell, but directly from the hand of God.'[48] As Henry
Squander, manager of the Squander estate, in the wake of his own father's
death midway through the novel, watches starving tenants evicted from
their homes, he comments:

> We feel that the people must die off—die out of the way—and it is not the
> first landlord I have heard say as much. This is a blessed famine, God be
> praised! If we could only get one or two more of them we would be able to
> reconstruct our property, and proceed with success, because we could then
> get rid, in a natural way, of the superabundant.[49]

Carleton, however, includes these views in his novel, not to endorse, but
to critique them and show the limits of English and Anglo-Irish responses.
Trollope, on the other hand, broadly subscribed to the providential
interpretation, and endorsed the belief that the Famine checked the lack
of responsibility that had long dominated the lifestyles both of the Anglo-
Irish gentry and the peasantry, thus paving the way for the growth of a
more responsible, duty-bound middle class, exemplified by the Fitzgeralds
of Castle Richmond.

Trollope was also keen to make clear that Ireland's woes were not
caused by 'the idolatry of popery, or by the sedition of demagogues, or
even mainly by the idleness of the people'. Although these elements were,
like 'sedition', 'bad', they were no worse in Ireland than elsewhere. Thus,

---

[45] Peter Gray, 'The Triumph of Dogma: The Ideology of Famine Relief', *18th–19th
Century History*, 3/2 (1995), 3.

[46] Kinealy, *Great Calamity*, 33.   [47] Carleton, *Black Prophet*, 250.

[48] William Carleton. *The Squanders of Castle Squander*, 2 vols (London: Office of the
Illustrated London Library, 1852), 2, 391.

[49] Carleton, *Castle Squander*, 2, 278.

for the narrator, it is off the mark to criticize the 'idleness of Ireland's people' who, if given the chance, 'will work under the same compulsion and same persuasion which produce work in other countries'. What has undone Ireland is 'the lowness of education and consequent want of principle among the middle classes; and this fault had been found as strongly marked among the Protestants as it had been among the Roman Catholics'. Too many men 'were brought up to do nothing', with no sense of duty and an overwhelming desire to exploit the land without working it. Absentee landlords played their part, but worse was done by their agents, 'those they left behind them on the soil. The scourge of Ireland was the existence of a class who looked to be gentlemen living on their property, but who should have earned their bread by the work of their brain, or, failing that, by the sweat of their brow' (*CR*, 67). That God put a stop to all of this was a manifestation of his goodness:

> But though I do not believe in exhibitions of God's anger, I do believe in exhibitions of his mercy. When men by their folly and by the shortness of their vision have brought upon themselves penalties which seem to be overwhelming, to which no end can be seen, which would be overwhelming were no aid coming to us but our own, then God raises his hand, not in anger, but in mercy, and by his wisdom does for us that for which our own wisdom has been insufficient (*CR*, 66).

Because the Irish were not capable of seeing the error of their ways, God sent the disaster of the Famine, which ultimately was for the good of the Irish tenants who lived beyond their means and did not know the meaning of hard work:

> But the Irish tenant would by no means consent to be a farmer. It was needful to him that he should be a gentleman, and that his sons should be taught to live and amuse themselves as the sons of gentlemen—barring any such small trifle as education. They did live in this way; and to enable them to do so, they underlet their land in small patches, and at an amount of rent to collect which took the whole labour of their tenants, and the whole produce of the small patch, over and above the quantity of potatoes absolutely necessary to keep that tenant's body and soul together (*CR*, 67).

Although Trollope's grasp of the social and economic realities of Ireland was solid, his note in favour of the changes facilitated by Famine is at best strident, showing a shocking disregard for the dead. He risks sounding like Swift in *A Modest Proposal* but without any of the irony:

> Change is good: It is with thorough rejoicing, almost with triumph, that I declare that the idle, genteel class has been cut up root and branch, has been driven forth out of its holding into the wide world, and has been punished

with the penalty of extermination. The poor cotter suffered sorely under the famine, and under the pestilence which followed the famine; but he, as a class, has risen from his bed of suffering a better man. He is thriving as a labourer either in his own country or in some newer—for him better—land to which he has emigrated. He, even in Ireland, can now get eight and nine shillings a-week easier and with more constancy than he could get four some fifteen years since. But the other man has gone, and his place is left happily vacant (*CR*, 68).

In the aftermath of the Famine, the Irish economy did, as Trollope repeatedly points out, gradually recover, and therefore people erred in thinking that 'God's anger' was turned against them. Quite the contrary: 'lo! the famine passes by, and a land that had been brought to the dust by man's folly is once more prosperous and happy' (*CR*, 66). As a result, Ireland found itself with a thinned but strengthened ascendancy; a routed Irish farmer class; and a much reduced but more economically viable peasantry. The fittest, as it were, had survived and could now begin to prosper. Trollope was far from alone in this belief. Harriet Martineau, a visitor who was always sympathetic to Ireland, believed that the Famine would 'bring in a better time than Ireland has ever known yet . . . freedom, in short, to begin afresh, with the advantage of modern knowledge and manageable numbers. It was this view that consoled us during many a day's journey'.[50]

Trollope assumes almost biblical tones to explain the purging effects of the Famine:

> Such having been the state of the country, such its wretchedness, a merciful God sent the remedy which might avail to arrest it; and we—we deprecated his wrath. But all this will soon be known and acknowledged; acknowledged as it is acknowledged that new cities rise up in splendour from the ashes into which old cities have been consumed by fire. If this beneficent agency did not from time to time disencumber our crowded places, we should ever be living in narrow alleys with stinking gutters, and supply of water at the minimum (*CR*, 68).

Toward the conclusion of *Castle Richmond*, the narrator expounds the moral, straining once again for biblical resonance:

> But if one did in truth write a tale of the famine, after that it would behove the author to write a tale of the pestilence; and then another, a tale of the exodus. These three wonderful events, following each other, were the blessings coming from Omniscience and Omnipotence by which the black clouds were driven from the Irish firmament. If one through it all could have dared to hope, and

---

[50] Martineau's letter is dated 17 September 1852. Quoted in Glenn Hooper, ed., *Letters from Ireland* (Dublin: Irish Academic Press, 2001), 111.

have had from the first that wisdom which has learned to acknowledge that His mercy endureth for ever! And then the same author going on with his series would give in his last set, Ireland in her prosperity (*CR*, 347).

The Divine, therefore, has intervened to bring good to the 'Irish firmament', or so we are told by the narrator, who widens the lens to take the longest possible perspective on what has occurred, moving beyond the day-to-day account to embrace a historical reading that minimizes the suffering and death that was involved. In *The Landleaguers*, Trollope would continue to endorse the providentialist reading: 'God will step in, and will cause famine, and plague, and pestilence—even poverty itself—with His own Right Arm' (*LL*, 298).

Later in *Castle Richmond*, however, the frivolous tone with which Trollope remakes this point, with an allusion to Sir Toby Belch in *Twelfth Night*, is inopportune and crassly insensitive, seeming only to show regard for the benefits accruing to the landlords:

> Ah me! how little do we know what is coming to us! Irish cakes and ale were done and over for this world, we all thought. But in truth the Irish cakes were only then a-baking, and the Irish ale was being brewed. I am not sure that these good things are yet quite fit for the palates of the guest;—not as fit as a little more time will make them. The cake is still too new,—cakes often are; and the ale is not sufficiently mellowed. But of this I am sure, that the cakes and ale are there;—and the ginger, too, very hot in the mouth. Let a committee of Irish landlords say how the rents are paid now, and what amount of arrears was due through the country when the famine came among them. Rents paid to the day: that is the ginger hot in the mouth which best pleases the palate of a country gentleman (*CR*, 489).

The fact that, ten years after the Famine, rent collection is easier, may, from the landlords' point of view, be 'progress', but from a novelist who knew Ireland so intimately, it is politically and morally questionable; the sheer volume of death which left so many farms and houses 'happily vacant' (*CR*, 66) cannot be brushed away so lightly.

At various times throughout *Castle Richmond*, the reader finds himself being shifted between the 'then' of the actual core plot and the 'now' in which the narrator explains the changes in the country with the benefit of hindsight. At times, this robs the actual moment of the novel of much of its immediacy, trivializes the already creaky plot, and serves principally to diminish the effects of the Famine. For example, in chapter eight, the narrator embarks on an interpolation about Famine relief, only to abruptly cut it short so as to refocus on the fiction:

> How they all spent their day at the soup kitchen, which however, though so called, partook quite as much of the character of a bake-house; how they

studied the art of making yellow Indian meal into puddings; how the girls wanted to add milk and sugar, not understanding at first the deep principles of political economy, which soon taught them not to waste on the comforts of a few that which was so necessary for the life of many; how the poor women brought in their sick ailing children, accepting the proffered food, but bitterly complaining of it as they took it,—complaining of it because they wanted money, with which they still thought that they could buy potatoes—all this need not here or now be described. Our present business is to get them all back to Castle Richmond (*CR*, 77–8).

At the end of chapter sixteen, in the scene in which Herbert gives some money to a beggar-woman, after Clara has pleaded with him to do so, the narrator again intervenes, pulling back from the immediate description and lengthening the perspective:

'Go on now, my good woman,' said he, 'and take your children where they may be warm. If you will be advised by me, you will go to the Union at Kanturk.' And so the woman passed on still blessing them. Very shortly after this none of them required pressing to go to the workhouse. Every building that could be arranged for the purpose was filled to overflowing as soon as it was ready (*CR*, 192).

The awkwardness of this dual take on time is exacerbated in the discon-nection between the two concluding sentences, which encapsulates the strain in tying the domestic or familial and the national or Famine plots together: 'But the worst of the famine had not come upon them as yet. And then Herbert rode back to Castle Richmond' (*CR*, 192). In another narratorial intrusion of this type, describing a discussion between Father Bernard and his cousins, Mrs O'Dwyer and her daughter, Fanny, we see the strain caused by this temporal double-take, whereby the narrative voice alternates between telling in the moment and generalizing from the point of view of the moment of writing rather than the time being described. The narrative vantage point of the 'now' functions like a camera close-up, but this is thrown out of focus by the narrative's overall point of view, which is that of a distant camera putting the events in the perspective of a much longer time-frame. On hearing the priest describing the suffering in his area, his cousins are moved:

'Glory be to God, the poor cratures!' said the soft-hearted lady.

'It isn't much the like of us have to give away, Father Bernard; I needn't be telling you that. But we'll help, you know,—we'll help.'

'And so will father, uncle Bernard. If you're so bad off about here I know he'll give you a thrifle for the asking.' In a short time, however, it came to pass that those in the cities could spare no aid to the country. Indeed it may be a question whether the city poverty was not the harder of the two (*CR*, 199).

According to the narrator, God sent the Famine so as to bring Ireland to sense, to remedy her social ills so that the country could be reborn in a more rational and, indeed, more English, way. Because this was the work of God, then all that man can do is to accept it and learn from it. Hence there is no point in attempting to circumvent God's plans by helping people who are beyond help. Providence must take its course and providence—guidance and control through the hand of God—can only be praised. If this is the case, and Trollope evidently believed that it was, what was to be made of those many who devoted themselves to bettering the people's lot through charity? Trollope was always sceptical about the benefits of charity and philanthropy, of giving money or succour to those in need. No matter how well intended the relief-work schemes may have been, he believed—like Thomas Malthus—that it was counterproductive to provide public or private short-term relief without addressing the deep-rooted causes of poverty and distress. Trevelyan too regarded 'dependence on others' as 'a moral disease' and saw the Famine as 'the judgment of God on an indolent and unself-reliant people.'[51] The giving of charity, in Trollope's view, bred inertia and the need for further assistance, and for this reason 'the Irish cry for charity' was unceasing and 'universal' (*Examiner*, 77). In 1882, some forty years after the Famine, he would write to Alfred Austin in connection with a fund, established by the Association for the Relief of Ladies in Distress, intended to help women in difficulty for non-payment of rent in Ireland, in tones that show that his opinions had not budged an inch:

> I have seen your wife's name as collector for the Irish fund. What does she mean to do with the money? She cannot walk into a gentleman's house and offer him a £10 note. Of course her money will go to a common fund. But what will the common fund do with it? The fact is all charity is wrong,—and only to be excused by the comfort it gives to the giver (*Letters II*, 942).

Trollope's letters to the *Examiner* further motivate his opposition to charity:

> The sufferings of the poor were awful; very awful in their extent and severity, but almost more tremendous from the patience, nay, the apathy, with which they were borne; but perhaps the most fearful feature of the time was the inactivity and want of self-denial of those who shrieked to Government their loud demand that the famine should be taken from their doors . . . in the spring of 1847 the energies of the country were expended in petitions for relief (*Examiner*, 80).

---

[51] Boyd Hilton, *The Age of Atonement: The Influence of Evangelicalism on Social and Economic Thought, 1795–1865* (Oxford: Clarendon Press, 1988), 113.

An excess of relief, in Trollope's view, engendered 'idle habits', while 'fraud was made easy, and the temptation to it affected more or less all classes; ... people were taught to know that if they do not work and feed themselves, others must work and feed them. These, let us own, were dreadful consequences' (*Examiner*, 83). Therefore he argued that some work should always be required in exchange for charity: 'The supply provided should not be gratuitous, for dependence on charity for daily bread destroys the feeling of independence. To prevent habits of idleness ample work should be required in exchange for the means of livelihood' (*Examiner*, 84).

Trollope was still making this point more than twenty years later in the pages of *Mr Scarborough's Family*, where the down-at-heel Captain Carroll relies on his brother-in-law in order to feed his family of six girls. A drinker, who boasts of royal blood among his ancestors, he seems to incarnate all the worst traits of idleness, vanity, and ill-supported notions of grandeur that Trollope saw as the cause of so many of the troubles of the Irish. His daughters have been raised in his image and, caught in a spiral of dependence, will stop at nothing in demanding charity and extracting money from their relatively well-off uncle while at the same time boasting about their own dubious prospects in marriage. Although Trollope's line is harsh in the extreme, it was not out of sync with mainstream Victorian views:

> [e]motional continence was an indispensable character trait, and it has a lot in common with the suppression of instincts that evangelicals preached and practiced. When political economists and evangelicals persuaded people to desist from giving money to beggars, it was more than just clearing the streets. It was the first object lesson in both evangelical morality and political economy. It taught people to master their benevolent instincts in the pursuit of a higher goal. And it had worked; people, and especially the middle classes in town and cities throughout the country, had imbibed the religious and economic arguments. 'I remember the time,' wrote Brougham in 1825, 'when money given to beggars was supposed to be well bestowed—a notion now exploded.' Anti-mendicity propaganda stressed that one small coin conferred on an unworthy supplicant was a crime against natural law, fuel to the fire of unproductive labor and an encouragement to a surplus population.[52]

Although Trollope took regular issue with the Evangelicals, this anti-charity message would be reiterated many times over in the pages of *Castle Richmond*, where charity is seen as self-serving—it makes the giver feel

---

[52] Ben Wilson, *The Making of Victorian Values: Decency & Dissent in Britain: 1789–1837* (New York: Penguin Press, 2007), 329.

better but solves nothing. In the chapter entitled 'The Last Stage', Herbert visits the home of a dying woman and child. The shocking scene is described by the narrator in detached, almost scientific terms, and is followed by a consideration on how 'it was difficult to be delicate when the hands were so full':

> In those days there was a form of face which came upon the sufferers when their state of misery was far advanced, and which was a sure sign that their last stage of misery was nearly run. The mouth would fall and seem to hang, the lips at the two ends of the mouth would be dragged down, and the lower parts of the cheeks would fall as though they had been dragged and pulled. There were no signs of acute agony when this phasis of countenance was to be seen, none of the horrid symptoms of gnawing hunger by which one generally supposes that famine is accompanied. The look is one of apathy, desolation, and death (*CR*, 369–70).

Herbert tries to help and struggles to find the right words, perhaps knowing all too well that there are no right words. He gives the woman a few coins and promises to send someone to help her. However, both of them know it will be too late and 'the promise brought her no joy' (*CR*, 374). The only one to benefit from his charity is Herbert himself, who is able to put his own new-found situation of dispossession into perspective in the light of what he has witnessed:

> Whatever might be the extent of his own calamity, how could he think himself unhappy after what he had seen? How could he repine at aught that the world had done for him, having now witnessed to how low a state of misery a fellow human being might be brought? Could he, after that, dare to consider himself unfortunate? (*CR*, 374).

In other cases in the novel, charity is shown to function not as an end in itself, but as a means to religious conversion to Protestantism (souperism) through the characters of Aunt Letty and the Reverend and Mrs Townsend. This practice is consistently condemned by Trollope, who is also reluctant to endorse the more disinterested charity practised by the Fitzgerald family, even if he is well aware of the human desire to attempt to alleviate suffering. Indeed, much of the novel's most powerful writing depicts the harrowing effects of the Famine as seen through the caring eyes of the Fitzgeralds or Clara. The scene in which the Fitzgerald women say goodbye to their tenants before leaving their home forever rings true and backs up this sense of connection between well-meaning resident landlord families and their tenants:

> And then Aunt Letty found that there was no necessity for her to continue her speech, and indeed no possibility of her doing so even if she were so

minded. The children began to wail and cry, and the mothers also mixed loud sobbings with their loud prayers; and Emmeline and Mary, dissolved in tears, sat themselves down, drawing to them the youngest bairns and those whom they had loved the best, kissing their sallow, famine-stricken, unwholesome faces, and weeping over them with a love of which hitherto they had been hardly conscious (*CR*, 362).

To understand that this is not merely wishful thinking on Trollope's part, we need only quote from John Mitchel's *The Last Conquest of Ireland (Perhaps)*, where Mitchel recounts how

the resident landlords and their families did, in many cases, devote themselves to the task of saving their poor people alive. Many remitted their rents, or half their rents; and ladies kept their servants busy and their kitchens smoking with continual preparation of food for the poor. Local Committees soon purchased all the corn in the government depots (at market price, however), and distributed it gratuitously.[53]

While Herbert Fitzgerald, the hero of the novel, is praised for his efforts on behalf of the poor living around his father's estate, he is far more convincingly backed by the narrator for his awareness of the limits of what charity can achieve: 'Herbert had learned deep lessons of political economy, and was by no means disposed to give promiscuous charity on the road-side' (*CR*, 190). Charity should not be casual or unrestrained, and Herbert plays what for Trollope is a useful role in limiting the work his sisters are willing to carry out. Nothing, in Trollope's view, should be given free of charge:

And then two great rules seemed to get themselves laid down—not by general consent, for there were many who greatly contested their wisdom—but by some force strong enough to make itself dominant. The first was, that the food to be provided should be earned and not given away. And the second was, that the providing of that food should be left to private competition, and not in any way be undertaken by the Government. I make bold to say that both these rules were wise and good (*CR*, 200).

Charity, in the narrator's view, should be earned and relief supplies should be paid for. This belief is tested, however, when Herbert's conscience is appealed to by Bridget Sheehy, the starving young Irish mother in rags who appears unexpectedly before him and Clara (at times the effectiveness of the Famine depictions is increased by the abruptness with which they are sprung on the reader):

---

[53] John Mitchel, *The Last Conquest of Ireland (Perhaps)* (Glasgow: Cameron, Ferguson & Co., 1876), 115.

A woman was standing there, of whom you could hardly say that she was clothed, though she was involved in a mass of rags which covered her nakedness. Her head was all uncovered, and her wild black hair was stream-ing round her face. Behind her back hung two children enveloped among the rags in some mysterious way; and round about her on the road stood three others, of whom the two younger were almost absolutely naked (*CR*, 189).

The babies Bridget Sheehy carries on her back are in a piteous state: 'she undid the bundle at her back, and laying the two babes down on the road showed that the elder of them was in truth in a fearful state.... [I]ts little legs seemed to have withered away; its cheeks were wan, and yellow and sunken' (*CR*, 191). Just as the sympathy of the reader, along with that of Herbert and Clara, is being won over by this vision of the 'wretchedly thin' mother and her children whose 'naked limbs...were like yellow sticks' (*CR*, 189), the narrator interrupts with a needless and contextually offensive reflection about the relative beauty of the Irish peasantry, increasing the sense that this woman, whose semi-nakedness is underlined, is being violated by the gaze of Herbert, Clara, and indeed the reader at a moment of terrible personal suffering:

> It is strange how various are the kinds of physical development among the Celtic peasantry in Ireland. In many places they are singularly beautiful, especially as children; and even after labour and sickness shall have told on them as labour and sickness will tell, they still retain a certain softness and grace which is very nearly akin to beauty. But then again in a neighbouring district they will be found to be squat, uncouth, and in no way attractive to the eye. The tint of the complexion, the nature of the hair, the colour of the eyes, shall be the same.... (*CR*, 189).

This jarring interpolation reads as if the narrator were classifying a strange species, with Trollope suggesting that in normal times the peasantry is 'beautiful' and that these Famine images are a temporary blip. Eventually, the woman is individualized and identifies herself: 'And my name is Bridget Sheehy. Shure, an' yer ladyship remembers me at Clady the first day ye war over there about the biler' (*CR*, 190). Herbert initially tries to fend her off by asking where her husband is and then by suggesting she go to the poorhouse in Kanturk; a choice which would mean giving up her house and home and possibly being separated from her children. Bridget continues to plead her case and mentions Owen, his rival for Clara's love:

> Shure thin an' I'll jist tramp on as fur as Hap House, I and my childher; that is av' they do not die by the road-side. Come on, bairns. Mr Owen won't be after sending me to the Kanturk union when I tell him that I've travelled all thim miles to get a dhrink of milk for a sick babe; more by token when I tells him also that I'm one of the Desmond tinantry. It's he that loves the

Desmonds, Lady Clara,—loves them as his own heart's blood. And it's I that
wish him good luck with his love, in spite of all that's come and gone yet.
Come on, bairns, come along; we have seven weary miles to walk (*CR*, 191).

Clara is moved by her appeals and encourages Herbert: '"Do give her
something, Herbert, pray do," said Clara, with her whole face suffused
with tears' (*CR*, 191). Morash claims that Herbert eventually does help
because 'the woman threatens to go to Herbert's rival, Owen Fitzgerald',[54]
but this is not to do Herbert full justice. The narrator is careful to note
that 'Herbert Fitzgerald, from the first moment of his interrogating the
woman, had of course known that he would give her somewhat' (*CR*,
192). Furthermore, although he argues against easy charity, he too at times
cannot resist offering immediate help: 'In spite of all his political economy,
there were but few days in which he did not empty his pocket of his loose
silver, with these culpable deviations from his theoretical philosophy. But
yet he felt that it was his duty to insist on his rules, as far as his heart would
allow him to do so' (*CR*, 192). In a sense, this sums up Trollope's own
stance on the Famine, but it also contradicts Morash's assertion that 'issues
of economic theory and individual suffering are here resolved through
the conventions of the fictional romantic narrative.'[55] Yes, Herbert ensures agreement with Clara, but he, like the author, remains troubled as to
how to react to the Famine, how to reconcile his ideological principles
with the depth and vastness of the suffering that he encounters. In the end
he yields and gives some money, believing, all the while, that it will be to
no avail:

> It was a settled thing at their relief committee that there should be no giving
> away of money to chance applicants for alms. What money each had to
> bestow would go twice further by being brought to the general fund—by
> being expended with forethought and discrimination. This was the system
> which all attempted, which all resolved to adopt who were then living in the
> south of Ireland. But the system was impracticable, for it required frames
> of iron and hearts of adamant. It was impossible not to waste money in
> almsgiving (*CR*, 192).

Trollope's choice of the noun 'adamant' is interesting. It was more
common in the nineteenth century than it is today to use this word as a
noun meaning a very hard or impenetrable stone. In a sense this definition
sums up the uncompromising toughness of Trollope's position on how
the Famine should be dealt with: that is, on economic rather than
charitable terms, by appeal to the head despite the claims of the heart
which cry out for charitable action. This, the narrator claims, is how those

---

[54] Morash, *Writing the Famine*, 42–3.   [55] Morash, *Writing the Famine*, 43.

living on a day-to-day basis with the realities of the Famine react. 'Men', the narrator states, 'ceased to be uncomfortable about it' and learnt to deal in a matter-of-fact way with the misery they encountered:

> And dying paupers, with 'the drag' in their face—that certain sign of coming death of which I have spoken—no longer struck men to the heart. Like the skilled surgeon, they worked hard enough at what good they could do, and worked the better in that they could treat the cases without express compassion for the individuals that met their eyes. In administering relief one may rob five unseen sufferers of what would keep them in life if one is moved to bestow all that is comfortable on one sufferer that is seen (*CR*, 413).

Those who worked most wisely for the common good denied help to those victims 'whose doom was already spoken' because 'money, if duly used, might save the lives of others not yet so far gone in misery'. Those 'who worked the hardest for the poor and spent their time most completely among them, became the hardest of heart, and most obdurate in their denials. It was strange to see devoted women neglecting the wants of the dying, so that they might husband their strength and time and means for the wants of those who might still be kept among the living' (*CR*, 413). Armed with these beliefs, it is not surprising that the narrator is almost invariably critical of charity and claims it does more good to the giver than to the receiver. For Clara, acts of benevolence afford the compensatory distraction she needs to get over her problems in love:

> For some time after the love adventure, Clara had been pale and drooping, and the countess had been frightened about her; but latterly she had got over this. The misfortune which had fallen so heavily upon them all seemed to have done her good. She had devoted herself from the first to do her little quota of work towards lessening the suffering around her, and the effort had been salutary to her (*CR*, 75).

Trollope deals ironically with the Fitzgeralds' philanthropy by describing how the siblings patronizingly discuss the poor and starving before sitting down to their own large dinner: 'And so they went on, till I fear they kept the Castle Richmond dinner waiting for full fifteen minutes' (*CR*, 79). The allusion to this 'normal' dinner is also testimony to what is now historically believed, which is that 'for many life went on normally' or, to quote L. M. Cullen, 'Comfortable people lived their normal lives'.[56] When the entire Fitzgerald family discuss charitable works around

---

[56] W. F. Vaughan, 'Reflections on the Great Famine', *Ulster Local Studies*, 17/2 (1995), 7–8, and L. M. Cullen, 'The politics of the Famine and Famine Historiography', in *Comhdháil and Chraoibhín 1996* (Roscommon, 1997), 24, both quoted in Ó'Gráda, 'Famine, trauma, and memory', 126.

the estate, Sir Thomas is glad of the respite from his own domestic problems:

> Lady Fitzgerald took a part in all this, and so occasionally did Sir Thomas. Indeed, on this evening he was more active than was usual with him. He got up from his armchair, and came to the table, in order that he might pore over the map of the estate with them; for they were dividing the property into districts, and seeing how best the poor might be visited in their own localities. And then, as he did so, he became liberal. Liberal, indeed, he always was; but now he made offers of assistance more than his son had dared to ask; and they were all busy, contented, and in a great degree joyous— joyous, though their work arose from the contiguity of such infinite misery. But what can ever be more joyous than efforts made for lessening misery? (*CR*, 79).

Charity, in this description, is as much a form of entertainment for the giver as it is an attempt to reduce suffering. Thus we read that when Clara's visit to the Fitzgeralds and her helping in the soup kitchen is to come to an end this 'created some little feeling of awkwardness, for Clara had put her whole heart into the work at Gortnaclough, and it was evident that she would have been so delighted to continue with them' (*CR*, 80). At 'times it reads as if the narrator is ironically describing a light social scene reminiscent of an excursion in a Jane Austen novel, rather than work among the starving and the dying.

Trollope's novel has been criticized for his comments on the lack of gratitude of the poor for the efforts made on their behalf: 'The hardest burden', the narrator states, 'which had to be borne by those who exerted themselves at this period was the ingratitude of the poor for whom they worked;—or rather I should say thanklessness' (*CR*, 86). The narrator then qualifies this and excuses the peasants for feeling less than grateful:

> To call them ungrateful would imply too deep a reproach, for their convictions were that they were being ill used by the upper classes. When they received bad meal which they could not cook, and even in their extreme hunger could hardly eat half-cooked; when they were desired to leave their cabins and gardens, and flock into the wretched barracks which were prepared for them; when they saw their children wasting away under a suddenly altered system of diet, it would have been unreasonable to expect that they should have been grateful. Grateful for what? Had they not at any rate a right to claim life, to demand food that should keep them and their young ones alive? But not the less was it a hard task for delicate women to work hard, and to feel that all their work was unappreciated by those whom they so thoroughly commiserated, whose sufferings they were so anxious to relieve (*CR*, 86).

Some suffering, however, cannot be relieved and must be endured. This is the case for so many victims of the Famine, but it is also true, albeit in a different way, for the Fitzgeralds. Trollope casts their story in a manner that makes it parallel to that of the peasantry. The family's loss of their property and of their future parallels the losses of so many of their tenants. In the fullness of time, however, Herbert accepts what providence sends his way, reacts as strongly as he can and ultimately triumphs over these adversities. This is in marked contrast to his father, who meekly submits, and whose failure to stand up to those English criminals who are blackmailing him is the cause of his and his family's seeming ruin. One of a litany of weak, culpable Trollopian fathers, he is not even capable of opposing what seems, given their sudden financial destruction, to be his son's impossible marriage to Clara: 'Sir Thomas certainly did disapprove his son's marrying, but he lacked the courage to say so. Much misery that had hitherto come upon him, and that was about to come on all those whom he loved so well, arose from this lack of courage' (*CR*, 132). His death is made to mirror that of the Famine poor and is seen as a passive yielding to the inevitable:

> Such battle as it had been in his power to make he had made to save his son's heritage and his wife's name and happiness, even at the expense of his own conscience. That battle had gone altogether against him, and now there was nothing left for him but to turn his face to the wall and die. Absolute ruin, through his fault, had come upon him and all that belonged to him,—ruin that would now be known to the world at large; and it was beyond his power to face that world again. . . . The mind of that poor man was diseased past all curing in this world, and there was nothing left for him but to die (*CR*, 324).

The fact that his dying will leave his family homeless and penniless is underlined again and again, as in this exchange between the Townsends: '"And when he dies all will be gone?" "Everything"' (*CR*, 329). The Fitzgeralds' dispossession on the death of the father is not unlike that of the Irish peasants. Sir Thomas's apathy, his acceptance of his ruin, his utter helplessness and hopelessness mirrors that, in the narrator's view, of the Irish at large:

> The fault of the people was apathy. It was the feeling of the multitude that the world and all that was good in it was passing away from them; that exertion was useless, and hope hopeless. 'Ah, me! your honour,' said a man to me, 'there'll never be a bit and a sup again in the county Cork! The life of the world is fairly gone!' (*CR*, 345).

The painfully 'altered world' (*CR*, 307) of the Fitzgeralds mirrors the radically changed world of Ireland and the domestic dispossession plot is worked so as to parallel the national one.

Herbert's riches-to-rags story means that all his life plans are in disarray: he will not be able to marry Clara and must break the news to her and to her mother, something he understandably finds traumatic and which parallels the role of the writer in trying to tell of the Famine, even if the parallel may seem insensitive. His is a tragedy of dispossession (the loss of the family estate) and death (of his father) which will, it seems, cause great suffering to two families; similarly, the Famine is a tragedy of dispossession and death which devastates countless peasant families:

> Herbert then sat for a few minutes silent, thinking how best he should tell them his story. He had been all the morning resolving to tell it, but he had in nowise as yet fixed upon any method. It was all so terribly tragic, so frightful in the extent of its reality, that he hardly knew how it would be possible for him to get through his task (*CR*, 292).

The story of Herbert's fall becomes a morality tale of decline, near destruction, and resurrection. At his lowest ebb, Herbert is described in terms that make him resemble a Famine victim. He feels the doom of his dispossession heavily:

> He was still his father's son, though he had lost the right to bear his father's name. He was nameless now, a man utterly without respect or standing-place in the world, a being whom the law ignored except as the possessor of a mere life; such was he now, instead of one whose rights and privileges, whose property and rank all the statutes of the realm and customs of his country delighted to honour and protect (*CR*, 254).

Albeit briefly, he does come to live something partly paralleling the experience of his own tenants and of the hundreds of thousands of nameless victims of the Famine, finding himself owning little or nothing but the clothes in which he stands up, and feeling, like the rest of his family, 'that they were outcasts in the world' (*CR*, 345). He is subject to Lady Desmond's scorn because she believes he is lacking in fight and compares him negatively to Owen, who would not have yielded so tamely to his fate:

> How was she to decide, sitting here with Herbert Fitzgerald before her, gloomy as death, cold, shivering, and muddy, telling of his own disasters with no more courage than a whipped dog? As she looked at him she declared to herself twenty times in half a second that he had not about him a tithe of the manhood of his cousin Owen.... Had Owen come there with such a story, he would have claimed his right boldly to the lady's hand, in spite of all that the world had done to him (*CR*, 297).

Herbert is depicted as a passive victim and the 'harsh and cruel' (*CR*, 298) anti-model, Lady Desmond, who personifies the worst of the landlord

class, looks on him with the same sort of contempt—'weak with hunger
...he looked like a whipped dog' (*CR*, 299)—normally reserved for
the starving peasantry, who are inevitably blamed for their destitution.
Despite this, he manages to tell her of his downfall,

> that he was no longer Fitzgerald of Castle Richmond, but a nameless,
> pennyless outcast, without the hope of portion or position, doomed from
> henceforth to earn his bread in the sweat of his brow—if only he could be
> fortunate enough to find the means of earning it (*CR*, 293).

Herbert's story is told in such a way as to encourage the reader to see it as
an allegory of the tragic individual Famine stories:

> Was not his story one that would have melted the heart of a stranger—at
> which men would weep? He himself had seen tears in the eyes of that dry, time-
> worn, world-used London lawyer, as the full depth of the calamity had forced
> itself upon his heart. Yes, Mr. Prendergast had not been able to repress his tears
> when he told the tale; but Lady Desmond had shed no tears when the tale had
> been told to her. No soft woman's message had been sent to the afflicted mother
> on whom it had pleased God to allow so heavy a hand to fall (*CR*, 302).

Eventually, Herbert manages to return home on foot but is so physically
exhausted that 'his strength almost failed him' (*CR*, 302). Comfort finally
comes from his mother, who encourages him to trust in providence, let
Clara go, and understand that 'God is good, and will teach you to bear
even that' (*CR*, 304). He tells his sister, Emmeline, that he is now 'a
beggar' (*CR*, 308) and writes telling Clara that 'it would be unmanly in me
to wish to ruin you because I myself am ruined' (*CR*, 309). Herbert shows,
like his father before him, little strength, finding resolve only when Clara
writes to say that she will stand by him despite everything.

Lady Desmond's comments bolster the Famine parallel. She feels more
for Lady Fitzgerald than she does for Herbert: 'How terrible, overwhelming, and fatal! What calamity could fall upon a woman so calamitous
as this which had now overtaken that poor lady at Castle Richmond?' (*CR*,
314). In her view, the Fitzgerald family's fall is a 'horrible catastrophe'
(*CR*, 322), ' "They will be beggars!" she said to herself—"beggars" ' (*CR*,
323). Words like 'calamity', 'poverty', and 'beggar', more normally associated with the Famine, are employed repeatedly to describe this fallen
Ascendancy family. Terms like 'penniless' and 'poverty' are used more
often to describe the Desmonds and Herbert Fitzgerald than to depict the
starving peasants—a sign, this, of Trollope's attempt to render the main
plot an allegory of Ireland's fall and possible resurgence.

The family's seeming collapse into poverty is interpreted by Aunt Letty
in a providentialist key in a manner which connects it, inexorably, with

the larger Famine context: 'The Lord giveth, and the Lord taketh away. Blessed be the name of the Lord. Oh! Herbert, my darling boy. I hope this may be a lesson and a warning to you, so that you may flee from the wrath to come' (*CR*, 469). This message is reiterated throughout the narrative. Thus we read:

> It is astonishing how quickly in this world of ours chaos will settle itself into decent and graceful order, when it is properly looked in the face, and handled with a steady hand which is not sparing of the broom. Some three months since, everything at Castle Richmond was ruin; such ruin, indeed, that the very power of living under it seemed to be doubtful... A broken world was in truth falling about their ears, and it was felt to be impossible that they should endure its convulsions and yet live (*CR*, 356).

From this ruinous calamity, hope can be reclaimed:

> But now the world had fallen, the ruin had come, and they were already strong in future hopes. They had dared to look at their chaos, and found that it still contained the elements of order (*CR*, 356).

Despite everything: 'chaos was conquered, and there was hope that the fields of life would again show themselves green and fruitful' (*CR*, 357). Initially Herbert decides to start over and to train for a legal career. In other words, he seeks a new, middle-class route to an income by seeking gainful employment. Ireland, the text reasons, can do the same. Acceptance of providence, an insistence on taking logical steps rather than being overcome by pathos, and an embrace of industry and hard work will see Ireland back on its feet. This is the message that Trollope hammers home through the love and disinheritance plots, but also through the Famine vignettes that accompany them. It is also the essential lesson of his *Examiner* letters.

Foster has argued that there 'were opinions which he shared with the majority of middle-class English clubmen and politicians—but the majority of them did not know Ireland as Trollope did. Perhaps because of this, he argued with a stridency and vehemence which suggests an underlying doubt.'[57] In a similar vein, Melissa Fegan claims that Trollope is in less than full agreement with his narrator and that 'Trollope, freed from the dead weight of his own official stance, resurrects the polemic of the factual Six Letters in the fictional *Castle Richmond* in order to subvert it.'[58] To our contemporary sensibilities it would be nice to believe it were so. Although

[57] Foster, *Irish Story*, 134.
[58] Melissa Fegan, *Literature and the Irish Famine, 1845–1919* (Oxford: Clarendon Press, 2002), 123.

elsewhere in this volume I have written of Trollope's internal counter-narratives, in this case I am inclined to believe that *Castle Richmond*, long vilified for its contradictions, is, in fact, unified by the desire to communicate the need for peasant and landlord to accept and respond to what providence has sent to Ireland, and to its people, rich and poor. Thus the narrator claims that things had come to such a pass that by the end of 1847, 'there was no longer any difference of opinion between rich and poor, between Protestant and Roman Catholic.... The famine was an established fact, and all men knew that it was God's doing,—all men knew this, though few could recognize as yet with how much mercy God's hand was stretched out over the country' (*CR*, 344–5). Although in places the narrator denies the actual scale and horror of the Famine, there are enough sketches of suffering, hunger, and death to suggest that Trollope knew exactly what he was doing.

That said, the Famine sketches counter Trollope's attempts to play down the catastrophe more powerfully than he ever intended. Although they were occasional, they linger more strongly in the readers' minds than anything else in the novel. Ironically, they can usefully be compared to some of the Famine descriptions and sketches so often seen in those very newspapers that Trollope complained were distorting and exaggerating the state of things in Ireland. James Mahoney's sketches in the *Illustrated London News* were among the best known of these, graphically describing the suffering that was so commonplace in the poorer parts of Ireland. They capture moments of Famine horror, yet they are to some extent incomplete, showing a lack of context, leaving absences that are sometimes filled by Mahoney's accompanying note, but also are left to be filled by the viewer. One picture showed a woman holding a sick infant. The woman looks very much like the Madonna. On reading the description we find, however, that the infant is actually dead:

> I started from Cork, by the mail, for Skibbereen and saw little until we came to Clonakilty, where the coach stopped for breakfast; and here, for the first time, the horrors of the poverty became visible, in the vast number of famished poor, who flocked around the coach to beg alms: amongst them was a woman carrying in her arms the corpse of a fine child, and making the most distressing appeal to the passengers for aid to enable her to purchase a coffin and bury her dear little baby. This horrible spectacle induced me to make some inquiry about her, when I learned from the people of the hotel that each day brings dozens of such applicants into the town.[59]

[59] Quoted in James Michael Farrell, '"This Horrible Spectacle": Visual and Verbal Sketches of the Famine in Skibereen', in Lawrence J. Prelli, ed., *Rhetorics of Display* (Columbia: University of South Carolina Press, 2006), 69–70.

What Mahoney offers is a 'horrible spectacle', not a mother seeking alms for a starving child, but a grief-stricken woman unable to separate herself from the corpse of her baby. The lady is never personalized and the viewer/reader is left wanting to know more. She is a representative figure of so many women in Ireland at this time. Famine vignettes of similar power are interspersed in Trollope's novel, given context, and personalized.

Trollope admits to the inevitability of the sympathetic and charitable reaction to such awful suffering while hoping, at the same time, to instil in his readers a sense of the greater necessity for an economic response. He confronts the reader with these sketches, not to elicit easy sympathy, nor to turn his gaze on Famine victims for aesthetic ends; rather, he hopes to take the reader beyond sympathy and to explain the necessity of a sterner stand, a position based on economics. Just as it seemed for a time that no kindly intervention could save Herbert and his family from ruin—the narrative of harsh justice as enacted by Mr Prendergast must run its course and they must accept their destiny—so too the Irish must submit to the omniscient justice that has handed down such a tough but ultimately improving sentence upon them. No social class is spared; all must learn their lesson and ultimately rejoice 'that the idle, genteel class has been cut up root and branch' and that the poor peasant 'has risen from his bed of suffering a better man' (*CR*, 68). Just as it pains Mr Prendergast to bring so harsh a judgement on people like the Fitzgeralds who deserve better, so too it troubles Trollope to deliver such a stern verdict on the Irish in his novel: 'It was sad and piteous. Stern and hard as was the man who pronounced this doom, nevertheless the salt tear collected in his eyes and blinded him as he looked upon the anguish which his judgment had occasioned' (*CR*, 216).

The fact is, however, that Herbert and his family *are* rescued from what seems like a certain doom while the Irish are not. The Fitzgeralds are saved because of the intervention, not of providence, but of an act of justice which sees the English conspirators and blackmailers being found out and rightful land ownership being reasserted. No such just reprieve is possible for the mass of Famine victims sporadically displayed in the narrative. Despite its attempt to establish a parallel between the family plots and the national calamity, ultimately the novel only renders full justice to the privileged, insisting on the fatalistic economic-providentialist reading of the Famine tragedy. It is as if Trollope believes that all he can do, beyond providing an incontrovertible admittance of suffering and death, is to put his hands up in the face of such misery, and argue that it is God's will. But this is to fail and, not for the first time, to draw the political conclusions from the evidence on the ground of which he is all too aware.

The justice that he evoked and sought for Ireland and the poorer Irish in *The Macdermots of Ballycloran* is reduced here to justice for the Anglo-Irish, while the starving natives are left with little more than mere pity and pathos, and the camouflage of Providence which is used to justify the horrific economic inequities of Ireland in the Famine years.

4

A Question of Character—The Many Lives of Phineas Finn

I. *PHINEAS FINN*: 'THE BEST IRISHMAN WE EVER GOT HOLD OF' (*PR*, 10)

One of the outstanding characters in the Palliser series, Trollope's extraordinary *roman-fleuve*, is the Irish politician, Phineas Finn, whose public and private careers are traced through the novels *Phineas Finn* (1869), *Phineas Redux* (1874), *The Prime Minister* (1876), and *The Duke's Children* (1880). Collectively these novels cover a troubled period of Anglo-Irish political relations which see Trollope's vision of Ireland darken and become increasingly unsympathetic and out of touch. The life story of Phineas is that of a young Irish lawyer who, like so many Irishmen before and after him, comes to England and builds a successful career there. Phineas's rise is, however, punctuated by false starts and more than a fair share of tragedy (the premature death of his young Irish wife, Mary Flood, in *Phineas Finn*) and trauma (his imprisonment, trial, and eventual acquittal for murder, in *Phineas Redux*). In the latter two novels, even if he has slipped out of central focus, it is hard to ignore Finn's assured social prominence and enduring political success. He has become, for his creator, an exemplary Irish character in Britain.

In the first novel, Phineas starts steadily in law before chance and good connections afford him an extraordinary opportunity to run to represent Lord Tulla's pocket Irish Loughshane constituency at Westminster. The young Phineas is initially almost overwhelmed by the 'beautiful dream' of running for election for the Liberals:

> When the proposition was first made to him in the smoking-room at the Reform Club by his friend Erle, he was aware that he blushed like a girl, and that he was unable at the moment to express himself plainly,—so great was his astonishment and so great his gratification (*PF*, 49).

Once elected, he proves himself to be adept at playing (English) party politics and is subsequently re-elected in different English constituencies. His political career will not all be smooth, however, and the seeds of his difficulties are visible from the start when the Liberal party man, Barrington Erle, makes it clear to him that he will be expected, above all else, to be 'a safe man' and not 'a cantankerous, red-hot semi-Fenian . . . with views of his own about tenant-right and the Irish Church' (*PF*, 50). Erle's confident assertion that Finn's opinions will merge with those of his party will soon be tested.

Side by side with this public career, Finn's private life develops through a series of romances with Lady Laura Brentford (later Kennedy), daughter of the Earl of Brentford, Liberal cabinet minister and one of his early political supporters; with orphan and heiress Lady Violet Effingham, who later marries Lord Chiltern, and with the fashionable, rich, and exotic Madame Max Goesler, who also receives a proposal of marriage from the elderly Duke of Omnium. Phineas genuinely falls for each of these women, despite his distant but lingering relationship with Mary Flood Jones, who patiently waits for him to return and marry her in Ireland. If he is something of an ingenuous rogue in love (the narrator admires his charm and, in *Phineas Redux*, contrasts his success with the plodding romantic clumsiness of Mr Spooner), he is also a winning opportunist in politics. His political career is punctuated with success while his romantic one brings a series of conquests that are inevitably followed by disappointments. These disappointments, coupled with his political accomplishments, combine to play an important role in Finn's personal growth, especially in *Phineas Finn*, a work which is essentially a *Bildungsroman*.

The political and the personal merge in the character of Phineas, whom Trollope uses to explore the nature of his nation, England, but herein lies a contradiction: in casting an Irishman at the centre of this very English novel, the writer essentially blurs the traditional demarcations and borders between the two peoples, and shows the extent to which they are interconnected and similar. Trollope later claimed that it had been a mistake to have his hero come from John Bull's other island.

> There was nothing to be gained by the peculiarity, and there was an added difficulty in obtaining a sympathy and affection for a politician belonging to a nationality whose politics are not respected in England (*Auto*, 318).

If it was actually an error it was also volitional. However, in the light of the very different situation in the changing Ireland of the later decades of the nineteenth century, Trollope eventually diluted Phineas's Irishness in *The Prime Minister* and *The Duke's Children*, and insisted on his placement within the upper echelons of the British Liberal Party rather than in the Irish Home Rule Party, which by then attracted almost all the prominent Irish politicians at Westminster. Despite this, the initial gesture of making his protagonist Irish is a vital choice which reveals the author's earlier positive feelings about Ireland and his continued belief in the Union between the two countries at the time he was conceiving *Phineas Finn* and, indeed, *Phineas Redux*. In the very act of attempting to recuperate the figure of an Irish politician before a hostile British reading public, Trollope was striking out a singular position within English letters.

The choice of the hybrid name, 'Phineas Finn', shows Trollope playing with stereotypes and preconceptions. The name Phineas cannot pass unnoticed and provokes animosity in many of the characters he encounters, such as Lady Eustace, who 'always hated the very name of that Phineas' (*PR*, 324). Trollope ensures that his oddly named Irish hero has 'a look of breeding about him which had come to him, no doubt, from the royal Finns of old, which ever served him in great stead.... but he looked as though he might have been anybody,—a royal Finn himself' (*PF*, 172–3).

The name may echo the Hebrew, Phinehas, a High Priest of Israel in the wilderness, or allude to the Phineas of Greek mythology who was a King of Thrace, son of Agenor, with the gift of prophecy. For all his charisma, Phineas's role will be rather more prosaic: at best he will be a member, at times prominent, of the Liberal clique that holds power in Britain. In an Irish context, it is hard not to hear an echo of Fénius Farsaid, sometimes known as Fénius the Ancient, an ancestor of the Milesians and thus of the Irish people. Clearest of all is the echo of Fionn MacCumhaill, a figure more usually connected in the 1860s with the Fenian Brotherhood and the armed struggle for Irish independence. Trollope may also have wished to catch an echo of the word 'Faineant', which derives from the French and describes an idle person with no inclination to work. Trollope uses the term to describe the Duke of Omnium in *Phineas Redux*, and again in *The Prime Minister* to describe Phineas's rather unconvincing efforts at giving increased power to Irish municipalities 'as to make the Home Rulers believe that a certain amount of Home Rule was being conceded to them. It was not a great measure, and poor Phineas himself hardly believed in it. And thus the Duke's ministry came to be called the Faineants' (*PM*, 316). Here a play on Fenian/Faineant is also apparent, even if the Irish Phineas is, ironically, the most active member of this English government.

Giving his industrious Irish character such an ambiguous name was part of Trollope's strategy of interrogating deepening English prejudices about Ireland. Trollope was not alone in seeing the growing need to combat negative opinion about the Irish in the late 1860s. As Charles Lever, writing under his Cornelius O'Dowd hat, put it in 1865:

> Englishmen are so firmly possessed with the idea that everything in Ireland is absurd, anomalous and upside-down that they are ever ready to accept the most ridiculous explanations of whatever occurs there, and hear a policy defended which, if applied to any other portion of the kingdom, they would scout with indignation ... Men are not permitted to talk of India as people talk of Ireland: the references to national peculiarities and the tendencies of race would not be tolerated if applied to the Bengalee.

Lever, still very much a Unionist, went on to complain that the 'leading journal [*The Times*] especially has adopted this line, and the adjective Irish has been acclaimed as a disqualifier to all and everything it can be applied to ... we are treated as such acknowledged admitted inferiors as makes it a very polite piece of condescension of Englishmen to occupy themselves, even in their leisure hours, by admonishing us of our faults', resulting in that 'everlasting depreciation of Ireland which is the stock theme of newspapers.'[1] The English public was particularly disturbed by the political events of the mid- and late 1860s, especially by the protests in the period before the 1867 Second Reform Act, and by the rise of Fenian activity, which caused an increase in anti-Irish sentiment. Trollope was therefore taking a risk in creating Phineas and persisting with him, and he was, in a sense, repaying his debt to the country which had given him so much. He was mostly praised for doing so in Irish notices. The *Dublin Review* (founded in 1836 by Michael Joseph Quinn, Cardinal Wiseman, and Daniel O'Connell, and published in London) reviewed *Phineas Finn* warmly,[2] while the *Irish Times* praised the serialization of the novel in Trollope's *Saint Pauls Magazine*: 'His own story opens well, and he is so completely in his second best element (his best being that of Barchester) when he deals with phases of Irish social life, that "Phineas Finn" is certain to deserve and enjoy popularity.'[3]

Throughout the Palliser series, Trollope challenges English preconceptions about Ireland through reversals, by giving significant English characters Irish or Irish-sounding surnames and, sometimes, stereotypical Irish traits. Thus the Irish surname, Barrington (perhaps an echo of George Barrington, the notorious Irish adventurer and pickpocket famous in England in the late eighteenth century), becomes an English Christian

---

[1] Cornelius O'Dowd [Charles Lever] quoted in Andrew Blake, 'Writing from the Outside In: Charles Lever', in Neil McCaw, ed., *Writing Irishness in Nineteenth-Century British Culture* (Aldershot: Ashgate, 2007), [116–27], 122–3.

[2] John Halperin. *Trollope and Politics. A Study of the Pallisers and Others* (London: Macmillan, 1977), 70.

[3] *Irish Times* (30 September 1867), 2.

name in the case of Barrington Erle. The very English Laura Standish (later Kennedy) bears 'a noteworthy Irish Christian name' as her surname,[4] while her brother Oswald (Lord Chiltern) has traits more usually associated with stage Irish characters and 'with his red hair and blackguardly dare-devilry was much more Hibernian than Phineas.'[5] The English Chiltern, whose portrait may owe a debt to Spencer Compton Cavendish, the then Lord Hartington and later the eighth Duke of Devonshire, functions in both *Phineas Finn* and *Phineas Redux* as a foil to Phineas, given his penchant for wild behaviour, gambling, and racing. The adjective 'savage' is used to describe him, and he is seen as being 'outside the pale of decent society', even if he was born at its heart. Known for his 'towering passion' (*PR*, 124), Chiltern takes part in a duel over Violet Effingham with Phineas, who has already been gifted what he considered should have been his seat in Parliament. Chiltern shoots to kill while Phineas shoots to miss, and this sums up the profound differences between the two characters.

Phineas comes from a relatively well-to-do middle-class Irish back-ground, the son of a successful Catholic country doctor who is married to a Protestant. Dudley Edwards argues that 'mixed marriages between the religions were easier and more common in Trollope's time than in the first half of the twentieth century after the Vatican issued the *Ne Temere* decree (1908).[6] However, Trollope was swimming against the tide in holding up the mixed marriage as something to be wished for in Ireland, even if the Palatine pact continued to obtain, whereby the sons of a Catholic father and a Protestant mother would be Catholic, while the daughters would be Protestant (as is the case in Phineas's family, where he is brought up a Catholic while his five sisters are Protestant). On both sides of the religious divide, there was a fear that mixed marriage would weaken the stock or would result in land passing from one community to the other, as was depicted in *The Kellys and the O'Kellys*, where Simeon Lynch was a Protestant married to a Catholic, and Barry consequently followed his father's religion while Anty followed her mother's. With Anty's marriage to Martin Kelly, her family land passed definitively into Catholic hands. Despite the economic benefits of intermarriage, it met increasing hostility within the Church as the century proceeded (and was also, of course, a source of much fear among the Ascendancy):

> If the church's canon law permitted plenty of scope for the exercise of discretion by local parish priests, as the nineteenth century progressed,

[4] Owen Dudley Edwards, 'Anthony Trollope, Irish Writer', *Nineteenth-Century Fiction*, 38/1 (June 1983), 23.

[5] Shane Leslie, 'Preface' to Anthony Trollope, *Phineas Finn* (Oxford: Oxford University Press, 1973), ix–x.

[6] Edwards, 'Irish Writer', 26.

clerical attitudes hardened, and from roughly mid-century onwards, mixed marriages were a staple item of pastoral denunciation by the prelates and the clergy. The evils of intermarriage were the particular concern of the century's mightiest churchman, Paul Cullen.[7]

Throughout the series, Phineas represents the pro-English, Catholic middle class that Trollope hoped to see emerging in Ireland. A fairly non-committed Catholic, he has the benefit of being the son of an upper-class Protestant mother, while his father's Catholicism 'was not of that bitter kind in which we in England are apt to suppose that all the Irish Roman Catholics indulge' (*PF*, 45). Phineas's father can afford to maintain him at Trinity College Dublin, then as an apprentice lawyer in London, and later again as an unpaid parliamentarian. Yet, by the standards of those sitting in Westminster, Phineas is, as he tells his great sponsor and friend, Lady Laura, 'very poor' (*PF*, 168). He is a gentleman more in manner than in substance. Finn's poverty, at least as much as his Irishness, appears, in this first novel, to compromise his political career; indeed, 'poverty' and 'Irishness' become almost synonymous terms, and both complicate the enterprise of holding down a government position. Given that individual members of Parliament were 'entitled to nothing more than a peg for their hats and a locker',[8] to be independent and vote for one's principles was a privilege in which few could indulge. Even in the early years before he chooses to vote by following his principles rather than his party, Finn vows that he 'would throw up his position, resign his seat... if he found that his independence as a man required him to do so' (*PF*, 634–5). At the same time, he lives the life of a gentleman, thanks to the potentially compromising generosity of his English friends, and perhaps for this reason strives to merit the promotions that come his way.

Finn stands in contrast with his fellow Irish member, Laurence Fitzgibbon, who corresponds to an Irish type in English nineteenth-century fiction as an irresponsible and indebted idler (of noble but poor birth), who cares little about the people he is elected to represent. And yet, he is offered the position of Under-Secretary (for the Colonies) instead of Phineas. When Phineas receives a letter on this subject from Lord Brentford, he thinks his moment has come but 'his great triumph' is immediately checked when he reads that the Prime Minister has 'offered the place

---

[7] Donald Harman Akenson, *Small Differences: Irish Catholics and Irish Protestants, 1815–1922: An International Perspective* (Kingston and Montreal: McGill-Queen's University Press, 1988), 113.

[8] James McConnel, 'The Irish Parliamentary Party in Victorian and Edwardian London', in Peter Gray, ed., *Victoria's Ireland? Irishness and Britishness, 1837–1901* (Dublin: Four Courts Press, 2004), 38.

at the colonies to his old supporter, Mr Laurence Fitzgibbon', while Phineas is to take up Fitzgibbon's unremunerated Irish seat at the Treasury Board (*PF*, 419–20). His disappointment at not being chosen as paid Under-Secretary is compounded by the realization that his industry has been passed over in favour of Fitzgibbon's 'great zeal for his party', and he feels slighted because his rival 'had eaten the bread of idleness, and yet he was promoted'. Within weeks, however, it is clear that Fitzgibbon has no intention of actually doing the work required in his new position; he is relieved of his duties and the path is cleared for Phineas. He immediately distinguishes himself as Under-Secretary by working hard, and is praised by Prime Minister Gresham as 'the first Irishman we've had that has been worth his salt', while Fitzgibbon is seen, in Lord Cantrip's words, as that 'other Irishman . . . a terrible fellow' (*PF*, 516).

Fitzgibbon's political approach is summed up in his declaration that he hates 'all change as a rule' (*PF*, 69). After fifteen years in Parliament he has achieved little, although his friends admit 'that he might have been high up in office long since if he would have taken the trouble to work' (*PF*, 69). He is too cynical to bother, and is more concerned with using politics as a means to personal gain than as an instrument for public change. Early in the novel, he risks jeopardizing Phineas's career by asking him to endorse a loan that neither of them is in a position to repay. This debt will eventually be paid off by his sister, Aspasia, in what is an unusual reversal of gender roles, as both men are rescued from irresponsibility by a financially independent woman (a dynamic that repeats, times over, in other Trollope novels, including *Can You Forgive Her?* and *Framley Parsonage*). This event also underlines the fragility of the foothold that these two Irish representatives have in London, with Phineas, in particular, always dependent on the patronage and advocacy of wealthy women.

While Phineas is an idealized figure, Fitzgibbon is little more than an opportunistic stage-Irishman and as such is a permanent outsider in the House of Commons and within the greater English community. He speaks in a mixture of stage Irish and affected English, both of which combine to underline his falseness and lack of belonging, his being caught between two worlds without fully being part of either of them. He uses both ways of speaking to flatter Phineas into signing a bill for £250 as guarantor with his anglicized 'By George, my dear fellow' (*PF*, 148), before later switching into consciously stage Irish-English syntax with the cleft sentence: 'Bedad, it's my father would be glad to see you' (*PF*, 150).

When, later in the novel, Phineas discusses the issue of his voting against his own government and in favour of an Irish Reform Bill, Trollope again has Fitzgibbon adopt a stage-Irish turn of phrase (with pronunciation and syntax carried over from the Irish): the 'i' instead of 'e'

('niver' for 'never'), and the insertion of 'th' where there should only be a
't', as in 'thrue', 'throubles', and 'thry', as an overcompensation for the
difficulties of Irish-English speakers with the 'th' sound. This is not
Trollope getting his Irish-English wrong; rather, it is Fitzgibbon playing
the Paddy. His deviation from Standard English, his lack of competence in
refined language, sets him apart from his fellow members and contributes
to his unsuitability for office. He is not short of 'a gift of the gab', but lacks
the 'competence in "refined language" [which] . . . was a prerequisite for
political power.'[9] 'A specifically English linguistic standard was also a vital
instrument in creating a normative sense of the English nation, with full
membership accruing to those who could speak and write in the newly
"correct" fashion'.[10] Finn's mastery of the necessary Standard English
forms renders his Irishness almost inaudible, and thus a major obstacle
is removed along his path to a place at the centre of English government.

Finn's linguistic neutrality allows Trollope to imbue him with a strong
sense of belonging within England and the English institutions, while
Fitzgibbon remains an outsider, his alterity underlined by his linguistic
ventriloquism, his shifting from Irish-English to a conspicuously upper-
class Received Pronunciation to Cockney. His many voices are the outward sign of his non-belonging, of his lack of a genuine identity after
fifteen years in Britain. Phineas is cut from a different cloth. Thus the
Dublin Review would write approvingly that he was a good deal better
than the 'not very elevated' average Irish member who got elected to
Parliament, a cut above that 'curious hybrid of lawyer and grazier that
seems to be the favourite type of candidate rising steadily in popular
favour . . . a combination of Smithfield and the Four Courts'.[11] Shortly
after Phineas takes his seat, he notes 'that Irish members of parliament
were generally treated with more indifference than any others' (*PF*, 65),
and this is in line with Whitty's 1853 assertion that '[h]istorically, Parliament had laughed at, rather than with, Irish members', and that the
House was grateful to 'Celtic Gentlemen' for the amusement they provided: '[they] are as silly, as brogue, as useless, as quarrelsome, and as
contemptible as ever they were.'[12] Phineas is well aware of the poor
standing of his fellow Irish members:

[9] Mary Jean Corbett. *Allegories of Union in Irish and English Writing* (Cambridge:
Cambridge University Press, 2000), 42.
[10] John Barrell. *English Literature in History, 1730–80: An Equal, Wide Survey* (New
York: St. Martin's Press, 1983), 127.
[11] *Dublin Review*, 13 (July–October, 1869), 362.
[12] E. M. Whitty, *History of the Session 1852–3: A Parliamentary Retrospect* (London:
1853), 127–8.

to whom no outward respect or sign of honour was ever given by any one; . . . that Irish members of Parliament were generally treated with more indifference than any others. There were O'B—— and O'C—— and O'D——, for whom no one cared a straw, . . . and yet they were genuine members of Parliament. Why should he ever be better than O'B——, or O'C——, or O'D——? And in what way should he begin to be better? He had an idea of the fashion after which it would be his duty to strive that he might excel those gentlemen. . . . He would go to his work honestly and conscientiously, determined to do his duty as best he might (*PF*, 66).

Despite these many negative stereotypes, Trollope could draw on a rich range of Irish politicians who enjoyed successful careers in Britain. Religion apart, Finn corresponds quite closely to Jennifer Ridden's identikit of the Irish Liberals as mainly Protestant but broadly supportive of the extension of full civil and political participation to Catholics, proudly Irish but also enthusiastic participants in Britain, subscribing 'to a broad and flexible notion of imperial Britishness', refusing to accept that Irish and British identities were opposed.[13] The nominally Catholic Finn is probably more than a generic fit, and there is good reason to believe that Trollope had various Irish models in mind when constructing his character and career, including John Sadleir (1813–1856), Chichester Fortescue (1823–1888), John Pope Hennessy, and William Gregory. Sadleir was an Irish financier and politician who first entered the House of Commons in 1847 as an MP for Carlow, and became a leading member of the Independent Irish Party which, after it formed in 1852, held the balance of power in the House of Commons. He held minor office in Lord Aberdeen's coalition government from 1852 to 1854 but was forced to resign when he was found guilty of being involved in a plot to imprison a depositor of the Tipperary Bank because the individual in question had refused to vote for him. He was also known for his disastrous financial affairs, which, among other things, caused the insolvency of the same bank. He committed suicide in 1856. Although Phineas would also resign and would also undergo a trial, his career is very different to that of Sadleir, and the connection seems fragile (the hypothesis that Sadleir is a model for Melmotte, who also commits suicide in Trollope's *The Way We Live Now*, is more plausible).

In all probability Phineas was a composite figure. One early model may have been the Limerick-born Thomas Spring Rice (1790–1866), initially elected to represent Cambridge as a Whig politician, who went on to serve in various governments as joint Secretary to the Treasury from 1830 to

---

[13] Jennifer Ridden, 'Britishness as an imperial and diasporic identity: Irish elite perspectives, c. 1820–1870s', in Gray, *Victoria's Ireland?*, 89.

1834 under Lord Grey, and then as Secretary of State for War and the
Colonies, with a seat in the Cabinet. He later served as Chancellor of
the Exchequer and became Lord Mounteagle in 1839. A strong Unionist
(and a supporter of Catholic emancipation), he went so far as to suggest
that Ireland should be renamed 'West Britain.'[14] In Escott's view,

> As regards good looks, Phineas may have had something in common with
> Colonel King-Harman, whom the novelist occasionally met at the Arts Club,
> but at all other points Trollope's Irish member, by his fine presence, winning
> manners, and his return to St. Stephen's after an interval of absence, suggests
> Sir John Pope Hennessy rather than any other representative of the Emerald
> Isle during the Pre-Household Suffrage portion of the Victorian Age.[15]

Michael Sadleir believed that '[p]hysically Phineas was Joe Parkinson, an
English journalist who married a millionaire's daughter and became a
wealthy director of companies', while 'intellectually and politically he was
John Pope Hennessy, a young Irish politician of brilliant parts who was a
protégé of Disraeli and married the daughter of Sir Hugh Low.'[16] Roy
Foster is a little more circumspect in speculating that Finn's career may
have been suggested by Irish adventurers like William Gregory (for the
precocious political advancement) and Chichester Fortescue (for the grand
marriage). Fortescue (1823–1898) is by a long way the most convincing
prototype for Phineas. A graduate of Oxford, he became MP for Louth in
1847 and served until 1874, when he was created Lord Carlingford. He
was 'spectacular in his social attainments', mostly thanks to his marriage to
the Dowager Countess Waldegrave, but was also a politician to be
reckoned with, serving in the Liberal administrations of Palmerston,
Russell, and Gladstone as Lord of the Treasury, Under-Secretary of
State for the Colonies, Chief Secretary, and President of the Board of
Trade.

He played a key role in drafting the Church of Ireland Disestablishment
Act in 1869 and the Landlord and Tenant Act—the beginning of a new
Land Code in 1870,[17] although he was criticized, in 1865, by John Stuart
Mill for an earlier Land Bill. Mill denounced the policy of clearing away
the small tenants to make room for larger farmers: '"You cannot," he said,

---

[14] Richard Brent, *Liberal Anglican Politics: Whiggery, Religion, and Reform, 1830–1841*
(Oxford: Oxford University Press, 1987), 51.
[15] T. H. S. Escott, *Anthony Trollope. His Work, Associates and Literary Originals* (London: John Lane/The Bodley Head, 1913), 264.
[16] Michael Sadleir, *Trollope: A Commentary* (London: Oxford University Press, 1961),
418.
[17] Pádraig Ó Néill, 'The Fortescues of County Louth', *Journal of the County Louth
Archaeological and Historical Society*, 24/1(1997), 8–9.

"evict a whole nation."[18] His somewhat exotic marriage to the Dowager Countess Waldegrave (born Frances Braham, daughter of the great Jewish tenor John Braham) also carries prototypical elements of Phineas's marriage to Madame Max Goesler in *Phineas Redux*. Although he was much appreciated by figures including Charles Gavan Duffy and George Moore for his work for Ireland, and was on very friendly terms with Protestants and Catholics alike, and with many Catholic clergy, he was criticized at home for accepting the office of Under-Secretary for the Colonies. According to the *Dundalk Democrat* of 9 July 1859:

> Mr Fortescue has deserted his post, betrayed the people and clergy . . . Mr Fortescue despises the priests, the people and the bailiffs who elected him. He has sold his anxiety for reform, religious equality, tenant right and the rights of the people of Louth for £2,000 a year.[19]

Finn too is caught between two cultures and fails to identify completely with either. Several times in the novel, he vacillates between Irishness and Englishness. When Lady Laura calls him, in terms that could be seen as demeaning, an 'impetuous Irish boy', he makes no objections (*PF*, 114). Although he is silver-tongued in his private affairs and able to hold his own at every level of encounter, his initial attempts to find a public voice in Parliament are faltering. At the end of the first session of Parliament, his conservative lawyer friend, Mr Low, congratulates him on not having spoken, and for having been able to restrain his 'hot Irish blood' (*PF*, 151). Phineas, however, is distraught at having failed to make his maiden speech, and likens himself rather melodramatically to his fellow Celt, the clan chieftain Conachar in Sir Walter Scott's 'Fair Maid of Perth'—'how his heart refused to give him blood enough to fight? He had been suckled with the milk of a timid creature, and, though he could die, there was none of the strength of manhood in him. It is about the same thing with me, I take it' (*PF*, 221). Eventually, he does find his voice, only to be attacked by the scurrilous radical newspaper, the *People's Banner*, for doing so:

> During the late debate . . . Mr Finn, Lord Brentford's Irish nominee for his pocket-borough at Loughton, did at last manage to stand on his legs and open his mouth. If we're not mistaken, this is Mr Finn's third session in Parliament, and hitherto he has been unable to articulate three sentences, though he has on more than one occasion made the attempt. For what special merit this young man has been selected for aristocratic patronage we

---

[18] Mill is quoted in J. H. Morgan, *The New Irish Constitution* (London: Hodder and Stoughton, 1912), 179.
[19] Quoted in Ó Néill, 'The Fortescues', 9.

do not know,—but that there must be some merit recognisable by aristocratic eyes, we surmise (*PF*, 386–7).

Phineas suffers because of his inability to find a political voice as an
Irishman somewhat ill at ease in an English Parliament. Always something
of an outsider, he can never be properly independent. Even his very seat in
Parliament is not his own—firstly, it falls into his lap as a favour from Lord
Tulla, and later, when this seat is abolished, he is gifted the English
constituency of Loughton by the Earl of Brentford at the behest of his
daughter Laura. Phineas remains acutely aware of his lack of financial and
political autonomy and of the anomaly of representing a pocket borough.

One of Finn's essential problems is that his Irish persona is at odds with
the identity he assumes in England. On the one hand, he appears to have
no trouble referring to himself and Madame Max Goesler (a German
Jewess!) as 'us Britons' (*PF*, 441), but then, as Ridden has argued, it was
not untypical for an Irish Liberal to claim Britishness while at the same
time renouncing Englishness in favour of Irishness.[20] At the same time,
when Phineas is in Ireland, his sense of his Irish identity and indeed his
double identity returns:

> Now that he was in Ireland, he thought that he did love dear Mary very
> dearly. He felt that he had two identities,—that he was, as it were, two
> separate persons,—and that he could, without any real faithlessness, be very
> much in love with Violet Effingham in his position of man of fashion and
> member of Parliament in England, and also warmly attached to dear little
> Mary Flood Jones as an Irishman of Killaloe (*PF*, 354–5).

Gradually, as the series of novels progresses, this Irish Finn will fade. In the
first novels, however, Finn's Irishness is negatively evoked by those who
do not like him, such as the dowager Lady Baldock, who tells her niece,
Violet Effingham, not to allow herself 'to be talked of with an adventurer,
a young man without a shilling, a person who has come from nobody
knows where in the bogs of Ireland' (*PF*, 417). Mr Bonteen and Mr
Ratler, two of his chief Liberal rivals, also attack him in terms of his
Irishness: 'The fact is, Finn,' said Bonteen, 'you are made of clay too fine
for office. I've always found it has been so with men from your country.
You are the grandest horses in the world to look at out on a prairie, but
you don't like the slavery of harness.' Finn ironically replies: 'And the
sound of a whip over our shoulders sets us kicking;—does it not, Ratler?'
(*PF*, 660). Given that this is the way Bonteen and his ilk talk to their Irish
'equals', it is no wonder that 'Finn carries within himself the divide that

<hr>

[20] See Jennifer Ridden, *Making Good Citizens: National Identity, Religion and Liberalism
among the Irish Elite c.1800–1850* (PhD thesis, University of London, 1998).

makes his own experience of the English nation always vicarious, even when he occupies the center.'[21]

Finn manages to attain a key position in Britain's government and sees no contradiction as an Irishman in assuming the post of Under-Secretary for the Colonies. In reality, many Irish Liberal political figures occupied this position in the mid-nineteenth century, including John Ball, Liberal MP for Carlow, who held the post from 1855 to 1857, his successor, Chichester Fortescue, from 1857 to 1858, and Limerick-born William Monsell (1868–71), who later became the First Baron Emly. Finn works with enthusiasm and competence, pushing along projects such as the 'contemplated railway from Halifax, in Nova Scotia, to the foot of the Rocky Mountains' (*PF*, 502). He sees the Canada Railway Bill 'through the House in a manner which redounded infinitely to his credit' and makes him 'conspicuous among Under-secretaries' (*PF*, 600). His success is built on precarious foundations, however. He must follow the party line and not express himself on Irish issues. As long as he does this, he is listened to with respect. Even at the moment, however, when Phineas takes office, he is already aware of how his independent scruples might clash with 'his duty as a subaltern to vote as he was directed' (*PF*, 423). 'It was only when he said a word to any leaders of his party about other matters,—about Irish Tenant-Right, for instance . . . that he found himself to be snubbed.' This limitation makes him worry about being treated 'like a proxy in Mr Gresham's pocket' (*PF*, 534). Mr Monk, his chief political confidant, tells him this is the price of office and urges patience.

It is the arrival of a Reform Bill for Ireland that places Finn's loyalty at risk. He cannot help being aware of the gross inequalities in his country with regard to Irish tenant rights, and it is precisely because of this issue that he helps to organize Mr Monk's visit to Ireland:

> This trip to Ireland had been proposed in consequence of certain ideas respecting tenant-right which Mr Monk was beginning to adopt, and as to which the minds of politicians were becoming moved. It had been all very well to put down Fenianism, and Ribandmen and Repeal,—and everything that had been put down in Ireland in the way of rebellion for the last seventy-five years. England and Ireland had been apparently joined together by laws of nature so fixed, that even politicians as liberal as was Mr Monk,—liberal as was Mr Turnbull,—could not trust themselves to think that disunion could be for the good of the Irish. They had taught themselves that it certainly could not be good for the English. But if it was incumbent on England to force upon Ireland the maintenance of the Union for her own sake, and for

---

[21] Sara L. Maurer, *The Dispossessed State: Narratives of Ownership in 19th-Century Britain and Ireland* (Baltimore: Johns Hopkins University Press, 2012), 163.

England's sake,—because England could not afford independence established so close against her own ribs,—it was at any rate necessary to
England's character that the bride thus bound in a compulsory wedding
should be endowed with all the best privileges that a wife can enjoy. Let her
at least not be a kept mistress. Let it be bone of my bone and flesh of my
flesh, if we are to live together in the married state. Between husband and
wife a warm word now and then matters but little, if there be a thoroughly
good understanding at bottom (*PF*, 550–1).

The image of the marriage of masculine England (despite the reference to
'her ribs') and feminine Ireland as the dependent spouse in an indissoluble
marriage was an enduring one in Victorian writing, but also one in which
Trollope had a personal investment. Again and again, and usually in
paternalistic terms, he stresses the need for England to treat Ireland better
and to make the union real and not simply a question of force. Carleton,
in *Traits and Stories of the Irish Peasantry* (1843–4), asserted that Ireland,
or the idealized female figure of Hibernia, could not live on her own but
must, as Martine Monacelli put it, 'be uplifted by England through a
gentle matrimonial embrace'.[22] A similar premise lay at the base of many
Irish travel guides, such as *Ireland: Its Scenery and Character* by Anna
Maria and Samuel Carter Hall (1841–3), which expressed 'the belief that
the British Isles were in the process of consummating a marriage that
would lead to mutual prosperity and happiness: "A union, based on
mutual interests is rapidly cementing", they wrote confidently'.[23]

By the time Trollope was writing *Phineas Finn*, such confidence was
flagging, and much of the blame for this was to be laid, he believed, at the
door of the members of the Ascendancy. In *Phineas Finn*, the limits and
excesses of the Anglo-Irish are personified in Lord Tulla, who disrespects
the people within his constituency and his country and believes that the
native Irish are racially incapable of self-rule. For him, the only hope is
direct British colonial rule and he wishes 'they'd disenfranchise the whole
country, and send us a military governor' (*PF*, 56). Even at his most
pessimistic, these were never views shared by Trollope, although he does
favour a strong English hand in the country.

Phineas Finn's positions on Irish tenant rights and on Irish affairs more
generally loosely match Trollope's own. Like the author, Phineas believes
in achieving better administration for Ireland, making the Union work
more effectively, and in repealing the laws governing landlord-tenant
relations. He bridles at the iniquitous situation by which most Irish land

---

[22] Monacelli, Martine, 'England's re-imagining of Ireland in the nineteenth century',
Études irlandaises, 35/1 (2010), 18.
[23] Monacelli, 'England's re-imagining', 18.

occupiers have no guarantees, are tenants-at-will and receive notices to quit yearly or half-yearly, and therefore live under constant threat of eviction. This situation removes any incentive to improve the land and leaves the tenant in a precarious situation where mere survival is an achievement. To the detriment of his own career and contrary to the advice of his mentor, Mr Monk, Phineas makes outspoken comments on these issues at public meetings in Ireland, knowing that he is putting his career at risk: 'I must', he declares, 'take my chance of that. I am not going to tie myself down forever and ever for the sake of being Under-Secretary to the Colonies' (*PF*, 626). The far more established Monk can afford to speak with greater clarity:

> The only difficulty was in this, that the men who were to produce the wealth had no guarantee that it would be theirs when it was created. In England and elsewhere such guarantees were in existence. Might it not be possible to introduce them into Ireland? (*PF*, 628).

Phineas shares these views and takes the radical step of supporting 'a bill advocating tenant right'. This leads him into direct conflict with the government of which he is part. He is attacked by the Chief Whip, Barrington Erle: 'Convictions! There is nothing on earth that I'm so much afraid of in a young member of Parliament as convictions. . . . A fellow with convictions is worst of all' (*PF*, 638). Earlier Erle had been equally blunt when Finn told him that he wanted 'not to support a party, but to do the best I can for the country'. Erle 'turned away in disgust. Such language was to him simply disgusting' (*PF*, 57). Soon the cost of his position is spelled out to him and his immediate superior, Lord Cantrip, advises him that he should not have opinions outside of his professional brief within government.

Phineas sticks to his guns and makes a dignified speech declaring his vote in the House, expressing his pride at having been able to serve, and in being Irish, along with his sorrow that his nationality now bars his way to continuing. He chooses what he terms 'independent action' on behalf of Ireland over loyalty to his government. His choice is somewhat undermined by Trollope's reluctance to explain the Irish tenant-right issue in detail, on the grounds that 'no English reader will desire to know much' (*PF*, 703). The political potency of the issue behind his resignation is diluted as the narrator turns the substance of Phineas's objections into performance.

In the vote which follows the debate, Gresham's government is defeated, but before dissolving the house, the Prime Minister pushes through an alternative, watered-down Irish Reform Bill to cancel various rotten boroughs in Ireland. Despite the 'loud opposition' of 'very many recalcitrant Irish members', the measure is passed and has important ramifications for Finn, who 'voted for the measure which deprived Loughshane forever of its parliamentary honours' (*PF*, 704). Far from being his 'great fall',[24] Finn's resignation is his defining moment in the first novel. In his parliamentary journalism Trollope asks the question: 'How shall you argue with a man that he is bound in conscience to give up the crotchet to which he finds that his conscience directs him?'[25] His study of Finn's motivations seems analogous to the implied response. Phineas shows strength in supporting the fight for Irish tenant rights that would (and, in reality, did, in 1870) give tenants security for improvements they made to their holdings. This is a moment in which Phineas's Irishness is made to matter, but also one in which he is seen to rise to a Victorian ideal of manliness through his show of independence.[26]

This newly acquired autonomy is given further symbolic weight by his decision to return to Ireland after Parliament has been dissolved, and by his rejection of the rich, worldly-wise German heiress, Madame Max Goesler, so that he can marry his poor Irish sweetheart, Mary Flood Jones. The easier decision, if he had wanted to prioritize his career and his material comfort, would have been to settle down with Madame Max, but this would also have meant risking an emasculation of his new-found independence. These events show him to be more than a mere opportunist in love or a gadfly willing to jump to his party's bidding in politics. Rather, he emerges as a man of character by choosing to be loyal to the Ireland he has left behind, although this means being stripped of office.

Beliefs and convictions in political life are rare and, in so far as Finn holds them, he is, for Trollope, who tried and failed to get elected himself, something of a hero, but also something of a self-portrait. Finn is in a sense the politician Trollope himself never became, but he is also his vision of the patriotic Irishman—that is, an Irishman with a sense both of his own identity and of his place within the larger scheme of things—within the unbreakable Union between Britain and Ireland, and within the empire. In somewhat limited and ultimately patronizing terms then, the Phineas of the first novel is Trollope's exemplary, patriotic Catholic, middle-class Irishman, but by the time he reappears in *Phineas Redux*, several years

---

[24] John Sutherland, 'Introduction' to Anthony Trollope, *Phineas Finn, The Irish Member* [1869] (London: Penguin, 1972), 14.

[25] Anthony Trollope, 'Whom Shall We Make Leader of the New House of Commons?', *Saint Pauls Magazine*, 1 (1867–8), 533–4.

[26] According to John Tosh, for the Victorians, the key attribute of manliness was independence and 'Independence could only be acquired at the cost of competitive relations with one's peers.' John Tosh, *A Man's Place: Masculinity and the Middle-Class Home in Victorian England* (New Haven: Yale, 2007), 111.

later, everything that he has achieved in the eyes of his creator and of the reader will be placed under renewed scrutiny.

II. *PHINEAS REDUX*: 'AND NOW HERE HE IS BEGINNING ALL OVER AGAIN' (*PR*, 104)

Phineas Redux was written in 1870–1. It was published in the *Graphic* from July 1873 to January 1874, and in book form in 1873, in the aftermath of Gladstone's disestablishment of the Church of Ireland and Trollope's unsuccessful 1868 run for election in Beverley, an adventure which saw him spend some £400 on his campaign and poll last of four candidates. An investigation carried out by a Royal Commission soon found that there had been widespread corruption and the borough was disenfranchised two years later, but this was poor consolation for Trollope.

The theme of establishment and disestablishment is prominent in *Phineas Redux*, a work which reflects its author's increasing disenchantment with politics. However, just as the issue of conspiracy in *The Kellys and the O'Kellys* was introduced in connection with O'Connell and Repeal, only to be displaced and treated within the domestic plots, here the theme of Church disestablishment seems central at the outset, only to yield to the more vital issue of Phineas's own establishment/disestablishment within the political elite in London. The idea of sundering the marriage of Church and State in Britain (as actually happened with the minority Anglican Church in Ireland) is paralleled by the prospect of several other separations or reconciliations in the novel. At the level of national politics there is the 'compulsory wedding' (*PF*, 551), or the Union between the bride, Ireland, and her English groom; at party level, there is Phineas's connection with the Liberals. He is initially described as 'the blushing bride' by his colleagues, from whom he later separates, but in *Phineas Redux* he lives a complex reconciliation after the period in which he had been 'driven out into the cold' (*PR*, 10). On a domestic level, there are the various marriages which are broken in the novel—those of Phineas and Mary Flood Jones, Kennedy and Laura Standish, and Mr and Mrs Bonteen (all broken by death), as well as the marriage of Emilius and Lizzie Eustace, which is nullified by his bigamy. Two marriages are made—between Phineas and Madame Goesler, and Gerald Maule and Adelaide Palliser—both of which owe as much to convenience and mutual benefit as they do to love.

Much of the novel is concerned with questioning Phineas's belonging/ non-belonging to the establishment, to the closed, self-selective social elite that holds power and authority. Even if the term 'the establishment' came to be used in this sense only in the early twentieth century, what it conveys lies at the heart of everything Phineas tries to do in the two novels. Arriving in London as an outsider, he initially seeks stability; he seeks to belong. His mistake is to seek stability in politics and love before he has a firm financial base. Like many of Trollope's protagonists, he shows excessive ambition by 'beginning at the wrong end' (*PF*, 84), as Mr Low, his tutor, puts it. At the outset, he lacks both a financial base and a sufficient sense of who he is, and is defined more by his roles as politician and man about town than by any deeper sense of his own identity. At the end of *Phineas Finn*, he chooses Ireland and an Irish spouse, but only the first of those choices is convincing. At the close of *Phineas Redux*, on the other hand, having found a firmer individual stability outside his public persona, it is clear that his future will be England and that his marriage to Madame Goesler will ensure a permanent place within the establishment there. If Phineas entered politics, in Emerson's terms, to adhere to 'the party of the future', hoping to change how things worked, and if, as such, he represented the younger Trollope's belief in slow, progressive change, by the end of *Phineas Redux* he belongs more closely to what Emerson called 'the party of the Past', of 'the Establishment'.[27] Again, in this he is a reflection of his increasingly conservative and disillusioned creator, for whom Ireland is increasingly an encumbrance.

But all this is to put the cart before the horse. Following his return to Ireland, Phineas had taken up a dull but well-paid Inspectorship of Poor Houses in Cork, and married Mary Flood Jones. This decision had more to do with the author's need to define his manly character through having him take a number of difficult personal decisions than it had with any sense of Mary as a credible partner for the hero. Sadly for Phineas, necessarily for Trollope, fortuitously for the second novel, we learn at the outset that this marriage has come to a premature end with her death during childbirth. Having made Mary such a one-dimensional, stock Irish character, utterly resolute in her devotion to Finn and inspired in her passive and immature acceptance of him by her Catholicism (she 'swore before a figure of the Virgin that she would be true to Phineas forever and ever, in spite of her mother, in spite of all the world, in spite, should it be necessary, even of himself' (*PF* 182), it is clear that her continued presence would have impeded Phineas's development as he faces a series of public and private choices over the course of the second novel. Thus Trollope wastes little time in eliminating her and clearing the way for Phineas's

---

[27] Ralph Waldo Emerson, *The Early Lectures of Ralph Waldo Emerson, Volume III: 1838–1842*, eds. Robert E. Spiller and Wallace E. Williams (Cambridge: Harvard University Press, 1972), 187.

re-entry into English political life. It is a harsh destiny for this 'little girl about twenty years of age', who was cast, from the outset, as a victim, first of her intended husband's lack of interest, then of her creator's disregard: 'She was one of those girls, so common in Ireland, whom men with tastes that way given, feel inclined to take up and devour on the spur of the moment; and when she liked her lion, she had a look about her which seemed to ask to be devoured' (*PF*, 61). Trollope would later comment on his own embarrassment at 'the awkward and unpleasant necessity' of having to kill this blameless Irish girl who had become an 'encumbrance' (*Auto*, 318). The removal of Mary allows Trollope to seamlessly construct *Phineas Redux* as the second part of one long novel and to keep the focus on Phineas's development over many years. It also leaves the door open for the return of Madame Max.

Left without a wife and caught in a less than exciting sinecure in Ireland, Phineas is happy to accept his fortuitous recall to England to be a candidate in the by-election in Tankerville. His appetite for working hard continues to be appreciated, even by semi-idlers like his compatriot, and constant foil, Laurence Fitzgibbon:

> 'He's the best Irishman we ever got hold of,' said Barrington Erle—'present company always excepted, Laurence.'
>
> 'Bedad, you needn't except me, Barrington. I know what a man's made of, and what a man can do. And I know what he can't do. I'm not bad at the outside skirmishing. I'm worth me salt. I say that with a just reliance on me own powers. But Phinny is a different sort of man. Phinny can stick to a desk from twelve to seven, and wish to come back again after dinner' (*PR*, 10).

Another convenient removal is accomplished over the course of *Phineas Redux*, that of Robert Kennedy, unhappy husband of the equally unhappy Laura, Phineas's first London flame. Laura is so depressed by her marriage to the morose but hugely wealthy Kennedy that she has left him and is living in exile with her father in Dresden. Her sin is to always have been in love with Phineas, but not to have followed her heart when he proposed to her. Now, altogether belatedly, she realizes her great mistake and can see no way out (the divorce option, rather like the Repeal of the Union, is one that Trollope refuses to countenance). Although Phineas is kind to her in her distress, it is clear that he no longer loves her and that he has successfully moved on after she turned down his marriage proposal. While Phineas has 'almost forgotten his love' and realizes that the 'indulgence of a hopeless passion was a folly . . . a weakness showing want of fibre and of muscle in the character', Laura remains mired in misery and cannot

> rid herself of her passion in the course of years, although she felt its existence to be an intolerable burden on her conscience. On which side lay strength of character and on which side weakness? Was he strong or was she? (*PR*, 142).

The plot of the novel suggests that strength and, perhaps more importantly, balance lies on his side, and that his courage will win out in the end,
while Laura will pay for her 'sin' with a lonely life of miserable spinster-
hood and self-pity. But Phineas's final affirmation will not come about
until he has survived several trials. The first is political. Finn's return is far
less smooth than he would have hoped. He loses the election by the
narrowest of margins but, on appeal, it is found that his opponent, the
Conservative, Mr Browborough, bribed voters, and Finn is elected in his
stead. Much to Finn's chagrin, however, Browborough's trial for bribery
results in his acquittal, despite his evident guilt. This takes some of
the gloss off Finn's victory, and is an early signal of the limits of the
justice system, which shies away from punishing a wrong-doer for political
motives.

Phineas's acceptance on his return to London faces other obstacles,
most of which arise from his original 'sin' of having been 'in advance of his
party' (*PR*, 10) and having voted against his government. As a result, he
is vulnerable to Mr Bonteen's disparaging remarks about his political
trustworthiness, which undermine his campaign to return to a minor
position in government. A further complication for Finn comes when
he is attacked in the pages of the *People's Banner* by his old enemy, the
'indefatigable, unscrupulous' journalist, Quintus Slide. Slide now firmly
supports the Conservatives 'with great zeal, and with an assumption of
consistency and infallibility which was charming' (*PR*, 156) and relishes
the thought of bringing Phineas down. He shows him a letter from Robert
Kennedy, which is to be published in his paper and which will expose
Phineas as the cause of his wife's refusal to return to her marital home.
Slide is full of righteous indignation, and seeks to destroy Phineas in the
name of what he calls 'Purity of morals . . . punishment for the guilty;—
defence for the innocent;—support for the weak;—safety for the
oppressed;—and a rod of iron for the oppressors!' (*PR*, 162). Thanks to
Kennedy's letter, his armoury against Phineas is full as he seeks to exploit
the Irishman's complicated romantic and political past and to connect him
publicly with Lady Laura and her wronged husband, Phineas's former
colleague in government. Slide cares little that Kennedy has become
a religious fanatic and is sinking into madness, such is his desire to
target Phineas.

Earlier in the novel, Phineas had travelled, at Kennedy's request, to his
home in Loughlinter, ostensibly to be given a message to take on his behalf
to Laura in Dresden. What transpired in the heated conversation between
the two men was Kennedy's outraged identification of Phineas as an
'adulterer' who led his wife astray. Kennedy asks Phineas to cut all contact
with Laura and physically threatens him with a poker. Phineas would have

been well advised to take Kennedy's threats seriously, but such is his loyalty to Laura that he insists that he will go to Dresden to see her and offers to take a message to her from Kennedy, only to be told:

> 'Then you will be accursed among adulterers,' said the laird of Loughlinter. 'By such a one I will send no message. From the first moment that I saw you I knew you for a child of Apollyon. But the sin was my own. Why did I ask to my house an idolater, one who pretends to believe that a crumb of bread is my God, a Papist, untrue alike to his country and to his Saviour? When she desired it of me I knew that I was wrong to yield. Yes;—it is you who have done it all, you, you, you' (*PR*, 75).

Kennedy has made similar accusations of his wife, and continues to make them in letters to her, the contents of which she shares with Phineas, who seems to be one of the very few people to whom she can turn in her despair:

> I repent my sin in sackcloth and ashes. But I did not leave him after I married him till he had brought against me horrid accusations,—accusations which a woman could not bear, which, if he believed them himself, must have made it impossible for him to live with me. Could any wife live with a husband who declared to her face that he believed that she had a lover? And in this very letter he says that which almost repeats the accusation. He has asked me how I can have dared to receive you, and desires me never either to see you or to wish to see you again. And yet he sent for you to Loughlinter before you came, in order that you might act as a friend between us. How could I possibly return to a man whose power of judgment has so absolutely left him? . . . He now threatens me with publicity. He declares that unless I return to him he will put into some of the papers a statement of the whole case (*PR*, 139–40).

The narrative repeatedly makes it clear that, contrary to what might have been supposed, there has been no physical adultery. But this does not lessen Lady Laura's pain for what she calls her 'continual sin': her abiding, unquenchable, and by now tragically hopeless love for Phineas, a love which has destroyed her and her marriage, and which threatens to bring Phineas down too.

When Phineas manages to get an injunction to block the publication of Kennedy's letter, a 'wailing record of his own desolation', which with 'a marvellous absence of reticence' names 'the names of all persons concerned' (*PR*, 160), he is met with Slide's vows to 'crush' him (*PR*, 193) and Kennedy's resolve to eliminate him. When Phineas attempts to reason, Kennedy turns on him violently and tries to shoot him; Phineas is lucky to escape unscathed. As Lady Glencora tells Madame Goesler, 'Mr Finn is one of those Irish gentlemen who always seem to be under some special protection. The ball went through his whiskers and didn't hurt him' (*PR*, 177–8). Shortly after the shooting incident which Phineas, kindly but naively, does not report to the police, Kennedy is taken back to his home in Loughlinter, where he succumbs to despair, madness, and an early death. Phineas is left with the taint of adultery, which, added to his earlier 'sin' of having voted against his party with regard to the Irish land question, leaves him vulnerable to further attack. He is exposed to further criticism when Lady Laura openly reveals the intensity of her love for him to her brother, Lord Chiltern, and to his wife Violet.

But it will be in the political arena where Finn will be more seriously hindered by his controversial reputation. The fact that for many he becomes 'something of a hero' (*PR*, 223) causes great envy among his colleagues:

> Other ladies besides Madame Goesler were anxious to have the story from the very lips of the hero, and in this way Phineas Finn became a conspicuous man. But Fame begets envy, and there were some who said that the member for Tankerville had injured his prospects with his party (*PR*, 223).

But there is more to Phineas than notoriety. He is a popular man with a personal charisma that most of his colleagues lack. Like the leadership figure described by Max Weber, Finn necessarily comes from outside the system and his rise is unpredictable.[28] His notoriety, however, contains the roots of his second fall when Slide, and a group of liberals led by Bonteen, not only block his return to government, but put his very survival at risk. His relationship with his rival, Mr Bonteen, is particularly bitter. Bonteen is set to become Chancellor of the Exchequer, but Finn considers him an overreacher, even if he has already served as 'a junior Lord, a Vice-President, a Deputy Controller, a Chief Commissioner, and a Joint Secretary' (*PR*, 227). Bonteen is intent on blocking Finn's return to the fold through insinuations about his being as unreliable in politics as he is in love. He also sees this unreliability as being a consequence of Finn's Irishness, telling Barrington Erle: 'I never liked him from the first, and always knew he would not run straight. No Irishman ever does' (*PR*, 224). Ironically, Finn and Bonteen have much in common and the Phineas/Laura/Kennedy triangle is paralleled by a similar one involving Bonteen, Mr Emilius, and Lizzie Eustace. More importantly, the two men share a common self-belief and feeling of moral superiority, and a common overweening ambition. This helps to explain their mutual distrust,

---

[28] Max Weber, 'The Vocation Lectures: Science As a Vocation, Politics As a Vocation', eds., David S. Owen, Tracy B. Strong, and Rodney Livingstone (Indianapolis: Hackett, 2004).

which verges on loathing. Finn is deeply resentful that Bonteen is destined for high office while he, despite all his industry and integrity, will be left to languish on the sidelines of power:

> He had despised almost as soon as he had known Mr Bonteen. . . . He had regarded Mr Bonteen as a useful, dull, unscrupulous politician, well accustomed to Parliament, acquainted with the bye-paths and back doors of official life,—and therefore certain of employment when the Liberals were in power; but there was no one in the party he had thought less likely to be selected for high place. And yet this man was to be made Chancellor of the Exchequer, while he, Phineas Finn, very probably at this man's instance, was to be left out in the cold (*PR*, 247–8).

Despite his disappointment, Finn follows the party line in the vote in which the Liberals oppose Conservative Prime Minister Daubeny's cynical attempt to pass a Reform Bill to disestablish the Church of England, a measure which he has pilfered from the Liberal Party's platform but in which neither Daubeny nor his party believe. Finn and his colleagues oppose the measure because it is little more than a ruse intended to allow Daubeny (a version of Trollope's *bête noire*, Disraeli) to cling on to power. But they must engage in serious rhetorical contortions in order to justify their position. This is especially true for Phineas, who feels that 'as a Roman Catholic, this was a delicate subject', and initially declares himself 'not particularly' (*PR*, 30) in favour of disestablishment. However, as it had represented his best shot at election in Tankerville, Finn had campaigned hotly in favour of disestablishment as 'the sworn foe to all Church endowments' (*PR*, 32). Thus he finds it somewhat difficult to justify his change of heart, even if his colleagues pressure him to toe the party line:

> 'I wonder then that you should have asked me to come forward again after what I did about the Irish land question,' said Phineas.
>
> 'A first fault may be forgiven when the sinner has in other respects been useful. The long and the short of it is that you must vote with us against Daubeny's bill' (*PR*, 144).

All of Finn's friends encourage him to vote with his party, but his sense of alienation in this political world, where opportunism triumphs over principle, is marked. Before outlining his position in the Commons, Phineas wishes he was 'back in Dublin' (*PR*, 255) and feels a sense of futility in even taking part in the debate. His speech is a dignified explanation of his position and a highly effective assault on the government's motives. Once more, in adversity Phineas shows his strength, having come to realize the importance of party loyalty as a means to eventually winning change:

He began by saying that he should not have added to the difficulty of the debate . . . were it not that he had been accused in advance of voting against a measure as to which he had pledged himself at the hustings to do all that he could to further it. No man was more anxious than he, an Irish Roman Catholic, to abolish that which he thought to be the anomaly of a State Church, and he did not in the least doubt that he should now be doing the best in his power with that object in voting against the second reading of the present bill. That such a measure should be carried by the gentlemen opposite, in their own teeth, at the bidding of the right honourable gentleman who led them, he thought to be impossible. Upon this he was hooted at from the other side with many gestures of indignant denial, and was, of course, equally cheered by those around him. Such interruptions are new breath to the nostrils of all orators, and Phineas enjoyed the noise. (*PR*, 258).

Phineas is oversensitive to criticism made of him in the party because of his earlier vote, which had led him to leave office and unnecessarily alludes to 'that former scuttling of the ship,—an accusation as to which had been made against him so injuriously by Mr Bonteen'. He defends his earlier position and notes that he had since 'had the gratification of knowing that he had been so far practical as to have then foreseen the necessity of a measure which had since been passed' (*PR*, 258). He justifies his contrary vote in the belief that a proper measure of disestablishment would soon be introduced and that his Tankerville promises would be fulfilled. Despite the success of his speech and the general consensus that the Conservative Party would lose the vote and relinquish power, Phineas realizes now more than ever that he will be shut out from the future Liberal government: 'nothing occurred then or at the conclusion of the debate to make him think that he had won his way back to Elysium' (*PR*, 257). Even if he finds himself in political exile, Phineas insists that his vote then was non-negotiable:

How easy, thought Phineas, must be the sacrifices of rich men, who can stay their time, and wait in perfect security for their rewards! But for such a one as he, truth to a principle was political annihilation. Two or three years ago he had done what he knew to be a noble thing;—and now, because he had done that noble thing, he was to be regarded as unfit for that very employment for which he was peculiarly fitted (*PR*, 261).

Despite voting, this time round, with his party on the disestablishment issue, Finn will continue to pay for his early show of principle. He also contributes to his own undoing by mishandling his row with Bonteen. This leaves him with a growing sense of resentment at how politics is practised by conjurers like Daubeny, Ratler, and Bonteen. Phineas is also deeply troubled about his long-term financial situation, which will not permit him to remain outside the fold for long. As he tells Madame Max, he is completely dependent on being in office for financial survival. His poverty is partly what fuels his annoyance at seeing the Duke of Omnium fail to put to use the independence afforded him by his great wealth. Phineas far prefers the industry and seriousness of Plantagenet Palliser. Without it ever being clearly stated, it is clear that Phineas believes in usefulness and utilitarianism on the lines set out by influential thinkers of the time such as Smith, Bentham, and Mill, and he reads Palliser's life in these terms even if Madame Max argues against him on this: 'I dare say that Mr Palliser, as Mr Palliser, has been a useful man. But so is a coal-heaver a useful man. The grace and beauty of life will be clean gone when we all become useful men' (*PR*, 215). In the end Phineas will come to learn that usefulness is not enough and it certainly does not guarantee him the life he wishes for.

For many of his colleagues, Finn's Irishness is enough to disqualify him for high office, regardless of how hard he may be willing to work, and it is no consolation to him that his supporters will work to trim Bonteen's sails. The anti-Irish attacks aimed at Phineas come from characters who are negatively drawn, and from the clique most openly opposed to Phineas, which includes Bonteen and his wife, as well as Lord Fawn and Lady Eustace, and consider him 'one of those conceited Irish upstarts that are never good for anything' (*PR*, 324). Not that Lord Fawn's opinions count for much. The son of an Irish peer who was given an English peerage by Lord Melbourne, he is, like Phineas, a young man on the make, in search of a wealthy wife, and has served as 'an Under-Secretary of State, very prudent and very diligent'. He is also, however, as Lizzie Eustace says, 'dull as a blue book, and possessed of little beyond his peerage to recommend him' (*Eustace Diamonds*, 82).

It is, however, Bonteen rather than Fawn who will cause Finn's undoing when their rivalry spirals out of control, reaching its climax in a verbal bust up which takes place in full public view at the Universe club. Both men leave the club, more or less at the same time, but separately, to walk home. Bonteen never reaches home, however, because he is bludgeoned to death on the way by a man, supposedly similar to Finn, wearing a grey coat. As it turns out, Finn was not Bonteen's only enemy. He had also fallen foul of Mr Emilius because of his attempts to prove that Emilius's marriage to the wealthy Lizzie Eustace was bigamous and therefore void. Mr Emilius is arrested and accused, but manages, through a fraudulent alibi, to be released, leaving Finn as the only suspect. He is charged with murder as all the circumstantial evidence points against him. Thankfully, Finn can count on the support of many influential friends, including

Mr Low, Lord Chiltern, and Lady Chiltern, all of whom visit him, as well as the Duchess of Omnium, Madame Goesler, and Lady Laura Kennedy who sustain and maintain their friendship with him from afar. The Duchess and Madame Max work hard to convince his lawyers of his undoubted innocence, outraged at the idea that he 'is to be hung because Lord Fawn says that he saw a man running along the street in a grey coat' (*PR*, 388). He is also grateful for the encouragement that comes from his Irish family—two of his sisters coming to London to be with him: 'They were sure that he was innocent, as was every one, they said, throughout the length and breadth of Ireland (*PR*, 393).

Despite such support, Phineas is hurt that the general public as well as many of his colleagues and friends assume that he is guilty: 'certainly four-fifths of the members had made up their minds that Phineas Finn was the murderer' (*PR*, 355). Even his mentor Mr Monk has doubts:

> Mr Monk, as Phineas himself well knew, had doubted. . . . He had visited Phineas in prison, and Phineas had accused him of doubting. 'You need not answer me,' the unhappy man had said, 'but do not come unless you are able to tell me from your heart that you are sure of my innocence. There is no person living who could comfort me by such assurance as you could do.' Mr Monk had thought about it very much, but he had not repeated his visit (*PR*, 435).

On being told by Mr Low that he must show himself now 'to be a man', Phineas responds by voicing his terror that he will be executed. When Mr Low exclaims 'May God, in His mercy, forbid', Phineas insists that he does not want mercy but justice: 'No;—not in His mercy; in His justice. There can be no need for mercy here,—not even from Heaven.' (*PR*, 394–5). His attorney, Mr Wickerby, and his barrister, Mr Chaffanbrass, like Mr Low, doubt his innocence. Chaffanbrass, this 'most experienced practitioner' who 'rescued more culprits from the fangs of the law' than any of his rivals (*PR*, 408), believes, initially at least, that Phineas is guilty, and will endeavour not so much to prove his innocence as to create doubts in the jury:

> 'But I don't want to hear his own story. What good will his own story do me? He'll tell me either one of two things. He'll swear he didn't murder the man——'
>
> 'That's what he'll say.'
>
> 'Which can have no effect upon me one way or the other; or else he'll say that he did,—which would cripple me altogether' (*PR*, 427–8).

While Phineas's legal representatives show little interest in 'the truth' or 'his own story', this is precisely the terrain that captivates Trollope. Once again in this novel, justice is at centre stage. Once again, as in *The Macdermots*, there is an Irishman in the dock for murder and the system will be sorely stretched in its attempts to render him justice. Trollope does not hold the reader in suspense about his hero's innocence, even if he backs away from exposing the reader directly to Phineas's diary, in which he 'never tired of expatiating on the terrible injustice of his position' (*PR*, 429), and instead gives summary accounts of his dark thoughts:

> He assured himself from hour to hour that it was not death he feared,—not even death from the hangman's hand. It was the condemnation of those who had known him that was so terrible to him; the feeling that they with whom he had aspired to work and live, the leading men and women of his day, Ministers of the Government and their wives, statesmen and their daughters, peers and members of the House in which he himself had sat;—that these should think that, after all, he had been a base adventurer unworthy of their society! That was the sorrow that broke him down, and drew him to confess that his whole life had been a failure (*PR*, 429).

Phineas demands of his barrister that there be 'No subterfuges, no escaping by a side wind, no advantage taken of little forms, no objection taken to this and that as though delay would avail us anything', but they have very divergent ideas on how the defence should be conducted. When Chaffanbrass asserts that 'Character will go a great way', Phineas answers that it 'should go for nothing. Though no one would speak a word for me, still am I innocent' (*PR*, 431). The barrister doubts the truth will ever be known and argues that 'a verdict of acquittal from the jury is the one object that we must have before us.' Still not convinced, Phineas retorts: 'The one object that I shall have before me is the verdict of the public.... I am treated with so much injustice in being thought a murderer that they can hardly add anything to it by hanging me' (*PR*, 432). Only the author, the readers, and Phineas himself are sure of his innocence:

> The reader need hardly be told that, as regards this great offence, Phineas Finn was as white as snow. The maintenance of any doubt on that matter,— were it even desirable to maintain a doubt,—would be altogether beyond the power of the present writer. The reader has probably perceived, from the first moment of the discovery of the body on the steps at the end of the passage, that Mr Bonteen had been killed by that ingenious gentleman, the Rev. Mr Emilius, who found it to be worth his while to take the step with the view of suppressing his enemy's evidence as to his former marriage (*PR*, 350).

This reiteration of innocence is not clumsy plot construction by Trollope. His interest does not lie in pulling the wool over his readers' eyes, but elsewhere—in exploring the effects on Phineas's character of this trial and in examining the criminal justice system as it deals with this high-profile

Irishman in Britain. What *Phineas Redux* shows is that the instruments of law are at times blunt and ineffective, and they need a personal investment, belief, or commitment, which usually comes from outside the legal system, if something like justice is to be attained.

When the judgment day finally comes, Phineas is collapsing physically under the strain. However, help is at hand: Madame Max has travelled to Bohemia and found convincing evidence that will show that Emilius is the guilty party. Finn is acquitted and the judge apologizes to 'the poor broken wretch' for what has happened, reassuring him that his reputation is intact:

> I need not say that you will leave that dock with no stain on your character. . . . It is, and it has been, a great sorrow to me to see such a one as you subjected to so unmerited an ignominy; but a man educated in the laws of his country, as you have been, and understanding its constitution fundamentally, as you do, will probably have acknowledged that, great as has been the misfortune to you personally, nothing more than a proper attempt has been made to execute justice (*PR*, 475).

The speaker for the jury goes so far as to say that the trial should not have taken place. Although Phineas has been acquitted and has become something of a hero, 'merely because I didn't kill Mr Bonteen', the inadequacies of the judicial systems have been amply exposed. Without the personal intervention of Madame Max, Phineas would have been condemned. Without friends in high places, he would have got even less of a hearing. Trollope stresses the inequalities inherently built into a justice system in which only those who can pay will enjoy a proper defence:

> And it will probably strike you that the length of the trial is proportioned not to the complicity but to the importance, or rather to the public interest, of the case,—so that the trial which has been suggested of a disappointed and bloody-minded ex-Prime Minister would certainly take at least a fortnight, even though the Speaker of the House of Commons and the Lord Chancellor had seen the blow struck, whereas a collier may knock his wife's brains out in the dark and be sent to the gallows with a trial that shall not last three hours. And yet the collier has to be hung,—if found guilty,—and no one thinks that his life is improperly endangered by reckless haste (*PR*, 433).

With his acquittal, the path is opened for Finn to re-establish himself in politics, and for the return of business as usual in the House of Commons, where his arrest had meant—even for the Conservatives—that it was 'out of the question that they should bring in any Church bill this session' (*PR*, 358). While, for his friends, there is huge relief—'Phineas was acquitted, and cakes and ale again became permissible' (*PR*, 491)—for Phineas himself, the attempt to return to normal life is traumatic. His experience has taken a great toll on him and he is left 'doubting his own identity' (*PR*, 478). He initially leads a somewhat ghostly experience, afraid to enter old haunts, to resume old habits, and he tells Monk: 'I feel that I am broken, past any patching up or mending' (*PR*, 483). Chiltern tells him that he is 'weak and womanly' because he has not yet been able 'to return to his usual mode of life' after the trial (*PR*, 483–4), but this signals more Chiltern's lack of sensitivity than any evidence of weakness on Phineas's side. His depth and self-awareness are evident when he says: 'I am womanly . . . I begin to feel it. But I can't alter my nature' (*PR*, 484).

Gradually Finn gets back on his feet and, having resigned his seat, is resoundingly re-elected to Parliament. But his lifelong desire for office has waned and Phineas turns down Gresham's offer of a return to his old position as Under-Secretary for the Colonies:

> That a change had come upon himself was certain, but he did not at all believe that it had sprung from any weakness caused by his sufferings in regard to the murder. He rather believed that he had become stronger than weaker from all that he had endured (*PR*, 548).

He is not willing to sacrifice his newly found independence just for the sake of office. Once again, at this turn in the novel, Laurence Fitzibbon reappears as a *controfigura*, in a vignette which describes the ease with which Fitzgibbon backs down from a publicly assumed commitment made on behalf of the government when challenged to do so by the Chancellor of the Exchequer. Fitzgibbon all too willingly gives way and, 'with all his usual fluency and beautiful Irish brogue', tells the House 'that the money would be absolutely thrown away if expended on a purpose so futile as that proposed' (*PR*, 563). Given that he had made the proposal, his weak backdown puts him in stark contrast with Finn, even if Finn himself did something of a U-turn on Church disestablishment at the start of the novel, but this was with a view to blocking Daubeny, the conjuring Conservative leader who is likened to Cagliostro, and to ensuring the introduction of the measure in due time. Fitzgibbon's lack of principle would be unthinkable for Finn, who reveals, in conversation with Madame Max, all his disillusionment—not only with what his Irish colleague has done, but also with politics more in general, with the seemingly unavoidable compromises that erode personal principles, and with the willing conformism of his peers. Having refused his chance of being in government on the grounds that he does not possess the financial independence necessary to allow him to act with dignity, Phineas decides to marry Madame Max. Unlike their possible marriage in *Phineas Finn*, in which the 'frank' and 'handsome' Madame Max held all the cards and was the one proposing, here the risk of emasculation is more contained;

Phineas is controlling his own destiny, and not, for the time being at least, using this marriage as a springboard for political security. Of course he will be guaranteed financial stability, but there is also a sense that Madame Max, always proud of her independence, needs him every bit as much as he needs her.

Thus, in this second novel, Finn's journey towards self-knowledge and individuality continues, and the hero is shown coming to understand and ultimately to fight and save his individuality against challenges from multiple forces, including political enemies, scurrilous journalists, and complacent legal eagles. Far from simply following a straightforward mid-Victorian upwardly mobile career, Phineas spends most of the novel merely trying to survive. His journey towards self-knowledge has been a more profound one than might have been expected at the outset, and causes him to suffer a personal breakdown before a slow and painful rebuilding.

III. PHINEAS REDUCED

Phineas's political reward comes early in the next instalment in the series, *The Prime Minister* (1876), which focuses on the Duke of Omnium as Trollope's exemplary leader and Daubeny, the Conservative leader. Finn is relegated to a position of secondary importance in the work's priorities, even if he continues to be chosen for high government office, mostly thanks to the Duke's wife, Glencora, supporting his cause. As far as she is concerned, no office is too high for this Irishman; she clearly considers him a gentleman deserving of his place in the establishment.

'Mr. Finn is to go to Ireland.'

'Go to Ireland!—How do you mean?'

'It is looked upon as being very great promotion. Indeed I am told that he is considered to be the luckiest man in all the scramble.'

'You don't mean as Chief Secretary?'

'Yes, I do. He certainly couldn't go as Lord Lieutenant.'

'...And so Phineas is to be Secretary for Ireland! Not in the Cabinet?'

'No; – not in the Cabinet. It is not by any means usual that he should be' (*PM*, 70).

The role of Chief Secretary for Ireland is a significant posting for Phineas, even if Trollope cannot resist having a swipe at Glencora's stereotyping of the 'murderous' Irish:

'Poor Phineas! I hope they won't murder him, or anything of that kind. They do murder people, you know, sometimes.'

'He's an Irishman himself.'

'That's just the reason why they should. He must put up with that of course' (*PM*, 70).

Glencora's passing comment was to become all too true some ten years later, when Lord Frederick Cavendish, the newly appointed Chief Secretary for Ireland, and Thomas Henry Burke, the Permanent Under-Secretary, were assassinated in the Phoenix Park, Dublin, in May 1882 by a Fenian group called the 'Invincibles'.

Sending Phineas to Ireland also partly solves the problem for Trollope of what to do with his now somewhat inconvenient Irish hero in the politically fraught 1870s, which saw Fenian activity grow and a rise in agrarian violence, coupled with ever-louder demands for Home Rule. Dispatching Phineas to Ireland meant that Trollope could mostly keep him out of focus. His more than occasional appearances, however, suggest Trollope's enduring interest in Ireland. Not long in his new position, 'our old friend Phineas Finn' soon becomes 'bent on unriddling the Irish sphinx'. The narrator's implication is that this is a doomed venture, but he is keener to discredit the politics of Home Rule and its proponents than he is to dismiss Phineas's faltering efforts. Like Trollope, Finn believes that Home Rule would be bad for Ireland and that the Home Rulers are the first to think this (privately). His chief task in Ireland is to concoct measures designed to keep the growing calls for Home Rule at bay:

> Surely something might be done to prove to his susceptible countrymen that at the present moment no curse could be laid upon them so heavy as that of having to rule themselves apart from England; and he thought that this might be the easier, as he became from day to day more thoroughly convinced that those Home Rulers who were all around him in the House were altogether of the same opinion (*PM*, 92).

Not for the first or last time, Trollope conveys Irish politics and politicians in a dismissive, second-hand manner and neglects to allow an Irish argument in favour of Home Rule to be adequately articulated. The reader must rely on the opinions of Phineas, an 'honest and patriotic' Irishman, but only on Trollope's rather limited terms. Phineas sets about trying to invent

> some remedy for the present ill-boding ferment of the country. . . . He found himself beating about among rocks as to Catholic education and Papal interference, the passage among which might be made clearer to him in Irish atmosphere than in that of Westminster (*PM*, 93).

Having started out as a representative character in *Phineas Finn* and *Phineas Redux*, he becomes, in *The Prime Minister*, a more aspirational figure, even if Trollope does acknowledge that it might have been easier for Phineas to come up with something for Ireland while in Ireland, rather than from Westminster, which somewhat contradicts the novel's blanket refusal of any serious consideration of Home Rule.

Part of Finn's difficulties in Ireland lie in the fact that he is in constant disagreement with the Lord Lieutenant, the Marquis of Tyrone, who 'had in his time been a very strong Conservative' and who finds Finn 'troublesome':

> How should it be otherwise? What can he and I have in sympathy with one another? He has been brought up with all an Orangeman's hatred for a Papist. Now that he is in high office, he can abandon the display of the feeling,—perhaps the feeling itself as regards the country at large. He knows that it doesn't become a Lord Lieutenant to be Orange. But how can he put himself into a boat with me? (*PM*, 103).

On being asked if the government to which he belongs has any 'great measure to pass', Phineas replies that 'they've a great measure that they wish to pass.' He is referring to the Irish desire for Home Rule. His fellow Irish have become 'they', and Finn despairs that 'if you were to poll the people, Home Rule would carry nearly every voter' (*PM*, 104). But Finn would fight against conceding such a measure on the grounds that it would be akin to allowing

> a son to ruin himself because he asked me. But I would endeavour to teach them that they can get nothing by Home Rule,—that their taxes would be heavier, their property less secure, their lives less safe, their general position more debased, and their chances of national success more remote than ever (*PM*, 104).

Finn's distance from his own people is striking, as is his mode of considering them as children incapable of running their affairs. He has essentially adopted a paternalistic attitude of superiority towards the Irish, which contradicts his views in the early novels. At the same time, like Trollope, he still has some belief in the possibility that a growing middle class might step up in Ireland, even if Catholicism is increasingly seen as a hindrance:

> I feel sure that even in Ireland there is a stratum of men, above the working peasants, who would understand, and make those below them understand, the position of the country, if they could only be got to give up fighting about religion. Even now Home Rule is regarded by the multitude as a weapon to be used against Protestantism on behalf of the Pope (*PM*, 104).

The Catholic Finn sees the temporal power of the Church declining in Continental Europe and Ireland seems to be the sole exception to this: 'the power of the Church is going to the wall,—yet in Ireland it is infinitely stronger now than it was fifty, or even twenty years ago' (*PM*, 104–5). The growth of the structure, strength, and influence of the Catholic Church under Cardinal Cullen's guiding hand in the second half of the nineteenth century is well attested, and Phineas's take is not off the mark. Nor is his criticism of the difficulties faced by English Catholics: 'all England does not return one Catholic to the House, while we have Jews in plenty. You have a Jew among your English judges, but at present not a single Roman Catholic' (*PM*, 105). There are many things that Finn would like to change in England and, more immediately, in Ireland, but he wearily concludes that he will probably never

> 'cure anything, or even make any real attempt. My patriotism just goes far enough to make me unhappy, and Lord Tyrone thinks that while Dublin ladies dance at the Castle, and the list of agrarian murders is kept low, the country is admirably managed. I don't quite agree with him;—that's all' (*PM*, 105).

Phineas is part of a weak coalition, capable only of continuing the ordinary administration of the country. Only Phineas has anything close to a reform that he wishes to propose, and both he and the Prime Minister feel the government is at a dead end:

> 'I wish it were broken up,' said the Prime Minister.
>
> Thus it came to pass that the only real measure which the Government had in hand was one by which Phineas Finn hoped so to increase the power of Irish municipalities as to make the Home Rulers believe that a certain amount of Home Rule was being conceded to them. It was not a great measure, and poor Phineas himself hardly believed in it. And thus the Duke's ministry came to be called the Faineants (*PM*, 316).

Following a government crisis brought on by the resignation of the 'old Tory', Sir Orlando Drought, as First Lord of the Admiralty, Phineas is appointed in his place. He is as unenthusiastic about accepting this position as the Prime Minister is about offering it to him. He knows that his chance of effecting any meaningful change in Ireland will evaporate with this new appointment. At the same time, Phineas's stature is growing within the party and he is one of the colleagues with whom the Prime Minister regularly consults in his attempts to keep his fragile government afloat. Palliser's time as Prime Minister is clouded by the Silverbridge election scandal, in which Glencora unwisely encourages Ferdinand Lopez, a shady City adventurer, to run for the Silverbridge seat that was always in the giving of the Duke of Omnium. Convinced he has the Duke's backing, Lopez campaigns against a popular local candidate called Arthur Fletcher, but withdraws when he realizes that he will not be elected and that the Duke does not support him. He then insists that Omnium reimburse him for the considerable expenses he has incurred. Furious with Glencora, the Prime Minister foolishly agrees to pay off Lopez, and a minor scandal ensues when news of this payment is leaked and it is assumed that Palliser has used his wealth to buy the election. Nothing could have been further from his honest intentions. The task of defending the Prime Minister in the House of Commons falls to Finn, now an accomplished debater, and he carries the day with great aplomb.

Phineas's old problems with Quintus Slide reignite in the novel, following his defence of the Prime Minister, and he is singled out for attack. By now, however, Phineas is a lot less thin-skinned and has the strength to elect not to reply, not to take action, and not to sue despite the Prime Minister's insistence that he does. This restraint is admiringly depicted by the narrator and contrasts with the Prime Minister's tetchy responses. Phineas is wise enough to know that raking over old stories can do him little service and is willing to risk demotion and indeed the wrath of the man who has given him high office. He tells the Prime Minister's secretary: 'in this matter others are concerned, and I cannot make my judgment subordinate to his' (*PM*, 537).

By now, Finn is sufficiently independent to be able to say no and will have no problem resigning if this is asked of him. The bottom line is 'that he certainly would bring no action for libel against the *People's Banner* (*PM*, 538). As it turns out, the Prime Minister does not take action against him because he fully understands his value within the government. Towards the end of the novel, when the Prime Minister is isolated politically because of an unpopular appointment as Knight of the Garter, Finn is identified as his most loyal minister by Slide, who claims 'that the only ally the Prime Minister had in his own Cabinet was the Irish adventurer, Mr. Phineas Finn' (*PM*, 565), but in reality Finn by now is his own man and has amply shown when to exercise his personal judgement and when to be loyal.

In the eyes of the narrator, Finn shows many similarities with his chief, none more so than his appetite for steady labour. He plays a key role in drafting legislation with the Prime Minister and Mr Monk, although all three realize their reform of the election franchise—the new County Suffrage Bill—is likely to be doomed: when the Bill comes to Parliament and is attacked by the opposition's Sir Orlando Drought, Phineas is its chief defender. Despite his strenuous efforts, the Duke's government falls and he retires from public office, making way for the return of Mr Gresham, who sets about forming a new Liberal administration. Once again, Finn is chosen for office.

Despite or perhaps because of his political successes, increasingly Phineas reads like a throwback, a product of his author's wishful thinking. Now he is 'a very convenient man', an uncontroversial and well-regarded member of the Whig establishment, having been shaped by his experiences into an almost ideal servant of the party and government. He has shown capacity to absorb change and to be domesticated. Others are not so lucky, or not so needy: Chiltern, for example, is left to sit aloft his elevated title and busy himself with being a master of hounds. Finn's career, on the other hand, takes him to the pinnacle of Liberal power, first as Chief Secretary for Ireland, then as First Lord of the Admiralty, before he finally accepts the sinecure of Chancellor of the Duchy of Lancaster. Yet his success makes Phineas an ever more anomalous Irishman, given that at the time Trollope was writing *The Prime Minister*, most Irish members of Parliament had joined forces in the Home Rule Party, which would eventually decide the balance of power in the House and push Gladstone towards legislating for Irish Home Rule.

Phineas also seems to have lost some of the steel that made him, twice over, capable of saying no to measures regarding Ireland with which he was in disagreement. A one-time proponent of change, he is now reduced to being a conformist establishment figure (even if his growing ambivalence about change and the promise of progress might also be read as more representative of the darkening mood of the later Victorian age). His early casting as an optimistic and even idealistic young politician has given way to his being drawn as a more calculating figure, who realizes he has to work the system and work within the system in order to get things done. For all his upward movement and success, he is, in the latter novels, a less appealing character than he was in his more impetuous younger phase.

Trollope's novels are full of politicians for whom the tactics of parliamentary survival is an end in itself, full of lawyers for whom law and legalities count more than the achievement of justice. These politicians Trollope describes as 'the intriguers, the clever conjurers, to whom politics is simply such a game as is billiards or rackets' (*Auto*, 295). Rather forlornly, in both *The Prime Minister* and *The Duke's Children*, Palliser tries to battle against such politics, expressing the belief that a 'Member of Parliament should feel himself to be the servant of his country,—and like every other servant, he should serve. If this be distasteful to a man he need not go into Parliament. If the harness gall him he need not wear it. But if he takes the trappings, then he should draw the coach' (*Duke's Children*, 103). Finn is, in many ways, Palliser's most loyal lieutenant; he never ceases to work hard—too hard, if Madame Max is to be believed. His commitment to making things better yields him little more than frustration and leads his political fellows to dismiss him, believing, as Erle puts it, that there is 'always a little too much zeal about Finn' (*PM*, 97). With good reason, Madame Max fears that his 'unjustifiable expectations' will lead to 'biting despair, and contempt of others', and doubts that 'he was made for a politician'. Finn, she believes, would do well to learn from the example of Lord Brock, 'the very model of an English statesman', who 'loved his country dearly' but had 'no belief in perpetuating her greatness by any grand improvements'. Instead he

> let things take their way naturally,—with a slight direction hither or thither as things might require. That was his method of ruling. . . . Your man with a thin skin, a vehement ambition, a scrupulous conscience, and a sanguine desire for rapid improvement, is never a happy, and seldom a fortunate politician (*PM*, 97–8).

In *The Duke's Children*, Trollope's final Palliser novel, Phineas is an occasional but positive presence, seen as being particularly active on the Liberal benches in opposition to the negatively cast Sir Timothy Beeswax, Conservative Leader of the House, who has 'no idea as to the necessity or non-necessity of any measure whatever in reference to the well-being of the country' (*Duke's Children*, 135). Although he is overshadowed by his wife in this novel, which privileges the private over the political in its thematic explorations, Phineas stands out, once again, for his industry, intelligence, and loyalty. His Irishness is no longer an issue, even if the Conservatives point to it when speaking of him as a 'bellicose Irishman'. By now, Phineas is older and wiser. In an early draft of the novel, which gave Phineas a more central role, he plays a very significant part in bringing the Duke of Omnium's son, Lord Silverbridge, who is elected for the Conservatives, back into the Liberal fold. A deleted passage from Chapter 45 describes Phineas's crucial role in Silverbridge's eventual defection from the Conservative cause: 'Phineas Finn demolished one after another the juvenile arguments of the young deserter. "He'll come back to us, Duke, before long," said Phineas one morning.'[29] Silverbridge's eventual return mirrors that, decades earlier, of Finn himself.

Having starting out his political life in London as one of 'them', Phineas has come full circle. His Irishness has been diluted to allow him to fit in perfectly with his political peers; to be, in a very concrete sense, one of 'us'. Over the course of the novels, Trollope has come to terms with his own

[29] Quoted in Dinah Birch, 'A note on the manuscript', in Anthony Trollope, *The Duke's Children* (London: Penguin, 1995), 508.

initial rejection by England, his outsider status, and his subsequent feelings for—and debt to—Ireland, which saw him initially create Phineas as a kind of a guilty projection of himself as he made his way towards success in London. After Trollope resettled in England and became an establishment figure there, he gradually came to keep Ireland, for professional and creative reasons, increasingly on the margins and, as a consequence, to deprive his Irish, almost English gentleman Phineas of most of his Irishness and to make him an increasingly minor character. The young man, Phineas, who started out with such promise in the first novel bearing his name, and became a figure of considerable depth and complexity in *Phineas Redux*, deserved a better end.

5

Gentlemen Priests and Rebellious Curates

Trollope's Irish Catholic Clergy

Long before Trollope settled in Ireland, Maynooth College, the country's main Catholic seminary, was looked upon with suspicion and even fear from Britain. The college was founded in 1795 and had grown with extraordinary rapidity, becoming, by 1850, the world's largest seminary. It was partially funded by the government, which provided an annual grant of £9,000, which rose to £26,000 in 1845. Many, especially in Tory circles, opposed State support for Catholicism and felt that Maynooth was a breeding ground for a substantial army of rebellious Irish priests, which should be suppressed rather than encouraged with an annual subvention. Many were particularly alarmed by a renewed zeal in Irish Catholic demands in the 1830s and 1840. In 1835, an article entitled 'The O'Connell Domination', published in the pro-Tory *Blackwood's Edinburgh Magazine*, described the 'disastrous change' in the Irish clergy that had come about with the rise of Maynooth:

> The truth is that a great and most disastrous change in the composition and character of the Romish clergy has taken place, not only since Catholic emancipation was granted, but since the operation of Maynooth College in Ireland itself began to be fully experienced. Never was a more fatal measure to the peace of Ireland than that well meant, but ill-judged step. Before its establishment, the Catholic students were sent to St Omer, Salamanca, or some other foreign seminary; and if they received little practical benefit from the tenets which were there taught, they at least mingled with young persons of all nations, and insensibly contracted a certain portion of liberality from their intercourse with men of many different countries and professions, or shades. Thence the many liberal and enlightened priests, who, in the last twenty years, adorned the Romish priesthood of Ireland. But since the influence of the education of almost all the Catholic clergy at Maynooth, the influence of these counteracting principles of good has been entirely lost.

The young Irish priests, drawn almost exclusively from the ranks of the peasantry, are sent universally to Maynooth, where, instead of enlightened foreign ecclesiastics, or young foreigners of the world, they meet nothing but furious zealots in the teachers, and barbarian bigots in the students themselves.[1]

Maynooth, and the Maynooth grant, were the subject of loud debate, often tinged with anti-Catholic sentiment. In Kenneth Hylson-Smith's words, the 'determination to be faithful to the Protestant Reformation, and thus to oppose Roman Catholicism or anything approximating to it, was a powerful factor in English religious life in the eighteen-thirties and forties.'[2] But it had implications and consequences well beyond the world of 'religious life'. The institutional and popular instances of anti-Catholicism were numerous and Irish Catholicism was sometimes singled out for attack. The success of Daniel O'Connell in the 1828 Clare election and the subsequent winning of Catholic Emancipation had been ill digested by many, while the influence of and faith in Catholicism was often identified as the major cause of Ireland's troubles. The stream of Irish Catholic immigrants into Britain in these decades was seen as a threat, and these new arrivals were often seen as bringing violence and filth. Two important studies into the condition of the Irish in Britain during the 1830s, James Phillips Kay-Shuttleworth's *The Moral and Physical Condition of the Working Classes . . . in Manchester* (1832) and Sir George Cornewall-Lewis's 'Report on the State of the Irish Poor in Great Britain' (1836), connected the presumed depravity and immorality of Irish immigrants with their Catholic beliefs. The influential Whig *Edinburgh Review* was as hostile as its Tory equivalent and claimed that Catholicism contributed 'to the backwardness and barbarism of Ireland. Its debasing superstition, childish ceremonies, and profound submission to the priesthood' would 'prevent Ireland from becoming as free, as powerful, and as rich as the sister kingdom.'[3] But anti-Catholicism was not predominantly directed against Ireland. For many, it was far more important than that. The continued repression of Catholicism ensured progressive, Protestant Britain's very survival and its continued growth. English Victorian greatness was directly to be attributed to the triumph of the Protestant work ethic, to the solid Protestant domestic model, and to the assumption of individual responsibility. Anything that

---

[1] 'The O'Connell Domination', *Blackwood's Edinburgh Magazine*, 37/242 (December 1835), 721.

[2] Kenneth Hylson-Smith, *Evangelicals in the Church of England, 1734–1984* (Edinburgh: T&T Clark International, 1989), 115.

[3] *Edinburgh Review*, 49 (1829), 218.

was seen to pose a threat to the structures built around these values was to be opposed.

In 1845, to cite a couple of examples that are but the tip of the iceberg, the British Reformation Society started a magazine called *British Protestant* and republished Bishop William Gibson's *Preservative against Popery*. The following year, the Evangelical Alliance was formed to defend the faith of the Reformation and opposition to Popery and Puseyism was central to its platform.[4]

English fiction played a key role in opposing what Sir Walter Scott called the 'mean and depriving superstition' that was Popery,[5] contributing a constant stream of dark and sometimes gothic images of evil priests, corrupt and sexually depraved nuns, and conniving Jesuits, all serving to illustrate the underlying evil of Catholicism.[6] Examples abound such as Charlotte Brontë's *Villette* (1853) and Catherine Sinclair's *Beatrice, or the Unknown Relatives* (1852). Trollope's mother, Frances, also contributed to the anti-Catholic (and anti-Tractarian), often gothic genre in works such as *The Abbess* (1833) and *Father Eustace* (1847), which were influenced both by Diderot's *La Religieuse* (1796) and by Maturin's *Melmoth the Wanderer* (1820). Dissatisfied Catholic convert Elizabeth Furlong Shipton Harris chipped in with *From Oxford to Rome* (1847), the subplot of which describes how an Anglican minister abandons his wife and children to become a Roman Catholic priest. Harris's novel presented conversion to Popery as a threat not only to the English Church, but to the English nation itself.[7] In Ireland, from the late 1830s onwards, the fervent evangelical writer, Charlotte Elizabeth Tonna, produced virulently anti-Catholic novels such as *The Rockite*, a polemical answer to Thomas Moore's *Memoirs of Captain Rock* (1824) and his assumption that the causes of Irish violence should be looked for in misgovernment, in the repression of Catholicism, and in the financial exactions of the Church of Ireland. Mass conversion to Protestantism represented the only hope for Tonna.[8] Although far more moderate, even Charles Lever, in *The Daltons* (1852), would create the Abbé D'Esmonde as a paragon of pure

---

[4] Hylson-Smith, *Evangelicals*, 115.

[5] Walter Scott, *The Journal of Sir Walter Scott*, ed. W. E. K. Anderson (Oxford: Clarendon, 1972), 526.

[6] See Susan M. Griffin, *Anti-Catholicism and Nineteenth-Century Fiction* (Cambridge and New York: Cambridge University Press, 2004).

[7] Pierce Connelly, *Domestic Emancipation from Roman Rule in England* (London: T. Hatchard, 1852), 9.

[8] See Francesca Scarpato, *Women Writing Ireland, 1798–1921: il popular novel tra identità nazionale e immaginario religioso nelle autrici cattoliche e protestanti*, unpublished doctoral thesis, University of Bologna, 2012.

evil, a nefarious character embodying an amoral, worldly, and militant Catholicism.

Ireland's stubborn adherence to Catholicism was seen by many as the cause of its troubles. Gavan Duffy recorded Carlyle's influential view that 'Ireland had brought all her misfortunes on herself. She had committed a great sin in refusing and resisting the Reformation. . . . It was a great sin for nations to darken their eyes against light like this, and Ireland, which had persistently done so, was punished accordingly. . . . Ireland refused to believe and must take the consequences', one of which, he believed, was a population preternaturally ignorant and lazy.[9]

It is clear that Trollope, before and during his time in Catholic Ireland, would have been no stranger to popular preconceptions about Catholics and to a large volume of anti-Catholic writing that ranged from pamphlet to fiction, some of which was produced within his own family. He was also aware of a large body of Catholic Irish fiction which had been written in the 1820s, by writers such as Thomas Moore, John and Michael Banim, and Gerald Griffin, whose works reflect a growing confidence that was part of the movement towards Catholic emancipation and which form a kind of positive literary Catholic hinterland for Trollope's own writings on Irish Catholicism.[10]

He was well informed about the opinions regarding the seminary at Maynooth, and of the 1845 decision to provide substantially increased direct government funding. This financial support came at a time when the college was already in the midst of rapid growth, as Caesar Otway noted in 1839:

> It is now celebrated as containing the great Roman Catholic College, which stands fronting you as you drive down the street. The centre building was erected by a butler of the late Duke of Leinster, who, out of his savings, built it as a private mansion; he little thought of all the Latin, and logic, and dogmatic theology it would subsequently contain. This college is daily enlarging itself; and so it should, if meant to supply the immense and rapidly increasing Roman Catholic population of Ireland with pastors.

Otway complained about the ragged nature and the sheer scale of Maynooth, which compared poorly with equivalent institutions in Britain or on the continent, and was 'more like a workhouse than a college':

> Looking on it as a great factory, where strong machinery is applied to the purpose of bending mind, and assuming that it is more notable for its

---

[9] Charles Gavan Duffy, *Conversations with Carlyle* (New York: Scribner, 1892), 223–4.
[10] For more on this strand in Irish fiction see Emer Nolan, *Catholic Emancipations: Irish Fiction from Thomas Moore to James Joyce* (Syracuse: Syracuse University Press, 2007).

discipline than its learning, I say, it is deficient in the air, the unction, the scholastic, grey sobriety that characterizes Oxford and Cambridge in England, or Padua or Salamanca on the continent.[11]

An initial lump sum of £30,000 for improvements to Maynooth was committed in 1845, followed by an annual grant of £26,000 in perpetuity. Prime Minister Peel allowed only five days between the first and second readings of the highly controversial bill introducing these measures, presumably in the hope of getting it passed with a minimum of debate (thus causing the resignation of one of his ministers, none other than William Gladstone, who did, however, vote in favour). An Anti-Maynooth Committee was set up, composed of Protestant 'men of firmness, who will not be trifled with'. Its aim was to unite Anglicans and Dissenters in opposition to government aid for the Irish Catholic College. The committee expressed its shock that:

> For the first time since the Reformation, our Representatives have consented to a permanent connexion between the State and Popery, and to the name of England being withdrawn, as that of Geneva had been before withdrawn, from the list of Nations protesting against Rome. If the House of Lords, and the Crown, should adopt the Maynooth Bill, all the great powers of Europe will be in the situation of conniving at Popery. The last great exception to this fearful dereliction of duty among Protestant Nations will have ceased. Let us strain every nerve to avert this consummation![12]

Many Presbyterians came to view the Famine as an act of divine vengeance on both Irish Catholics and English politicians guilty of 'sins' including the endowment of Maynooth College. Some Catholics, on the other hand, believed that 'God was extracting a penance for the Irish people accepting money from the British government to finance Maynooth College.'[13]

Soon, English Protestants would have to tolerate an even more explosive development at home: the Papal Aggression which, in 1850, and for the first time since the reign of Mary Tudor, saw the reinstatement of a full Catholic hierarchy in the country. The appointment of the outspoken Dr Nicholas Wiseman as Cardinal and Catholic Archbishop of Westminster caused dismay, fear, and even violence among English Protestants

---

[11] Caesar Otway, *A Tour in Connaught, Comprising Sketches of Clonmacnoise, Joyce Country and Achill* (Dublin: William Curry, 1839), 15.

[12] A. S. Thelwall, ed., *Proceedings of the Anti-Maynooth Conference of 1845: With an Historical Introduction, and an Appendix* (London: Seeley, Burnside, 1845). http://www.archive.org/stream/a609499200antiuoft/a609499200antiuoft_djvu.txt.

[13] Christine Kinealy, *This Great Calamity: The Irish Famine, 1845–1852* (Dublin: Gill & MacMillan, 1994), 33.

already feeling threatened by the Oxford Movement. *Punch* depicted Wiseman as Guy Fawkes while effigies of the Cardinal were burnt, Catholic churches damaged, and 'No Popery' processions held throughout England. In Ireland, the 1850s also saw the beginnings of what is now termed the 'devotional revolution', and which saw a strengthening of the Catholic Church through a transformation of popular religious practice, increased Mass-going and standardization of religious practices.[14]

As 'a nominal, latitudinarian, tolerant, Church of England adherent, more worldly than otherwise',[15] Trollope was largely contrary to anti-Catholic reaction. Although he was anything but a fan of O'Connell and his campaigns for Repeal, he belatedly supported the quest for Catholic Emancipation, writing, in 1850, that 'the Irish made a good and a successful fight for Catholic emancipation. I would not deny their merits, certainly not that of O'Connell, whose career at the period of the contest shines with a brilliance from which I would not detract, and I cannot enhance'. At the same time he tries to cut O'Connell's role down to size and to rather absurdly deny his and indeed Ireland's centrality in the campaign: 'but in that struggle the cause had many friends in England as in Ireland the battle was fought as warmly at Westminster as in the County Clare' (*Examiner*, 99). Trollope saw little point in responding to Pius IX's re-establishment of the Roman Catholic hierarchy, nor did he support Lord John Russell's Ecclesiastical Titles Act (1851), introduced as a reaction designed to prevent Roman Catholic prelates in England from accepting titles bearing the names of the districts in which they served. He believed 'it was better to leave things be, let the whole thing sink by its own weight'.[16] Nor would he have had much time for literary reactions such as Charles Kingsley's *Westward, Ho!* (1851). Furthermore, there is evidence that Trollope, a High Church Anglican, was interested in and sympathetic to the Oxford Movement and well versed in the issues dividing High Church Anglicans from the evangelical brothers (most brilliantly satirized in the tensions between Archdeacon Grantly and Bishop Proudie in the Barsetshire Chronicles). In his positive and sensitive portrayal of Mr Arabin in *Barchester Towers*, Trollope showed that he had a comprehensive understanding of the spiritual draw of the Oxford Movement. In *The Bertrams*, set in the early 1840s, he wrote of the early days of Tractarianism when 'what has since been called Puseyism was in its robust infancy' (*Bertrams*, 13). Presumably, he was among those who had

---

[14] See Emmet Larkin, 'The Devotional Revolution in Ireland, 1850–75', *American Historical Review*, 77 (1972), 625–52.

[15] N. John Hall, *Trollope: A Biography* (Oxford: Oxford University Press, 1991), 118.

[16] Quoted in Hall, *Trollope*, 119.

indeed read the tracts with some care. He also looked with respect at some English Catholic leaders and he valued a letter from Cardinal Henry Edward Manning—Wiseman's successor—among just a handful that he considered worth keeping. He had earlier been deeply impressed upon hearing Newman preach at Oxford in the 1830s and the two kept quite regularly in touch. In the Barchester series, 'The Reverend Francis Arabin, fellow of Lazarus, late professor of poetry at Oxford, and present vicar of St Ewold . . . took up the cudgels on the side of the Tractarians and at Oxford he sat for a while at the feet of the great Newman'. The great convert 'did not carry off Mr Arabin, but the escape which that gentleman had was a very narrow one' (*BT*, 162–5). The irony is aimed not at the Catholic Church, but at those within the Anglican Communion who feared mass conversion. Trollope clearly did not share the general panic that Newman's conversion caused among Tractarians and that many believed would contribute to the revival of Roman Catholicism in England.

In *The Three Clerks*, Trollope makes fun of anti-Catholic sentiment in England at the time. He describes the proposed 'novel' by Charley Tudor, to be titled, on his editor's instructions, 'Sir Anthony Allan-a-dale and the Baron of Ballyporeen', a name suggesting a character from the Robin Hood legend and an unlikely nobleman from the tiny Tipperary town, two rival knights in love with the same beautiful young lady. Tudor is often read as a light-hearted autobiographical portrait of Trollope himself in his hobbledehoy days. The ridiculously improbable plot summary of the proposed novel, commissioned by the *Daily Delight*, and crafted by an aptly named 'Tudor', openly derides anti-Catholic fiction, describing how at the end of a long feud between the two title characters, 'Sir Anthony reforms, leaves off drinking, and takes to going to church every day. He becomes a Puseyite, puts up a memorial window to the Baron, and reads the Tracts. At last he goes over to the Pope, walks about in nasty dirty clothes all full of vermin, and gives over his estate to Cardinal Wiseman' (*Three Clerks*, 193–6).

Elsewhere in his English novels, Trollope shows interest in the Oxford Movement as a possible force for good and enjoys satirizing those alarmed by changes there. In his Irish novels, on the other hand, he goes further by taking an approving view of Catholicism, which he pitches in positive terms against the excesses of evangelical Irish Protestantism. In his depictions of the Irish clergy, Trollope shows empathy with those Irish Catholic clerics educated on the continent—and hence belonging to a slightly higher social class—and is, at the same time, wholly dismissive of the clerical products of Maynooth, even if he remains cautiously supportive of the Maynooth project.

On his journey to Dublin to make an appeal on Thady's behalf at the end of *The Macdermots of Ballycloran* (in a chapter cut from a later edition of the book), Father McGrath passes 'the College of Maynooth', which offers Trollope the opportunity to reflect on the Maynooth question in one of those lengthy explanatory digressions which punctuate his Irish novels: 'In that college is to be implanted the seeds, all the piety which is to retain the vice and animate the virtue of thirty-two counties, and which not only is to do it, but which does it'. He also pokes fun at the 'wrath and sorrow . . . indignation and vexation lately given rise in the minds of the truly orthodox members of the Church of England' on the mere mention of Maynooth. The narrator mocks their objection that 'its students should be fattened by the contributions of Protestants, and that the wealth of the orthodox should be squandered in enabling them to sleep in separate beds' (*Macdermots*, 642–3). This is, of course, ironic, given the hated tithe imposed on the Catholic Irish to maintain the Anglican Church of Ireland. Trollope was a staunch and early supporter of the disestablishment and disendowment of the Church of Ireland, which he considered an unfair tax on the Irish people for a Church that was not theirs (at the same time he had considerable sympathy for individual Anglican priests struggling for survival in parishes with insufficient parishioners to contribute to their upkeep).

In a forthright review of the Rev. Alfred T. Lees's *Facts Respecting the Present State of the Church in Ireland* and of William Maurière Brady's *Remarks on the Irish Church Temporalities*, published in the *Fortnightly Review*,[17] Trollope made clear his belief in the necessity of disendowment, largely sharing Brady's authoritative reading (he had served as chaplain to several successive viceroys, corresponded with Gladstone, and, from 1861, was Vicar of Clonfert, County Cork, before later converting to Catholicism). Trollope shares Brady's view of the established Church as an anachronism, writing of 'the crying injustice of the present arrangement' and 'the monstrous injustice of the State Church as at present established in Ireland' (*Irish Church*, 87, 89).

> An ascendant church, numbering six hundred thousand souls, stands amidst a population of six millions, and is in the receipt of funds intended for the religious teaching of the whole people! Is it possible that under such circumstances the populace of the country should not execrate the church of the minority? (*Irish Church*, 87).

---

[17] Anthony Trollope, 'The Irish Church', *Fortnightly Review* (15 August 1865), reprinted in *Anthony Trollope, Miscellaneous Essays and Reviews*, introd. Michael Y. Mason (New York: Arno Press, 1981), 82–90.

Three years later, in 1868, when Trollope contested the parliamentary election in Beverley, he saw disestablishment and disendowment of the Irish Church as the 'great question' of the coming session, telling his constituents:

> for many years I have been one of those who have denounced the gross injustice of the absurd uselessness of the Irish Church establishment. The Protestant Church, as it now stands established in Ireland means the ascendancy of the rich over the poor, of the great over the little, of the high over the low. It has none of those attributes which should grace a Church. It does not open its bosom to the poor. It lacks charity. It assumes the virtue of the Pharisee. It is hated instead of loved by the people. That the Irish Protestant Church will speedily be disendowed and disestablished no intelligent politician in England or Ireland now doubts.[18]

Trollope's views are well represented, with regard to this issue, by Mr Monk in *Phineas Finn*:

> But, as Mr. Monk well knew, the subject of the Protestant Endowments in Ireland was so difficult that it would require almost more than human wisdom to adjust it. It was one of those matters which almost seemed to require the interposition of some higher power,—the coming of some apparently chance event,—to clear away the evil; as a fire comes, and pestilential alleys are removed; as a famine comes, and men are driven from want and ignorance and dirt to seek new homes and new thoughts across the broad waters; as a war comes, and slavery is banished from the face of the earth (*PF*, 181).

As it turned out, Trollope was overly pessimistic. The Irish Church Act was passed in 1869 and became law in 1871.

Trollope was nothing if not a practical realist, preferring reform to come 'by slow steps', as he puts it in his article on the Irish Church,[19] and given that Catholicism was not going to go away in Ireland and played an important role in attempting to address the problems of the people, he thought it best to guide it to good ends by educating the clergy. As the narrator puts it in *The Macdermots of Ballycloran*:

> we cannot convert these staunch Romanists to Protestantism—that they will adhere to their old tenets and principles, and that they are likely to remain in the errors which they love so well—nay more, it is pretended by many that they are re-converting us—that if any essential movement is being made by either party, that it is the Church of Rome, which is advancing. Priests, therefore, of the Roman persuasion are, it is to be presumed, necessary, and

---

yet it is considered better to have untaught, or poorly taught clergymen among the poor, than men, who, by having their minds opened by the process of a more liberal education, will enter on their duties with abated prejudices, and enlightened feelings (*Macdermots*, 643).

By educating the clergy, Trollope believed, it would be easier to moderate and indeed 'enlighten' their political views, and if that were achieved, the knock-on effects on the country would be considerable:

It is alleged that the priests of the present day are dangerous men—enthusiasts—political fanatics and bigots, if it is so are these faults most likely to be found in an imperfectly, or in a highly educated character? If in the former, surely the more that is done for the priests of the next generation, the less likely are they to be imbued with the crimes which are now attributed to their predecessors (*Macdermots*, 643).

Views such as these would have cut little mustard among Protestants of various hues in England (or, even more so, in Ireland), and would have offended more militant Catholics in Ireland, but Trollope never repented these opinions and made them the basis of his studies of the Irish Catholic clergy in his novels.

Trollope schematically divided the Irish priesthood into two types. Firstly, there is the older, Continentally educated parish priest, who is concerned about his parishioners' well-being and does his all to dampen down their politics; secondly, there is the rebel-rousing, uncouth curate, educated (with little success) at Maynooth College. Trollope's respect for the older priests was considerable, as can be seen from this 1874 letter to Mary Holmes:

The parish priest I knew myself, & loved, & opened my house to him, and fed him when he was fearfully, horribly, hungry, from sheer want,—and he was a gentleman at all points; but I could not go on with him, not because he would say nasty things of my religion which could only be answered by nasty things as to his, which I could not say to any guest, or to any sincere Christian. But he was a man who will certainly go to heaven, if a mortal may presume to say so much of any man (*Letters II*, 321).

The curates, on the other hand, were treated with no such indulgence. In his last novel, *The Landleaguers*, Trollope drew attention to his schematic view of the Irish priesthood as he had found it more than thirty years earlier:

There used to be two distinct sorts of priests; of whom the elder, who had probably been abroad, was the better educated; whereas the younger, who was home-nurtured, had less to say for himself on general topics. He was generally the more zealous in his religious duties, but the elder was the better read in doctrinal theology. As to the political question of the day, they were both apt to be on the list against the Government, though not so with such violence as to make themselves often obnoxious to the laws. It was natural that they should be opposed to the Government, as long as the Protestant Church claimed an ascendency over them. But their feelings and aspirations were based then on their religious opinions (*LL*, 18).

Over time, Trollope suggests, the clergy became more radicalized:

The parish priest is not so frequently opposed to the law, as is his curate. The parish priest is willing that the landlord shall receive his rents, is not at least anxious, that he shall be dispossessed of his land. But the curate has ideas of peasant proprietors; is very hot for Home Rule, is less obedient to the authority of the bishops than he was of yore, and thinks more of the political, and less of the religious state of his country (*LL*, 18–19).

In his novels, the first type is represented by Father John McGrath in *The Macdermots*, Father Bernard M'Carthy in *Castle Richmond*, Father Marty in *An Eye for an Eye*, and Father Giles in *The Landleaguers*, although the prototype for them all is the eponymous priest of his first Irish short story, 'Fr Giles of Ballymoy'. The unkempt curates are represented by Father Cullen in *The Macdermots*, Father Creagh in *Castle Richmond*, and Father Brosnan in *The Landleaguers*. In *The Macdermots*, Father McGrath is portrayed with indulgent sympathy, while his curate, Father Cullen, is depicted with slighting disdain and not given the dignity of a first name. Father McGrath is, at least in part, based on a real Father Gerary, who was the parish priest of Drumsna when Trollope lived in the town, but also has some prototypes in Irish fiction, such as the French-educated Father John in Owenson's *The Wild Irish Girl*, who himself was based on 'the real-life attributes of Father Arthur O'Leary, a controversial Catholic apologist who insisted on his co-religionists' loyalty to the crown.'[20] Trollope may also have drawn on the description of the priest in Maria Edgeworth's glossary to *Castle Rackrent*, which distinguishes between the Continentally educated priests and the Maynooth rebels:

I THOUGHT TO MAKE HIM A PRIEST.—It was customary amongst those of Thady's rank in Ireland, whenever they could get a little money, to send their sons abroad to St. Omer's, or to Spain, to be educated as priests. Now they are educated at Maynooth. The Editor has lately known a young lad, who began by being a post-boy, afterwards turned into a carpenter, then quit his plane and work-bench to study his HUMANITIES, as he said, at the

[20] Claire Connolly, *A Cultural History of the Irish Novel, 1790–1829* (Cambridge: Cambridge University Press, 2012), 146.

college of Maynooth; but after he had gone through his course of Humanities, he determined to be a soldier instead of a priest.[21]

William Parnell's *Maurice and Berghetta, or, the Priest of Rahery* (1819)
also 'shows the influence of both *The Wild Irish Girl* and *Castle Rackrent* in
having the action focalized via an honourable priest character who presides
over the novel's love plot and also serves as narrator',[22] and may have
influenced Trollope. Parnell's work caused the *Quarterly Review* to accuse
its author of apostasy and the *Eclectic Review* to stigmatize Parnell's stance
in speaking 'of Popery as in itself of innocuous or of beneficial tendency'.[23] Parnell's priest-narrator, trained at St Omer, 'returns to his
parish with enlightened and improving views that are not only reflected
in but developed and progressed by his exemplary young ward, Maurice'.
He is an explicit representation of 'the figure of the kind of aristocratic and
anti-revolutionary Catholicism' which Owenson had advanced, some
years earlier, in *The Wild Irish Girl*.[24]

Like Edgeworth's and Parnell's priests, Trollope's Father McGrath was
educated at St Omer and was 'a thorough French scholar' who had also
'officiated as a curé there'. He is 'a man of taste', of 'good family', and well
dressed; in many ways the work's most sensitive and sophisticated character. Living in one of Ireland's poorest parishes, he is 'always in want of
money', and yet is noted for his ability 'to mix in society', for his 'natural
bonhomie, and perpetual good temper' (*Macdermots*, 40–1). His house is
'exteriorly, the prettiest house in his parish, interiorly, it was discomfort
personified', and yet a 'more hospitable man than Father McGrath never
lived even in Connaught'. He allows himself to be extravagant in only two
things: clothes and books. He dresses 'like a gentleman', with hat and
gloves, and cannot resist buying 'books of every sort, from voluminous
editions of St. Chrysostom to Nicholas Nicklebys and Charles O'Malleys;
and consequently he had a great many' (*Macdermots*, 43).

In contrast, Father Cullen is presented with 'lank and yellow features,
much worn dress and dirty' (*Macdermots*, 88), and seems to correspond to
'the vulgar illiterate herd of the Maynooth priests' venomously described by
the expelled Maynooth seminarian Eugene Francis O'Beirne in 1840.[25]

[21] Maria Edgeworth, *Castle Rackrent*, ed. Marilyn Butler (London: Penguin, 1992), 232.

[22] Connolly, *A Cultural History*, 146.

[23] Quoted in Claire Connolly, 'Irish Romanticism, 1800–1830', in Margaret Kelleher
and Philip O'Leary, eds., *The Cambridge History of Irish Literature*, I (Cambridge University
Press, 2006), 2.

[24] Connolly, *A Cultural History*, 147.

[25] Eugene Francis O'Beirne, *A Succinct Account and Accurate Account of the System of
Discipline, Education, and Theology, Adopted and pursued in The Popish College of Maynooth*
(Hereford: W. H. Vale, 1840), 83.

Drawn from a lower social class, he is a narrow-minded and intolerant anti-Protestant, a Repealing priest with, in the narrator's view, too much interest in politics:

> He was educated at Maynooth, was the son of a little farmer in the neighbourhood, was perfectly illiterate,—but chiefly showed his dissimilarity to the parish priest by his dirt and untidiness. He was a violent politician; the Catholic Emancipation had become law, and he therefore had no longer that grievance to complain of; but he still had national grievances, respecting which he zealously declaimed, when he could find a hearer. Repeal of the Union was not, at that time, the common topic, morning and night, at work and at rest, at table and even at the altar, as it afterwards became; but there were, even then, some who maintained that Ireland would never be herself, till the Union was repealed; and among these was Father Cullen (*Macdermots*, 44).

Trollope lays it on a little thick in his determination to discredit Father Cullen and, as would be his wont, always associated Repeal with his most ignorant characters. It is inconceivable that a priest, even a product of Maynooth College, could have been 'perfectly illiterate' in the middle of the nineteenth century. The only redeeming feature of this humourless curate appears to be his earnestness on behalf of 'the ould church as it stood always down from Christ', if such fanaticism can be seen as redeeming:

> He was as zealous for his religion as for his politics; and he could become tolerably intimate with no Protestant, without thinking he was specially called on to convert him. A disciple less likely to make converts than Father Cullen it would be difficult to imagine, seeing that in language he was most violent and ungrammatical—in appearance most uncouth—in argument most unfair. He was impatient if any one spoke but himself. He relied in all such arguments on his power of proving logically that his own church was the true church, and as his education had been logical, he put all his arguments into syllogisms. If you could not answer him in syllogisms, he conceived that you must be, evidently to yourself, in the wrong, and that obstinacy alone prevented you from owning it. Father Cullen's redeeming point was his earnestness,—his reality; he had no humbug about him; whatever was there, was real; he had no possible appreciation for a joke, and he understood no ridicule (*Macdermots*, 44–5).

Father Cullen is treated as a figure of fun, and it is not outside the realms of possibility that in thus naming him, Trollope was having a cut at the ultramontane Cardinal Cullen of Dublin, then the dominant force in the Irish Church. Cardinal Cullen was regularly depicted battling 'with Protestant proselytisers who "perverted" the Catholic people, he sought to restore his church's numerical strength by using every possible enticement to persuade Protestants of privilege to "convert." '[26]

The chief target of Trollope's attack is the priest's politics, which Trollope refuses to take seriously. Occasionally Cullen has a point worth making, such as when he complains about the changing of the parish boundaries, but Trollope trivializes these valid opinions by making Cullen insist too much:

> And bad manners to them Commissioners and people they sent over bothering and altering the people! Couldn't we have our own parishes as we like, and fix them ourselves, but they must be sending English people to give us English parishes, altering the meerings just to be doing something? (*Macdermots*, 89).

More worrying for Trollope is Cullen's hope that the country can be rid of men like Captain Ussher, 'till he and all of the sort is put down intirely in the country; and that'll only be when the country rights herself as she should do' (*Macdermots*, 90). At the same time Trollope stops short of Edgeworth's position of looking fearfully at Maynooth priests as representative of 'the dangerous spirit and tendency of Catholicism' which is fostered behind 'closed doors' and 'concealment',[27] even if, as we have seen, secrecy and 'concealment' is treated as a major theme in *The Macdermots* and the Catholic clergyman in that novel is shown to have a part in it. Father Cullen takes the revelation that Thady and others are planning to kill Keegan very seriously, but Father McGrath essentially pretends not to believe this in order to protect Thady. He believes it is better not to tell so as to save Thady, whom he considers a good man. It is a crucial error. If Father McGrath had acted immediately and more decisively on this information, the tragic events of the novel might have been avoided. Trollope presents the priest's behaviour, on this occasion, in ambivalent terms, but makes it clear that the priest's intentions are good.

Of similar fibre to Father McGrath is Father Marty in *An Eye for an Eye*. He is another priest close to Trollope's own heart, being 'no great politician, and desiring no rebellion against England. Even in the days of O'Connell and repeal, he had been but lukewarm' (*Eye*, 45). In its review of the novel, the *Spectator* enthused that 'the finest picture in the tale...is that of the Irish priest, Father Marty....Nothing truer or stronger in drawing has ever proceeded from Mr. Trollope's pen than

[26] Desmond Bowen, *Paul Cardinal Cullen and the Shaping of Modern Irish Catholicism* (Waterloo, Ontario: Wilfrid Laurier University Press, 1983), 294.

[27] Edgeworth, quoted in Michael Hurst, *Maria Edgeworth and the Public Scene* (Coral Gables: University of Miami Press, 1969), 98.

this vigorous sketch.'[28] Father Marty is a decent, disinterested, 'improving' priest, who does his utmost to look out for his flock, believes his country has been badly treated by British misrule, but also that the solution to its problems are to be found in better administration and through building a stronger union rather than campaigning for Home Rule. Trollope uses Father Marty as an instrument of union—that of Kate with Army Lieutenant Fred Neville—and, by implied extension, of Ireland with England. But of course, as we will see in the final chapter, Neville tragically fails to honour his side of the bargain, making Trollope's constant calls for an English assumption of responsibility little more than aspirational. This does not stop Trollope continuing to hope (at least until the late 1870s) and to cast positively drawn senior Irish priests who can favour reconciliation and be part of an alliance between English temporal powers and Irish spiritual powers for the betterment of the country (what Joyce, among many others, sees as collusion, and stigmatizes in the 'Wandering Rocks' episode of *Ulysses*, in a Dublin symbolically occupied by Father Conmee SJ and the Viceroy). Trollope communicates the aspiration towards this type of alliance through descriptions of Father Marty's hopes, but it is hard to believe that many Irish priests would have shared his position:

> But justice for Ireland in the guise of wealthy English husbands for pretty Irish girls he desired with all his heart. He was true to his own faith, to the backbone, but he entertained no prejudice against a good looking Protestant youth when a fortunate marriage was in question. So little had been given to the Irish in these days that they were bound to take what they could get (*Eye*, 45).

Father Bernard McCarthy in *Castle Richmond* is another of Trollope's virtuous Irish priests, although he is presented in more ambivalent terms. As the parish priest of Drumbarrow he is seen, rather patronizingly, as a worthy and decent man, almost, but not quite, a gentleman, praiseworthy for his 'spruce and glossy' black clothes, his 'quite new' gloves and his 'shiny, bright, ebon appearance . . . that quite did a credit to his side of the church' (*CR*, 200). In this as in many other aspects, he is in contrast with the negatively drawn, 'discreditably shabby' Mr Townsend, the Anglican parson.

> His clothes were all brown, his white neck-tie could hardly have been clean during the last forty-eight hours, and was tied in a knot, which had worked itself nearly round to his ear as he had sat sideways on the car; his boots were ugly and badly brushed, and his hat was very little better than some of those worn by the workmen—so called—at Ballydahan Hill (*CR*, 207).

[28] *Spectator*, 52 (15 February 1879), 210–11.

Mr Townsend is also criticized for taking advantage of the hardship caused by Famine to try to win converts to his Church, and this is something his Catholic counterpart is not willing to forgive:

> What he called the 'souping' system of the Protestant clergyman stank in his nostrils—that system by which, as he stated, the most ignorant of men were to be induced to leave their faith by the hope of soup, or other food (*CR,* 103).

Trollope consistently stigmatizes this practice, commonly engaged in by those Irish Protestants who saw Famine as 'punishment for the prevalence of popery',[29] and took their chance to rescue people from the priests with the result that many 'Irish Catholics were unashamedly pushed into converting to Protestantism in return for bowls of soup.'[30] Much Protestant Famine charity was dependent on the poor converting, so although Trollope sketches the Townsends' activities in a humorous tone, he takes the issue seriously:

> But neither Mr nor Mrs Townsend were content to bestow their charities without some other object than that of relieving material wants by their alms. Many infidels, Mr Townsend argued, had been made believers by the miracle of the loaves and fishes; and therefore it was permissible for him to make use of the same means for drawing over proselytes to the true church. If he could find hungry Papists and convert them into well-fed Protestants by one and the same process, he must be doing a double good, he argued;— could by no possibility be doing an evil (*CR,* 103).

Trollope shows this as a peculiarly Irish practice. When the English parson, Mr Carter, comes to Ireland to help the relief effort during the Famine, he is firmly against souperism, telling his Irish colleagues: ' "There was to be no making of Protestants," he said, "by giving away of soup purchased with his money" ' (*CR,* 418). As late as *The Landleaguers,* Trollope continued to condemn the divisive souping system as practised, in that novel, by the 'charitable' Rev. Joseph Armstrong, who 'passed his time in making rude and unavailing attempts to convert his poorer neighbours'. He holds it to be 'an established fact that a Roman Catholic must necessarily go to the devil' and tries to save souls by carrying 'morsels of meat in his pocket on Friday', in the hope that 'the poor wretches who had flown in the face of their priest by eating the unhallowed morsels, would then have made a first step towards Protestantism' (*LL,* 90).

---

[29] D. A. Kerr, *A Nation of Beggars: Priests, People & Politics in Famine Ireland, 1846–1852* (Oxford: Clarendon Press, 1994), 207.

[30] C. Kinealy and G. MacAtasney, *The Hidden Famine: Hunger, Poverty & Sectarianism in Belfast, 1840–1850* (London: Pluto, 2000).

Trollope's most ungenerous descriptions are saved for Father McCarthy's curate, Father Creagh, who corresponds to his stereotype of the younger, Maynooth-educated priest. Once again, the appearance marks the man. Father Creagh is denoted in condescending, rascist tones, as if he were genetically inferior: 'To tell the truth, Father Columb was not a nice-looking young man. He was red-haired, slightly marked with the small-pox, and had a low forehead and cunning eyes' (*CR*, 207). Father Creagh engages in far too much politics for Trollope's liking, as can be seen during the meeting of the Famine relief committee. At first Creagh attempts to win over the committee with his 'bland', ingratiating smile, but soon, instead of dealing with practical measures, he embarks on a pointless political tangent, 'as he thought, to speak up for the people'. Sounding a little like Joyce's Citizen, he launches into a denunciation of government policy, lamenting the 'eight millions of the finest pisantry on God's earth—' before he is 'cruelly and ruthlessly stopped by his own parish priest' and, we might say, by Trollope himself. It is a weakness rather than a strength of Trollope's Irish work that he cannot bring himself to give fair voice to ideas such as those held by Father Creagh.

The fact that Trollope actually allows Creagh to attend the relief committee is perhaps a positive sign and an optimistic one. In reality, many Catholic priests were excluded from involvement, despite the intro-duction, in 1846, of the Labour Rate Act, which specified that the lieutenant of each county was to make sure that both a Catholic and a Protestant clergyman served on the relief bodies. This was ignored on a widespread basis, with Catholic priests and bishops being refused mem-bership.[31] Trollope, however, would have done better to allow his curate to have his say, and to have him convey the real issues affecting the Irish peasantry he seeks to represent, rather than turn him into a 'fool', to use the Reverend Townsend's term for him (*CR*, 110).

At the same time, Trollope paints a rather idealized picture of the parish priest and the parson, 'men who had hitherto never been in a room together', working hand in hand during the Famine, 'each for the moment' laying aside 'his religious ferocity' (*CR*, 70). Later, while stres-sing that it was not common, he adds: 'I myself have met a priest at a parson's table, and have known more than one parish in which the Protestant and Roman Catholic clergymen lived together on amicable terms' (*CR*, 105). This contrasts with Thackeray's reading of Ireland as 'the most priest-ridden of countries', and his denunciation of Catholic clergymen who 'lord it over their ragged flocks', as do 'Protestant

---

[31] R. Dudley Edwards and T. Desmond Williams, *The Great Famine: Studies in Irish History, 1845–1852* (Dublin: Lilliput, 1994), 151.

preachers, lay and clerical, over their more genteel co-religionists. Bound to inculcate peace and good-will, their whole life is one of enmity and distrust.'[32] Trollope is almost rhapsodic in reiterating his more optimistic view of Protestant–Catholic relations in the seventh letter to the *Examiner*, where differences of religion, 'that frequent source of former quarrels', are said to be much less common, the domain of no more than a minority of colourful eccentrics:

> In the north the fag-end of the wretched fight is still occasionally battled out; and the magistrates of the county Down are vexed, because they dare not hope to repeat the glorious action of Dolly's Brae; in the south a zealous but intemperate parson occasionally runs a-tilt at the altars of Rome, and meets with some discomfiture at the hands of those whom he assails; and in the far west, the Lion of Judah, John of Tuam, still makes himself heard from time to time by the virulence of his anathemas, and dismays those of his own creed rather than his opponents, by his efforts to bring back the animosities of former times. These, however, are exceptions, the more conspicuous from the general good feeling existing on the subject, which a few years since was made the ground for a feud in every parish. Few gentlemen now care to show their loyalty by drinking confusion to wooden shoes and warming pans, and the eccentricities of those who do are becoming interesting from their rarity (*Examiner*, 97).

This runs contrary to much of the hysterical anti-Catholic reaction that Trollope undoubtedly encountered in the country and ridiculed in his fiction. As his narrator puts it in *Castle Richmond*:

> In Ireland stanch Protestantism consists too much in a hatred of Papistry— in that rather than in a hatred of those errors against which we Protestants are supposed to protest. Hence the cross—which should, I presume, be the emblem of salvation to us all—creates a feeling of dismay and often of disgust instead of love and reverence; and the very name of a saint savours in Irish Protestant ears of idolatry, although Irish Protestants on every Sunday profess to believe in a communion of such. These are the feelings rather than the opinions of the most Protestant of Irish Protestants, and it is intelligible that they should have been produced by the close vicinity of Roman Catholic worship in the minds of men who are energetic and excitable, but not always discreet or argumentative (*CR*, 101–2).

Among Trollope's extremist Irish Anglicans, the Reverend Townsend and the Reverend O'Joscelyn, rector of Kilcullen, 'a most ultra and even furious Protestant' in *The Kellys and The O'Kellys* (*Kellys*, 398), stand

---

[32] William Makepeace Thackeray, *The Irish Sketchbook* (New York: Scribner, 1911), 433.

out. Trollope's contempt is evident in the ironic descriptions of O'Joscelyn's Christian principles, which do not extend to his Catholic neighbours (and they anticipate later treatments of Low Church figures such as Obadiah Slope and Mrs Proudie). His sentences, which initially offer a positive generalization, turn back on themselves with a correction or explanation that negates the initial proposition; a narrative ploy, this, that was, even in this early stage in his career, characteristic of Trollope's style:

> He was, by principle, a charitable man to his neighbours; but he hated popery, and he carried the feeling to such a length, that he almost hated Papists. He had not, generally speaking, a bad opinion of human nature; but he would not have considered his life or property safe in the hands of any Roman Catholic (*Kellys*, 398).

In O'Joscelyn's view, the Catholic is even more to be hated than those belonging to non-Christian religions:

> He pitied the ignorance of the heathen, the credulity of the Mahommedan, the desolateness of the Jew, even the infidelity of the atheist; but he execrated, abhorred, and abominated the Church of Rome. '*Anathema Maranatha*; get thee from me, thou child of Satan—go out into utter darkness, thou worker of iniquity—into everlasting lakes of fiery brimstone, thou doer of the devil's work—thou false prophet—thou ravenous wolf!' (*Kellys*, 398).

Trollope contrasts O'Joscelyn with the Rev. Joseph Armstrong, a good and sociable man with a sense of humour who struggles to provide for his large family of 'helpless, uneducated, and improvident' children (*Kellys*, 218) in the tiny and remote Mayo parish of Ballindine. Although Trollope admits that he 'could hardly be called a good clergyman', this is because he does not have the chance to be: 'How could a Protestant rector be a good parish clergyman, with but one old lady and her daughters, for the exercise of his clerical energies and talents?' (*Kellys*, 218). Trollope is forgiving but makes it clear that his clergyman is no saint:

> He often regretted the want of work, and grieved that his profession, as far as he saw and had been instructed, required nothing of him but a short service on every Sunday morning, and the celebration of the Eucharist four times a-year; but such were the facts; and the idleness which this want of work engendered, and the habits which his poverty induced, had given him a character as a clergyman, very different from that which the high feelings and strict principles which animated him at his ordination would have seemed to ensure. He was, in fact, a loose, slovenly man, somewhat too fond of his tumbler of punch; a little lax, perhaps, as to clerical discipline, but very staunch as to doctrine. He possessed no industry or energy of any kind; but he was good-natured and charitable, lived on friendly terms with all his

neighbours, and was intimate with every one that dwelt within ten miles of him, priest and parson, lord and commoner (*Kellys*, 219).

Armstrong finds himself preaching to just a handful of people every Sunday:

> 'We're not very strong down in the West. . . . There are usually two or three in the Kelly's Court pew. The vicarage pew musters pretty well, for Mrs Armstrong and five of the children are always there. Then there are usually two policemen, and the clerk; though, by the bye, he doesn't belong to the parish. I borrowed him from Claremorris' (*Kellys*, 399).

Mr O'Joscelyn reacts to this information with 'horror and astonishment', but Armstrong defends himself and his congregation, which is 'friendly and neighbourly, if not important in point of numbers', and argues that 'if I wanted to fill my church, the Roman Catholics think so well of me, that they'd flock in crowds there if I asked them; and the priest would show them the way—for any special occasion, I mean; if the bishop came to see me, or anything of that kind.' This reflects a situation narrated in W. H. Maxwell's *Wild Sports of the West* (1832), where the Catholic priest, Father Patt Joyce, lends his congregation to his Protestant counterpart, Mr Carson, on the occasion of the visit of Bishop Beresford. This was possible because the two clergymen are 'as thick as inkle-weavers'.[33] Maxwell recounts the deal reached by the two clergymen with typical colour:

> 'I'm ruined,' says he; 'for some bad member has wrote to the bishop, and told him that I have no congregation, because you and I are so intimate, and he's coming down to-morrow, with the dane, to see the state of things. Och, hone!' says he, 'I'm fairly ruined.' 'And is that all that's frettin' ye?' says the priest, 'Arrah, dear Dick' for they called each other be their cristen names, 'is this all? If it's a congregation ye want, ye shall have a decent one to-morrow, and lave that to me; and now we'll take our drink, and not matter the bishop a fig.' . . . that blessed morning, Father Patt whipped mass over before ye had time to bless yourself, and the clanest of the flock was before the bishop in the church, and ready for his holiness.[34]

The prefatory note to the 1910 edition of Maxwell's book notes that after his career in the army, he 'took holy orders, obtaining the living of Ballagh, in Connemara, a place without a congregation, but full of game', which would make Maxwell, even more than his character, Mr Carson, the perfect model for Trollope's Mr Armstrong.

---

[33] William Hamilton Maxwell, *Wild Sports of the West* (Dublin: Talbot Press, 1910), 246.
[34] Maxwell, *Wild Sports*, 248.

Trollope's descriptions of the varying shades of Irish Protestantism are, like his other Irish 'digressions'—on the Famine, the Irish Church, and Irish agrarian agitation, to name but three—elements of Irish reality which he believes cannot be taken for granted and which need to be illustrated even if they cannot always be smoothly inserted into the comfortable folds of a go-ahead narrative. The question of the audience that Trollope hoped to reach is also vital. Just as he could assume a lot from his readership when writing about England for the English, he clearly felt he could assume little when writing about Ireland for the same English audience, whose popular ideas about Ireland were often, in his view, 'somewhat incorrect',[35] hence the digressive but always informative insertions. The empty benches of Mr Armstrong's church are a vivid illustration of the minority position of the Anglican Church in Ireland, and a *de facto* demonstration of why it needs to be disestablished. On the other hand, it should be recalled that the parson is painted as a sensible and good man who plays an important role in the resolution of both plots in the novel. Clearly Trollope believed that clerics of both persuasions could be voices of reason and restraint.

O'Joscelyn would not be Trollope's last overweening evangelical. The Barsetshire Chronicles teem with such figures, led by Mr Slope, who, Dudley Edwards suggests, 'has a formal Irish antecedent in his supposed descent from Steren's Slop: "slop" and "slob" are pleasing terms of abuse in rural Ireland, and the contemptuous "slopeen" is noted by Somerville and Ross'.[36] Similarly, the evangelical bishop, Dr Proudie, also has Irish family connections, being related to 'an Irish baron by his mother's side' (*BT*, 21). In *Castle Richmond*, the elderly, 'woebegone' spinster Aunt Letty Fitzgerald, described as 'not ill-natured' but 'strongly prejudiced' (*CR*, 47, 52), is another voice of extreme 'horror and hatred of popery':

> As she lived in a country in which the Roman Catholic was the religion of all the poorer classes, and of very many persons who were not poor, there was ample scope in which her horror and hatred could work. She was charitable to a fault, and would exercise that charity for the good of Papists as willingly as for the good of Protestants; but in doing so she always remembered the good cause. She always clogged the flannel petticoat with some Protestant teaching, or burdened the little coat and trousers with the pains and penalties of idolatry (*CR*, 53).

She is possibly outflanked by the Rev. Townsend's wife, who believes

---

[35] Anthony Trollope, 'The Irish Beneficed Clergyman', in Anthony Trollope, *Clergymen of the Church of England*, with an introduction by Ruth Roberts (Leicester: Leicester University Press, 1974), 105–6. Hereafter this text is referred to as *CCE*.
[36] Owen Dudley Edwards, 'Anthony Trollope, Irish Writer', *Nineteenth-Century Fiction*, 38/1 (June 1983), 35.

that priest M'Carthy was pitch, pitch itself in its blackest turpitude, and as such could not be touched without defilement. Had not all the Protestant clergymen of Ireland in a body, or, at any rate, all those who were worth anything, who could with truth be called Protestant clergymen, had they not all refused to enter the doors of the National schools because they could not do so without sharing their ministration there with papist priests; with priests of the altar of Baal, as Mrs Townsend called them? (*CR*, 104).

Mrs Townsend is referring to the scheme proposed by the Anglican Archbishop of Dublin, Dr Whately, to introduce non-sectarian National education in Ireland. This is referred to by Lord Cashel in *The Kellys and the O'Kellys* as 'the abominations of the National system' (*Kellys*, 397). Talking to Aunt Letty, Herbert questions Mrs Townsend's hating Catholics 'as a mad dog hates water', pointing out that Father McCarthy was deserving of respect as 'an ordained priest', and ridiculing her as 'the quintessence of absurdity and prejudice' (*CR*, 128). Aunt Letty defends her 'thoroughly Protestant' friend as a woman who 'cannot abide the sorceries of popery' and whose beliefs are the 'substantial, true, and holy doctrines of the Protestant religion, founded on the gospel' (*CR*, 128, 129):

> 'But there are no good qualities in popery,' said Aunt Letty, with her most extreme energy.
>
> 'Are there not?' said Herbert. 'I should have thought that belief in Christ, belief in the Bible, belief in the doctrine of a Saviour's atonement, were good qualities. Even the Mahommedan's religion has some qualities that are good.'
>
> 'I would sooner be a Mahommedan than a Papist,' said Aunt Letty, somewhat thoughtlessly, but very stoutly.
>
> 'You would alter your opinion after the first week in a harem,' said Herbert. And then there was a burst of laughter, in which Aunt Letty herself joined. 'I would sooner go there than go to confession,' she whispered to Mary, as they all walked off to dinner (*CR*, 129).

Possessed by a 'chronic hatred of the Irish Roman Catholic hierarchy', Mrs Townsend sees Trinity College Dublin as a last bastion, and Aunt Letty concurs that it is 'the only place left for good Church of England sacerdotal life' (*CR*, 359) because Oxford has succumbed to the devil and produces 'perverts to the Church of Rome' (*CR*, 106):

> Indeed, at Oxford a man had no chance against the devil. Things were better at Cambridge; though even there there was great danger. Look at A— and Z— ; and she would name two perverts to the Church of Rome, of whom she had learned that they were Cambridge men. But, thank God, Trinity College still stood firm. Her idea was, that if there were left any real

Protestant truth in the Church of England, that Church should look to feed her lambs by the hands of shepherds chosen from that seminary, and from that seminary only (*CR*, 106).

She echoes Mr O'Joscelyn's opinion that Oxford is 'a Jesuitical seminary, devoted to the secret propagation of Romish falsehood' (*Kellys*, 401). In *Miss Mackenzie* (1865), the squinting and presumptuous evangelical, the Rev. Jeremiah Maguire, a product of Trinity College, Dublin, corresponds to the type of parson of whom Mrs Townsend would approve as a fervent anti-Catholic, who believes it 'is such a blessing' to have no 'Papists' in his parish (*Miss Mack*, 136).

Aunt Letty worries that Herbert is 'tainted with the venom of Puseyism' (*CR*, 355) and thus hopes that he will be ordained in Ireland and not Oxford, which is, in Mrs Townsend's words, 'the most dangerous place to which a young man can be sent'. She even claims that she would 'sooner send a young man to Rome than to Oxford. At the one he might be shocked and disgusted; but at the other he is cajoled, and cheated, and ruined' (*CR*, 106). Their worry is representative of concerns in both England and Ireland in the 1840s with the growing influence of the Puseyite movement. This concern deepened in a genuine fear that the trickle of high-profile conversions to Catholicism among the intellectual elite, especially in Oxford (John Henry Newman *in primis*), could turn into a flood. In Chadwick's words: 'By prestige and history Oxford University weighed heavily in the establishment. It nurtured English statesman, guarded orthodoxy, educated future clergyman.'[37] Trollope, whose sister Cecilia became a Puseyite before her death from tuberculosis,[38] clearly enjoyed poking fun at this fear as it was lived in Protestant Ireland:

> Now that means much with some ladies in England; but with most ladies of the Protestant religion in Ireland, it means, one may almost say, the very Father of Mischief himself. In their minds, the pope, with his lady of Babylon, his college of cardinals, and all his community of pinchbeck saints, holds a sort of second head-quarters of his own at Oxford. And there his high priest is supposed to be one wicked infamous Pusey, and his worshippers are wicked infamous Puseyites (*CR*, 45).

Thus Aunt Letty and Mrs Townsend believe that Herbert 'should get himself ordained ... in good, wholesome, Protestant Ireland, where a Church of England clergyman was a clergyman of the Church of England, and not a priest, slipping about in the mud halfway between England and

---

[37] Owen Chadwick, *The Victorian Church*, vol.1, 1966 (London: SCM, 1987), 41.
[38] Hall, *Trollope*, 118.

Rome' (*CR*, 355). The point is made again when Herbert and Aunt Letty are in conversation with the English solicitor, Mr Prendergast. Herbert's tolerance contrasts with Aunt Letty's hysteria:

> Mr. Prendergast was desirous of information; but the statements which were made to him one moment by young Fitzgerald were contradicted in the next by his aunt. He would declare that the better educated of the Roman Catholics were prepared to do their duty by their country, whereas Aunt Letty would consider herself bound both by party feeling and religious duty, to prove that the Roman Catholics were bad in everything.
>
> 'Oh, Herbert, to hear you say so!' she exclaimed at one time, 'it makes me tremble in my shoes. It is dreadful to think that those people should have got such a hold over you.'
>
> 'I really think that the Roman Catholic priests are liberal in their ideas and moral in their conduct.' This was the speech which had made Aunt Letty tremble in her shoes (*CR*, 214).

Mr Prendergast is left, like many an English visitor to Ireland, none the wiser, and, according to the narrator, 'set them both down as "Wild Irish," whom it would be insane to trust, and of whom it was absurd to make inquiries' (*CR*, 214–5).

These scenes can leave little doubt as to Trollope's attitudes to prevalent anti-Catholic views, which he sees as based on unthinking prejudice made all the more dangerous by the fact that they are held by otherwise respected, thinking people (even O'Joscelyn, Trollope acknowledges, is '[a]part from his fanatical enthusiasm...a good man, of pure life, and simple habits' (*Kellys*, 399)). In his essay 'The Irish Beneficed Clergyman', Trollope largely confirms in serious terms what he portrayed with comic effect in the novels, complaining that the Irish Anglican clergyman's activities 'are always at work against enemies and not on behalf of friends', and that he is 'a severe, sombre man' who 'has no doubts' (*CCE*, 109):

> He is preaching every moment of his life, preaching in his gait, preaching in every tone of his voice, preaching in every act that he does, preaching in every turn of his eyes. Find him asleep and you will find him preaching with a long protracted, indignant, low-church Protestant snore, very eloquent as to the scarlet women (*CCE*, 105–6).

It is the Irish Protestant clergyman's misfortune to be 'always in a state of feud, not only against the devil, as should be the case with all of us whether clergymen or laymen, but against the Antichrist on the Seven Hills, against the scarlet woman who goes about devouring, against the Pope who is to him a ravenous old woman as to whom he cannot say whether he is most ravenous or most old-womanish' (*CCE*, 107). No bishop—not the 'liberal Whatelys' or the 'orthodox Trenches'—can have any impact on the vast body of the clergy who remain set in their ways and beliefs. Aunt Letty's words also find an echo in Trollope's essay when he points out that the Anglican priest sees in Catholicism 'only the small points of divergence from his own [beliefs]', making him a much more insidious opponent than the 'Mussulman' or the 'Jew' (*CCE*, 107).

Dismissive of Protestant attempts to 'lead troops of the Roman Catholics of Ireland in triumph to the top of the Tarpeian rock of conversion' (*CCE*, 107), Trollope saw Irish Catholicism as something that could be embraced as an instrument for the better management of the country. And he was not entirely wrong. William O'Brien would later charge that in the latter half of the nineteenth century, the Church had betrayed the nationalist cause 'for certain pieces of government silver' and, as a result, the British had been able to rule the island by 'Canon law instead of martial law.'[39] It is in this spirit that Trollope supports Maynooth, believing that the Catholic Church, if properly encouraged, can contribute to calming the country. In *The Macdermots* the narrator clearly admires Father McGrath, whom Trollope later described as 'as thoroughly good and fine a man as I know how to depict' (*Letters II*, 645). Father John's worries correspond exactly to Trollope's vision of the role of the Catholic priest in Ireland; that is, to serve and encourage his flock, to understand them, and to help keep them out of trouble, and thus render the country more peaceful:

> He had also had a sad morning's work with his curate, his parishioners were in great troubles, the times were very bad on them; many of them were in gaol for illegal distillation; more were engaged in the business, and were determined so to continue in open defiance of the police; many of them were becoming ribbonmen, or, at any rate, were joining secret and illegal societies. Driven from their cabins and little holdings, their crops and cattle taken from them, they were everywhere around desperate with poverty, and discontented equally with their own landlords and the restraints put upon them by government. All this weighed heavily on Father John's mind (*Macdermots*, 91–2).

In his lengthy chapter describing Father McGrath's visit to Dublin, Trollope indulges in substantial digressions about the nature of Irish Catholicism. Although ultimately they slow the pace of the novel, they reveal the author's genuine admiration for the faith of the people that he experienced at first hand. Father McGrath visits Dublin's Pro Cathedral and notes that even if it bears no comparison with the great Continental churches, 'the zeal and faith of the multitude so richly merited

---

[39] William O'Brien, *When We Were Boys* (London: 1890), 168.

such a prize'.[40] What impresses the priest is 'the devout submission with
which the enormous congregation of poor there assembled, attended to
their religious duties, he could not but reflect that what they wanted
in edifices they made up in faith, and that they gained more in sincerity
than they lacked in wealth' (*Macdermots*, 652). Father McGrath's voice in
this passage doubles with that of the author; such a straight appreciation of
Irish Catholic faith was unusual and ran contrary to popular discourses
about Irish Catholic backwardness.

That said, Trollope's view was that this simple faith was somewhat out
of touch with the real world. For this reason, in *North America* he would,
on the one hand, describe Catholicism as being a brake on progress while,
on the other, openly admit his admiration for the child-like faith and
obedience of the people:

> Surely one may declare as a fact that a Roman Catholic population can never
> hold its ground against one that is Protestant. I do not speak of numbers; for
> the Roman Catholics will increase and multiply, and stick by their religion,
> although their religion entails poverty and dependence, as they have done
> and still do in Ireland. But in progress and wealth the Romanists have always
> gone to the wall when the two have been made to compete together. And yet
> I love their religion. There is something beautiful, and almost divine, in the
> faith and obedience of a true son of the Holy Mother. I sometimes fancy that
> I would fain be a Roman Catholic—if I could; as also I would often wish to
> be still a child—if that were possible (*NA*, 48–9).

In *The Macdermots*, Father McGrath compares the obedient Catholicism
in Ireland with the more superficial variety practised in Europe: 'there is
no country where the religion of Rome is so sincerely trusted to, and acted
on as in Ireland'. Its influence has subsided in France, Spain, even in the
Papal States. Rarely in these countries can one find 'men of education
believing in, submitting to, and guided by the religion which they
possess, and allowing that by that only can they regulate their conduct
in this world, and hope to meet salvation in the next'. In Ireland, on the
other hand,

> the people have a real though sincere belief in their creed—whether they act
> according to its tenets or no—whether they are good or bad they no more
> doubt the truth of the doctrines they have learnt than they doubt their own
> existence. I have met no Romanist Irishman who would express the remotest

---

[40] James Joyce, in his 'Ireland at the Bar' article, published in *Il Piccolo della Sera* in
1907, would similarly single out Ireland's devotion to Catholic practice, noting that the
Irish were 'the only Catholic people to whom faith also means the exercise of faith', in
Ellsworth Mason and Richard Ellmann, eds., *The Critical Writings of James Joyce* (New
York: Viking Press, 1959), 198.

doubt as to any portion of the doctrines of the creed of his church—miraculous and difficult to believe as they are and it is this unshaken belief—this firm sincerity of trust which has kept Ireland so faithful to her church, through all the frightful means which have been taken to convert her (*Macdermots*, 653).

Ireland's religious attachment to Catholicism becomes the subject of praise rather than condemnation. Trollope's position, ultimately, was not unlike that of Aubrey de Vere, who dissented from the view that Irish Roman Catholic priests were 'the instigators of Whiteboys', and saw them instead as 'the chief barrier which at present exists between us and anarchy.'[41] Like De Vere, Trollope for the most part respected Irish priests and saw them as a bulwark against any radicalization of their flocks. The Catholicism that Trollope praises is one separated from Irish nationalist politics, which he believes could be channelled as a force if priests were paid by the government as their Protestant colleagues were. However, he grew increasingly worried, as the century wore on, that the more nationalist priests were gaining the upper hand. In *Lord Palmerston* he quotes Palmerston's wish, as expressed in a letter to the ambassador extraordinary to the Papal States, Lord Minto, that the new Pope (Pius IX) would 'exert his authority over the Irish priesthood, to induce them to abstain from meddling in politics' and 'confine themselves to their spiritual duties'. He increasingly shared Palmerston's opinion that 'at present in Ireland, misconduct is the rule, and good conduct the exception in the Catholic priests' (*Palmerston*, 97). Trollope worried about the growing influence of nationalist-leaning Maynooth-trained priests, but laid much of the blame for this on the British government and rather simplistically assumed that the Irish clergy could be brought over (or better bought over) to support the status quo:

> Of course it would be so, human nature being the same with Roman Catholics as with Protestants. Had we paid the priests, as we paid, and still pay, the parsons, out of the funds collected by the Government, the priests would have worked for the Government. To expect that they should do so under other circumstances is to dream of a Utopia (*Palmerston*, 97).

---

[41] Aubrey De Vere, *English Misrule and Irish Misdeed. Four Letters from Ireland, addressed to an English Member of Parliament* (London: John Murray, 1848), 43.

6

Problems of Form

Trollope's Irish Short Stories

Mostly, when we think of Victorian prose fiction, we focus on the novel, usually the hefty three-volume or triple-decker work. Less attention is given to what Brander Matthews, in one of the first cogent discussions of the genre, described, in 1885, as 'the minor art of the Short-story.'[1] In his view, English writers, unlike their American counterparts, failed to understand the formal requisites of the shorter model. Too often, the 'English short story . . . is only a little English Novel, or an incident or episode from an English Novel. . . . Most of the brief tales in the English magazines are not true Short-stories at all . . . they belong to a lower form of the art of fiction, in the department with the amplified anecdote.'[2]

In Trollope's case, his massive output of novels inevitably dwarfs what might otherwise seem a substantial body of more than forty short stories, which are sometimes unfairly dismissed as little more than fillers or novels that he did not have the time to write. Very often Trollope's short stories are the locus of what Bareham calls 'the restless energy with which he tried out new forms and modes for his fiction.'[3] They show the author trying out new styles, exploring marginal and ambiguous themes, characters, and settings, and interrogating those very Victorian values which he so often endorses and embodies.[4] In this he exemplifies Pratt's conception of the short story as a site for formal experimentation, a genre which can be used 'to introduce new (and possibly stigmatized) subject matters.'[5] At times, as Niles has argued, Trollope revels in this genre, which 'resists closure,

---

[1] Brander Matthews, *The Philosophy of the Short-Story* (New York: Peter Smith, 1931), 12–13.

[2] Matthews, *Philosophy of the Short-Story*, 59–60.

[3] Tony Bareham, ed., *Trollope, The Barsetshire Novels: A Casebook* (London: Macmillan, 1983), xvii.

[4] Anthony Trollope, *The Complete Shorter Fiction*, ed. Julian Thompson (New York: Carroll & Graf, 1992). This volume will hereafter be referred to as *CSF*.

[5] Mary Louise Pratt, 'The Short Story. The Long and the Short of It', in Charles E. May, ed., *The New Short Story Theories* (Athens: Ohio University Press, 1994), 104.

mediating a far more complex narrative strategy', and finds the 'margin-alization' of the short story form 'liberating.'[6]

Trollope himself drew attention to the problematics of the nineteenth-century short story in his 1870 collection, *An Editor's Tales*. As the narrator in one of those tales, 'The Panjandrum', learns to his cost, the short story is too often seen not as a literary genre with its own rules, but merely as a short version of a novel. 'The Panjandrum' tells of the ill-fated attempt made by a group of young intellectuals to establish a new journal of the same name in London. Although they decide to adopt a policy not to publish novels, the first-person narrator chooses to write a short story because he feels that his work will qualify for publication and will lighten up an otherwise heavy table of contents. However, his fellow contributors refuse to allow him to read his piece. One of his colleagues, Mr Churchill Smith—a distinctly uncomplimentary version of George Eliot's partner, George Lewes, who is described as 'generally dirty, unshorn, and, as I thought, disagreeable' (*CSF*, 573)—dogmatically declares that 'a novel is not a novel because it is long or short. Such is the matter which we intended to declare that we would not put forth in our magazine' (*CSF*, 597). Thus, for the bickering, self-centred members of the editorial board of this new journal, prose fiction of any kind, be it long or short, is essentially judged to be a form of the novel. Consequently, the narrator's story is not even accepted for consideration. As it turns out, this is only one of many issues to divide the contributors, and the periodical dies before it can be properly born. The story ends in a mood of anticlimactic frustration while the disappointed narrator is left to ponder what might have been.

One of the after-effects of reading this short work is that the reader is also called on to consider the formal problematics of the short story. Fifteen years after this story was first published in 1870 in both *Saint Pauls Magazine* and, in the United States, in *The Galaxy*, Matthews would give belated and, presumably unconscious, backing to Trollope's frus-trated narrator's attempts to assert the essential difference of the short story. In Matthews's words:

> The difference between a Novel and a Short story is a difference of kind,
> A true Short-story is something other and something more than a mere story
> which is short. A true Short-story differs from the Novel chiefly in its
> essential unity of impression. . . . A Short-story deals with a single character,

---

a single event, a single emotion, or the series of emotions called forth by a single situation.[7]

Later in his article, however, Matthews calls into question the abilities of the novelist to write short stories and, to make his point, focuses on Trollope. In Matthews's prescriptive view, the writer of 'Short-stories' is called on for originality and ingenuity, while the novelist can make do with representing 'a cross-section of real life'. Therefore it may be possible for a writer such as Trollope to be a novelist of success while remaining a dismal failure as a short-story writer because of his lack of 'fantasy and compression . . . ingenuity and originality':

> If an example must be given, the name of Anthony Trollope will occur to all. Fantasy was a thing he abhorred, compression he knew not, and originality and ingenuity can be conceded to him only by a strong stretch of the ordinary meaning of the words. Other qualities he had in plenty, but not these. And, not having them, he was not a writer of Short-stories. Judging from his essay on Hawthorne, one may even go so far as to say that Trollope did not know a good Short-story when he saw it.[8]

In this description, Matthews is alluding to Trollope's rather apt description of the contrast between his own work and that of Hawthorne. Trollope's own declared purpose was

> to draw my little pictures as like to life as possible, so that my readers should feel that they were dealing with people whom they might probably have known, but so to do it that the everyday good to be found among them should allure, and the every-day evil repel; and this I have attempted, believing that such ordinary good and ordinary evil would be more powerful in repelling or alluring than great and glowing incidents which, though they might interest, would not come home to the minds of readers. Hawthorne, on the other hand, has dealt with persons and incidents which were often but barely within the bounds of possibility,—which were sometimes altogether without those bounds,—and has determined that his readers should be carried out of their own little mundane ways, and brought into a world of imagination in which their intelligence might be raised, if only for a time, to something higher than the common needs of common life.[9]

Matthews goes on to define the short story with reference to Trollope:

> I have written Short-story with a capital S and a hyphen because I wished to emphasize the distinction between the Short-story and the story which is

[7] Matthews, *Philosophy of the Short-Story*, 15.
[8] Matthews, *Philosophy of the Short-Story*, 24.
[9] Anthony Trollope, 'The Genius of Nathaniel Hawthorne', *The North American Review*, 129/274 (September 1879), 204–5.

merely short. The Short-story is a high and difficult department of fiction. The story which is short can be written by anybody who can write at all; and it may be good, bad, or indifferent, but at its best it is wholly unlike the Short-story. In 'An Editor's Tales' Trollope has given us excellent specimens of the story which is short; and the stories which make up this book are amusing enough and clever enough, but they are wanting in the individuality and in the completeness of the genuine Short-story. Like the brief tales to be seen in the English monthly magazines and in the Sunday editions of American newspapers into which they are copied, they are, for the most part, either merely amplified anecdotes or else incidents which might have been used in a Novel just as well as not.[10]

This dismissal of Trollope as a writer who did not have the imagination or the discipline to write a short story or to understand its essential make-up was not untypical. The normally sympathetic Stebbins, for example, contended that Trollope's short stories 'were not even second-rate, since they were neither cleverly plotted nor sufficiently rapid in character development.'[11] Trollope, however, was not alone among the Victorians in having his shorter fiction summarily dismissed. Dickens's short stories were written off in similar manner, as 'by-products and on occasion only filler materials.'[12]

Matthews's opinions of Trollope's stories seems to be based more on how he imagined Trollope would write a short story than on any careful reading of the actual texts. At their best, to use Matthews' terminology, Trollope's are short stories 'with a capital S and a hyphen', brimming with individuality, and not compressed or truncated novels. They fulfil Matthews's demands that stories show '[a]n idea logically developed by one possessing the sense of form and the gift of style', and are amply revelatory of Trollope's own awareness of the form. Sometimes too, the Trollopian short story reveals a sensibility for the genre which is closer to the models and demands of a more modern aesthetic than to Matthews's nineteenth-century demand that 'in a Short-story there must be something done, there must be an action'. Trollope centres each story around a revelatory single event in the protagonist's and/or narrator's life. Often he chooses seemingly minor events or non-events, sometimes eschewing action in favour of the creation of mood and the evocation of a moment of change or intuition arising from overcoming a misunderstanding or a disagreement,

---

[10] Matthews, *Philosophy of the Short-Story*, 26.
[11] Lucy Poate Stebbins and Richard Poate Stebbins, *The Trollopes: The Chronicle of a Writing Family* (New York: Columbia University Press, 1945), 187.
[12] Harold Orel, *The Victorian Short Story: Development and Triumph of a Literary Genre* (New York: Cambridge University Press, 1986), 64.

and his stories explore delicate, uncertain issues, leaving the reader to ponder ambiguities and enigmas, and to draw his or her own conclusions.

Trollope's Irish stories form a representative sample of his varying stylistic and formal achievements in the genre. Two stories, 'The O'Conors of Castle Conor' and 'Father Giles of Ballymoy', are set in Ireland and relate directly to events that took place early in Trollope's time there. A second group includes stories with significant Irish characters set in London ('The Panjandrum' and 'The Turkish Bath') and on mainland Europe ('Mrs General Talboys' and 'The Man Who Kept His Money in a Box'). Other stories contain minor Irish characters, such as Kate O'Brien, 'a thick-set, noisy, good-natured old Irishwoman' (*CSF*, 19), who appears as Mrs Bell's servant in 'The Courtship of Susan Bell', or major characters, such as Emily Viner in 'The Journey to Panama', but their Irishness seems of only passing significance.

The first two stories fall into the category of light-hearted tales or 'amplified anecdotes' of Ireland and owe a debt to Lever's early style. Trollope admitted as much when he commented on the autobiographical backgrounds and therefore on what he considered the authenticity of the stories.

> Some adventures I had;—two of which I told in the *Tales of All Countries* under the names of 'The O'Conors of Castle Conor', and 'Father Giles of Ballymoy'. I will not swear to every detail in these stories, but the main purport of each is true (*Auto*, 66).

'The O'Conors' was published in *Harpers* in 1860 and reprinted in *Tales of All Countries* the following year. It was one of three stories in the volume (the others being 'John Bull on the Guadalquivir' and 'Relics of General Chassé') that dealt 'with the chastening of Britons blundering abroad'.[13] 'The O'Conors' tells of Trollopian alter ego Archibald Green and the time he spends in Castle Conor in County Mayo, and is named to ironically recall the O'Conor surname, one of the most influential in Irish history (the O'Conors provided twenty-four kings of Connacht and eleven High Kings of Ireland). In the first-person narrative, Green describes how he presented himself at a small Irish hunt, only to be invited by the important O'Conor family to spend the evening at their castle. On arrival, he is delighted to meet the two charming older daughters of the house, one of whom he immediately thinks might make an ideal wife for him. Soon, however, he becomes disconcerted at the knowing smiles from the rather impertinent youngest sister, who appears to have sensed the danger posed

---

[13] Donald D. Stone, 'Trollope as a Short Story Writer', *Nineteenth-Century Fiction*, 31/1 (June 1976), 33.

by Green and determines to upset his plans. On going upstairs to dress for dinner and after-dinner dancing, he discovers the reason for the smiles: the servant back at the inn where he had been staying has sent his huge, heavy-nailed hunting shoes instead of the pumps for which he had asked. Green is thrown into a panic until he manages to bully Larry, the compliant servant, into lending him his own down-at-heel shoes. Larry belongs to the tradition of faithful Irish retainers inaugurated by Thady in *Castle Rackrent* and put most successfully on stage by Dion Boucicault. His subsequent strange behaviour—he falls over himself and keeps complaining about the uncomfortable boots Green has forced him to wear—eventually causes the protagonist's secret that he is without his proper shoes to become known to all, amidst great general hilarity.

The light-heartedly theatrical and Leveresque story, a homage to Irish hospitality and to Irish mischief, was written (or rewritten) during a visit to the Pyrenees in the autumn of 1859, and may have served Trollope as a distraction from the rather darker and more onerous task of writing *Castle Richmond*. The second story, 'Father Giles of Ballymoy', which appeared in the *Argosy* in May 1866 and was reprinted in *Lotta Schmidt and Other Stories*, has slightly more sinister tones; in this case the protagonist-narrator runs a risk greater than mere embarrassment. The use of the 'I' narrator in both stories is striking and serves as a reminder of a presumed link between the modern short story and the older Irish oral tradition. The narrator, Archibald Green, incarnates something of Trollope's own initial hesitancy as a 'stranger' (Irish shorthand for 'Englishman') in Ireland. In 'Father Giles of Ballymoy' he poses as a 'traveller' and a 'spectator' (*CSF*, 438), thus allowing Trollope to treat Ireland with the amused detachment of an outsider rather than with the engaged narratorial voice adopted in his Irish novels. Trollope underlines that the inexperienced narrator Green lives up to his name in his initial attempts to find his feet shortly after his arrival in Ireland. Neither of the stories could stand up without a protagonist who is wet behind the ears. His general ignorance of customs and habits in Ireland is an indispensable device for the dynamic development and flow of the narrative. It is precisely his 'typical' English lack of knowledge of Irish ways that provides the pretext for these minor tales.

'Father Giles of Ballymoy' describes Green as he enters the town of Ballymoy:

> Ireland is not very well known now to all Englishmen, but it is much better known than it was in those days. On this my first visit into Connaught, I own that I was somewhat scared lest I should be made a victim to the wild lawlessness and general savagery of the people, and I fancied, as in the wet, windy gloom of the night, I could see the crowd of natives standing round

the doors of the inn, and just discern their naked legs and old battered hats, that Ballymoy was probably one of those places so far removed from civilisation and law, as to be an unsafe residence for an English Protestant (*CSF*, 440).

In writing this description, Trollope was drawing on his own apprehensions about Ireland, but also ironically challenging the preconceptions of what he calls, in *West Indies and the Spanish Main*, 'dear good old thickly-prejudiced native England' (*West Indies*, 46). The story tells of how Green is shocked to find a strange man getting into his bed in Larry Kirwan's small hotel in Ballymoy. Unfortunately, Green had earlier failed to understand the maid's telling him that he would be sharing his bed with the priest, and he reacts violently when he sees 'a tall, stout, elderly man standing with his back towards me, in the middle of the room, brushing his clothes with the utmost care' (*CSF*, 441). Subsequently, the man tries to get into his bed, causing Archibald to throw him out of his room and down the stairs, seriously injuring him in the process. Although the story proceeds in an almost slapstick manner, Mr Green has clearly committed, at the very least, a major *faux pas*:

> So, when I got him through the aperture of the door, I gave him a push, as was most natural, I think, for me to do. Down he went backwards,—down the stairs, all in a heap, and I could hear that in his falls he had stumbled against Mrs Kirwan, who was coming up, doubtless to ascertain the cause of all the trouble above her head (*CSF*, 443).

Pandemonium ensues. The people of Ballymoy are incensed at what they see as an attack on their beloved priest. One shouts: 'He shall be hanged if there's law in Ireland' (*CSF*, 444), while the landlady is equally indignant: 'Oh, you born blagghuard!... You thief of the world! That the like of you should ever have darkened my door!' (*CSF*, 445). Archibald is concerned for his own safety:

> I had heard of Irish murders, and heard also of the love of the people for their priests, and I really began to doubt whether my life might not be in danger. ... For vengeance they were now beginning to clamour, and even before the sergeant of police had come, the two sub-constables were standing over me; and I felt they were protecting me from the people in order that they might give me up—to the gallows! (*CSF*, 445–7).

The arrival of the doctor makes matters worse, as he insists 'on the terrible nature of the outrage and the brutality shown by the assailant' (*CSF*, 447). Green is locked up for the night for his own protection, only to be ultimately saved by Father Giles himself, who calms his defenders and invites Archibald to breakfast the following morning so as to persuade the locals to forgive him. Victim and assailant become close friends in the story's happy ending.

This story, like 'The O'Conors', is a reflection on Irish hospitality and an augury of improving English–Irish relations. Green's fault has been that he had no awareness of the Irish habit of bed-sharing at an inn. Sharing was seen as a better alternative to turning a person away, and Green was lucky to have been given a bed, even if it was a shared one. This story gets much of its energy from misunderstandings between its Irish and English protagonists, and from moments of knock-about, physical humour. But it also carries grains of truth, and Trollope is careful not to create offence by noting that the narrated events are set twenty years after he first became 'acquainted with one of the honestest fellows and best Christians whom it has ever been my good fortune to know. . . . As he has now been ten years beneath the sod, I may tell the story of our first meeting' (*CSF*, 438). That this Catholic clergyman is the agent of forgiveness, tolerance, and reconciliation is also important, as Trollope would, as we have seen, later portray a series of older Irish priests in this manner in his novels.

Even if we can read hints of deeper themes in Trollope's early Irish stories, they largely remain within the terms of once oral anecdotes, and presumably were part of the author's store of amusing conversational tales about Ireland. His more accomplished later stories pose rather more complicated questions, very often through the means of dark and somewhat risqué comedy such as that to be found in 'Mrs General Talboys', a story that was rejected by Thackeray for *Cornhill* on the grounds that it was indelicate. Despite himself, Trollope was irked by Thackeray's decision, and wrote to his older colleague: 'I will not allow that I am indecent, and profess that squeamishness—in so far as it is squeamishness and not delicacy—should be disregarded by a writer'. He concludes that 'history perhaps should be told even to the squeamish' (*Letters I*, 127–9); in other words, the writer should not be afraid of upsetting those who are too easily offended at trifling improprieties. Given the growing interest in the 1860s in authors of sensation fiction, such as Wilkie Collins and Ouida (Marie Louise Ramé), and in works like Mary Elizabeth Braddon's *Lady Audley's Secret* (1862), which enjoyed massive popular success, it is easy to understand Trollope's frustration with Thackeray's objections, given the fairly timid nature of his own story of potential bigamy.

'Mrs General Talboys' was published in the *London Review* in 1861, and later in *Tales of All Countries*, but it provoked precisely the complaints about its low moral tone that Thackeray had feared. Its central theme, adultery, was one that could be treated only with extreme reserve and for some readers Trollope had crossed a line. Seduction, betrayal, and unhappy marriages, as H. H. Lancaster commented in 1866, 'like any of the other crimes or calamities of life, may be proper subjects of fiction. But to make them so, they must be treated with studious reserve and delicacy.'[14]

The story is set among a group of mostly English and American expatriates in Rome in 1859, and grew from Trollope's visits to his brother Thomas at the Villino Trollope in Florence. Trollope used his experience there to capture the smallness of the anglophile community abroad, even if he diplomatically located the events further south in Rome. The gossipy nature of the community is communicated through the narrator, who is very much an insider. The story is dominated by an Englishwoman called General Mrs Talboys, who has gone to spend a year in Rome with her twelve-year-old daughter, Ida, but without her husband and her four other children. She is a loud, opinionated member of the expatriate community of artists and their spouses, and she is looked on with suspicion by the other women, who do not appreciate her flirting with their husbands. The men in the story know better than to get involved, with the exception of a rather green young Irishman, the twenty-five-year-old Mr Charles O'Brien, who becomes 'her own indiscreet enthusiasm' (the word enthusiasm, suggesting violent passion or excitement, occurs ten times in the story and is the defining characteristic of this sexually frustrated middle-aged woman seeking temporary respite from an unhappy marriage). Rather like Phineas Finn, O'Brien is a handsome young Irishman with a penchant for older women, although Mrs Talboys is far older than any of Finn's partners, and is, as one character claims, 'old enough to be his mother' (*CSF*, 197). O'Brien is seen by the expatriate community as being 'as free from blame as a man can be', even if it is acknowledged that he has 'a wife in Ireland, some ten years older than himself'. Given his general propriety, O'Brien is distinguished from the other unhappily married man in the story, Mr Brown, who has two illegitimate Italian children, is 'an ill-tempered, bad-hearted man' (*CSF*, 196), and is the author of his own marital problems.

Mrs Talboys and O'Brien become 'strictly confidential' and she gives him advice on how to deal with his difficult marriage, asking him: '"Why should his soul submit to bonds which the world had now declared to be intolerable? Divorce was not now the privilege of the dissolute rich". . . . In short she had recommended him to go to England and get rid of his wife' (*CSF*, 200). The other members of the group see the danger awaiting

---

[14] H. H. Lancaster, 'George Eliot's Novels', *North British Review*, 45 (September 1866): 197–228. Reprinted in John Olmsted, ed., *The Victorian Art of Fiction: Essays on the Novel in British Periodicals* (New York: Garland, 1979), 2, 585.

O'Brien and speculate that 'we shall have a row in the house if we don't take care. O'Brien will be making love to Mrs Talboys' (*CSF*, 197). Things come to a head during a picnic at the tomb of Cecilia Metella, where both O'Brien and Mrs Talboys drink too much, with O'Brien playing the role of 'Ganymede'—for the Greeks, the most beautiful and virile of mortals. The two become increasingly intimate and disappear together after Mrs Talboys has pointedly told her daughter not to come with them. Thus encouraged, O'Brien makes a declaration of love and invites her to depart with him the following morning for Naples. She indignantly refuses and rejoins the group, proclaiming her shock at his outrageous behaviour. He is seen skulking back to Rome, alone, having overplayed his hand. As one unmarried female bystander points out: 'If poor Mr. O'Brien had not shown so much premature energy with reference to that little journey to Naples, things might have gone quietly after all' (*CSF*, 206). However, O'Brien is given the last word and it is his version of events which the reader will remember: 'What the deuce is a fellow to do when a woman goes on that way? She told me . . . that matrimonial bonds were made for fools and slaves.' She also tells him that her husband, the general, is old enough to be her father, and he replies with excessive passion:

> 'I wish he were,' said I, 'because then you'd be free.' 'I am free,' said she, stamping on the ground, and looking up at me as much as to say that she cared for no one. 'Then,' said I, 'accept all that is left of the heart of Wenceslaus O'Brien,' and I threw myself before her in her path. 'Hand,' said I, 'I have none to give, but the blood which runs red through my veins is descended from a double line of kings.' I said that because she is always fond of riding a high horse (*CSF*, 207).

O'Brien, however, is superficially drawn by Trollope, and his Irishness seems to be little more than colouring in a story more concerned with adultery, illegitimacy, entrapment within marriage, and with the difficulties of age difference within relationships. What the narrator makes clear, however, is that Mrs Talboys has misbehaved, and that the Irishman, in his naivety, has been her victim in what is a gender reversal of the traditional plot of the young Irish girl being taken advantage of by the older Englishman.

Mrs Greene in the story 'The Man Who Kept His Money in a Box', which first appeared in *Public Opinion* in 1861 and later in *Tales of All Countries*, is another character whose Irishness is not denoted with great care. She is a strident, loud, objectionable woman, who has married only for money. In the story, she stands guilty of hastily accusing the narrator, Mr Robinson, of robbing her jewel box, which was placed in his room by mistake. As her stepdaughter complains: 'Papa had to pay the bill for every stitch she had when he married her'. Her Irishness is conveyed through her 'considerable brogue superinduced by her energy' (*CSF*, 253), but seems of little consequence in this story of a comically vulgar English family putting their worst face forward when abroad, terrorizing their fellow travellers—and indeed their hosts—on Lake Como. In depicting the English as poor and often annoying travellers, Trollope's story should be read within the tradition of describing the English behaving badly in Europe, and which includes Thomas Moore's epistolary verse novel, *The Fudge Family in Paris* (1818), Frances Trollope's *The Robertses on Their Travels* (1846) and Lever's *The Dodd Family Abroad* (1854).

The story 'The Panjandrum' is a more sombre piece. Its title suggests a nonsense word coined by the playwright Samuel Foote in the mid-eighteenth century (Trollope kept a copy of Foote's *Dramatic Works* in his library at Waltham Cross); the term went into disuse before being brought back into popular circulation by Maria Edgeworth, who refers to 'the great panjandrum' in *Harry and Lucy Concluded* (1825).[15] The term was used to describe a person who takes him/herself too seriously and is a fitting title for the earnest and self-important group of writers who attempt to establish a periodical of the same name in Trollope's story. Prominent among them is the young Irish barrister, Patrick Regan, who is struggling at the English Bar while also trying to launch a literary career. He wins all the narrator's rather patronizing sympathy. 'The world', the narrator suggests, 'would have used him better had his name been John Tomkins.... What attorney, with any serious matter in hand, would willingly go to a barrister who called himself Pat Regan?' (*CSF*, 573). It would be easy to take issue with this passage for being anti-Irish, but that would be to miss the point. The text is playing with and challenging English preconceptions of the Irish and pointing to the inevitable resistance that an Irish name causes among those in the legal professions. Trollope is also exposing the limits of the perspective offered by his narrator—a partial self-portrait of the author as a younger man and unpublished writer in the years before he went to Ireland—rather than offering an unfiltered reading of the Irishman. Regan stands out for his creativity and his poverty:

> Pat has told me a score of times that he was born so, and I believe him. He had a most happy knack of writing verses, which I used to think quite equal to Mr. Barham's and he could rival the droll Latinity of Father Prout who was coming out at that time with his 'Dulcis Julia Callage,' and the like. Pat's father was an attorney at Cork; but not prospering, I think, for poor Pat was always short of money (*CSF*, 573–4).

[15] Maria Edgeworth, *Harry and Lucy Concluded: Being the Last Part of Early Lessons* (London: R. Hunter, Baldwin, Cradock, and Joyce, 1825), 2, 46.

As an Irish lawyer in London, Regan follows in the tradition of Phineas Finn, but pays a far higher price for his Irishness in Britain where, as the text puts it, the merest 'hint of a brogue' is enough to jeopardize his legal career. Regan is made more unappealing by his physical features, especially his pug nose. The narrator, however, suggests that the supposed physical differences of the Irish is a matter of birth and is not the result of violent behaviour: 'I do not believe that all the Irishmen with flattened noses have had the bone of the feature broken by a crushing blow in a street row; and yet they certainly look as though that peculiar appearance had been the result of a fight with sticks' (*CSF*, 573). Despite the ambivalence of this description, Pat Regan is sketched in positive terms, and remembered for the 'undoubted brilliance of his intellect, and his irrepressible personal humour and good-humour', for which he is linked to Richard Harris Barham, the English Anglican priest, better known by his *nom de plume*, Thomas Ingoldsby, author of a series of grotesque metrical tales known as *The Ingoldsby Legends*. Regan is also connected with the pseudonymous Father Prout, otherwise known as the Rev. Francis Sylvester Mahony, a former priest and author of the popular poem, 'The Bells of Shandon', as well as many satirical poems and mock translations in Latin and Greek. Mahony also wrote under the pen name Don Jeremy Savonarola. Pat Regan also gives thought, like the other contributors to the new periodical, to changing his name. Initially he considers 'The O'Blazes' but is 'persuaded to adopt the quieter name of "Tipperary"'. With Regan's choice of pen name, Trollope is criticizing a habit common among some of the Irish who made it in London by playing stereotypical Irish roles.

Trollope's linking of Regan with Prout and Barham gives his would-be Irish writer a certain amount of credibility. Like Prout he is a skilled translator and his rendering of 'Lord Bateman' in Latin is 'so excellent that it will go far to make us at any rate equal to anything else in that line' (*CSF*, 583). The poem in question is 'The Loving Ballad of Lord Bateman', transcribed in 1839 by Thackeray with notes by Dickens and illustrations by George Cruikshank, and topical around the time 'The Panjandrum' is set, 1840.[16] Although the narrator believes that Regan's 'translation was certainly as good as the ballad', it is rejected by the self-serving board members who are shown to care little either about producing a publication that will sell or about nurturing a young literary voice.

The young Trollope knew a thing or two about literary rejection and Regan's portrayal seems based on a lightly disguised version of Trollope,

---

[16] Regan is not the only Trollope character to translate this poem. The Reverend Josiah Crawley, the impoverished curate of Hogglestock in *The Last Chronicle of Barset* (1867), also penned a Greek version.

who is, in effect, doubly present in the story, since the narrator, who holds political ideas with regard to the Corn Laws and the Irish Church which are essentially Trollope's own, is also a partial self-portrait. The story conveys Regan's intelligence, friendship, and wit, as if to underline how much this Irishman has to offer to the English world. Ultimately, he does not find his way in England, but accepts the second chance offered to so many Victorians by Empire by taking up the position of Attorney General on 'Turtle Island'—possibly the bare, bleak, and remote Ascension Island, or the Fijian Turtle Island. Both were British colonies. Whichever it is, Regan is relegated to a marginal role in a remote corner of the Empire.

Another marginal and ultimately disappointed literary Irishman, Mr Molloy, is the protagonist of 'A Turkish Bath', written following Trollope's appointment as editor of *Saint Pauls Magazine* in 1867 and published there in October 1869, and subsequently in *An Editor's Tales* (1870). A complex story, it hints, rather like 'A Ride Across Palestine', at various issues that were certainly not standard material in Victorian fiction, most prominently homosexuality, even if the exploration of this theme yields to a focus on the undefined madness of the struggling London-based Irish writer/journalist Mr Molloy. This story gives weight to Kate Flint's contention that Trollope felt freer in the shorter form to experiment with queer relationships, to be 'at his most socially ludic in this developing mode, where he could set forth unconventional scenarios without any risk of them upending the ordinariness of the world that his novels depict.'[17] The story tells of the editor's encounter with a mysterious Irishman (Mr Molloy) in a Turkish bath in London, and of their subsequent meetings at the editor's office, during which Mr Molloy unsuccessfully attempts to have some of his articles published. The story is resolved when the editor visits Mr Molloy's home and is informed of his 'madness' by his hard-working wife. This story and its protagonist fit closely into Frank O'Connor's conception of the short story as the locus for 'outlawed figures wandering about the fringes of society.'[18]

From the outset, the depictions of both the sauna and the Irishman's state of undress suggest a borderline situation of sexual ambiguity. A detailed sketch is given of the gentlemen's bathing house, with close-up views of the behaviour of the partly naked men and lingering descriptions of towels and seating arrangements:

---

[17] Kate Flint, 'Queer Trollope', in Dever and Niles, *Cambridge Companion*, 110.
[18] Frank O'Connor, *The Lonely Voice: A Study of the Short Story* (Cleveland: The World Publishing Co., 1963), 19.

some there are who carry it under the arm,—simply as a towel; but these are they who, from English perversity, wilfully rob the institution of that picturesque orientalism which should be its greatest charm. A few are able to wear the article as a turban, and that no doubt should be done by all who are competent to achieve the position. We have observed that men who can do so enter the bathroom with an air and are received there with a respect which no other arrangement of the towel will produce (*CSF*, 515).

The narrator acknowledges that it is 'not every man who can carry a blue towel as a turban, and look like an Arab in the streets of Cairo, as he slowly walks down the room in Jermyn Street with his arms crossed on his naked breast', but concludes 'that the second towel should be trailed. The effect is good, and there is no difficulty in the trailing which may not be overcome' (*CSF*, 515). Although as a novelist Trollope often indulges in lengthy digressions, his short stories tend to be tightly crafted, and descriptions of this nature cannot be dismissed as padding. His choice of the highly topical location of the sauna is also deeply significant in the context of a short-story genre which leaves an onus on the reader to fill gaps and supply what is not or cannot be said. 'Telling', in Seán Ó Faoláin's words, 'by means of suggestion or implication is one of the most important of all the modern short-story's shorthand conventions. It means that a short-story writer does not directly tell us things so much as let us guess or know them by implying them. . . . Telling never dilates the mind with suggestion as implication does.'[19] The reader is empowered to bring what Frank O'Connor calls his 'moral imagination' and 'moral judgment' to bear in order to 'see into the shadows' of the story.[20]

Turkish baths had only recently been introduced into Britain and Ireland by the Scottish diplomat and politician David Urquhart, who had been greatly impressed by the system of dry hot-air baths in use in Spain, Morocco, and in the Ottoman Empire, and had described them in his *The Pillars of Hercules* (1850). Six years later, the first modern Turkish bath in the United Kingdom was opened in Ireland by Dr Richard Barter, in Blarney, County Cork. The following year a bath was built in Manchester and 1860 saw the establishment of the first Turkish bath in London, near Marble Arch. In 1862, the *Illustrated London News* reported that Urquhart had formed the London and Provincial Turkish Bath Company, in order to build a genuine hammam or hot-air bath on St Jermyn Street.

Charles Gavan Duffy, who was Premier in Victoria when Trollope visited there, left a vivid description of the always colourful Urquhart, whom he

19 Seán Ó Faoláin, *The Short Story* (London: Collins, 1948), 198–200.
20 O'Connor, *Lonely Voice*, 25.

valued as a supporter of Home Rule Repeal. According to Gavan Duffy, Urquhart, who served as a Member of Parliament from 1847 to 1852, 'received me, arrayed in Orange silk trousers, and a caftan of some green material, and looked like an Oriental Pasha condescending to mate for a moment with the dullards of the West'. He described him as 'manifestly a man of ability, overshadowed by a self-esteem so prodigious that it cast an air of ridicule on whatever he proposed', and remembered with surprise being told by him that 'my business is in the generous, simple, noble East, not among the mean intrigues and cabals called Parliamentary Government.'[21]

In choosing to locate his story in the Jermyn Street Turkish Baths, built under Urquhart's direction, Trollope would have been very conscious of the setting's topicality and of the lively debate as to the physical and moral benefits or risks of such baths he describes with 'delicious wonder'. According to John Potvin, Urquhart's Jermyn Street hammam

> figured prominently in the Victorian imaginary as a privatized public space erected for the cleaning, cleansing, detoxification and relaxation of the male body. Located in the ultra fashionable West end, Urquhart's Jermyn Street hammam offered its patrons a location distinct from the harried and polluted streets outside its exotic doors.[22]

Trollope cannot but have been conscious of the exotic, oriental aura of the sauna, a liminal zone on the edge of respectability, a twilight arena for middle-class men to meet and enjoy the attention of what the narrator describes as 'those Asiatic slaves who administer to our comfort' (*CSF*, 516). While most users were respectably married Victorian gentlemen, a minority would have frequented such a locale attracted by its Oriental (a by word for homosexual) allure. The ambiguously modulated spaces

> furnished an ideal venue for a queer constituency to safely experience—at the levels of the visual and the corporeal—homoerotic desire in this all-male environment, the performances enacted in the baths centred on a scopic and somatic pleasure which enlivened a distinctly illicit homoerotic desiring gaze with the subsequent queer appropriation of its space, despite attempts to keep things clean and pure.[23]

Such are the connotations attached to this 'all-male environment' in Trollope's story that Turner has suggested it was written to appeal to

---

[21] Charles Gavan Duffy, *My Life in Two Hemispheres* (New York: Macmillan, 1898), 1, 212–13.

[22] John Potvin, *Material and Visual Cultures Beyond Male Bonding, 1870–1914; Bodies, Boundaries and Intimacy* (London: Ashgate, 2007), 13.

[23] Potvin, *Material and Visual Cultures*, 13.

the sexual fantasies of a mostly male readership, citing its homoerotic undertones in the descriptions of 'young oriental boys, the heat, the steam, the nudity, the silence, the tension about etiquette, the supply of men.'[24] A further layer of interpretation is possible if we remember that the sauna was also seen to offer protection against 'the harried and polluted streets' to the middle-class gentlemen who believed 'that cleanliness was central to the fight against both physical and moral decline, and ultimately, against the threat of the "great unwashed" '.[25] This protective screen is challenged by the unwanted intrusion of the cigar-smoking Irishman, given that images of dirty, diseased, dying, and dead Irish from the Famine were far from excised from Victorian memory at the time of this story.

Noting that 'men do depend much on their outward paraphernalia', the narrator encourages his reader to pay close attention to clothes codes, to observe 'a stout, middle-aged gentleman', who is not identified as Mr Molloy until later in the story, 'clad in vestments somewhat the worse for wear, and to our eyes particularly noticeable by reason of the tattered condition of his gloves' (*CSF*, 514). Trollope was well aware of the social significance of gloves, summed up by the saying, 'A gentleman is known by his gloves', and the narrator's clear social superiority to the down-at-heel Irishman is underlined in his comment that a tattered glove is 'the surest sign of a futile attempt at outer respectability' and in his asking if there is 'an editor whose heart has not been softened by the feminine tattered glove' before stressing that in 'this instance the tattered glove was worn by a man'. The editor's digression about the 'feminine' glove suggests that there is something sexually 'different' about this tattered Irishman whose cigar he accepts. While Freud is, of course, correct to suggest that 'sometimes a cigar is just a cigar', in Victorian fiction it is normally more (we think, for example, of Alec d'Urberville's cigars in *Tess of the d'Urbervilles*, but we might well consider this to be true of Trollope's story as well). The day after the sauna encounter, the editor receives a visit from Molloy in his office and notes:

> The first thing we saw was the tattered glove; and then we immediately recognised the stout middle-aged gentleman whom we had seen on the other side of Jermyn Street as we entered the bathing establishment. It had never before occurred to us that the two persons were the same . . . Nevertheless we had known and distinctly recognised his outward gait and mien, both with

[24] Mark W. Turner, *Trollope and the Magazines: Gendered Issues in Mid-Victorian Britain* (London: Macmillan, 2000), 204.
[25] Teresa Breathnach, 'For health and pleasure: the Turkish Bath in Victorian Ireland', *Victorian Literature and Culture*, 32/1 (2004), 164.

and without his clothes. One tattered glove he now wore, and the other he carried in his gloved hand (*CSF*, 521–2).

The repeated use of the adjective 'tattered' suggests a number of inter-pretations within the context of the story. The owner of the glove will be revealed to be tattered in the standard sense of 'shabby' and 'worn', but he is also revealed to be 'disordered'. His behaviour, in what he calls 'the little ruse' of tricking the editor, is shabby, but beneath it we see a more complex disorder, his 'madness' (which is hard to credit given his sane determination in seeking out the editor both in the sauna and at work). The nature of the disorder is the question posed but not fully resolved by this story. The early sections of the narrative suggest that his presumed homosexuality—which seems to be what the editor/narrator initially finds attractive about him—is the cause of his ruin, but many of the later parts and especially the descriptions of his wife and children, and his wife's diagnosis of her husband's condition, run against this initial impression. Trollope shies away from openly pushing the homosexual option to its conclusion (much as he did not push the adultery issue to its resolution in 'General Mrs Talboys') for fear of provoking the prescriptive policing, so dear to Victorian moralizers (of which he himself was often one), and concluded the story in terms of the Irish journalist's mental derangement. This was to duck the issue, but clearly Trollope felt he could not push it any further. This ending comes, however, only after awkward unanswered questions have been raised and left for the reader to ponder.

What the story effectively stages is a veiled study of homosexual desire in a homoerotic *locus par excellence*, and in so doing it presents another gender reversal, that of Mr Molloy as a feminized Irishman utterly dependent on his English wife, the 'strong hearty-looking' domestic breadwinner 'with that mixture in her face of practical kindness with severity in details, which we often see in strong-minded women who are forced to take upon themselves the management and government of those around them' (*CSF*, 529). Mr Molloy seems the perfect exemplar of Ernest Renan's 1860 description of the Irish as an 'essentially feminine race',[26] and perhaps Trollope is playing with similar ideas about the Celts and the Saxons that were being enunciated by Matthew Arnold in articles in the *Cornhill Magazine* in the 1860s (Arnold and Trollope often appeared in the same issues) and later collected as *On the Study of Celtic Literature*. Molloy's wife, on the other hand, incarnates the typically solid

---

[26] Ernest Renan, *The Poetry of the Celtic Races, and Other Essays*. Translated and with an introduction by William Hutchinson (London: Walter Scott, 1896), 8. Renan's *Poésie des Races Celtiques* was first published in French in 1860.

'Saxon' qualities he lacks and the couple can be read in the light of Robert Young's descriptions of how nineteenth-century racial theories were 'covert theories of desire', based on the perceived results of sexual unions between different peoples.[27] Here the union is between the English and the Irish (once again), but the English woman is given all the Saxon male qualities while the Irish man is rendered as being unmanly and even effeminate. But this scenario is complicated by the English editor's evident attraction to the Irishman who uses, above all else, his semi-naked body to catch his attention. The editor does not hesitate in appreciating the 'peculiar and captivating grace' (*CSF*, 517) of the feminized Irishman, and the story's only description of desire is that felt by the English editor for his Irish sauna companion.

At a key moment in their exchange, Trollope has the narrator slip from the 'we' of public decorum into the private first-person singular. This use of the singular form is unusual in a story pointedly told in the plural, a choice which Trollope took the trouble to justify in the *incipit*:

> This little story records the experience of one individual man; but our readers, we hope, will, without a grudge, allow us the use of the editorial we. We doubt whether the story could be told at all in any other form (*CSF*, 514).

Why could the story not have been told in another form? Why, for the greater part of the narrative, does Trollope choose to deprive himself of a first- or third-person singular narration and thus of a more intimate, layered, and complex narrative voice and presence, and to rely instead on a rather indistinct but collegial 'we'? Why does he subsequently choose to disrupt the cohesive 'we' relationship established between the narrator and the reader? The answer seems to lie in the fact that the story, in attempting to deal with the taboo subjects of sexual ambiguity and homosexuality, had to be placed at a distance from a first-person singular narration that might have been more uncompromisingly identified with Trollope himself. It is as if the narrator wants to be identified with what might be presumed to be the conservative views and morals of the majority of his readers. As in Trollope's novels, the established narratorial voice of the short stories possesses a distinctive, common-sense personality, is 'always male or at least "manly"' displaying 'good intentions, and sound moral values'.[28] This 'manly' narrator establishes a relationship of trust with the reader,

---

[27] Robert Young, *Colonial Desire: Hybridity in Theory, Culture and Race* (New York: Routledge, 1995), 9.

[28] Francine Navakas, 'The Case for Trollope's Short Stories', *Modern Philology*, 83/2 (1985), 177. Review of *Anthony Trollope: The Complete Short Stories*, ed. Betty Jane Slemp Breyer.

who is assumed to be of like mind. To break this established connection, to shift from the collegial 'we' to the individual 'I', is important, especially as the 'I' here is the private 'I' of prohibited desire. This is seen on two occasions. The first comes when the narrator realizes the stranger is Irish: 'I thought that I detected just a hint of an Irish accent in his tone; but if so the dear brogue of his country, which is always delightful to me, had been so nearly banished by intercourse with other tongues as to leave the matter still a suspicion,—a suspicion, or rather a hope. . . . My hope had now become an assurance' (*CSF*, 517). The second comes when the narrator describes how the Irishman offers him a cigar and then comments on his attractiveness: 'I accepted his offer, and when we had walked round the chamber to a light provided for the purpose we reseated ourselves. His manner of moving about the place was so good that I felt it to be a pity that he should ever have a rag on more than he wore at present' (*CSF*, 518).

These two moments see the editor using the 'I' form to express admiration for Molloy's Irishness and his sexualized physical presence. These two moments are out of sync with the stiff upper lip of the first-person plural narrative. It is as if the first-person plural narrating voice functions like the much-talked-of clothes in the story—it presents the public man with his decorous and manly public thoughts while the first-person singular corresponds to the naked man, and is used to communicate private and forbidden thoughts. Society is built on the decorous third person, but beneath the surface lurk desires and thoughts that subvert the public front:

> 'And yet,' said we, 'men do depend much on their outward paraphernalia.'
> 'Indeed and they do,' said our friend. 'And why? Because they can trust their tailors when they can't trust themselves' (*CSF*, 517).

Trusting convention allows society to keep functioning according to Victorian mores, but occasionally—and this story is a good example of it—Trollope allows a chink of light to fall on alternative lives and lifestyles, counter discourses, and on the complications that lie below the surface.

The issue of clothing and nakedness is also focalized in the image of the glove. In presenting himself to the English editor in the sauna, Molloy is effectively throwing 'down the gauntlet', challenging him to giving him a hearing. It is as if the Irishman must present himself before an English court of appeal and go to great extremes to get a hearing. In this case, the court is accommodating and willing to listen. Ultimately, what this feminized Irishman has to offer, alas, is nonsense. Another expression of the time was 'to take off the gloves'. As gloves were the symbol of a gentleman, to take off the gloves meant to end gentlemanly restraint—to go beyond what was publicly acceptable—and pursue a dispute with vigour. The strange Irishman with the tattered gloves does not pursue a dispute, but he certainly pursues the editor with vigour; it is hard not to read the Irishman's desperate tactics as the necessary response to his failing to get a hearing in London, and as being symbolic of the difficulties of the Irish more generally in securing a proper audience there.

Practically all of Trollope's Irish short stories dramatize moments in which an English 'stranger' or outsider fails to understand or fit into an Irish situation or, perhaps better, fails to gracefully accept Irish hospitality—we see this with Archibald Green in 'Father Giles of Ballymoy' and 'The O'Conors of Castle Conor'; or situations in which an Irish outsider struggles to belong in an English world. We see this with Mr Molloy in 'The Turkish Bath' and Pat Regan in 'The Panjandrum'. The mutual incomprehension between the inhabitants of the two islands is dramatized with effects that range from the comic to the almost tragic. In both 'The Panjandrum' and 'The Turkish Bath', Trollope portrays the dramatic situation of the marginalized Irishman in London and in doing so writes two short stories which give voice not only to the difficulties experienced by Irish writers and professionals in London, but also to often obscured themes, such as Irishness itself and (homo)sexuality—which sees an Irish woman like Mistress Morony appearing as a virago, that is as 'a female who has the robust body and masculine mind of a man', and various Irish men appearing to be playing out feminine roles.

Trollope's more complex Irish stories offer substantial and skilful use of the short-story form, fully deserving to be categorized under Matthews's capital 'S', and are written with a knowing reader in mind, one with the capacity to read between the lines of his risky counter-hegemonic narratives and to find much lurking within its shadows. In this sense, these stories are representative of all his output in this genre and offer significant evidence of what John Sutherland calls 'the unexpected image of a morally embattled writer, one at odds with, and sadly hampered by, the "squeamishness" (his word) of the times.'[29]

---

[29] John Sutherland, ed., *Early Short Stories by Anthony Trollope* (Oxford: Oxford University Press, 1994), ix.

7

Trollope's Irish English

Much of the nineteenth-century Irish fiction writer's authority comes from a capacity to reproduce Irish-English speech. In fact, even though Irish English was not yet the subject for scholarly investigation, it was already abundantly present in Irish fiction.[1] Even today, nineteenth-century fiction remains one of the most significant sources for studies of the contact variety that is Irish English, the product of a gradual language shift among the Irish population from the original Gaelic into a vernacular form of English. Irish English was partially shaped from its indigenous Irish substratum in a process which took several generations, but was also influenced by a superstratal input from early modern English:

> In the pronunciation and vocabulary of southern Hiberno-English it is possible to trace the influence both of older strata of the English language and of the Irish language; in grammar, syntax and idiom the peculiarities of south Hiberno-English depend exclusively on the Irish language.[2]

Attempting to capture as slippery and unstable a dialect as Irish English, awash with local usages and inflections, is hazardous, and P. L. Henry is at least partly correct in describing the use of Hiberno-English language in fiction and theatre as necessarily 'fabricated',[3] as is O'Maolain when he claims that its authenticity is undermined because of its frequent use of

---

[1] P. W. Joyce's *English As We Speak It in Ireland* (1910) was the first significant publication containing a broad view of scholarship on the subject of Hiberno-English. The most comprehensive work available today is Raymond Hickey's *Irish English: History and Present-Day Forms* (Cambridge: Cambridge University Press, 2007).

[2] A. J. Bliss, 'English in the South of Ireland', in P. Trudgill, ed., *Language in the British Isles* (Cambridge: Cambridge University Press, 1984), 150. The influence of the Irish language was probably overemphasized in early studies and was subsequently challenged by scholars, who argued that many of the alleged Irishisms of Hiberno-English phonology are actually residues of earlier (seventeenth-century) varieties of 'mainland' English and that Irish English is less a contact variety and more a retentionist language. The Gaelic-English contact thesis has gathered weight again in recent years.

[3] P. L. Henry, *An Anglo-Irish Dialect of North Roscommon: Phonology, Accidence, Syntax* (Dublin: University College Dublin, 1957), 319.

parody, caricature, and ethnic slurring.[4] For Elizabeth Butler Cullingford, when Irish playwright Dion Boucicault adorns his Irish characters in plays such as *Arrah-na-Pogue* and *The Colleen Bawn* with verbal wit and eloquence played off against the duller Queen's English which maintains linguistic hegemony, he is in danger of falling into the trap of linking Irishness and Hiberno-English 'with eloquence and rhetorical excess, the markers of a stage "character", while Englishness is identified with unadorned and therefore "normal" (or truthful) speech'.[5] Even J. M. Synge found himself being attacked as 'a faker of peasant speech', his Hiberno-English coming under fire as 'contrived, literary stuff, entirely unrepresentative of peasant speech.'[6] More sympathetic critics have concluded that 'Synge writes English as if it carried Irish inside it',[7] and the same is true to greater and lesser extents of practically all the attempts to give voice to the Irish on stage and page.

Too often in the hands of both English and Irish writers, Hiberno-English was equated with phonology, with efforts to transcribe an accent which is distinguishable in England as 'Irish' but is recognizable in Ireland only as 'stage-Irish', rather than with any real attempt to properly hibernicize English, to repeat the syntactic constructions of English as it was actually spoken in Ireland. Too often 'Irishness' was suggested solely through recourse to eye-dialect, the deliberate misspelling of words to suggest in writing a non-standard or dialectal pronunciation. This was then coupled with frequent references to God, the devil, and religious sentiments as proof that the primitive native culture was, as Lord Mountjoy put it back in the seventeenth century, 'obstinate in Popish superstition'.[8] Some writers did, however, manage to get beyond the stereotypes and to transcribe something approximating the complex and variable Englishes heard in Ireland, and yet, by faithfully reproducing the dialect, they ran the risk of alienating an English readership often hard-pressed to understand.

To explain how he avoided making things too inaccessible to his English and Anglo-Irish audiences, William Carleton described how he decided not to have his stories narrated directly by the peasants because

---

[4] S. O'Maolain, 'Alan Bliss, *Spoken English in Ireland, 1600–1740*. Representative texts assembled and analysed', *English World-Wide*, 1 (1980), 139–40.

[5] Elizabeth Butler Cullingford, *Ireland's Others: Gender and Ethnicity in Irish Literature and Popular Culture* (Notre Dame: University of Notre Dame Press/Field Day, 2001), 23.

[6] St John Ervine, *Some Impressions of My Elders* (London: Allen & Unwin, 1923), 201.

[7] Robert Welch, *Changing States: Transformation in Modern Irish Writing* (London: Routledge, 1993), 100.

[8] Quoted in D. B. Quinn, *The Elizabethans and the Irish* (Ithaca: Cornell University Press, 1966), 119.

this would 'narrow the sphere of the work, and perhaps fatigue the reader
by a superfluity of Irish dialogue and its peculiarities of phraseology.'[9] Like
his fellow novelists, Carleton did not share the view of some later Irish
writers that dialect ought to be used in more formal discourse as well.
Thus, as Declan Kiberd has shown, the 'dialect is deliberately framed
by the "learned" discourse, with which it must never be confused.'[10] This
put the Irish author writing in standard English on a par with his readers,
even if this was at the cost of distancing himself linguistically from his
subjects. By and large, Carleton's solution of a standard English frame
with Hiberno-English dialogue would be replicated by Trollope even if he
could only come at the dialect as an outsider. But Trollope went to serious
lengths to get his Irish English right and was openly critical of writers who
took less care (or who were not blessed, perhaps, with an ear as sensitive as
his). He had little choice but to rely on what he heard on the street in his
attempt to render Hiberno-English on the page. There was no dictionary
or comprehensive glossary of the dialect available and so he must have
written in the knowledge that he would never succeed in more than
partially cracking the dialect's code. His situation, as a representative of
British power in Ireland, was not unlike that of Lieutenant Yolland in
Friel's *Translations*. Yolland, who is responsible for anglicizing the Irish
place names in Donegal, complains to his Irish collaborator, Owen:

> Even if I did speak Irish I'd always be an outsider here, wouldn't I? I may
> learn the password but the language of the tribe will always elude me, won't
> it? The private core will always be . . . hermetic, won't it?[11]

Owen, in response, suggests that Yolland 'can learn to decode us' and
there seems little doubt that Trollope, even if his Irish never went beyond
a single '*ceade mille faltha*' in *The Macdermots*,[12] felt that even if Irish
would remain beyond him, he could crack the Irish-English linguistic
codes. Proving he could capture the peculiarities of Irish speech in his
fiction was another way of exercising control over his Irish literary subjects
and of asserting what he believed was his unrivalled knowledge of the
country.

Summing up the linguistic situation pertaining in Trollope's Ireland,
Glendinning writes: 'In most places, Irish was spoken by the poorer

---

[9] William Carleton, *Traits and Stories of the Irish Peasantry* (Gerrards Cross: Colin
Smythe, 1990), 144.
[10] Declan Kiberd, *Irish Classics* (London: Granta, 2000), 281.
[11] Brian Friel, *Translations* (London: Faber and Faber, 1981), 40.
[12] Trollope would have found '*ceade mille faltha!*' written in this way in John and
Michael Banim's (the O'Hara family), *Canvassing, A Tale* (Philadelphia: Carey, Lea &
Blanchard, 1835), 8.

people; all the Irish, when speaking English, brought to it the intonation, syntax, idioms and imagery of their native tongue'. She praises Trollope's capacity to transcribe 'this Irish English in his dialogue . . . the confidence he brought to the attempt carries the day. In retrospect he was sure he had it right, as he was sure that Thackeray in *Pendennis* did not.'[13] In fact, in his study of Thackeray, Trollope takes issue with the rendering of Irish English in Thackeray's '*The Crystal Palace*,—not that at Sydenham, but its forerunner, the palace of the Great Exhibition'. He quotes the ballad's crude and sometimes extravagant attempts to render Irish-English pronunciation through spellings such as 'Maydiayval' (Medieval), 'vayhycles' (vehicles), 'staym ingynes' (steam engines) rhyming with 'in lines', and the city of St Petersburg rendered as 'Paytersbug'. This, for Trollope, would all be good fun

> were it not that Thackeray has made for himself a reputation by his writing of Irish. In this he has been so entirely successful that for many English readers he has established a new language which may not improperly be called Hybernico-Thackerayan. If comedy is to be got from peculiarities of dialect, as no doubt it is, one form will do as well as another, so long as those who read it know no better. So it has been with Thackeray's Irish, for in truth he was not familiar with the modes of pronunciation which make up Irish brogue. Therefore, though he is always droll, he is not true to nature (*Thackeray*, 174).

Thackeray's fault was that he was not sufficiently acquainted with real Irish speech and he mistook the voices of the Irish in England, who attempted 'to imitate the talk of Londoners', with those of the Irish at home:

> It was these mistakes which Thackeray took for the natural Irish tone. He was amused to hear a major called 'Meejor,' but was unaware that the sound arose from Pat's affection of English softness of speech. The expression natural to the unadulterated Irishman would rather be 'Ma-ajor.' He discovers his own provincialism, and trying to be polite and urbane, he says 'Meejor.' In one of the lines I have quoted there occurs the word 'troat.' Such a sound never came naturally from the mouth of an Irishman. He puts in an h instead of omitting it, and says 'dhrink.' He comes to London, and finding out that he is wrong with his 'dhrink,' he leaves out all the h's he can, and thus comes to 'troat.' It is this which Thackeray has heard. There is a little piece called the *Last Irish Grievance*, to which Thackeray adds a still later grievance, by the false sounds which he elicits from the calumniated mouth of the pretended Irish poet. Slaves are 'sleeves,' places are 'pleeces,' Lord John is 'Lard Jahn,' fatal is 'fetal,' danger is 'deenger,' and native is 'neetive.' All

---

[13] Victoria Glendinning, *Trollope* (London: Hutchinson, 1992), 158.

these are unintended slanders. Tea, Hibernicé, is 'tay,' please is 'plaise,' sea is 'say,' and ease is 'aise' (*Thackeray*, 174–5).

Although Trollope's focus is on pointing out pronunciation errors, it would be wrong to imagine that his own rendering of Irish English was simply based on this aspect of the dialect. He was not above occasionally making fun of Irish pronunciation for comic effect, however. An example of this is to be found in *The Kellys and the O'Kellys* in the vignette about Savarius or Savy O'Leary from County Mayo:

> Well; some time ago—that is, since London began to fill, O'Leary was seen walking down Regent Street, with a parson. How the deuce he'd ever got hold of the parson, or the parson of him, was never explained; but Phil Mahon saw him, and asked him who his friend in the white choker was. 'Is it my friend in black, you mane?' says Savy, 'thin, my frind was the Honourable and the Riverind Augustus Howard, the Dane.' 'Howard the Dane,' said Mahon, 'how the duce did any of the Howards become Danes?' 'Ah, bother!' said Savy, 'it's not of thim Danes he is; it's not the Danes of Shwaden I mane, at all, man; but a rural Dane of the Church of England' (*Kellys*, 149–50).

What is interesting about this tale is that it is told by a middle-class Irishman poking fun at a strongly accented fellow Irishman and is not intended as stage-Irishry. The paragraph contains various noted features of Hiberno-English pronunciation, including the 'i' in place of 'e' in 'river-ind' as well as 'mane' and 'dane' for 'mean' and 'dean', examples of how Hiberno-English did not raise /e:/ to /i:/ and instead pronounced it with an /ɛ/ monophthong. Elsewhere, Trollope gets it right in transcribing Irish English pronunciation with 'plazes' for 'pleases', 'aisy' for 'easy' and 'baich' for 'beach', 'dacently' and 'discreatly' for 'decently' and 'discreetly' (*Macdermots*, 204), all of which are common examples of linguistically conservative Ireland's failure to adapt to the Great Vowel Shift and a retention from early modern English.

When Trollope spells 'true' as 'thrue' and places an 'h' sound after 't' where it is not required, as in 'nathural', 'sthranger', 'Protesthant' (*Eye*, 49, 94, 100), and even 'Prothesthant' (*Macdermots*, 361), he is successfully mimicking Irish pronunciation and drawing readers' attention to Irish confusion with 'th', which has been summed up by P. W. Joyce: 'As for the English *th*, it may be said that the general run of the Irish people never sound it at all; for it is a very difficult sound to anyone excepting a born Englishman.'[14] Trollope captures the common dentalization of /t/ before an /r/ as a characteristic feature of mid-nineteenth-century Irish English

---

[14] Joyce, *English As We Speak It*, 228.

in words like 'misther' and 'gutther', and he also hears the common habit of simply inserting a /d/ in place of the /th/ in words like 'widout'. The spelling of 'Misthress' is yet another example of Trollope's rendering of Irish problems with 'th' sounds, the confusion of the unvoiced as in, for example, 'thing', and the voiced in 'this' (sometimes pronounced 'dis' in Irish English, where fricatives are often pronounced as plosives). As Joyce has commented:

> The sounds of *English t* and *d* are not the same as those of the *Irish t* and *d*; and when the people began to exchange the Irish language for English, they did not quite abandon the Irish sounds of these two letters, but imported them into their English, especially *when they came before r*. That is why we hear among the people in every part of Ireland such vulgarisms as (for t) *bitther, butther, thrue* [for bitter, butter, true].[15]

Another example of Irish English's rejection of the Great Vowel Shift is to be found in the lingering /aʊ/ sound, as in the following example: 'you tould me to hould my tongue' (*Macdermots*, 360). Trollope also conveys the common raising of the vowel from /e/ to /i/ before /n/, which was a general feature of Irish English: 'a gintleman in Dublin recaved the rints, and a very stiff gintleman he was too' (*Macdermots*, 2).

Whatever about his mastery of Hiberno-English pronunciation, some critics have suggested that Trollope's grasp of Irish idiom was every bit as loose as that of Thackeray and he has been accused, with some justification, of inconsistency. Lionel Stevenson, for example, disputes the claim that Trollope had 'a very precise ear' and states that 'he did not undertake extensive phonetic imitation'. He complains that Trollope shifts 'back and forth between dialectical and formal spellings for the same or comparable words', and takes the ninth chapter of *The Macdermots*, set among the peasantry at the Widow Mulready's shebeen, to illustrate this:

> At the beginning of the scene the widow says, 'Send out the rint, Joe,' and four pages later when she uses the identical remark the first word is spelled 'sind.' 'Remember' in one speech is immediately followed by 'disremember.' 'Then' alternates with 'thin' and 'ten' with 'tin' though 'twenty' is never 'twinty.' Shifting to another vowel, we find 'dacent,' 'schaming,' 'tache' (teach), 'sazing' (seizing), 'spake' (speak), but 'thief' instead of 'thafe.' In the midst of frequent spelling of 'owld,' 'cowld,' 'sowl,' we find 'the old hag.' 'Raal' on one page is followed by 'really' on the next. As examples of consonant pronunciation there are 'sthrong' but 'stripped,' and 'draw' twice on one page but 'dhraw' on another and 'dhriving,' 'dhrying,' 'dhrink' *passim*. Although a few of these inconsistences might have been caused

by a printer's failure to follow the manuscript, they occur so frequently throughout the book that one must assume Trollope's own disregard for consistency.[16]

What Stevenson describes could alternatively be interpreted in the light of the fact that when Trollope replicates non-standard forms he intends them as representative of Irish-English pronunciation and not yet fixed or exhaustive. Trollope was rendering the uncertain nature of the English he was hearing in Ireland, particularly among the uneducated peasant classes, as well as his desire to transmit a flavour of the spoken language without overwhelming his English reader with an excessive quantity of Irishisms. English, in Trollope's Ireland, was a language in the making, which individual speakers often used inconsistently, depending on their level of education. To capture this sense, Trollope adopted more marked versions of Irish English to denote class and educational differences. Thus Trollope's Maynooth curates tend to speak thicker Irish English than their better-educated parish priests, while characters in the professions speak something close to standard English, adopting only occasional Hibernicisms, and poor tenants speak a more pronounced version of Irish English than do landlords or even land agents. As Robert Tracy points out, 'generally Trollope uses Irish English for accuracy rather than to make his characters seem quaint or ridiculous. They are not stage-Irish, but men and women who talk after the manner of their time and place and have important subjects to discuss with one another.'[17] In other words, Irish English is one of the tools employed by Trollope to bolster the realism of his Irish novels, to make them more 'true to nature', and to denote class difference.

Discussing the figure of Mrs Kelly in *The Kellys and the O'Kellys*, Dudley Edwards says that 'Trollope's ear for the speech of an Irish countrywoman dominated by the Gaelic forms and intonations so recently lost is outstanding. ... In their different locations O'Casey, Synge, and Somerville and Ross might be able to better it, but only debatably and marginally; and in cumulative effect, measurement of argument, categorization of wrongs, and perfection of rhythms, it can hold its own for authenticity anywhere.'[18] William Trevor concurs, asserting that

[16] Lionel Stevenson, 'Trollope As a Recorder of Verbal Usage', *Trollopian*, 3/2 (September 1948), 121.
[17] Robert Tracy, 'Introduction' to Anthony Trollope, *The Macdermots of Ballycloran* (New York: Oxford University Press, 1989), xx.
[18] Owen Dudley Edwards, 'Anthony Trollope, Irish Writer', *Nineteenth-Century Fiction*, 38/1 (June 1983), 11–12.

Trollope's eye and ear rarely let him down. His vernacular is as sound as any of the native Irish writers of his time, often more convincing than that of Gerald Griffin or William Carleton. In this respect, it is occasionally complained that the colourful Irish talk encountered in novels and short stories is exaggerated or unreal. This is not so; but the objection is understandable because so often such talk has been badly expressed and crudely represented on the page. Trollope subtly conveys its flavour without ever overreaching himself.[19]

The remainder of this chapter will offer an analysis of a sampling of Trollope's representations of the dialect's chief characteristics as seen in his Irish novels. Writing in a time of linguistic displacement, Trollope's novels demonstrate the advance of English, even among the peasants, but also occasional, passing examples of the resistance of Irish. One is to be found in *The Macdermots of Ballycloran* when Thady, hiding out in Aughacashel, finds himself with an 'old man [who] could not speak a word of English; but Thady could talk Irish, and he had no difficulty in getting plenty of potatoes from him' (*Macdermots*, 417). Trollope would have come across many such people as he travelled the country.

Trollope includes an impressive range of vocabulary directly derived from Irish, which he sometimes signals directly in the text, such as the following: 'Whilst Pat walked into the kitchen for a lighted piece of turf (*Hibernice*, coal) to kindle his patron's pipe' (*Macdermots*, 19). Later in the same novel he includes an arguably more obscure word, 'kishes', derived from the Irish *cis* (a large basket), without adding any gloss. More often than not, Trollope leaves the reader to figure out the meaning from the context. Examples abound, including terms of affection: 'Alanna', 'agra', 'avick', and 'Machree' (*Macdermots*, 109, 131, 195, 355), respectively from the Irish *a leanbh* (my child) *a ghrá*, *a mhic* (my boy), and *mo chroí* (my dear); religious imprecations: 'by Garra', from *Ba ghairid Dia* (by God); 'oh musha, musha, wirrasthrue', from *muise* (indeed), and *a Mhuire, is trua* (Mary, it's true); lamentations: 'Ochone! ochone! Miss Feemy, alanna, what'll we be doing widout you?' (*Macdermots*, 362), 'ochone' from *ochón* (woe); specific terms such as 'garron' (*Macdermots*, 304) from *gearrán* (gelding), and 'gossoon' from *garsún* (and the French *garçon*). Trollope includes a large number of pertinent examples which capture the morphological transfer to the '. . . een' ending in English from the Irish *ín* ending. These diminutive nouns often carry a connotation of contempt: 'not that I care a *thrawneen* for him and his company' (*Macdermots*, 23), with 'thrawneen' from *tráithnín* (straw); 'boreen' (*Macdermots*, 412) from

---

[19] William Trevor, 'Introduction' to Anthony Trollope, *The Kellys and the O'Kellys*, ed. W. J. McCormack (New York: Oxford University Press, 1982), xii.

bóithrín (a small road); 'the like of him, the spalpeen' (*Macdermots*, 32), from *spailpín* (rascal); 'young Macdermot was pulling hard at the dhudheen' (*Macdermots*, 23) from *dúidín* (a short pipe); the 'widow Mulready's shebeen shop' (*Macdermots*, 129), from *síbín* (an unlicensed drinking place); 'Thady had an alpine in his hand' (*Macdermots*, 239), from *ailpín*, meaning 'a thick ashplant'.[20] Other Irish English vocabulary to be found include words such as 'a hapoth' (*Kellys*, 164), which is more commonly written as 'ha'porth' (a halfpenny-worth); 'prates' for potatoes, which may today sound a little stage-Irishy but is also to be found, written as 'praties', in Patrick Kavanagh's *Tarry Flynn*, a text that no one would accuse of lacking in authenticity. We also find 'rapparee' from *rapaire* (robber) (*LL*, 103), 'bosthoon' from *bostún* (an idle fellow), and 'scraugh' in the phrase 'The very scraughs of which the roofs are composed are germinating afresh' (*Macdermots*, 125). This comes from *scraith* and denotes 'a strip of sod out of grassy or boggy land for making a fire or for protecting a thatched roof.'[21] Also present are familiar Irish words such as 'ruction' (row), as in 'there's a rucion between the Captain and Mr. Thady' (*Macdermots*, 231), 'Shilelahs' as the plural form of *shillelagh*, from the Irish *sail + éille*, and 'pailers' (*Macdermots*, 144) for *peelers* (the name for the police, deriving from Sir Robert Peel); and set idiomatic phrases, such as 'Av [if] that don't bang Banagher', uttered to express surprise by Mrs Kelly (*Kellys*, 182).

Trollope also transcribes common religious exclamations such as 'Bedad' and the popular discourse marker 'faith', roughly translatable as 'in truth', and the even more common 'faix' variable placed at the start of an exchange. We find these in 'Father Giles of Ballymoy', which also contains an example of 'and' as a subordinating adverbial conjunction followed by a pronoun,[22] a solecism in standard English but perfectly acceptable in Hiberno-English, as it is derived from Irish grammar:

'Is this Pat Kirwan's hotel?' said I.

'Faix, and it is then, yer honour,' said the driver (*CSF*, 439).

In *The Macdermots,* we similarly find 'Faix, Mr. Thady, and is that yerself?' (*Macdermots*, 403), which captures perfectly the Irish-English use of the reflexive. Other examples of this abound, so just a few will show Trollope's mastery of this Irish-English habit: 'Well, Feemy, how's yourself this

---

[20] T. P. Dolan, *A Dictionary of Hiberno-English* (Dublin: Gill and MacMillan, 1998), 6.
[21] Dolan, *Dictionary*, 230.
[22] Markku Filppula, 'Subordinating *and* in Hiberno-English Syntax: Irish or English origin?', in Ureland & Broderick, eds., *Language Contact in the British Isles* (Tübingen: Niemeyer, 1991), 618.

morning?' (*Macdermots*, 103); 'Faix, Mr. Thady, and is that yerself?' (*Macdermots*, 403), 'And God bless you, Mrs McKeon; it's yourself is a good woman' (*Macdermots*, 267). Trollope also provides examples of the substitution of the subjective 'they' with the third-person plural objective form 'them', which conveys an idea of respect, as in the following examples: 'There's none of 'em in the counthry so good as the Kellys. Hoorroo for the Kellys! them's the boys' (*Macdermots*, 342) and 'thim boys is fixed in gaol for the next twelve months any way' (*Macdermots*, 144).

In the next example, Trollope is spot on with the use of the erroneous reflexive 'meself' as an emphatic form of the nominative:

> That's thrue for you, Misthress O'Hara.... I don't know that I ever shot so much as a sparrow, meself, but I love to hear them talk of their shootings, and huntings, and the like of that. I've taken a fancy to that boy, and he might do pretty much as he plazes wid me (*Eye*, 43).

The Irish-English phrase, 'That's thrue for you', meaning 'you are correct', is a direct translation from the Irish *Is fíor duit*, while the phrase 'and the like of that', meaning 'and similar things', also comes from the Irish *leithéid*.

The following sentence: 'I'm thinking what will poor Pat be doing without me, and no one in it at all to bile the pratees and feed the pigs—the craturs!' (*Macdermots*, 112) captures various common Irish-English traits, such as the use of 'in it' as an adverbial phrase meaning 'there' (from Irish *ann*), followed by 'at all', an adverbial phrase used for emphasis (from Irish *ar chor ar bith*). Sometimes, the 'at all' is doubled, especially after a negative, again for emphasis: 'I don't believe, then, Mr. Thady, that Miss Feemy's gone home, at all at all' (*Macdermots*, 231). The word 'craturs' is a borrowing from Middle English, more usually spelt with a 'y' (we read 'God help the poor, the crayturs' early on in the same novel). Other English retentions in Irish English and to be found in Trollope's Irish works include 'the latter end of last winter' (*Macdermots*, 94), with latter meaning the last part, 'spliced' (married), and 'a sight' (*Macdermots*, 133), meaning a great number or quantity; 'blagguards' (*Kellys*, 242), meaning rogues, also written in the more standard 'blackguard': 'the blackguard nearly knocked the life out of her' (*Kellys*, 194); 'intirely' (altogether/completely): 'Well, Biddy, did you hear Captain Ussher's going away from this intirely?' (*Macdermots*, 360–1); 'afeard/afeared' (afraid) (*Macdermots*, 144, 206), 'foranenst' (against), as in 'Barney Egan was dancing foranenst her' (*Macdermots*, 231), and 'sup' (a small quantity): 'But, Captain, dear, sorrow a sup of dhrink did I see you take this blessed evening; shure then you'll let me get you a glass of wine before we all begin, jist to prevent

your being smothered with the dust like; shure, yer honour hasn't taken a
dhrop yet' (*Macdermots*, 209). This example also contains some interesting pronunciation quirks, such as 'shure', an example of eye-dialect
showing a perfectly standard pronunciation while implying dialect, in
place of the unstressed adjective 'sure', one of the commonest hedging
discourse markers in Hiberno-English.

Several more points of interest emerge in the following statement from
Father Marty in *An Eye for an Eye*:

> I'm getting to be a very ould man, Misthress O'Hara; but I'm not so ould
> but I like to have the young ones near me (*Eye*, 43).

In the first case 'but' functions in a fairly standard manner instead of the
conjunction 'although'; in the second it appears to be used ungrammat-
ically in the place of the conjunction 'that', although this construction has
a parallel in Irish by which it can be read as an example of what Henry calls
'a tendency towards negative statements at the expense of positive statements.' This tendency has 'a perfect match in the corresponding uses for
the Irish constructions involving *acht* (but)'. Thus Father Marty's second
'but' can be read as an example of the construction described by Henry as
'initial negation followed by exemptive *but*',[23] or, in Dolan's terms, 'a
conjunction heading clauses after negative verbs.'[24] The phrase 'the young
ones near me' does not refer to particular young people but to young
people in general, an example of what Filppula terms 'plural count nouns
with generic reference',[25] and is a typical feature of Hiberno-English use
of the definite article, which arises from the lack of an indefinite article
in Irish.

The following sentence: 'Bedad thin, Mistress O'Hara, I don't know a
fairer face to look on in all Corcomroe than your own—that is when you're
not in your tantrums, Misthress O'Hara' (*Eye*, 43) is exemplary of the Irish
penchant for exaggeration. Given Trollope's description of the miseries of
the county Clare Barony of Corcomroe, he is probably poking a little fun at
his flattering Irish priest. The pronunciation of 'then' as 'thin' is an example
of how short *e* is sounded before *n* and sometimes in other positions
like short *i*. Another example of this is the 'niver' of 'I niver like seeing
too many of 'em going that way, and them that are prittiest are the last I'd
send there' (*Eye*, 44), while the 'prittiest' is not a phonetic variation but an
accentuated vowel sound in the syllable 'pre', which is never pronounced

---

[23] Henry, *An Anglo-Irish Dialect*, 200.   [24] Dolan, *Dictionary*, 46.
[25] Markku Filppula, *The Grammar of Irish English. Language in Hibernian Style* (London: Routledge, 1999), 56.

'pre', even in standard English—a question of style then rather than of phonetics.

Father Marty's response—'I do thin, Misthress O'Hara'—to Mistress O'Hara's 'If you like to look at the fair face of a handsome lad' (*Eye*, 43)— is an example of the Hiberno-English manner of providing a response to a question with a repetition of the verbal element rather than with an elliptical 'yes' or 'no'. This repetition of the verbal phrase is a direct carry-over from the absence of Irish words for 'yes' or 'no'. Sometimes the Irish does not repeat the lexical verb of the question but substitutes it with *déan*, meaning 'make' or 'do'. Thus Father Marty's use of the finite 'I do' corresponds in Hiberno-English to the Irish 'déan'.

Trollope is careful to repeat characteristic Irish-English syntax and verbal use, such as the 'after-perfect' as recent or immediate perfect, a Hiberno-English compensatory ploy carried across from the perfective of Irish. An example would be: 'Denis McGovery is afther going to get married, I hear' (*Macdermots*, 46). He also captures the use of 'do be' to represent habitual aspect: 'Why I don't know why you do be hating him so' (*Macdermots*, 80).[26] In response to Fred's saying that he would be going to see Mistress O'Hara and her daughter, Father Marty says: 'In course you will. Sorrow a doubt of that' (*Eye*, 49). The use of the emphatic negative 'sorrow' is a commonly used borrowing from medieval English. The 'in course' begs for elucidation but finds little, apart from Filppula's rather vague statement about the preposition 'in' being part of 'another category' which 'is formed by cases in which in appears to have been used instead of some other preposition for some reason or another'[27]. Further features borrowed from the Irish language can be seen in the following sentences, uttered by Father Marty:

> What's the good of an ould man like me going bothering? And, signs on I'm going into Ennistimon to see Pat O'Leary about the milk he's sending to our Union. The thief of the world—it's wathering it he is before he sends it (*Eye*, 51).

In this context 'Signs on' means 'and I'm showing the effect of it [of being old]', from the Irish '*dá chomhartha sin*.'[28] In the phrase 'The thief of the world', we have an example of the definite article being used for rhetorical effect. We also find 'and' being overworked as a catch-all conjunction

---

[26] For a discussion of habitual aspect in Irish English, see Raymond Hickey, 'Models for describing aspect in Irish English', in Hildegard Tristram, ed., *The Celtic Englishes II* (Heidelberg: Carl Winter, 2000), 97–116.

[27] Markku Filppula, *Grammar of Irish English*, 232.

[28] Liam Ua Broin, 'A south-west Dublin glossary. A selection of south-west county Dublin words, idioms and phrases', *Béaloideas*, 14 (1944), 181.

linking to 'signs on', which means 'he looks it' or 'he shows the effect of it', and is a translation from the Gaelic '*tá a rian air*.'[29] The use of the copula, 'it's wathering it he is', rather than the standard English 'he is watering it', brings us to a key Hiberno-English usage, clefting. This derives from the necessity in Irish to start every main clause with a verb. This omission of the relative pronoun is another borrowing from Middle English. A further example of the Hiberno-English copula in Trollope comes when Father Marty addresses Fred: '"It's quite a sthranger you are, these days," said the priest' (*Eye*, 94).

Overall, Trollope succeeds surprisingly well in rendering the phonological, syntactic, and lexico-grammatical features of Hiberno-English through the voice of his fictional characters. In doing so he demonstrates the genuine nature of his attempts to understand the Irish through a rendering of their speech forms which is rarely mocking and is mostly reliable. This could, however, also be read as a form of colonial appropriation by this very English writer in Ireland whose Irish English is always presented against the normative backdrop of the Standard English that structures his texts.

Thus Trollope's sure command of Irish English serves in a sense as an act of linguistic containment, not only to make his Irish characters more believable and, at times, more endearing and 'authentic' (with all the difficulties this term contains), but also—and this is undoubtedly part of the political intent of his Irish novels—to domesticate the colourful Irish and make an appealing case for their belonging and their being well treated within the larger British family.

---

[29] Dolan, *Dictionary*, 240.

8

Countering Rebellion

I. *AN EYE FOR AN EYE*: TROLLOPE'S ADMONITORY PARABLE

Trollope's *An Eye for an Eye*, written in just four weeks in the autumn of 1870, was not published until 1878 (in instalments in the *Whitehall Review* and subsequently in book form by Chapman & Hall). Just why Trollope waited so long to place it is not clear, although he cannot but have been aware of growing British impatience with matters Irish in the 1870s, a decade dominated by Isaac Butt and Charles Stewart Parnell, and the intensification of both the Home Rule campaign and land reform agitation. Butt began life as a convinced Unionist (and an opponent of O'Connell) but had long since come to believe the only way forward for the country was to restore Ireland's Parliament. In 1870, he founded the Home Rule Association, which became the Home Rule League a couple of years later. He was given no thanks for doing so by Trollope, who belittled the battle for Home Rule and expressed doubts about its real levels of support:

> Home rule, no doubt, is a nuisance,—and especially a nuisance because the professors of the doctrine do not at all believe it themselves. There are probably no other twenty men in England or Ireland who would be so utterly dumfounded and prostrated were Home rule to have its way as the twenty Irish members who profess to support it in the House of Commons. But it is not to be expected that nuisances such as these should be abolished at a blow. Home rule is, at any rate, better and more easily managed than the rebellion at the close of the last century; it is better than the treachery of the Union; less troublesome than O'Connell's monster meetings; less dangerous than Smith O'Brien and the battle of the cabbage-garden at Ballingary, and very much less bloody than Fenianism. The descent from O'Connell to Mr. Butt has been the natural declension of a political disease, which we had no right to hope would be cured by any one remedy (*Auto*, 73).

Trollope's posthumous *Autobiography*, written before Parnell took Butt's place as leader of the Home Rule party, shows that he viewed the new leader with even greater disdain, and particularly disliked Parnell's aggressive twin policy of obstructing parliamentary business at Westminster and stoking up rural unrest at home. He was equally alarmed by the campaign of the Irish National Land League, founded in 1879 by Michael Davitt, for the 'three f's': fair rent, fixity of tenure, and free sale of land. The Land League held several large-scale protests in the west of Ireland in 1878 and 1879, in defence of Irish tenants increasingly unable to pay rents and in favour of a more flexible land tenure system and the elimination of rack-rents. Trollope was worried by the growing Irish protest movement, but equally alarmed by Gladstone's response, which he saw as a mixture of heavy-handed coercion and reckless concession.

Trollope believed that Ireland was on the verge of exploding into an uncontrollable spiral of violence such as he later depicted in *The Land-leaguers*. Long disappointed that the Ascendancy had failed to assume a more responsible leadership, Trollope failed to acknowledge that many or most of the Home Rule and Land League leaders were actually drawn from that same class; increasingly he identified only with the recalcitrant landlord class that was, in his view, being asked to make unreasonable and unsustainable concessions.

An Eye for an Eye makes no direct comment on current Irish troubles. Its remote setting, stark depictions, and biblical title and overtones give the text an almost archetypal quality. Offering yet another variation on the failed marriage plot, the novel describes the relationship between a poor, innocent, Irish girl called Kate, and Fred Neville, an English army officer stationed in Ireland for his last year of service and adventure abroad. Neville is set to return to England to take up his duties as heir to his uncle, the Earl of Scroope, in the large, unattractive, and time-locked Scroope Manor in Dorsetshire, but finds himself in an impossible bind. After a brief romance, he has promised to marry Kate, who is expecting his child, but he has also agreed to remain single and to return to England to take on his new-found responsibilities there. He attempts to satisfy pressures from both sides of the water but gradually begins to favour the social demands of his new position over the moral imperative to honour the pledge he has given to Kate. The situation precipitates when Kate's mother, who had warned him 'if you injure my child I will have the very blood from your heart', enacts a furious revenge by pushing him to his death off the cliffs of Moher.

This gothic and often melodramatic parable was greeted with mixed reviews. The *Academy* dismissed it as all too reminiscent of 'that preeminently painful story', *The Macdermots of Ballycloran*, and voiced the hope 'that Mr. Trollope will come back before long to his own better self, and be to us as the hierophant of Barchester and the whip of Downing Street once more.'[1] In the *Spectator*, R. H. Hutton, Trollope's most incisive contemporary critic, believed, on the other hand, that the novel would 'take a high place' among the author's works and praised its classic simplicity, commenting that 'there is something in the atmosphere of Ireland which appears to rouse [Trollope's] imagination and give force and simplicity to his pictures of life'. Hutton also enthused that to 'one emerging from the overladen atmosphere' of the 'sordid world' of *The Way We Live Now*

> this tragic story of mastering passion and over-mastering prejudice,—of a great sin, a great wrong, and a great revenge, is like the breath of that Atlantic to the shores of which it carries us, after the stifling atmosphere of a London alley.... Mr Trollope has hardly ever painted anything so striking as the mode in which the promise not to disgrace his house and name grows unconsciously and involuntary in the young Lord Scroope's mind, till it takes all the life out of the more binding and far more sacred promise under the faith of which he has gained from Kate O'Hara all she has to give; and this, though far from wishing to desert her, though he is really willing to give all he has to give in the world, except his rank and social position, to make atonement to her for what has been done....[2]

Other critics took issue with what they considered the insufficiently subtle or deep characterization and saw the novel as a sombre sermon preached as a 'warning to women, young and innocent, to men, young and honorable, that even they might not be entirely beyond the temptings of their own natures.'[3] While praising the perfect style, *The Nation* complained that the 'characters do not of themselves develop the story; they are used by the novelist to tell the story with', while the novel itself falls short of tragedy because Fred does not have the status of a tragic hero.[4]

In our own times, George Watt has described *An Eye for an Eye* as 'a remarkably unified and well-controlled work of art' and praised its innovatory nature, claiming that it is the first English novel to examine 'the fallen-woman crisis from the male point of view, making him the hero of the novel.'[5] Gertrude White has argued that the novel is 'curiously powerful and exercises an effect upon the reader that cannot be accounted

---

[1] Unsigned review of *An Eye for an Eye*, *Academy*, 15 (February 1879), 117.

[2] *Spectator*, 52 (February 15 1879), 210.

[3] S. C. Lasselle, 'Morality in Authorship', *The Author: A Monthly Magazine to Interest and Help all Literary Workers*, 6 (15 June 1889), 82.

[4] *Nation*, 28 (24 April 1879), 290.

[5] George Watt, *The Fallen Woman in the Nineteenth-Century English Novel* (London and Canberra: Croom Helm, 1984), 73, 65.

for simply in terms of melodrama'. She sees much that is of interest in its treatment of 'snobberies of class, of "good blood," of rank, of wealth, of race, of religion, and of the perils in a real world of preferring fantasies to reality.'[6] John Hynes sees Neville's psychological struggle between conflicting loyalties as the 'main intention' of this 'simple tale of passionate revenge.'[7]

An Eye for an Eye can profitably be read within the spheres of these thematic interests and as a study of the classic choice between love and duty seen in the light of unbridgeable class, religious, and gender differences, but the novel's dogged rootedness in both England and Ireland is also deserving of attention. This is a work that voices not only Trollope's darkening vision of Ireland, but also his worries about the relationship between the two islands which seems, to his growing despair, to be at least as problematic as it was when he started writing about the country in 1843.

The novel connects the two countries through its two strange and singularly unhomely locations—Scroope Manor in Dorset and the O'Hara cottage in County Clare—but, before that, the reader is presented in the 'Introduction' with the haunting image of a third location: a 'private asylum' housing an 'unfortunate lady', which 'is furnished with every luxury which it may be within the power of a maniac to enjoy'. She has 'no one left belonging to her' and does not even 'sigh for release' (*Eye*, 1) but spends her time repeating the Old Testament mantra: 'An eye for an eye, and a tooth for a tooth'. The narrator announces that 'the story shall be told of the lady who dwelt there—the story of her life till madness placed her within those walls' (*Eye*, 2), and reveals the novel's essentially circular structure by anticipating, at the outset, its tragic conclusion. From the asylum we pass to the large but unattractive Scroope Manor, 'an Elizabethan structure of some pretensions', which has 'none of that finished landscape beauty of which the owners of such "places" in England are so justly proud' (*Eye*, 3–4):

> The atmosphere of the whole place was gloomy. There were none of those charms of modern creation which now make the mansions of the wealthy among us bright and joyous.... To a stranger, and perhaps to the inmates, the idea of gloom about the place was greatly increased by the absence of any garden or lawn near the house (*Eye*, 4–5).

---

[6] Gertrude M. White, 'Truth or Consequences: the Real World of Trollope's Melodrama', *English Studies*, 64/6 (December 1983), 492–3.

[7] John G. Hynes, '*An Eye for an Eye*: Anthony Trollope's Irish Masterpiece', *Journal of Irish Literature*, 16/2 (May 1987), 54–5.

The Earl of Scroope's home is solid and transmits a sense of safety and continuity, seeming to embody what Eagleton terms 'a dominant ideological device in Britain', that is, the transmutation of 'history itself into a seamless evolutionary continuum, endowing social institutions with all the stolid inevitability of a boulder. Society itself, in this view, becomes a marvellous aesthetic organism, self-generating and self-contained.'[8]

> The earl could talk for ever about the estate, every field, every fence, almost every tree on which was familiar to him. That his tenants should be easy in their circumstances, a Protestant, church-going, rent-paying people, son following father, and daughters marrying as their mothers had married, unchanging, never sinking an inch in the social scale, or rising—this was the wish nearest to his heart (*Eye*, 82).

The Earl represents the responsible and conservative English landlord class (which Trollope shows in stark contrast to their Irish counterparts) and is a proud member of 'the oldest agrarian capitalist class in the world...a model of hegemonic rule, bound to their tenants by custom, affection and paternal care, and so able to evoke their grateful loyalty.'[9] Yet, for all the Earl's undoubted fidelity to his history and his land, both familial and national, Trollope, who cautiously believed that a certain amount of controlled change was necessary if society was to prosper, questions the myth of stability that he incarnates. The tranquil continuity that supposedly passes from generation to generation in Scroope soon reveals itself to be a façade. The Earl lost his first wife as well as his only daughter 'just as she became a bride', while his son, who was 'thoughtless, lavish, and prone to evil pleasure', had married a 'wife from out of the streets...a painted hussy from France' (*Eye*, 7). Shortly after the Earl's second marriage, his only son died and he had to turn to his nephew Fred Neville, the impoverished son of a renegade member of the family, as his heir. And despite all this hidden upheaval, the Earl insists that things must proceed according to the old rules, as though nothing has changed.

In an article in *Saint Pauls Magazine*, Trollope was critical of the stolid patriarchal politics of the Tory to whom 'it appears almost to be an ordinance of God that society should be composed of a squire in a big house, with a parson below him, with four farmers in a parish, and with a proportion of peasantry living in cottages.'[10] The Earl of Scroope appears as a version of what Trollope describes in his *Autobiography* as

---

[8] Terry Eagleton, *Heathcliff and the Great Hunger: Studies in Irish Culture* (London and New York: Verso, 1995), 4.

[9] Eagleton, *Heathcliff*, 53.

[10] Anthony Trollope, 'Whom Shall We Make Leader of the New House of Commons?', *Saint Pauls Magazine*, 1 (1867–8), 541.

the so-called Conservative, the conscientious, philanthropic Conservative . . . convinced that such inequalities are of divine origin, tells himself that it is his duty to preserve them. He thinks that the preservation of the welfare of the world depends on the maintenance of those distances between the prince and the peasant by which he finds himself to be surrounded; and, perhaps, I may add, that the duty is not unpleasant, as he feels himself to be one of the princes (*Auto*, 292–3).

Even if he never makes radical proposals for rapid change in the relationships between classes, Trollope recognizes that gaps could and should be narrowed, and derides the Earl's belief and investment in maintaining the status quo at all costs. When his will is read, there is much irony in the description of his bequest of 'his affectionate love to every tenant on the estate. All the world acknowledged that it was as good a will as the Earl could have made' (*Eye*, 124). Similarly, the novel contains criticism of the Earl of Scroope's anti-Catholic prejudice, which means that no one is 'taken into service but they who were or called themselves members of the Church Establishment' (*Eye*, 6). The Earl is a victim of his own rigidity, his incapacity to make any concessions to a changing world, and he is guilty of making hasty, harsh judgements with regard to his family. He initially does not want to meet his second nephew Jack, Fred's younger brother, because he does not like the name, but the 'strait-laced' Jack (*Eye*, 80) turns out to be everything that Fred is not and the Earl has to belatedly admit that he is 'a very well educated gentleman' (*Eye*, 24).

Fred Neville struggles to come to terms with the new life that is suddenly cast upon him in dismal Scroope. Not surprisingly, he favours the freedom and 'real life' of County Clare, where the cliffs are 'beautifully coloured, streaked with yellow veins, and with great masses of dark red rock', to the grey monotony and 'gloomy chambers' (*Eye*, 64) of the Dorsetshire manor. He sees Ireland, through the superficial lens offered him from his post in a regiment stationed at the Ennis cavalry barracks, as a romantic, exotic, and wild place in which he can be a character in a personal romantic fiction and fulfil his aunt's prophesy that he was 'exactly the man to fall in love with a wild Irish girl' *(Eye*, 17) and 'indulge in that wild district the spirit of adventure which was strong within him' (*Eye*, 13).

The Ireland in which Neville finds himself initially seems both wild and wonderful, a blank canvas on which he can sketch his shallow dreams. This liminal setting partly corresponds to George Levine's description of extreme locations outside England which are used to represent 'primal realities beyond the reach of social constraint',[11] but also to what Seamus

---

[11] George Levine, *The Realistic Imagination: English Fiction from Frankenstein to Lady Chatterley* (Chicago and London: University of Chicago Press, 1981), 206.

Deane calls the subverted 'urge to make what was strange—a recalcitrant Ireland—familiar, a part of the United Kingdom'. Often, however, rather than create familiarity, this urge served to underline difference and was 'predicated on the shared belief that the country had never been adequately represented before. The sense of an initiatory blankness, or emptiness, and the evolution of the techniques by which it could be filled is an abiding one in Irish writing'.[12] *An Eye for an Eye* contains several passages giving a vision of Ireland as a place which is strange, primal, and empty, although Trollope plays his own domesticating vision of Ireland off against more stereotypically biased English attitudes, based on an idea of the country as barbaric and intractable, as expressed by Lady Scroope and, at times, by Fred himself. Lady Scroope bemoans her nephew's refusal to leave the army and complains of his failure to assume his responsibilities as heir to Scroope Manor:

> But this had not been done; and now there was an Irish Roman Catholic widow with a daughter, with seal-shooting and a boat and high cliffs right in the young man's way! Lady Scroope could not analyse it, but felt all the danger as though it were by instinct. Partridge and pheasant shooting on a gentleman's own grounds, and an occasional day's hunting with the hounds in his own country, were, in Lady Scroope's estimation, becoming amusements for an English gentleman. They did not interfere with the exercise of his duties. She had by no means brought herself to like the yearly raids into Scotland made latterly by sportsmen. But if Scotch moors and forests were dangerous, what were Irish cliffs! (*Eye*, 18).

For Lady Scroope and her husband, safety, both physical and moral, is only guaranteed within the boundaries of 'a gentleman's own grounds' and within the borders of familiar England. Her vision is limited by the suffocatingly closed world in which she lives, and by her rigid adherence to what she believes are upright moral principles, but which are revealed to be prejudices. In her central role in forcing Neville not to marry his Irish sweetheart, she causes much of the novel's tragic conclusion.

Neville's initial error lies in his refusing to accept his destiny and his good fortune and remain at home in Scoope instead of insisting on a return to Ireland for one more year in which to indulge his 'spirit of adventure'. His straying is underlined by the fact that Kate O'Hara lives outside the confines and constraints of 'normal' society in a cottage which is half a mile from the neighbouring 'mud cabins'. The house is described

---

[12] Seamus Deane, 'The Production of Cultural Space in Irish Writing', *Boundary 2, An International Journal of Literature and Culture*, 21/3 (Fall 1994), 120.

in negative terms, defined in terms of what it is not. Thus it is 'very unlike an English cottage' and

> a blank place enough, and most unlike that sort of cottage which English ladies are supposed to inhabit, when they take to cottage life. There was no garden to it, beyond a small patch in which a few potatoes were planted. It was so near to the ocean, so exposed to winds from the Atlantic, that no shrubs would live there. Everything round it, even the herbage, was impregnated with salt, and told tales of the neighbouring waves (*Eye*, 30).

While elsewhere Trollope contributes to a domesticating strategy of integrating Ireland as a ragged but fundamentally similar version of England, *An Eye for an Eye* stresses the wildness, blankness, and otherness of the country. The representations of Clare are in stark contrast with the benign and pleasant pen pictures to be found in contemporary descriptions, such as the volume entitled *Holiday Haunts on the West Coast of Clare* (1891), which evokes 'the neat, white cottages of the farmers, and the handsome residences of the gentry, dotting the landscape here and there' as 'as nice a picture as any one could desire to see. . . . In Liscannor and its vicinity are laid many of the scenes and incidents recorded by Trollope, in his work, "An eye for an eye" [sic].'[13] This is a good example of the effort to integrate Ireland culturally with Britain as described by Deane: 'After 1800, travel literature had a more specific purpose than before—namely, to make Ireland recognizably a part of the United Kingdom, to represent it as a part of the larger system or to represent it in such a way that its refusal to be so could be explained, if not excused.'[14] *An Eye for an Eye* offers a truer topographical picture than is to be found in the domesticating strategies of *Holiday Haunts*, which adopts trite and inadequate adjectives to impose fictitious order on a desolate and impoverished landscape and social reality. Trollope's novel stresses the region's wild remoteness, as seen from Neville's point of view, as he thinks of the O'Hara ladies and their home:

> he liked them the better because they did not live as other people lived. Their solitude, the close vicinity of the ocean, the feeling that in meeting them none of the ordinary conventional usages of society were needed, the wildness and the strangeness of the scene, all had charms which he admitted to himself (*Eye*, 42).

---

[13] H. B. H. *Holiday Haunts on the West Coast of Clare* (Limerick: McKern & Sons, 1891). This volume is available at http://www.clarelibrary.ie/eolas/coclare/history/holiday_haunts/liscannor.htm.

[14] Deane, 'Cultural Space', 118.

Neville initially feels free in Ireland, where 'ideas occurred to him which his friends in England would have called wild, democratic, revolutionary and damnable, but which, owing perhaps to the Irish air and the Irish whiskey and the spirit of adventure fostered by the vicinity of rocks and ocean, appeared to him at the moment to be not only charming but reasonable also' (*Eye*, 53). He comes to Ireland believing 'that Irish hunting is good', more risky, and hence more rewarding than its English equivalent. Much is made of the metaphor of hunting as the pursuit, capture, and eventual destruction of a prey, and these terms frame Neville's predatory behaviour towards his Irish victim. When asked by Kate why he shoots seagulls, he tells her: 'Only because it is so difficult to get at them' (*Eye*, 47). His predatory interest in Kate, an innocent and defenceless Irish virgin, is similarly motivated. He enjoys the chase far more than the capture and 'dear, sweet, soft innocent … Kate who … worshipped the very ground on which he trod' (*Eye*, 85), is easy prey, mired as she is in a meaningless and desolate everyday existence, living for nothing more than the merest hope of eventual escape:

> Her life at Ardkill Cottage was certainly very dull. Memory did but little for her, and she hardly knew how to hope. She would read, till she had nearly learned all their books by heart, and would play such tunes as she knew by the hour together, till the poor instrument, subject to the sea air and away from any tuner's skill, was discordant with its limp strings. But still, with all this, her mind would become vacant and weary. 'Mother,' she would say, 'is it always to be like this?' (*Eye*, 36)

Her life is a sort of prison and is the exact counterpart to what Neville sees ahead of him at Scroope.

Despite her mother's efforts to defend her, Kate takes her place among the litany of 'unprotected females' that crowd Victorian fiction and suffer because of the absence of a strong male guide or guardian. Father Marty, although a good man, is too innocent and forgiving to adequately protect her. He is also overly keen to see her profitably married off: 'it was a pain to him to see a young girl, good-looking, healthy, fit to be the mother of children, pine away, unsought for, uncoupled,—as it would be a pain to see a fruit grow ripe upon the tree, and then fall and perish for the want of plucking' (*Eye*, 46). This desire to see her married impedes him from taking adequate account of her awkward social situation and sees him join Kate's mother in giving Neville the benefit of the doubt. They are not alone in hoping that Neville turns out for the best. Even his stern uncle falls into this trap when choosing to pin his hopes on his positive appearance—'well-made, active, quick, self-asserting, fair-haired, blue-eyed, short-lipped' (*Eye*, 9)—rather than despair at his evident waywardness. Given

Neville's capacity to win over experienced older people, Kate's capitulation to his advances is no surprise. Like Feemy Macdermot, Kate lets her impulse overwhelm her judgement and falls in love without giving any thought to what complications may accrue. In the narrator's words: 'In the eyes of Kate O'Hara he was an Apollo' (*Eye*, 38). Their relationship is exemplary of what Watt describes as Victorian novelists' tendency to 'give young men sexual impulses but endow their young women with romantic ones. It is this germ of romantic hope which makes them vulnerable when their Apollo appears on the scene.'[15] Part of Kate's appeal is her very vulnerability, which makes Neville feel all powerful: 'No other man had ever pressed her hand, or drank her sweet breath. Was not such a love a thousand times sweeter than that of some girl who had been hurried from drawing-room to drawing-room, and perhaps from one vow of constancy to another for half a dozen years?' (*Eye*, 57). Once she has become a 'plucked rose' (*Eye*, 99), however, she immediately loses her appeal:

> Alas, alas; there came a day in which the pricelessness of the girl he loved sank to nothing, vanished away, and was as a thing utterly lost, even in his eyes. The poor, unfortunate one,—to whom beauty had been given . . . but to whom, alas, had not been given a protector strong enough to protect her softness, or guardian wise enough to guard her innocence! . . . She gave him all; and her pricelessness in his eyes was gone forever (*Eye*, 91).

As his interest in Kate fades, his sense of his responsibility at home in Scroope grows, and Neville begins to hate the place whose very strangeness had offered the lure of adventure. Having violated the O'Haras' space and thrown their lives into turmoil, Neville now wants nothing more than escape. Far from being the sober law-giver Trollope would hope for, he proves himself to be utterly irresponsible when asked to honour his oath to marry the now-pregnant Kate. Quickly the country loses its romantic allure and its very poverty becomes for him a cause for blame:

> How ugly the country was to his eyes as he now saw it. Here and there stood a mud cabin, and the small, half-cultivated fields, or rather patches of land, in which the thin oat crops were beginning to be green, were surrounded by low loose ramshackle walls, which were little more than heaps of stone, so carelessly had they been built and so negligently preserved. . . . The burial ground which he passed was the liveliest sign of humanity about the place. . . . Now the place with all its attributes was hideous to him, distasteful, and abominable (*Eye*, 109–10).

15 Watt, *Fallen Woman*, 69.

He starts 'to hate the coast of Ireland, and to think that the gloom of Scroope Manor was preferable to it' (*Eye*, 121), and realizes '[w]hat an ass had he made himself, coming thither in quest of adventures!' At the same time he can see no way out of 'the ruin he had brought upon himself' (*Eye*, 161) and as a result is 'sick indeed, of everything Irish, and thought that the whole island was a mistake' (*Eye*, 131). He now despises the girl whom he all-too-briefly saw as a woman worthy of his love before relegating her to the role of 'plaything for an idle hour' (*Eye*, 150), and branding her 'a wretched, ignorant creature' *(Eye*, 161). There is much irony in the fact that the Irish Kate is far 'better educated than himself, and perhaps knew as much as Sophie Mellerby' (*Eye*, 75), the colourless English girl of high family who has been chosen by the Countess of Scroope as his future spouse. Kate has read widely and is familiar, among other things, with Tennyson's poem 'Mariana', which describes a woman, cut off from society, vainly awaiting the return of her lover. Although she was 'pretending to fear future misery', Neville's declaration of love is 'Elysium to her - the very joy of Paradise. She could sit and think of him now from morning to night, and never find the day an hour too long'. And yet such is her fear that she cites cites the poem in what is a premonition of her own future:

> I think that you like me—a little. Oh Fred, if you were to go and never to come back I should die. Do you remember Mariana? 'My life is dreary. He cometh not,' she said. She said, 'I am aweary, aweary; I would that I were dead!' Do you remember that? What has mother been saying to you?' (*Eye*, 56).

If Kate resembles Mariana, Neville is akin to Lothario, to whom he compares himself—that is, the unscrupulous seducer of women in *Don Quixote*, who reappears in Nicholas Rowe's play *The Fair Penitent* (1702), a drama of man's cruelty to women that prefigures popular eighteenth-century domestic tragedies. Although he refuses to marry Sophie, Neville at least partly falls into line with his aunt's demands and refuses Kate on class and social grounds, believing that to do otherwise would 'injure the position of the earldom' (*Eye*, 70), while describing her returned father as 'disreputable' so as to preclude any lingering claims she may make to marriage. As the narrative hurries towards a conclusion, even his fellow soldiers side against him: 'By Heaven, there's nothing like rank to spoil a fellow. He was a good fellow once' (*Eye*, 144).

Some blame for Kate's tragedy rests with Mrs O'Hara, who had consigned her to a life of solitude for class reasons, believing that 'the weight of good blood' should preclude her from meeting 'the butcher's son on equal terms. . . . The burden had been imposed and must be borne, even though it isolated them from all the world' (*Eye*, 37). Long before she falls prey to

Neville, Kate suffers as a victim of her mother's threadbare gentility. Both the Scroope and O'Hara families provide ironic evidence to interrogate the Earl's image of 'daughters marrying as their mothers had married, unchanging...' (*Eye*, 82). What the novel reveals is a parallel family dysfunctionality, with those living in both the O'Hara cottage and in Scroope Manor described as 'inmates', a word which was already in use to describe people confined in institutions. Despite all their differences in terms of class and nationality, their common dysfunctionality seems destined to be replicated in generation after generation, just as the malfunction in the English-Irish relationship continues to repeat.

Trollope also plays with the trope of the wronged Irish woman/victim by making Mrs O'Hara English in name but Irish in fact, in yet another twist on Irish-English interconnection. Years earlier she was abandoned with her daughter by her husband, Captain O'Hara, who, according to Father Marty, is 'a low blackguard' (*Eye*, 94), while now the 'sweet innocent' Kate (*Eye*, 97) falls victim to a similar fate when Neville decides that he cannot 'pollute himself by marriage with the child of so vile a father. Poor Kate! Her sufferings would have been occasioned not by him, but by her father' (*Eye*, 103). Neville's sense of his own social superiority allows him to believe that he is doing the right thing on his family's account: 'Moralists might tell him that let the girl's parentage be what it might, he ought to marry her; but he was stopped from that, not only by his oath, but by a conviction that his highest duty required him to preserve his family from degradation' (*Eye*, 107). But even the Earl of Scroope himself, ignorant of the fact that Kate was pregnant, cautions against a heartless abandoning of Kate, asking his nephew, 'Would you ruin her – seduce her by false promises and then leave her? Do you tell me that in cold blood you look forward to such a deed as that?' (*Eye*, 83). Neville will ruin her but will also ruin himself, becoming a victim of his own hubris, of his belief that his rank he will protect him as he prepares to discard Kate. Even if he admits that he 'had committed an error', his callous belief that he is among people who are 'his inferiors in rank, education, wealth, manners, religion and nationality', and that he has been generous in offering 'to sacrifice himself as no other man would have done? signals the extent to which he underestimates the bind he is in. He is caught between trying to find some way to honour the promise given at Scroope while not abandoning Kate entirely. Thus, on being challenged by Mrs O'Hara, he declares 'that under no pressure would he marry the daughter of O'Hara the galley-slave' (*Eye*, 105) while still claiming: 'I will be true to her all the same'. He considers a 'half-valid morganatic marriage', and then a 'viler proposal', to keep her as his mistress in 'some sunny distant clime, in which adventures might still be sweet' (*Eye*, 154). Father Marty expresses his horror at what he calls 'a false counterfeit marriage' (*Eye*, 149) and condemns Neville's behaviour: 'Have you thought of the life of that young girl who now bears in her womb the fruit of our body? Would you murder her—because she loved you, and trusted you, and gave you all simply because you asked her; and then think of your own life?' (*Eye*, 157). Although Neville worries that he may pay dearly for abandoning Kate, he never believes that he will pay with his life. But this is precisely what happens at the climax of the novel, when he is pushed to his death by Kate's mother, who is overwhelmed by an outraged sense of injustice, an injustice she herself had earlier lived and which she now sees repeated in her daughter's abandonment.

Neville's death does not exonerate his family from responsibility. Having arranged to pay off Captain O'Hara just to make him go away, Neville's brother has little choice but to make a liberal settlement on Kate and to guarantee the costs of keeping her mother in an asylum for the remainder of her life. At the novel's end, the two families, so obviously estranged socially and indeed nationally, are more interconnected than ever through their shared grief and responsibility. Their union, if only economic, will necessarily endure in a manner not unlike that between the England and Ireland they represent. Even if the two countries seek to separate, the narrative implies that they will remain irrevocably bound together.

The fallout is painful for the survivors. The Countess's punishment, in particular, is marked. Having apportioned all blame for the unsuitable liaison on Kate and pushed Neville to abandon her, the Countess is criticized by the narrator for entertaining 'an idea that young men' commonly make 'promises with very little thought of keeping them' and for not expecting 'young men to be governed by principles such as those to which young ladies are bound to submit themselves' (*Eye*, 62). Her views are mirrored by those of Lady Mary Quin, who believes Neville should not 'in any circumstances' marry 'a Kate O'Hara' and suggests that he has been taken advantage of by Kate rather than vice versa: 'If he should be seduced into a marriage, nothing could be more unfortunate' (*Eye*, 58). Lady Scroope draws censure from the narrator for her 'hardness of heart', for putting the dynasty on a higher footing than the individual, and for failing to show any solidarity with a fellow woman:

> In her heart of hearts she approved of a different code of morals for men and women. That which merited instant, and as regarded this world, perpetual condemnation in a woman, might in a man be very easily forgiven.... She knew that the world could not afford to ostracise the men,—though happily it might condemn the women (*Eye*, 133).

Social snobbery lies at the base of the Countess's stance. '[P]roud of her blood' (*Eye*, 8), she abhors the fact that Neville is engaged 'to a girl of whom he knew nothing, a Roman Catholic, Irish, fatherless, almost nameless,—to one who had never been seen in good society, one of whom no description could be given, of whom no record could be made in the peerage that would not be altogether disgraceful, a girl of whom he was ashamed to speak before those to whom he owed duty and submission!' (*Eye*, 62). Given that Kate lives an existence that is so far outside her social world, no generosity towards her is possible: 'no feeling of mercy would induce her to hold her hand in this task of saving her husband's nephew from an ill-assorted marriage. Mercy to Miss O'Hara! Lady Scroope had the name of being a very charitable woman. She gave away money. She visited the poor. She had laboured hard to make the cottages on the estate clean and comfortable. But she would have no more mercy on such a one as Miss O'Hara, than a farmer's labourer would have on a rat!' (*Eye*, 63). Thus she prays that 'the young Earl might be saved from the damning sin and also from the polluting marriage' (*Eye*, 138) at whatever cost.

Punishment comes to Kate's mother too for not adequately protecting her daughter. There is even a hint of impropriety in her behaviour. Rather like the Countess Desmond who, in *Castle Richmond*, is at least as attracted to Owen Fitzgerald as her daughter Clara is, there seems to be an initial attraction between Neville and Mrs O'Hara. She is cast as a sexually attractive woman, with a 'heaven-made nose', and a chin marked 'by as broad a dimple as ever Venus made with her finger on the face of a woman' (*Eye*, 33). But as a beautiful, older woman whose own life has been destroyed by a predatory male, Mrs O'Hara should have better guided her daughter from a danger of which she was very much aware. She should not have allowed history to repeat itself, even more tragically the second time round, and should have refused, on her daughter's behalf, Neville's initial gift of a sealskin and immediately banished him from their lives. Instead she 'was by no means that most prudent mamma' and made 'not only the seal-skin, but the donor also welcome', convincing herself that the 'man had been brought there by her only friend, the priest, and why should she fear him? And yet she did fear . . . there was a deep dread upon her when her eyes rested upon him, when her thoughts flew to him. Men are wolves to women, and utterly merciless when feeding high their lust' (*Eye*, 40–1). Mrs O'Hara's laxity is the product of her desperation on her daughter's behalf, but it means Kate is easy prey: 'Men so often are as ravenous wolves, merciless, rapacious, without hearts, full of greed, full of lust, looking on female beauty as prey, regarding the love of woman and her very life as a toy!' (*Eye*, 38).

As in all of Trollope's Irish novels, the issue of justice is central. In this case, however, no court will get the chance to pronounce because Mrs O'Hara takes the law into her own hands so as to avenge the daughter's ruin:

> During that walk it was that she first repeated to herself the words that were ever afterwards on her tongue; 'An Eye for an Eye.' Was not that justice? And, had she not taken the eye herself, would any Court in the world have given it to her? Yes;—an eye for an eye! Death in return for ruin! One destruction for another! The punishment had been just (*Eye*, 165).

In this novel Trollope avoids the sentimental distortion of a happy ending so as to grapple with Ireland's situation through the domestic plot. The ending is pure tragedy in this work that reads as a distilled rewriting of *The Macdermots of Ballycloran*, without the distractions of the earlier novel's episodic nature, its subplots, and distracting comic interludes. Like *The Macdermots*, it is also an adaptation of indigenous treatments of Ireland as victim, most commonly seen in the classic myth—as perpetuated in songs, orations, poems—of Ireland personified as a helpless and impoverished young maiden who is victimized and raped by a brutal English foreigner who inevitably represents England itself. This is the underlying theme of the Gaelic *aisling* or vision poem, in which the *speirbhean* or dream woman is seen as both innocent and sexually attractive, but also, in political terms, as the incarnation of the country that is abused. Lee Wolff has interpreted the Neville-Kate relationship as 'an allegory of England the aggressor and Ireland the helpless victim',[16] while Robert Tracy sees Trollope's Kate (and Feemy Macdermot) as two Irish heroines who 'are exploited in a way that would seem like deliberately allegorical propaganda if they had been created by an Irish novelist.'[17] He draws attention to how both are 'violated and abandoned by their English lovers, like symbolic Kathleen Ni Houlihan or Dark Rosaleen, the popular nineteenth-century emblems of violated and downtrodden Ireland.'[18]

Trollope's two novels can be read as retellings of Jonathan Swift's *The story of the injured lady* (1746), a pamphlet in the guise of a letter from a well-to-do lady (Ireland) who has been seduced and ill-used by an unscrupulous gentleman (England), and then rejected in favour of an unfaithful rival (Scotland). This would in all probability have been as close as the

---

[16] Robert Lee Wolff, 'Introduction' to Anthony Trollope, *An Eye for an Eye*, 2 vols (New York: Garland 1979), 1, xxi.

[17] Robert Tracy, *Trollope's Later Novels* (Berkeley and Los Angeles: University of California Press, 1978), 132.

[18] Robert Tracy, '"The Unnatural Ruin": Trollope and Nineteenth-Century Fiction', *Nineteenth-Century Fiction*, 37 (1982), 360.

author would have come to the *aisling* mode (although he may have been aware of the echoes of this tradition in both Edgeworth and Owenson. As Michael Griffin has written: 'Swift was adapting the narrative element of the *aisling* mode when he composed the story of the injured lady (1846), in which Ireland is represented, or represents herself, as a once-beautiful woman betrayed and left neglected, forlorn, and ragged by a fickle England'.[19] Swift's work opens with an admonition from the lady who has been 'ruined by the inconstancy and unkindness of a lover' and urges 'credulous maids, never to put too much trust in deceitful men'. The ruined lady is also at fault for having 'yielded to all his usurpations' and accepted 'a hundred other hardships' heaped upon her until her estate became indigent—'my poor tenants are so sunk and impoverished, that, instead of maintaining me suitable to my quality, they can hardly find me clothes to keep me warm, or provide the common necessaries of life for themselves.'[20] In the words of Timothy McLoughlin:

> What the allegory does is to make an imaginative appropriation of the violence of the master (England) in order to reproduce it as an indictment of him and to rouse sympathy for her. He is given no say. It is not in the nature of the letter to give him a voice. What we have instead is a woman's moral denunciation framed by the opening and closing remarks about his, and by analogy England's, 'inconstancy and unkindness.'[21]

The lady in Swift blames herself as much as the gentleman for her seduction and claims: 'I was undone by the common arts practised upon all easy credulous virgins, half by force, and half by consent, after solemn vows and protestations of marriage.'[22] These lines later reverberate in the terrible scenarios lived by both Feemy, 'the incarnation of her country',[23] and Kate. As in Swift, the brunt of Trollope's narrative protest in both *The Macdermots* and *An Eye for an Eye* falls less on the original seduction and more on the Englishman's behaviour thereafter. Unlike Swift, Trollope gives Neville a voice but does so only in order to expose his duplicity.

Thomas Tracy notes that Trollope portrays Mrs O'Hara's vengeance 'as understandable, if not justifiable' and that Trollope's vision is 'far more

[19] Michael Griffin, *Enlightenment in Ruins: The Geographies of Oliver Goldsmith* (Lewisburg, PA: Bucknell University Press, 2013), 89.

[20] Jonathan Swift, 'The Story of the Injured Lady,' in *The Prose Works of Jonathan Swift*, ed. Temple Scott, 12 vols (London: Bell, 1903), VII, 97, 99, 101.

[21] Timothy McLoughlin, 'An Irish Reaction to English Domination: Swift's *The Story of an Injured Lady*', *Cycnos*, 6 (June 2008). http://revel.unice.fr/cycnos/index.html?id=1140.

[22] Swift, 'Injured Lady', 99.

[23] T. H. S. Escott, *Anthony Trollope. His Work, Associates and Literary Originals* (London: John Lane/Bodley Head, 1913), 66.

sympathetic than many of his contemporary countrymen's.'[24] He reads the novel as a 'condemnation of a corrupt British colonial enterprise', which is, he claims, suggested through the evocation of the 'Elizabethan structure' that is Scroope Manor. The Scroope name is used, in Tracy's words, to refer 'to a period which is significant for the consolidation of British power in Ireland.' Trollope may well wish to allude to British colonialism in Ireland—also through references to Shakespeare's Henriad (the Scroope name, spelt without an 'e', appears both in Richard II and Henry IV), an almost obligatory model for historical fiction after Scott, but he does so not to castigate the British colonization of Ireland or to conclude that 'the impossibility of Union is insisted upon', but rather to point to the limits of subsequent British management of the country. In Tracy's words:

> Trollope suggests through the marriage plot that Britain's role in Ireland is illegitimate, insofar as its policies constitute a corrupt exercise of power by a ruling authority out of touch with its society's ideals. It is the irresponsibility of the superior partner of the Union toward the Irish, and the resulting intransigent disaffection of the weaker, that comprises the 'argument' of *An Eye for an Eye*.[25]

Tracy notes that several speeches by Richard Scroop, Archbishop of York in *Henry IV, Part II*, directly invoke rebellion against an irresponsible government, but to suggest that Trollope wishes to assert something similar against British government in Ireland, because of the mere use of the name 'Scroope', is a step too far, as is his claim that the 'nation which becomes visible in Trollope's novel is, however, a Great Britain which cannot include Ireland.'[26] On the contrary, Trollope, while castigating Britain for its ongoing mismanaging or even mistreatment of Ireland, continues to refuse to countenance a separation. Ireland's role of both victim and dependant is portrayed through Kate's neglect and destruction, and Mrs O'Hara's subsequent violence and long-term dependence on the Earl of Scroope. Trollope does not put the Union in question, even if he fundamentally believes that England has misunderstood, mistreated, and mis-administered Ireland by failing to honour it, and has, in short, been a poor partner. Joshua Monk probably speaks for Trollope, in *Phineas Finn*, when he says he would not have Ireland as 'a kept mistress' (*PF*, 551) but would have taken better care of her within the Union. In *An Eye for an Eye*, Trollope endorses the belief that Ireland has been wronged but sees

---

[24] Thomas Tracy, *Irishness and Womanhood in Nineteenth-Century British Writing* (London: Ashgate, 2009), 159.
[25] Tracy, *Irishness and Womanhood*, 156.
[26] Tracy, *Irishness and Womanhood*, 156.

the solution in terms of England righting the wrong and entering into a
fuller union with the Ireland it has mistreated, in terms of the Liberal
campaign to save the Union 'that English recklessness had endangered, by
instituting "justice for Ireland." '[27] Just as Neville is condemned for failing
to honour his promises and for offering Kate the chance only to be 'a wife
who should be half a wife and half not' (*Eye*, 53), so too England, by
analogy, is criticized for similar prevarication and warned that the inevitable outcome of Irish neglect will be costly and violent.

When Mrs O'Hara's reaction comes, it is both predictable and unstop-
pable, bearing all the hallmarks of a tragic climax. The victims pile up:
Fred is killed, the Countess of Scroope is driven 'to the verge of insanity',
Kate's mother is locked in an asylum (and will remain a financial drain on
the Scroope family for the duration of her life), and Kate herself is reduced
to an almost catatonic state and longs for death; 'But as death cannot be
barred from the door when he knocks at it, so neither can he be made to
come as a guest when summoned. She still lived, though life had so little
to offer her' (*Eye*, 167). Only two very secondary characters, Fred's brother
Jack and Sophie Mellerby, benefit by marrying and taking over the estate.
With them an unconvincing recomposition is achieved, a fragile status
quo is reaffirmed.

II. A REACTIONARY FINALE: *THE LANDLEAGUERS*

In the early 1880s, the elderly and ailing Trollope returned to matters Irish
one final time with his last work, *The Landleaguers*. This novel is today
seen as one of a group of 'Land War' novels which attempt to address this
difficult period in Irish history in fictional form. Some, such as Elizabeth
Casey's *The Heart of Erin, an Irish Story of To-day*, which was published in
the immediate aftermath of the Phoenix Park murders, was broadly
perceived as a 'pro-Land League novel.'[28] Other works attempted to
tread a course which allowed both support for the difficult plight of the
tenants and understanding for the landlord class. A case in point is Ellis
Carr's *An Eviction in Ireland, and Its Sequel* (1881),[29] which sympathetically recounts the rather contrived story of a family facing eviction

---

[27] Mary Jean Corbett, *Allegories of Union in Irish and English Writing* (Cambridge: Cambridge University Press, 2000), 187.

[28] Elizabeth Owens Blackburne [Elizabeth Casey], *The Heart of Erin, an Irish Story of To-day* (London: Sampson Low, Marston, Searle & Rivington, 1882). For more on this work see James Murphy, *Irish Novelists & the Victorian Age* (Oxford: Oxford University Press, 2011), 171–2.

[29] Ellis Carr, *An Eviction in Ireland, and Its Sequel* (Dublin: M.H. Gill & Son, 1881).

and concludes with the new landlord's son, who has taken over the property following his father's death, promising to reverse the wrongs done in his father's time. Letitia McClintock's *A Boycotted Household* has more in common with Trollope's work in its open hostility towards the Land League and its sometimes awkward combinations of real and fictional events.[30] Rather like Mr Jones, the boycotted landlord in *The Landleaguers*, the main character in McClintock's novel, Mr Hamilton, is an exemplary figure who finds himself reduced to living in difficult conditions because of the no-rent campaign being waged against him as part of the Land War. He and his family are victims of a boycotting campaign which makes no allowance for their previously good relations with their tenants. The novel comes to a close on a somewhat optimistic note with some tenants beginning to pay rent again.

A similar conclusion is signalled in the final chapters of Trollope's unfinished novel, *The Landleaguers*. Very different to *An Eye for an Eye*, an admonitory moral tale about a country on the brink of a tragic and uncontrollable spiral of violence, *The Landleaguers* makes a similar point in its attempt to capture the incendiary moment in Ireland in a fictional photograph, but does so in a form which discards the almost biblical tones of the earlier work in favour of quasi-journalistic contemporaneity. At times, the writing gives the impression that it is almost 'embedded', to borrow a journalistic term from our own times; that Trollope is reporting from a battlefield. He was not. Despite the occasional claim that he was 'in the midst of Irish difficulties and Irish rebels' (*Letters II*, 966), whatever fieldwork there was was done from comfortable hotel rooms (such as the Imperial in Cork and the Royal Marine in Kingstown, today Dún Laoghaire), or in the drawing rooms of the Anglo-Irish great and good. Trollope greatly enjoyed visiting old haunts and catching up with old acquaintances, regaling Rose in his daily letters with tales of his adventures and, when staying in Glendalough, reassuring her that 'the brook still warbles just beneath our windows' (*Letters II*, 978). During his two trips to Ireland, Trollope stayed in the homes of Lord Charles Monck, former Governor General of Canada from 1861 to 1868, whose family seat was Charleville in Enniskerry, with Count Edmond James De la Poer, a private chamberlain to Pope Pius X, who resided in Gurten-le Poer, on the Waterford–Tipperary border, and with Lord Carysfort, High Sheriff of Wicklow and a knight of the Order of Saint Patrick. He also spent time with William Monsell, the first Baron Emly, a respected Anglo-Irish landowner and Liberal politician, who shared Trollope's views on Home Rule and the Land League. He

---

[30] Letitia McClintock, *A Boycotted Household* (London: Smith and Elder, 1881).

appears to have interviewed everyone he met in the hope of picking up the mood of the country and told Rose on 18 May 1882, 'I have done nothing but talk since I have been here, till I am very tired of it' (*Letters II*, 962). He remained somewhat frustrated, however, at the difficulties in getting a clear view of how things stood, telling Rose: 'You can hardly bring yourself to understand the state of the country here, for among the men who are well-informed and thoroughly loyal, there are so many opinions' (*Letters II*, 963). In another letter, partly written to tranquillize his wife, but which is also revealing of his wilful downplaying of the gravity of successive waves of agitation in Ireland, he wrote: 'It is astonishing how one loses here all sense of rows and riots & how soon one begins to feel that the world is going on the same as ever' (*Letters II*, 963). This was an illusion that might have been broken if Trollope had spent a little more time beyond the confines of the Big Houses.

Although Trollope was largely sheltered from them, rows and riots there were aplenty in the Land-War Ireland that he twice visited. From the late 1870s onwards tenants were increasingly exasperated by a lack of progress on agrarian issues and found themselves having to deal with 'an unfortunate conjunction of low prices, bad weather and poor harvests that effectively increased the burden of the existing rents',[31] leaving many of them living in near-famine conditions. Although Gladstone's 1881 Second Land Act reduced the number of evictions and promised fair rent, fixity of tenure, and the free sale of land through the newly established Land Courts, for the campaigners, especially in the west of Ireland, it was too little, too late, and was imposed rather than properly negotiated. It 'brought little or nothing to the cottiers and small farmers of the west who had founded the agrarian campaign. Landless labourers, leaseholders and those in arrears of rent were excluded from the provisions of the measure. In addition, though there was a very modest provision for land purchase, the League's demand for compulsory purchase was effectively dismissed'.[32]

Further fuel was thrown onto the Irish fire when, on 24 January 1881, Trollope's friend and fellow whist player at the Garrick, and now Chief Secretary for Ireland, William Edward Forster, introduced a coercion Bill, hoping it would help check the growth of the Land League and restore law and order. The Bill passed, despite a forty-one-hour-long filibuster in the House of Commons by the Irish Parliamentary Party. Now it was possible to imprison without trial persons suspected of crime and conspiracy and,

---

[31] Alvin Jackson, *Home Rule: An Irish History, 1800–2000* (Oxford: Oxford University Press, 2003), 40.
[32] Jackson, *Home Rule*, 43.

on 13 October 1881, Charles Stewart Parnell became the most notorious arrestee after his newspaper, *United Ireland*, attacked the Land Act. The arrest of Parnell and the suppression of the Land League caused a further escalation of the Land War. Throughout the long winter of 1881, landlords were boycotted, injured, and killed, and destruction of property became routine, even after the release of Parnell and his fellow prisoners in Kilmainham on 2 May 1882.

Forster resigned as Chief Secretary as a result of the decision to release the prisoners. Four days later, his successor, Lord Frederick Cavendish, and Thomas Henry Burke, the permanent Under-Secretary, were murdered in the Phoenix Park by a splinter group of Fenians called the Invincibles. In killing Cavendish, the Invincibles struck at the family of the Dukes of Devonshire—at the very heart, that is, of Whig aristocracy. As Trollope had commented, years earlier, in *Phineas Redux*, 'the fragrance of Cavendish' was 'essential' in every Liberal administration and for this reason Cavendish was part of an almost untouchable elite of 'hereditary Whig Cabinet ministers' (*PR*, 358). Condemnation was almost universal, as Trollope's novel noted: 'All Ireland was grieving. All Ireland was repudiating the crime' (*LL*, 282). Trollope was so appalled by these murders and by reports on the general state of the country that he travelled to Ireland to gather material for 'a novel as to the condition of the country' which, he despondently confirmed, was 'lamentable enough' (*Letters II*, 957). In doing so, however, he over-simplistically connected the Phoenix Park murders with the Land War and ignored the fact that the Land League movement was 'technically legal and non-violent', that it favoured 'publicity and moral intimidation', and that 'the aggregate of homicides was low—sixty-seven for 1879–82, very few involving landlords or agents.'[33] In Trollope's skewed view, expressed in what probably should have been the opening chapter of *The Landleaguers* but is the forty-first, 'There can be no doubt that Ireland has been and still is in a most precarious condition, that life has been altogether unsafe there, and that property has been jeopardised in a degree unknown for many years in the British Islands' (*LL*, 296). Even before travelling over to Ireland, he would have been alarmed by the atmosphere in London, where an 'attempt to blow up the Mansion House was made . . . and the clubs where he dined buzzed with rumours of terrorists stalking the streets.'[34]

His novel, therefore, attempted to directly react to this inflamed situation which he believed was being worsened by Gladstone's overly

[33] R. F. Foster, *Modern Ireland, 1600–1972* (New York: Penguin, 1988), 405–6.
[34] Richard Mullen, *Anthony Trollope: A Victorian in his World* (Savannah: Frederic D. Beil, 1990), 646.

conciliatory position towards Irish demands: 'a period of rebellion is not a
time for concessions...coercion and concession cannot be applied
together' (*LL*, 304). Trollope openly criticized Gladstone's government
'for interfering with the price paid for land in the country,—for putting up
a new law devised by themselves in lieu of that time-honoured law by
which property has ever been protected in England', even if he acknowledged, 'Of my disagreement no one will take notice;—but my story
cannot be written without expressing it' (*LL*, 283). He also had harsh
words for Parnell and saw Irish-American involvement (in the form of
arms and finance) as being particularly ruinous. He was correct to see the
strategic importance of growing American influence and Parnell's skill at
channelling financial and political support from across the Atlantic. In
June 1879, Parnell came to an informal agreement with the American
Fenian leader John Devoy called the 'New Departure'. This called for
'full legislative autonomy for Ireland, compulsory land purchase (official
compulsion on landlords to sell out to their tenants), and an independent
Home Rule party at Westminster. In addition, the "New Departure"
asserted the integrity of the Fenian movement and of its armed
strategies.'[35]

In the light of such developments, Trollope undertook to use his novel
to expose what he considered the errors of such policies. As late as the mid-
1870s, even as Parnell's movement was evidently becoming dominant,
Trollope had insisted, in the pages of *The Prime Minister*, that 'there was
not even a necessity to pretend that Home Rule was anything but an
absurdity from beginning to end' (*PM*, 101). By 1882, however, he was
finally realizing that it was becoming a real risk and wrote to Rose: 'we
ought to see the Parnell set put down. We should try it out with them and
see whether we cannot conquer them. I do not doubt that we could, them
and the American host at their back' (*Letters II*, 963). He also felt the need
to combat the Land League and blithely ignored the complexities of its
position or the fact that, by 1881, even the government believed that the
League was 'actually restraining' rather than provoking 'anarchic elements', even as it pursued its central tactic of boycotting.[36]

In *The Landleaguers*, Trollope forgoes the usual safety valve of setting
his novel at an earlier time or, as was the case of *An Eye for an Eye*, out of
time, and, perhaps conscious that his own time is running out, writes to
the moment. The *Landleaguers* was written almost 'live'—with just a lag of
three months between the novel and the events it was narrating. The
resulting mix of fiction, fact, and politics is sometimes awkward but it

---

[35] Jackson, *Home Rule*, 40.   [36] Foster, *Modern Ireland*, 406.

should be recalled that ill-health meant that Trollope was working in difficult circumstances, mostly dictating to his amanuensis and niece, Florence Bland,[37] and that he had only managed to write forty-nine and revise none of the planned sixty chapters when his work was brought to an abrupt halt as a result of his fatal stroke. Breaking a lifelong rule of not beginning serialization until his manuscript was complete (*Framley Parsonage* was another exception), Trollope allowed his work-in-progress to be serialized in *Life: A Weekly Journal of Society, Literature, the Fine Arts and Finance* from November 1882. It ran for almost two years and a final incomplete volume was published by Chatto & Windus in 1883.

Thirty years earlier, Trollope had concluded his last letter on the Famine to the *Examiner* by exhorting his fellow Englishmen to take advantage of the Encumbered Estates Act (1849), which provided for the sale of mortgaged estates and encouraged investment in Ireland: 'The man who takes a farm in Ireland and lives on it is Ireland's best friend'. He believed such personal and financial investment in a country full of hopelessly indebted properties could favour new economic success: 'Let us trust that their number will increase; when we find it considerable, we may surmise that the long wished-for period of Irish prosperity is at hand' (*Examiner*, 101). Although Corbett has argued that Trollope 'envisioned something like a revived system of colonial plantation in post-Famine Ireland, which would draw clearer lines of class and culture between landed English capital and landless Irish labor',[38] evidence suggests that he was in favour of something more benign and that he sought English investment within the frame of the Union rather than out of some perfidious colonial design. In any case, the hoped-for mass arrival of British speculators did not materialize, even if some 3,000 estates totalling over five million acres were disposed of between 1849 and 1857. However, the Act's liberal aim of introducing wider ownership was frustrated by speculative purchasers, many of whom were Irish Landlords and large Catholic farmers, often referred to as land-grabbers, who often made the rents even more extortionate. Despite this, Trollope chose, in *The Landleaguers*, to tell the story of an exemplary Englishman, Philip Jones, whom he describes as having made the kind of investment he had encouraged in the *Examiner*. In the aftermath of the Famine, the fictional Jones spent £30,000 buying estates in Ballintubber and Morony in County Galway. A modest and also a model Protestant landlord, with 'no horror of a Catholic'

---

[37] Florence Nightingale Bland was the orphaned daughter of Joseph Bland and Rose Trollope's sister Isabella. Following her parents' deaths, she lived with the Trollopes at Waltham in 1863.

[38] Mary Jean Corbett, *Allegories of Union*, 135.

(*LL*, 4), he worked hard to improve his estate and, despite the burden of mortgages, came to enjoy a prosperous lifestyle and 'it was acknowledged that he could not in England have obtained so good a return in the way of rent' (*LL*, 2). Improbably and irritatingly, the narrator claims that before the Land War he 'was much respected as though he had been an O'Jones from the time of Queen Elizabeth' (*LL*, 1). At the time of the novel, however, things have turned sour in his family and in the greater community:

> When his wife had died, the nature of the man had apparently been changed. Of all men he had been the most cheerful, the most eager, and the most easily pleased. He had worked hard at his property, and had loved his work. He knew every man and woman about the place, and always had a word to say to them. . . . He had lately become quick and short-tempered, but always with a visible attempt to be kind to those around him (*LL*, 2–3).

He has four children, the 'elder and the younger were boys, and two girls came between them' (*LL*, 2); Frank, the elder, is twenty-two, and Florian just ten years of age. The girls, Ada and Edith, are nineteen and twenty.

After decades of peaceful coexistence, Jones suddenly finds himself at odds with his tenants, led by Pat Carroll, a Land Leaguer, who has stirred up agitation in the area and led a no-rent protest against him. Tensions overflow when the tenants flood a substantial part of Jones's farm, destroying his crops and effectively wiping out his means to an income. The young Florian witnesses the event. However, having just converted to Catholicism, Florian has given his solemn word to a local priest, Father Brosnan, that he will say nothing to incriminate the culprits. Just ten years of age, he is easily terrorized into silence by the priest, Carroll, and by a frightening masked man named Terry Lax. In the eyes of the narrator (whose simplistic and blanket anti-Catholic stance is at odds with the more open attitudes to the Church in Trollope's earlier works), it is clear that the boy has not been properly raised by his father following his mother's death and thus is easy prey to this Catholic conspiracy: 'the father had made a favourite' of him and thereby 'had done mischief' (*LL*, 4).

Mr Jones agonizes over how to convince Florian to name the culprits, but is also terrified that he will be killed if he speaks. His neighbour and friend, Mr Blake, 'standing up for his country', assures him that there 'is not a county in all Ireland in which such a deed could be done' and insists, 'I think that you are bound to punish him. For the sake of your country you are bound to do so' (*LL*, 30). The repeated use of 'country' ('his', 'your') induces the reader to ask to which country are Florian and Mr Jones bound? To England or to Ireland? The same question perhaps no longer needs to be asked of Trollope, who, in cancelling any pretence of differentiating himself from his narrator, marks his growing affective distance from Ireland. Gone now are the pages of partial justification for Irish agitation which were to be seen in his first two novels. The change, initiated in *Castle Richmond*, saw Trollope substantially disown his earlier identification with Ireland, and it becomes far more pronounced here. In *Castle Richmond*, the narrator observed that the 'hopes and aspirations of his eldest son are as the breath of his nostrils to an Englishman who has been born to land and fortune' (*CR*, 378) in reference to Thomas Fitzgerald's Irish-born but English-educated son, Herbert. Loyalty for the Irish Fitzgeralds is, for Trollope, first and foremost, loyalty to England. It is almost as if it is impossible to conceive of a loyalty to Ireland, a country which, increasingly for Trollope, exists only as an appendix to Britain.

Eventually, along with Carroll's brother Terry, Florian bows to pressure from his family and from Captain Yorke Clayton, who is leading the investigation, to behave in a manner fitting to his gentlemanly status, that is to 'break a promise' rather than 'tell a lie' (*LL*, 92) and to testify and ensure that Carroll is brought to trial. All too predictably and tragically, Florian is shot dead by Lax just as he begins his journey to court with his father, and Terry is later murdered in the courtroom. Their evidence and the entire case against Lax dies with them.

As always there is a secondary, domestic plot, but rarely in Trollope has the connection between the two plotlines seemed more awkward. This plot hinges on the engagement of Frank Jones and Rachel O'Mahony, a young Irish-American opera singer of some notoriety who is the daughter of the American-born but still very Irish Gerald O'Mahony. A rather incongruous friend of Mr Jones, O'Mahony is a rabble-rousing Home Rule MP, who lives with his daughter in rented accommodation in London: he to tend to his parliamentary duties, she to pursue her singing career, which is managed by the unscrupulous Jewish-American promoter, Mr Mahomet M. Moss. O'Mahony is a wrong-headed but good-natured freeloader who shamelessly lives off his daughter and is shown in sharp contrast with Frank Jones, whose pride prevents him from marrying Rachel because he does not have the means to be financially independent of her. In fact, because of his family's new-found poverty, Frank believes he is in no position to marry Rachel and their engagement is broken off. She subsequently gets engaged to Lord Castlewell, a shady but wealthy patron of Covent Garden, who has supported her singing career financially. Sadly, Rachel becomes ill and loses her voice. Her singing career is over. She subsequently breaks off this new engagement, partly out of annoyance with Castlewell's low opinion of her father, and a return to Frank seems imminent when the narrative breaks off.

The final strand of the novel involves the love story between Captain Clayton and Edith, the less beautiful but more intelligent of Jones's daughters. An energetic opponent of the Land Leaguers, Clayton spends as much time as possible at Castle Morony so as to see the two adoring sisters but also to impose order in the neighbourhood. He is a courageous officer who strives to bring Carroll to justice but is himself shot in an ambush. He is taken to Castle Morony to be nursed to health, and falls in love with Edith whom, it can be presumed, he is destined to marry. Thus, with these two marriages and a gradual diminution of Land League protest in the pipeline when the narrative stops, Trollope is on the cusp of suggesting a national and domestic recomposition.

Given that the novel was published in book form, unfinished, after his death, early critics were loath to be overly negative. The *Academy* probably spoke for many with its words: '*De mortuis nil* – for it would be affectation to say anything good of such a novel as *The Landleaguers*', which was seen as little more than a rehash of the previous three years of Irish history.[39] The *Spectator* thought the novel a mistake, neither a pamphlet nor a novel, but an uneasy mix soured by Trollope's lack of sympathy with any Irish 'policy that had any semblance of the heroic'. The *Athenaeum* thought it 'more interesting than the generality of his books, in as much as his minuteness of delineation is brought to bear on characters somewhat further removed from every-day English experience'.[40] The liberal *Westminster Review* felt the novel, even unfinished, 'worthy of [Trollope's] best days', and praised what it judged the dispassionate and knowledgeable 'State of Ireland' chapter with its attack on Gladstonian Liberalism, 'notwithstanding that he himself was, all his life, a consistent supporter of the great Liberal Party',[41] a view that reads more as a political endorsement than an acclamation of the work's aesthetic qualities.

When *The Landleaguers* is given attention in book-length critical studies, it is mostly fleeting and negative. The Stebbinses, for example, complain that the story was 'recounted without the slightest touch of sympathy. Trollope was like a bystander who witnesses an atrocity and is able to make an accurate report, but completely fails to grasp its inner meaning.'[42] Terry agreed, complaining that Trollope 'was crusading against law reform agitation, and made a story to fit his thesis. He broke his cardinal rule, writing not because he had a story to tell, but because he had to tell a

---

[39] *Academy*, 24 (November 17, 1883), 328.
[40] *Athenaeum*, 2926 (November 1883), 665.
[41] 'Belles Lettres', *Westminster Review*, 121 (January 1883), 276.
[42] Lucy Poate Stebbins and Richard Poate Stebbins, *The Trollopes*, 331.

story.'[43] Barbara Arnett Melchiori criticizes the novel as a partial failure, which neglects to look closely enough at the economics of the Irish situation. The author's 'orthodoxy', is all too evident 'in the rewards he distributed (a bride for Frank, a bullet for Florian) but in the very names he gives these characters. Florian, fussy and foreign for the Roman Catholic 10-year-old who lied to his family and Frank, a name which speaks for itself, for his Protestant anti-leaguing brother.'[44] Tony Bareham is more positive, noting that in 'both his first and last novels Trollope weaves patterns around themes which adumbrate attitudes drawn from experience of a country he had long loved, to which he felt he owed a great debt, and the reality of whose tragedy he grasped with more assurance than has been hitherto recognized.'[45]

It is little surprise that this reactionary novel, with its unlikely ten-year-old protagonist, inspired mixed responses. Whereas in his previous Irish works, Trollope gave reasonably fair voice to the various sides, here he writes for one side only, that of what he sees as the hard-done-by landlords whose centuries-long control of the land was being seriously questioned and challenged. If the early works arose from encounters with a broad selection of Irishmen ranging from the peasantry and the coachmen to the gentry, the *Landleaguers* is the fruit of conversations with a much narrower and more elite constituency, among them Charles Trevelyan's son George, Chief Secretary for Ireland from May 1882, and two members of the Land Commission, the prominent Catholic barrister, John O'Hagan (a son-in-law of the Lord Chancellor of Ireland), and Mr John E. Vernon. Trollope held O'Hagan in high regard while John E. Vernon, agent of Dublin's Pembroke estate, was in favour of peasant proprietorship, and was, according to the *Spectator*, 'the ablest, most cultivated, and most successful of all those land agents who sympathise with the reform. He has managed estates occupied by 5,000 farmers for many years, and has never had a contentious suit. Though entirely unknown in England, no one in Ireland doubted his competence, though Land Leaguers either doubt or affect to doubt his fairness to the tenantry.'[46] Despite the competence of its members, Trollope felt the remit of the commission was 'beyond the reach of any mortal wisdom' (*LL*, 299) and that it was wrong, in any case, to interfere with the free market. He also believed that the commission was overly sympathetic to the tenants.

[43] R. C. Terry, *Anthony Trollope: The Artist in Hiding* (Basingstoke: Macmillan, 1977), 192.

[44] Barbara Arnett Melchiori, *Terrorism in the Late Victorian Novel* (London: Croom Helm, 1985), 85.

[45] Anthony Bareham, 'First and Last: Towards a Re-Appraisal of Trollope's *The Macdermots of Ballycloran* and *The Landleaguers*', *Durham University Journal*, 47 (1986), 317.

[46] *Spectator* (23 July 1881), 5. http://archive.spectator.co.uk/article/23rd-july-1881/5/the-irish-land-commission.

So strong was Trollope's abhorrence for the forms of agitation in Ireland that it blinded him to see the injustices that caused them. Where, forty years earlier, he had given partial voice to that same sense of injustice, now all his sympathy is with the landed gentry. He shows himself to be out of touch in his inability to acknowledge that the Irish Party at Westminster was being led by exponents of the same landed gentry, fighting for a very different agenda to the retrenchment suggested in this novel. And yet, despite many necessary reservations about the novel's reactionary politics and Trollope's fading and by now unreliable (if not dishonest) feel for the country, there remains much of interest in the text. *The Landleaguers* provides a series of remarkable sketches of what life was like in Ireland during the Land War, sparing no details in evoking real moments of terror in fictionalized form. As Foster points out, when 'Florian is shot from behind a hedge, just as Lord Mountmorris was actually murdered earlier that year, Trollope meticulously relates the deed and the place to the disaster of the 1840s.'[47] Thus we read that the 'place was one where the commencement had been made of a cutting in the road during the potato failure of 1846', which shows Trollope's intent in connecting this fresh atrocity with the horrors of the Famine and its dreadful historical legacy.

At the heart of Trollope's analysis is the belief that Ireland must grow up and move on from its past. Instead the country is in the grip of an irrationality and immaturity which he attempts to portray through his depiction of the two almost out-of-control young protagonists, Florian and Rachel. Florian is 'filled with the idea of doing something remarkable' and is involved in things that he is too young to understand. He has, in short, been asked to partake in an adult world, without having the maturity to do so. He all too easily falls victim to Pat Carroll who, in his father's words, 'had been very intimate with him. . . . All this calamity has come of his intimacy. He has changed his religion and ceased to be a gentleman' (*LL*, 111). The boy's stubbornness and extreme youth are constantly underlined.

Just as the adults in the novel pressurize and exploit the young Florian, so too an analogous charge could be brought against Trollope, who centres most of his novel around the young boy's dilemma but does little to dignify him with an adequately developed character. Instead he uses Florian to stigmatize a new young Ireland he sees emerging and engages in an old habit of accusing the Irish of being immature and childlike, in need of discipline. When Florian partially repents and capitulates to Edith,

---

[47] R. F. Foster, *The Irish Story: Telling Tales and Making It Up in Ireland* (London: Penguin, 2001), 144.

she tells him she knew he 'would struggle to be a gentleman at last' (*LL*, 110). But this is absurd. He is only ten! In telling what he saw, however, he is signing his own death warrant, even if he wins precious little credit or sympathy for doing so from the narrator—or indeed his father, who thinks he has 'disgraced himself forever' (*LL*,11). He wins even less sympathy from the supporters of the Land League who believe he 'deserved his fate' (*LL*, 224).

Rachel, too, is seen by the narrator as being guilty of wilful, even reckless behaviour in pursuance of her remarkable career. Like Florian, she lost her mother and is too often left to her own devices by her father. When in London, she must provide for him and she is left alone to defend herself against the two predatory males who pursue her. Eventually, in order to repel her fawning agent, Moss, she is forced to turn to violence and stabs him. She is accused by the narrator of being 'almost manlike' and of lacking 'a feminine weakness, which of all her gifts is the most valuable to an English woman, till she makes the mistake of bartering it away for women's rights' (*LL*, 123). The lack of guidance for these two young characters suggests a more general lack of authority in the Ireland they are supposed to represent. This is a country run mad, in the narrator's eyes, a country, traditionally cast as female and in need, like Rachel, of authority and restraint. The government under Gladstone is in dereliction of its duty, and the Catholic Church, which Trollope considers the second great agent of social control in the country, has fallen into the hands of radical young members of the priesthood. The generational upheaval can also be seen in the Church, where the senior priest, Father Giles, his name a regretful echo of 'Fr Giles of Ballymoy' and of happier times (for Trollope), fails to hold his curate, an 'ignorant, impertinent puppy' (*LL*, 21), in check:

> But the older Father Giles became the more he thought of the good things of this world, on behalf of his people, and the less he liked being troubled with the political desires of his curate. He had gone so far as to forbid Father Brosnan to do this, or to do that on various occasions, to make a political speech here, or to attend a demonstration there;—in doing which, or in not doing it, the curate sometimes obeyed, but sometimes disobeyed the priest, thereby bringing Father Giles in his old age into infinite trouble (*LL*, 19).

Where in the earlier works the more conservative parish priests held the upper hand, now they have been usurped. Thus, Father Brosnan supports Pat Carroll and believes that

> no rent ought to be paid by any Irish tenant to any landlord—no rent, at least, to a Protestant landlord. . . . Mr. Brosnan thought that for the present a

tenant was, as a matter of course, entitled to abatement in his rent, as in a short time he must be entitled to his land without paying any (*LL*, 20).

While Trollope admits that it 'would have been unfair to Mr Brosnan to say that he sympathised with murderers, or that he agreed with those who considered that midnight outrages were fair atonements', he still implies the contrary and notes how the priest 'boiled with indignation' at every act of the British Parliament and boiled 'with joy' at 'every triumphant note that came over the water from America'. Worse again, he 'had gleams in his mind of a Republic' and thought 'the Chief Secretary was a minister of the evil one himself'. Trollope cannot conceal his contempt for this 'thoroughly disloyal . . . thoroughly ignorant' priest, who has 'no capability of perceiving political facts, and no honesty in teaching them' (*LL*, 20–1).

In focusing on the role he plays in forcing Florian to lie about what he has seen, Trollope, as Foster has commented, indulges in one of 'the oldest Protestant shibboleths about Catholicism, . . . that Catholics are taught it is no sin to lie to Protestants. . . . Trollope defiantly adopts this ancient bigotry, pivoting the first half of the book around the attempt to make Florian tell the truth about the flooding of his father's land.'[48] Equally defiantly, rather than explore the rights and wrongs of the causes for which most of the country was campaigning, he indulges in bigoted depictions of masked men dabbling in religious witchcraft in order to terrify the young Florian:

> But just at that moment the man in the mask, who had not spoken a word, extemporised a cross out of two bits of burned wood from the hearth, and put it right before Florian's nose; one hand held one stick, and the other, the other. 'Swear,' said the man in the mask (*LL*, 17).

While there may well have been priests of the type Trollope describes, the problem is that Trollope portrays Brosnan as though he were representative of the clergy more in general, ignoring the extent to which, in the 1880s as in the earlier decades, the Irish priesthood was anything but uniform in its stance on political issues. Trollope was well acquainted with priests of many hues from his earlier time in Ireland, but by the time he was writing this novel he was mostly relying on second-hand information. His visit to Clifford Lloyd, a resident magistrate on the front line in contrasting the Land Leaguers, may have contributed to his negative stances. The very fact of his meeting with Lloyd alarmed Rose to such an extent that Trollope felt the need to assure her in a letter of 23 May 1882: 'we are both of us safe hitherto. I do not think there is any danger

---

[48] Foster, *Irish Story*, 144.

that we shall be hurt. We are now, (in an hour) going out for a drive with Clifford Lloyd, and I won't send this off till we have got back—so that you may know we are over that danger' (*Letters II*, 963). Lloyd was well acquainted with a certain Father Eugene Sheehy, often called 'The Land League Priest', who may well have been a model for Father Brosnan. A curate in Kilmallock during the Land War, he was also president of the local branch of the Land League and present at a meeting convened by Parnell, in October 1879, to form a central body to coordinate land agitation. He was the seconder on the resolution proposed at the meeting by Parnell, and the proposer of a motion, seconded by Michael Davitt, to send Parnell to America to seek financial aid. Lloyd had him arrested in 1881 and interned in Kilmainham, where he joined Parnell, Davitt, Dillon, and the other Land Leaguers. He was released after the signing of the 'Kilmainham Treaty', in which Gladstone agreed to increase the rights of tenants under the Land Act and Parnell undertook to pacify the Irish people and co-operate with the government. Like many other radical Land Leaguers, Sheehy opposed this deal and continued his campaigning and fundraising in Ireland and America.

If Clifford Lloyd brought Trollope up to speed on various firebrand priests, he himself may have served as a model for the courageous but foolhardy Clayton Yorke, the novel's resident magistrate for Mayo, Galway, and Roscommon.[49] Lloyd was the subject of parliamentary questions in 1881 because of his arrest and sentencing to six months' imprisonment of 'an old woman named Mrs Colman, who was charged with trying to prevent people from buying milk from a milk woman named Reardan'. Essentially, she was imprisoned for boycotting but released on bail the following day.[50] According to J. H. McCarthy, Lloyd was 'one of Mr Forster's favourite subordinates in the carrying out of the Coercion Acts', and as such under constant threat of armed attack and heavily guarded.'[51] Another notoriously zealous resident magistrate, Major Traill, who also worked in Mayo, 'went about with a guard of two policemen, one armed with a Winchester repeating rifle . . . the other provided with a double-barrelled gun loaded with buckshot, and carrying eight rounds in reserve. He himself carried a revolver and six extra cartridges.'[52]

---

[49] Lloyd wrote his own account of his time in Ireland, entitled, *Ireland under the Land League: A Narrative of Personal Experience* (Edinburgh: Blackwood, 1892).

[50] House of Commons debate, Hansard 263 (12 July 1881), 638–9. http://hansard.millbanksystems.com/commons/1881/jul/12/state-of-ireland-the-magis-tracy-mr.

[51] Justin Huntly McCarthy, MP, *England under Gladstone, 1880–1884* (London: Chatto & Windus, 1884), 189–90.

[52] McCarthy, *England under Gladstone*, 192–3.

Before being posted in Ireland, the fictional Clayton Yorke was 'employed as adjutant in a volunteer regiment in England, having gone over there from the police force in the north of Ireland'. As his methods are borderline, many of his Land League adversaries believe 'that he might be detected in breaking out into illegal expressions of hatred, or, more unfortunately still, into illegal acts.' A constant target, he is accompanied by armed police and travels, like Traill, with 'half-a-dozen pistols stuck into his girdle' (*LL*, 105):

> A hundred men in Mayo had sworn that he should die. This was told to him very freely; but he had only laughed at it, and was generally called 'the woodcock,' as he rode about among his daily employments. The ordinary life of a woodcock calls upon him to be shot at; but yet a woodcock is not an easy bird to hit (*LL*, 102).

Yorke holds the Land League MPs in particular contempt for instilling in their followers the belief that they have 'the right to it all. The poor creatures are not so bad as them that is teaching them':

> If you allow such doctrines to be preached abroad by Members of Parliament and Landleague leaders,—to be preached as a doctrine fit for the people,— then you cannot be surprised if the people do as they are taught and hold their tongues afterwards (*LL*, 328–9).

Trollope essentially shares this paternalistic view and routinely condemns the Land Leaguers without ever allowing them an effective voice. The political motivations behind their actions are denied or derided as the violent actions of evil men who are associated with the notions of sin and sinners rather than politics and change. Early on, on being told that Florian will no longer go to church, his brother, Frank, wants to 'lick the young sinner' (*LL*, 5). Likewise, his father threatens the 'young sinner' (*LL*, 13) in the hope of scaring him into revealing what he knows. Later we read that 'Pat Carroll had been the sinner' (*LL*, 101), that is, the one who opened the sluice gates on the Jones estate. Mr Jones sees those who have acted against him as having 'sinned against him' (*LL*, 220). Even the killing of Terry Carroll, who had agreed to testify at the trial of his brother, is termed as 'the murder of the sinner' (*LL*, 243). When O'Mahony speaks out of turn in the House of Commons, the Speaker moves to 'order the sinner to be carried away by the Sergeant-at-Arms' (*LL*, 256) before O'Mahony withdraws his offending phrase. While Black Daly considers it 'bare justice' to 'shoot a man who should lay hold of him or his horse', he resolves first to 'give some spoken warning to the sinner. After that, God help the man; for he would find no help in Black Tom Daly' (*LL*, 74). Thus the term 'sinner' is used repeatedly to describe the supporters of the Land League, with Florian, Carroll, and O'Mahony all equated as agents of evil. Only once is it used to refer to the other side, and that is in an overheated narratorial intervention on the demands of tenants and the practice of boycotting. Having described one outrageous boycotting tactic after another, Trollope comes to a climax suggesting the mindset of the agitators: 'as a last resource, if all others fail, let the sinner be murdered' (*LL*, 305). The sinner in this case is the landlord, but clearly it is not a view shared by the narrator in what is a weak attempt at parody.

The Irish tragedy, in the narrator's view, is that the fickle Irish will follow whoever chooses to lead them: 'When an Irishman does make up his mind to serve the other side he is very much determined. There is but the meditation of two minutes between Landleaguing and Orangeism, between boycotting landlords and thorough devotion to the dear old landlord' (*LL*, 285). Worse still, more often than not they follow men unworthy of their loyalty, and O'Mahony is his prime example of this. Full of 'thoughts of Irish wrongs', he is devoted to 'Republicanism' and, although 'no Irishman, as he delighted to intimate, his heart was Irish'. For the narrator, he was bred in 'utter ignorance of all political truths', and yet is capable of enjoying conversation with Mr Jones, even if 'his theory was that the land should be taken from the present proprietors, and divided among the peasants who tilled it' (*LL*, 34). He also believes that 'something good for his old country would be achieved by Home Rule; though how the Home-Rulers would set to work when Home Rule should be the law of the land, he had not the remotest conception. There were many reasons, therefore, why he should be a fit member for an Irish county' (*LL*, 208). O'Mahony is, like his daughter, more than anything a performer in search of an audience, a man who 'no doubt, could speak well in a debating society or a music hall. Words came from his tongue sweeter than honey' (*LL*, 252). Trollope is disingenuous in making him the only parliamentary voice for a movement headed up by as complex and sophisticated a politician as Parnell, and in having him argue, in anarchic fashion, against British government, not only in Ireland, but also in Britain:

> But on the wrongs arising from the want of Home Rule he was warmer even than on those which the land question had produced. 'Why should Ireland be governed by a British Parliament, a British Lord-Lieutenant, a British Chief-Secretary, a British Commander-in-Chief, and trodden under foot by a British soldiery? Why should Scotland be so governed, why should Wales, why should Yorkshire?' (*LL*, 34).

The narrator will reinforce this trivializing of the Irish situation later in the novel when pretending to praise the Irish capacity for applying the techniques of boycotting, which a Yorkshire or a Lancashire man might 'in half a century learn' when 'County Mayo and County Galway rose to the requirements of the art almost in a night!' (*LL*, 139).

Soon, the disastrous consequences of the 'quickness and perfection with which this science was understood and practised' are revealed in the most patronising of terms. Unlike 'we Englishmen', 'at the first whisper of the word all Ireland knew how to ruin itself. This was done readily by people of the poorer class,—without any gifts of education, and certainly the immoderate practice of the science displays great national intelligence' (*LL*, 140). Once again, no credit is given for the personal cost incurred by supporters of this political movement for political change. Nor are Irish economic issues given anything other than slighting, parodic treatment. O'Mahony's not unreasonable suggestion that 'Irish knives should be made of Irish steel' is rebuffed by Mr Jones: 'Heaven help the man who would want to cut his mutton. His best chance would be that he would soon have no mutton to cut' (*LL*, 35), and this is not challenged by the narrator, even though plenty of meat was being produced in Ireland at the time—even if the English market was increasingly looking to suppliers elsewhere to the detriment of Irish farmers.

The Irish aspiration towards a strengthening of the economy is undermined by the author's choice to explain it, second-hand, through Rachel's letters to Frank. Rachel has many qualities, especially of self-preservation, but, by her own admission, understands and cares little about Ireland or its politics:

> how am I to know whether they [the Irish people] ought to be allowed to make their own petticoats, or why it is that they don't do so? He says it's the London Parliament; and that if they had members in College Green, the young women would go to work at once, and make petticoats for all the world. I don't understand it, and wish that he had someone else to lecture to (*LL*, 60).

Rachel is cast as another female embodiment of Ireland who, for a time, enjoys the success gained 'by her own efforts' (*LL*, 289). Ultimately, however, she does not have the strength to make her own way. Trollope conveys an image of Rachel (and by extension of Ireland) as both apparently forthright and fierce but substantially fragile and in need of help: 'she looked as though she might be blown away. She was very fair, and small and frail to look at' (*LL*, 48).

Within a short time of his election, the indisciplined O'Mahony, the very antithesis of Trollope's early Irish parliamentary hero, Phineas Finn, becomes the subject of annoyance and ridicule even among his own party, while the British establishment feels he is an unsuitable presence in Parliament. Foster is correct when he writes that in O'Mahony 'the career of Phineas Finn is reversed: the anti-hero, so far from being educated through exposure to the high-political world, brings it down to his own level of burlesque.'[53] O'Mahony is a scurrilous version of various Irish figures in Westminster, including John Dillon and Michael Davitt, and of John Francis O'Mahony (1816–1877), a founding member of the Fenian Brotherhood in the United States and a one-time ally of O'Connell, who became impatient with the lack of progress towards Repeal, joined Smith O'Brien's Young Ireland movement, and participated in the failed Rebellion of 1848.

When O'Mahony seeks the candidature for Cavan, he is opposed by a 'pork-butcher possessed of some small means and unlimited impudence' who 'had put himself forward'. O'Mahony is selected after his opponent is shown 'to be very ignorant in his use of the Queen's English' (*LL*, 209). By linking O'Mahony to a pork butcher, Trollope may have wished to allude to Joseph Gillies Biggar, an Irish Party MP and convert to Catholicism, who was elected for Cavan and became one of the leading practitioners of Irish Party obstructionism. Biggar was subjected, as a result, to racist and classist attack. As *The World* put it in 1875: 'When Mr Biggar rises to address the House, a whiff of salt pork seems to float upon the gale, and the air is heavy with the kippered herring.'[54] Biggar became notorious in 1875 when, in the Commons sitting of 27 April, he rose to tell the house that he 'espied strangers' and, in accordance with the then existing rules of the House of Commons

> all the occupants of the different galleries, excepting those of the ladies' gallery, had to retire. The Prince of Wales was among the distinguished visitors to the assembly on this particular evening, a fact which added considerable effect to the proceeding of the member for Cavan.

He was denounced by leaders on both sides of the House and held 'to be wanting in the instincts of a gentleman':

> 'I think,' said the late Mr. George Bryan, another member of Mr. Butt's party, 'that a man should be a gentleman first and a patriot afterwards,' a statement which was, of course, received with wild cheers.[55]

Trollope's O'Mahony is considered guilty of very similar failings by his parliamentary peers. However, seen in historical terms, Trollope's parliamentarian is a travesty of the actual Irish representatives in Westminster

---

[53] Foster, *Irish Story*, 139–40. [54] *The World*, 5 March 1875.

[55] T. P. O'Connor, *Gladstone-Parnell and the Great Irish Struggle. A Complete and Thrilling History of the Fearful Injustice and Oppression inflicted upon the Irish tenants by Landlordism supported by coercive legislation* (Toronto: J. S. Robertson & Bros., 1886), 63–4.

of the time, and is testimony to the author's desire to damage the Irish leadership through his fiction—to 'see the Parnell set put down' as he put it (*Letters II*, 963)—rather than to represent it fairly.

Trollope's Irish landlords, Protestant and Catholic, are, on the other hand, almost invariably presented in a positive light. As is so often the case, Trollope shows a sure touch in his choice of names—Blake, Morris, Bodkin, Daly, Persse—for these west-of-Ireland members of the gentry. 'Mr. Blake, of Carnlough' is 'the first Irishman with whom Mr. Jones had become acquainted in the County Galway' and a popular 'man of good property'. He is a Protestant who has 'not made himself odious to the Roman Catholics around him as an Orangeman', nor is he 'considered to be hard as a landlord' (*LL*, 27). Sir Nicholas Bodkin is also favourably presented as a popular and respected Catholic member of the gentry, 'a sporting man' with '£5000 a year', who 'spent every shilling of it' and 'preserved his foxes loyally'. Thirty years earlier, 'as a Roman Catholic he was hardly equal in standing to some of his Protestant neighbours', but progress has been made: 'things are changed now. Sir Nicholas's neighbours, such of them at least that are Protestants, regard Sir Nicholas as equal to themselves. They do not care much for his religion'. More importantly,

> they know that he is not a Home-Ruler, or . . . a Land Leaguer. He is, in fact, one of themselves as a county gentleman, and the question of religion has gone altogether into abeyance. . . . He liked to get his rents paid, and as long as his tenants would pay them, he was at one with them. They had begun now to have opinions of their own upon the subject, and he was at one with them no longer (*LL*, 63).

These landlords are shown to be responsible and moderate men and no attempt is made to see them through the eyes of the tenantry. They are in marked contrast to Black Daly, the bellicose Master of the Hunt who thinks that the Land Leaguers, who block hunts throughout the west of Ireland, are 'children of Satan' (*LL*, 95). While the various landlords and other members of the hunt accept that times are altered, for Daly, the stoppage is a personal catastrophe that spells the end of a way of life. 'If a crowd of disloyal Roman Catholics chose to prevent the gentry in their hunting . . . what would become of Black Daly if the people of the county refused to allow his hounds to run?' (*LL*, 78). He refuses to accept the inevitable when he finds crowds blocking his hunt, and his desperate persistence is brilliantly conveyed as he rides himself and his horses to exhaustion in the vain hope of finding a fox. In the end he rides on alone, 'as grim as death' (*LL*, 84), accompanied only by his servant, knowing that the 'occupation of his life was over' (*LL*, 81). Given the centrality of hunting for Trollope, it would be wrong not to underline the metaphorical importance of this depiction. The passing of hunting in Ireland signifies what Trollope refused to countenance: the passing of the status quo in Ireland. *The Landleaguers*, even if it gestures towards a partial recomposition, contains all his fear that such a change was becoming inevitable and was being facilitated by the political actions of the party that he had always supported, the Liberals:

> It does not suit the present writer to name any individual statesman. He neither wishes to assist in raising a friend to the gods, or to lend his little aid in crushing an enemy. But to the Liberal statesmen of the day, men in speaking well of whom—at a great distance—he has spent a long life, he is now bound to express himself as opposed (*LL*, 299).

Given that Trollope wrote that 'nothing can reconcile me to a man [Gladstone] who has behaved so badly about Ireland' (*Letters II*, 978), there is good reason to believe, as Mullen has argued, that if he had lived on 'he would have become a Liberal Unionist and followed his friends Forster and Sir Henry James in breaking with Gladstone over his Home Rule policy for Ireland.'[56] In Black Daly's black-and-white view, Gladstone and Bright are 'the two very worst men in the whole empire for governing a country':

> It was the business of a Protestant to take rent, and of a Roman Catholic to pay rent. There were certain deviations in this ordained rule of life, but they were only exceptions. The Roman Catholics had the worst of this position, and the Protestants the best. Therefore the Roman Catholics were of course quarrelling with it, and therefore the Roman Catholics must be kept down. Such had been Mr. Daly's general outlook into life (*LL*, 68).

Daly favours the introduction of 'Martial law with a regiment in each county, and a strong colonel to carry it out' (*LL*, 162–3), but there is no evidence that Trollope, even if he believed there had been a dangerous erosion of authority, favoured so radical a step. He did, however, have huge sympathy for those landlords who were being boycotted and he conveyed their difficulties movingly and effectively. Once more, the novel's domestic plot is used to do ideological work as Trollope, challenged by the radical nature of what he sees happening in Ireland, frets over his lifelong belief in slow, gradual change, and paints a vision of uncontrolled upheaval being led from below. He attempts to convey this by depicting parallel situations in which parents are either absent or ineffectual and where the young are allowed to assume responsibilities beyond their maturity (Florian and Rachel). All proper hierarchical

---

[56] Mullen, *A Victorian*, 643.

relations are seen to have broken down as children usurp their seniors: 'Father is more like my son than my father' (*LL*, 123), Rachel says, while the narrator later comments about the peculiarity of the connection 'which bound a violent Landleagueing Member of Parliament with the prima donna of the day. They were father and daughter, but they looked more like husband and wife, and it always seemed that Rachel had her own way' (*LL*, 244). Similarly, potential wives (Rachel and Edith) seem to hold command over their potential husbands, with Rachel believing that 'a wife ought to be equal to the husband' (*LL*, 3), but there is little evidence that Trollope shared this view. Just as his novels largely endorse the subordinate role of women in marriage, so too they argue that Ireland's interests are best served through her continued subordination to England. This was the natural order of things. Whereas in the past he urged England to treat Ireland well, as though in a marriage of almost equals, now his message has become one of tough love.

Trollope's narrative also expresses the worry that the Irish Catholic Church was allowing younger, rebellious priests to gain the upper hand over their more conservative seniors and doing damage by backing tenants in their heightening list of demands. Similarly, those belonging to the more fortunate classes are shown to err in not maintaining a distance from the tenantry. Florian's mistake, like that of Thady Macdermot before him, is that he does not stick to his class but gets involved with his father's tenants and is corrupted by them just as they have been corrupted by their leaders in the Irish Party, the Land League, and the Church.

In his earlier novels, Trollope individualized his Irish characters of all social levels, albeit treating those pertaining to the lower orders in a comic vein, but now there is not a shred of comedy. The protesting Land Leaguers are seen at best as unscrupulous opportunists. In the central chapter describing the blocking of the hunt, a certain Kit Mooney, 'a baker from Claregalway, who in these latter days had turned Landleaguer', is presented as 'one who simply thought that his bread might be better buttered for him on that side of the question. He was not an ardent politician; but few local Irishmen were so. Had no stirring spirits been wafted across the waters from America to teach Irishmen that one man is as good as another, or generally better, Kit Mooney would never have found it out' (*LL*, 78). It is mendacious of Trollope to sum up his, and the Land Leaguers' beliefs with the following formula: 'if a man did not pay his rent, but kept his money in his pocket, he manifestly did two good things; he enriched himself, and he so far pauperised the landlord, who was naturally his enemy' (*LL*, 78).

Throughout the novel the tenantry is viewed as a dangerous, child-like, monolithic body, led by men such as Pat Carroll who are 'going around the country as bold as brass' (*LL*, 88). Frank Jones declares that he 'never saw the boys swarm about a place so thick' (*LL*, 141), and the crowd in the courtroom are described as having 'swarmed into court' (*LL*, 228). The idea of a carefully delineated 'us' against the swarming mass of Irish peasants which, among other things, is capable of implementing the 'science' of boycotting with 'quickness and perfection' (*LL*, 139), is evoked times over in the novel. Mullen's contention that 'Trollope's basic position was a loving paternalism'[57] describes well his attitude in this latter Irish novel (even if the love seems in scarce supply) and helps explain his new-found sympathy towards the landlord class which he had castigated in earlier works. The landlords, he seems to suggest, attempt to govern the people, 'the swarm', in a fatherly manner, but instead of being thanked for this all they get are unreasonable demands for new rights and indeed for new politics, which are pursued with methods that prove 'all Ireland knew how to ruin itself' (*LL*, 140). Florian's precocious and ruinous rebellion against his own father, which is described by Mr Jones as being 'against his country, against his religion, and against his father' (*LL*, 86), mirrors in miniature the confrontational stance of the Irish Home Rulers and Land Leaguers against their betters—the Ascendancy and the British. No space is given to the possibility that the Irish rebels have just cause; on the contrary, they are dismissed as a childlike, ignorant, and poorly led 'swarm'. Florian's sister urges him to 'Tell the truth, and your father will at once send you to some school in England, where you will be educated as becomes my brother' (*LL*, 93). If the young Irish boy complies, he will be forgiven and re-educated to become more 'English'. Similarly, if Ireland repents, England will forgive her. It is as if Trollope was still capable of describing what was happening in Ireland but could not bring himself to convey the reasons for such events or to contemplate their underlying causes and consequences.

In his biography of *Lord Palmerston*, Trollope enthuses about the fact that his subject

> had an Irish property in County Sligo, partly in the town, but chiefly on the sea-coast. To this he paid great attention. I remember having been told on the spot nearly forty years ago that that wonderful 'Irishman,' Lord Palmerston, had for the last ten years spent all his income upon the estate. He had just then been over, and the beauty of his presence had probably enhanced the virtue of his operations (*Palmerston*, 13).

Trollope quotes Palmerston's own accounts of his efforts at improving his estate and at building a large harbour and planning for the building of a

---

[57] Mullen, *A Victorian*, 645.

railway so that it could 'become the exporting and importing harbour for a large tract of very fertile country lying on the banks of that lake' (*Palmerston*, 23). Instead of the steady, guiding hands of responsible Englishmen, like Lord Palmerston, who, with the Union, could also be considered 'Irish', and of the various landlords described in *The Landleaguers*, who have been 'beneficient or, occasionally a hard master, and the tenants have acknowledged themselves as dependent, generally with much affection' (*LL*, 297), Ireland is falling into the hands of what Trollope calls the 'new aristocracy' of the Land League (O'Mahony makes no bones about wanting to 'abolish' the aristocracy, *tout court*). Trollope is convinced that if the Land League and the Home Rule Party gain the upper hand, the old hierarchies will be overturned and the country will be plunged into a cycle of fear, poverty, and misery:

> A new and terrible aristocracy was growing up among them,—the aristocracy of hidden firearms. There was but little said among them, even by the husband to the wife, or by the father to the son; because the husband feared his wife, and the father his own child. There had been a feeling of old among them that they were being ground down by the old aristocracy. There must ever be such an idea on the part of those who do not have enough to eat in regard to their betters, who have more than plenty. It cannot be but that want should engender such feeling (*LL*, 339).

But that very suffering, Trollope suggests, will push the people to realize that the old ways were better:

> But now the dread of the new aristocracy was becoming worse than that of the old. In the dull, dim minds of these poor people there arose, gradually indeed but quickly, a conviction that the new aristocracy might be worse even than the old; and that law, as administered by Government, might be less tyrannical than the law of those who had no law to govern them (*LL*, 339).

This, perhaps, is wishful thinking, and what Trollope fails to acknowledge is that Irish politics is falling into the hands of the Irish themselves. But what is at stake for Trollope is not simply Ireland—now seen as a mere dependent 'province of England'—but England itself: 'It is necessary,—necessary at any rate for England's safety,–that Ireland should belong to her' (*LL*, 298). If the Irish landlord system is overthrown, the country's entire system of governance will fail, and that will have huge repercussions for England:

> It may be said that the existence of Ireland as a province of England depends on the tenure of the land. If the land were to be taken altogether from the present owners, and divided in perpetuity among any possible number of tenants, so as to be the property of each tenant, without payment of any rent,

all England's sense of justice would be outraged, the English power of governing would be destroyed, and all that could then be done by England would be to give a refuge to the present owners till the time should come for righting themselves, and they should be enabled to make some further attempt for the recovery of their possessions. This would probably arrive, if not sooner, from the annihilation of the new proprietors under the hands of their fellow-countrymen to whom none of the spoil had been awarded (*LL*, 298–9).

The yielding of too many concessions to Irish demands, especially tenant demands, is yet another example, for Trollope, of the dangers of the 'philanthropy' (not for nothing is O'Mahony described as the 'amiable and philanthropic gentleman') (*LL*, 41). Once again, Trollope takes arms against the philanthropic impulse that he had opposed at such length in *Castle Richmond*. Economics must prevail, and rents should be decided by the market, while granting fixity of tenure is to be dismissed as 'romantic' and 'unjust' (*LL*, 304). Land must not be transferred to 'mutineers' (*LL*, 305) and a stop must be put to the excessive 'benevolence' of the English government and its appointees—'the tear-laden commissioner' (*LL*, 301)—in Ireland. Just as he suggested in *Castle Richmond*, what was needed in Ireland was not charity and concession, but a renewal of loyalty to Britain and the hard line; not benevolence, but the harsh economics of the free market.

9

Afterword

Irish Letters

Anthony Trollope is perhaps the most conventionally English of the nineteenth-century novelists, a man and writer who embodies and represents the spirit of his Victorian age. Nothing in this work attempts to challenge this reading of the author whose Englishness remains clearly visible even—and, at times, especially—in his Irish novels. Everything I have written, however, argues that Trollope became the postman-penman we know today precisely because he left England, settled in Ireland, and launched his two successful, parallel, and intertwined careers there.

This book has attempted to reconceptualize Trollope as ambiguously, unstably, and sporadically a quasi-Irish writer who made a deeply significant contribution to the canon of the nineteenth-century Irish novel over a fifty-year period stretching from the 1840s to the 1880s. Although the bulk of his fiction is concerned with England, he could never let go of John Bull's other island and returned, times over, in his fiction, to interrogate the status and meaning of the Union between the two countries, feeling himself to somehow embody their ineluctable (as he saw it) connection. He is unique among the English novelists of the nineteenth century for the breadth and depth of his knowledge of Ireland, and for his persistence in dealing with Irish themes and issues in his writing. He has not been duly acknowledged for these efforts; nor has a fair hearing been given to his genuine affection for Ireland and the Irish, or to his nuanced if opinionable and sometimes even objectionable political positions with regard to Ireland in the nineteenth century.

In her *Irish Recollections*, English Victorian writer Charlotte Elizabeth Tonna describes Ireland as 'the nation of my second birth',[1] and so too it was for Trollope, who called his appointment to Ireland 'the first good

---

[1] Tonna is quoted by Patrick Maume in his introduction to Charlotte Elizabeth Tonna, *Irish Recollections* (Dublin: University College Dublin Press, 2004), xi.

fortune of my life' (*Auto*, 59). It was in Ireland that he came to understand and hone his own very English qualities which are so often associated with Victorian England: optimism, a belief in progress, self-reliance, and industry. He applied these virtues to his writing and to his Post Office career, and in so doing achieved a level of success, respect, and seniority that seemed hugely unlikely when he started out as a friendless junior clerk at the headquarters of the General Post Office of the United Kingdom of Great Britain and Ireland at St Martin's-le-Grand in London in November 1834, when he came to work in the obscure Offaly town of Banagher in 1843, and when he published his first novel, *The Macdermots of Ballycloran*, only thanks to his mother's literary clout, in 1847.

Having long been an unmotivated outsider and underachiever in London, Trollope was transformed in Ireland into a figure bearing some of the qualities of the Post Office clerk Bagwax who, in *John Caldigate* (1879), is described as being 'a little too energetic' and 'a little too sure'. As Trollope himself put it in a letter: 'There was a touch of downright love in the depicting of Bagwax. Was I not once a Bagwax myself?' (*Letters II*, 815). In the novel, Bagwax plays a vital role in getting Caldigate acquitted by identifying a 'fraudulently applied' postmark and an 'incriminating envelope'. This outcome bolsters Bagwax's belief in the importance of 'a proper understanding of post-office details',[2] a belief that Trollope ardently shared. Bagwax also emerges in the novel as a defence of the professionalism of Post Office workers, who were often seen, as Trollope all-too-well knew, as the 'idle, the weak in mind, the infirm in body, the unambitious, the jolterheads, the ne'er-do-wells, the punys, and the diseased.'[3] Bagwax is one of the most explicit examples of the manner in which the author's demanding and sometimes rewarding Post Office life directly influences his fiction, which is, in turn, regularly concerned with the writing, delivery, and reception of letters of all types.

Contrary, however, to what we might expect, for the most part Trollope avoids writing full epistolary novels, preferring to pepper his works with occasional letters, which usually provide a crucial turn in the development of the plot. As his lengthy essay on E. S. Dallas's 1868 abridgment of Samuel Richardson's *Clarissa* shows, he was sufficiently acquainted with the epistolary tradition to know that it was better to avoid embracing it directly. In his essay, Trollope criticizes Richardson for his prolixity, for

---

[2] For a discussion of the importance of the Post Office elements in this novel, see Laura Rotunno, *Postal Plots in British Fiction, 1840–1898: Readdressing Correspondence in Victorian Culture* (London: Palgrave, 2013), 94–118.
[3] Quoted in Lucy Poate Stebbins and Richard Poate Stebbins, *The Trollopes: The Chronicle of a Writing Family* (New York: Columbia University Press, 1945), 148.

writing a novel that failed in its essential task, which was to 'please', and asserted 'the impracticability of telling stories by means of letters between correspondents' (*Clarissa*, 168). He cites Fanny Burney's *Evelina* (1778) as a rare success in the genre, 'perhaps the best instance we have of a novel told by letters', but he might well have also made mention of Sydney Owenson's *The Wild Irish Girl*, a successful novel told in letters which was undoubtedly a quarry from which he mined much material for his early Irish works. Instead, in his essay, Trollope points to another epistolary failure, that of his literary hero, Sir Walter Scott, who tried and failed with this 'mode of structure' in *Redgauntlet* (*Clarissa*, 168). Trollope learned from Scott's failure and was, in any case, very much aware that by the time his own literary career was beginning, that of the epistolary novel was ending—somewhat ironically given the huge growth of the postal service in mid-century following the 1839 Postage Duties Bill, which ushered in the Penny Post and, for the first time, made affordable postage a reality.[4]

Trollope's first novel provides early evidence of the author confidently inserting letters (delivered by messengers) into his fiction to great strategic effect. The sparingly used but always pivotal letters in *The Macdermots* are testimony to the importance Trollope gave to letter-writing and letter-reading among an ever-wider social group. When Thady is baffled as to how to proceed in his attempts to stop Ussher from visiting his sister, the narrator suggests that a letter would have been the most effective approach. Unfortunately, Thady is poorly educated and barely literate, and does not possess the necessary skills to pen such a letter:

> Had he lived more in the world, he would have had recourse to the common resort in cases where speech is difficult; he would have written a letter to his sister. But this never occurred to him; even had it done so, Thady's epistolary powers were very small, and his practice very limited; a memento to the better sort of tenants, as to their 'thrifle of rint,' or a few written directions to Pat Brady, about seizing crops and driving pigs, was its extent; ... His writing too was very slow, and his choice of language not extensive; a letter on such a subject from a brother to a sister should be well turned, impressive, terse, sententious: that scheme would never have done for Thady (*Macdermots*, 85–6).

The letter never gets written and Feemy's fall becomes all the more inevitable.

Another turning point comes in the novel when Ussher is informed, by letter, of his promotion to a position in Cashel, which will necessitate his

---

[4] Catherine J. Golden, *Posting It: The Victorian Revolution in Letter Writing* (Gainesville: University of Florida Press, 2009).

leaving Mohill and, as a consequence, Feemy. Trollope does not provide this letter but filters it through Ussher's report to Feemy. He tells her that '"they've sent me a letter from Dublin, with a lot of blarney about praiseworthy energy and activity, and all that—" and she knows immediately that things have changed irrevocably: "Ah! I thought so!" exclaimed the poor girl; "you're to go away out of this!"' (*Macdermots*, 280). The narrator subsequently adds a synthesis; a technique, this, which would regularly be reissued throughout Trollope's fiction:

> What he had told Feemy was all true; he had unexpectedly received an official letter that morning from the Dublin office, complimenting him on his services, informing him that he was to be moved to a higher grade, and that on his promotion he was to leave Mohill, and take charge of the men stationed at Cashel (*Macdermots*, 281).

A second major plot element—the Macdermots' loss of their property—is also communicated through a letter. Once again, it is not quoted *verbatim*, but summarized and interpreted by the narrator who is sympathetic to the family's plight. What the letter conveys is that Flannelly would require

> not only the payment of the interest money which would then be due, but also the principal; and in this notice was set forth the exact sum to be paid for principal, for interest, for costs; and it further stated that if the sum was not paid on or before that day, writs would be issued for his body—that is the body of poor Larry Macdermot—and latitats, and sheriff's warrants, and Heaven knows what besides, for selling the property at Ballycloran; and that the mortgage would be immediately foreclosed, and the property itself disposed of for the final settlement of the debt (*Macdermots*, 325–6).

The use of various legal terms immediately suggests the panic with which 'this agreeable document' will be greeted. The physical reality of the letter, quite apart from the message that it contains, is shown to have a powerful effect on Thady: 'its unusual dimensions and appearance made Thady at once feel that it was some infernal missile come still further to harass him, and leave him, if possible, more miserable than it found him' (*Macdermots*, 326). It falls to Thady to break the news to his father, whose reaction is to attack the messenger rather than the source of the letter: 'After that he began to whimper piteously and cry, complaining that it was a most grievous thing that his own son should bring such a letter to him; and he ended by accusing Thady of leaguing with the attorney to turn him out of his own house, and even asked him whether, when they had effected their purpose, he and Keegan intended to live at Ballycloran together' (*Macdermots*, 327). After this scene of futile defiance, Thady 'quietly folded up the letter, put it in the old bureau'. Just as he fails to adequately respond to Ussher, so too, in this case, he avoids taking appropriate steps in order to oppose Flannelly and Keegan, and his family's slide towards ruin is accelerated.

A fourth important letter in *The Macdermots* plays a decisive role in sealing Thady's condemnation. This time it is the unsigned threatening note to Captain Furster which we have already seen in chapter two of this work (and which is echoed, later, in the short but sinister letter from Captain Moonlight to Peter McGrew, the butler at Morony Castle, in *The Landleaguers*). The note to Furster is part of a campaign of intimidation and violence designed to frighten Ussher's successor. It leads him to inform 'head office in Dublin that the country was in such a state, that he was unable, with the small body of men at his command, to carry on his business with anything approaching to security' (*Macdermots*, 449). The perception of general agitation conveyed by this letter becomes a significant element in the decision to hang Thady, and in its immediate implementation which is encouraged by the Lord Lieutenant himself in Dublin.

The final important letter in the *The Macdermots* is written by Feemy to Mrs McKeon to thank her for her kindness and inform her that she is leaving her care and returning home. This letter is given in full to render explicit Feemy's unfortunate habit of withholding the truth. The sting is in the tail of this letter, in the postscript, which reads: 'P.S.—Indeed—indeed—it isn't the case, what you were saying' (*Macdermots*, 485). Feemy's denial of the increasingly obvious fact that she is pregnant mirrors her father's denial of the inevitability of losing his home.

In his highly effective use of a handful of letters—printed in full or summarized, seen at the moment of their writing and of their reception—Trollope was establishing a *modus lavorandi* that would distinguish his fiction down through the decades. Examples that show the importance of letters abound throughout Trollope's *oeuvre*. In the Irish works alone we can cite Barry Lynch's letters, written through Daly, his lawyer, to intimidate Anty, as well as her reply in *The Kellys and the O'Kellys*. Important too are Dot Blake's letters to Lord Ballindine in the same novel, which earn him the title 'Love's ambassador' and play a vital role in keeping Frank abreast of events in the Cashel household. Letters are prominent in *Phineas Finn*, where we read the full text of Madame Max's dignified letter refusing the elderly Duke of Omnium's offer of his hand and his coronet, as well as Laura Kennedy's letter, which effectively announces her separation from her husband. In *Phineas Redux*, Finn is called back to politics from Ireland through a letter from Barrington Erle. Later he receives troubling letters from both Laura and Robert Kennedy, from Dresden and Loughlinter respectively, and then is victim of Slide's attempts to blackmail him over Kennedy's letter to the journalist accusing him of adultery with Laura. In *An Eye for an Eye*, the family at Scroope Manor are able to monitor Fred from a distance thanks to Lady Mary Quin's regular reports, which she sends to the Countess. Kate too writes many love letters to Fred, both when he is in Ennis and when he is in England, and her mother also writes on her behalf. *The Landleaguers* features Rachel O'Mahony's correspondence with Frank and with his sister Edith, as well as the letter (published in full) in which she sends back Lord Castlewell's cheque for £200. Just as poor capacity in speech is a negative mark in Trollope's characters, so too are sloppy letters, only more so. It is entirely in keeping with Castlewell's poor character that the cheque he sends to Rachel is accompanied by nothing better than 'a short scrawl' (*LL*, 197).

What emerges from these and other examples is that the narratorial choice to have characters 'put it in writing'—to communicate, that is, in letter form—almost always provides indelible confirmation of their personality and behaviour (we think of Clara's letter confirming her commitment to Herbert in *The Kellys and the O'Kellys*) and often also furnishes a key turn in the development of plot. The insertion of a letter irrevocably 'officializes', through its evocation of a written form, elements which have already been implied or 'spoken' by a character. This is true not only of the Irish fiction but is paralleled elsewhere in Trollope's writing and reflects his awareness of the mechanics of how letters were written, delivered, read, and more broadly received.

The early Irish novels also suggest that there was still much reliance in the mid-decades of the nineteenth century on private messengers rather than the official Postal Service, and Trollope himself played an important role in changing this situation. In the chapter entitled 'My First Success' in his *Autobiography*, Trollope describes how

> it was the ambition of my life to cover the country with rural letter-carriers.... Our law was that a man should not be required to walk more than sixteen miles a day. Had the work to be done been all on a measured road, there would have been no need for doubt as to the distances. But my letter-carriers went here and there across the fields. It was my special delight to take them by all short cuts; and as I measured on horseback the short cuts which they would have to make on foot, perhaps I was sometimes a little unjust to them.... I would ride up to farmhouses, or parsonages, or other lone residences, about the country, and ask the people how they got their letters, at what hour, and especially whether they were delivered free or at a certain charge.... In all these visits I was, in truth, a beneficent angel to the public, bringing everywhere with me an earlier, cheaper, and much more regular delivery of letters (*Auto*, 90).

In this passage Trollope is referring to his work in both Ireland and England and makes no distinction between the two countries. He presents himself almost as a frontiersman, opening up new territories on horseback so they could be better served by the Post Office. And his work paid off to the extent that by the time he came to write *Castle Richmond*, he could take the liberty of not so modestly illustrating the efficiency of the reinvigorated postal system in both of what he calls 'the British Islands' (*Landleaguers*, 26). At a certain juncture in the novel, Herbert Fitzgerald sets out from Castle Richmond to see his lawyer, Mr Prendergast, in London. On the same day, his agent Mr Somers writes to the lawyer and 'this letter, not having slept on the road as Herbert did in Dublin, and having been conveyed with that lightning rapidity for which the British Post-office has ever been remarkable—and especially that portion of it which has reference to the sister island,—was in Mr. Prendergast's pocket when Herbert dined with him in London' (*CR*, 412). The growth in the scale and efficiency of the Post Office's operations ran parallel with Trollope's achievements as a writer and owed much to his own professional endeavour.

A similar pioneering motivation drove his Irish writing. Rather than create an openly invented fictional world akin to Barsetshire, he sought to map what he saw as the 'real' Ireland in fiction, to naturalize it within the 'English' novel, and to normalize and render it more 'understandable' for his English reader. Just as he sought 'to cover the country with rural letter-carriers', so too he attempted to map as much of Ireland as possible, even if the west and south-west dominate. This form of literary cartography was also an act of cultural possession which mirrors Trollope's appropriation of Irish-English speech in his novels. Charting the land and possessing the language were, for Trollope, two important steps towards understanding and claiming the country anew within the Union. We need only cite the *incipit* of *The Macdermots*, which draws attention to this geographical dimension by locating 'the quiet little village of Drumsna, which is in the province of Connaught, County Leitrim, about 72 miles w.n.w. of Dublin, on the mail-coach road to Sligo' (*Macdermots*, 1). Although *The Macdermots* is for the most part set in County Leitrim, Dublin is also featured and reappears more prominently in *The Kellys and the O'Kellys*, which is mostly set between Galway, Mayo, and Kildare. *Castle Richmond* is located between Kanturk and Mallow in Cork but also takes in Kerry, while *Phineas Finn* connects to Clare (Finn is born there), Cork, and Dublin, with Phineas first standing for the imaginary Loughshane borough which is placed on the confines of Clare, Limerick, Tipperary, and Galway, near Killaloe. *An Eye for an Eye* returns to the stark and dramatic Clare coast, while *The Landleaguers* again is set in the west in the counties of Galway and Mayo.

Sometimes, as in *Phineas Finn* and *An Eye for an Eye*, Trollope fore-fronts his role as a messenger or mediator between Ireland and England, almost as if to blur the differences between them (as he also attempted in the opening of *Castle Richmond*). He wrote his Irish fiction fully aware of the power of his pen as a means of mediating between the two islands, of attempting to bridge gaps and disentangle stereotypes. Of course his views on Ireland hardened over the decades, but for the most part he attempted to put the country's best foot forward in his fiction and also in his private correspondence, where he downplays perceived danger in Ireland, as in this letter to Frances Trollope, written in the spring of that year of European revolution, 1848:

> And I get letters from England, asking me whether I am not afraid to have my wife and children in this country, whereas all I hear or see of Irish rows is the columns of the *Times* newspaper. . . . Here in Ireland the meaning of the word Communism—or even social revolution—is not understood. The people have not the remotest notion of attempting to improve their worldly condition by making the difference between the employer and the employed less marked. Revolution here means a row. Some like a row, having little or nothing to lose. These are revolutionists, and call for pikes. Others are anti-revolutionists, having something to lose and dreading a row. These condemn the pikes, and demand more soldiers and police. There is no notion of anything beyond this;—no conception of any theory such as that of Louis Blanc. My own idea is that here is no ground to fear any general rising either in England or Ireland. I think there is too much intelligence in England for any large body of men to look for any sudden improvement; and not enough intelligence in Ireland for any body of men at all to conceive the possibility of social improvement (*Letters I*, 17).

While on the one hand, Trollope was correct: the Young Ireland 'Cabbage Patch' rebellion of July 1848 was indeed to turn out to be a pathetic farce; on the other, his letter synthesizes all the limits of his way of looking at Ireland. It is written to reassure his English mother, but what it reveals most of all is both his failure to treat Irish politics with the seriousness it increasingly merited, and his belief that Ireland needed to be guided by what he essentially considered more evolved English practice. Just as happened in *The Macdermots*, where he purposefully deflated much of the political potential of the work by turning the murder into a domestic squabble and, in *Castle Richmond*, where he defused the political elements central to the Famine by seeing it all through a providentialist lens, here he openly mocks the possibility of Irish revolution or even of an articulate Irish political stance by essentially stating that the Irish do not possess enough intelligence to organize anything more significant than a local bust up.

Very often Trollope's offhand comments are at least as revealing as his more balanced novels as to where he really stood with regard to Ireland and the Irish. An example of this is to be found in *North America*, when he describes his landing at Queenstown (Cobh) on his return from the United States. His affection is warmly apparent:

> I also went ashore at the dear old place which I had known well in other days, when the people were not too grand to call it Cove, and were contented to run down from Cork in river steamers, before the Passage railway was built. I spent a pleasant summer there once in those times;—God be with the good old days! And now I went ashore at Queenstown, happy to feel that I should be again in a British isle, and happy also to know that I was once more in Ireland (*NA*, 599).

But patronizing old prejudices soon re-emerge and Trollope seems singularly blind to the offence they may cause:

> Or rather I should have been happy if I had not found myself instantly disgraced by the importunities of my friends! A legion of women surrounded me, imploring alms, begging my honour to bestow my charity on them for the love of the Virgin, using the most holy names in their adjurations for halfpence, clinging to me with that half joking, half lachrymose air of importunity which an Irish beggar has assumed as peculiarly her own. There were men too, who begged as well as women. And the women were sturdy and fat, and, not knowing me as well as I knew them, seemed resolved that their importunities should be successful. After all, I had an old world liking for them in their rags. They were endeared to me by certain memories and associations which I cannot define. . . . I myself am fond of Irish beggars. It is an acquired taste,—which comes upon one as does that for smoked whisky, or Limerick tobacco (*NA*, 600).

This well-meaning but singularly inopportune and offensive paragraph reduces Irish human suffering to a picturesque spectacle, even if it appreciates the fact that now (in 1862) there is less beggary 'than there was twenty years since. Things are mending there'. There is also much nostalgia in this vision, which prettifies Irish poverty and justifies itself in doing so by calling attention to the author's 'old world liking for them in their rags'. The fact is that the Irish in rags, the Irish as beggars, pose no threat that cannot be dismissed. The Irish who achieve success, those who manage to assume 'a dignity' which they have 'never known before' through emigration, are ambivalently applauded for doing so. However, they are also greeted with an overwhelming sense of regret because 'the Irishman when he expatriates himself to one of those American States loses much of that affectionate, confiding, master-worshipping nature which makes him so good a fellow when at home' (*NA*, 600).

Although Trollope's Irish politics today are 'out of time' and often cause discomfort, his Irish novels, even if they are frequently pitched stubbornly and uncomfortably against what today may seem like the inevitable movements of Irish history, are fully deserving of attention in their own right as a separate and distinct body of writing both within his own overall output—in the manner of the Barsetshire or Palliser novels—but also as a substantial contribution to the nineteenth-century Irish novel, *tout court*. Trollope remains one of a handful of significant novelists to write consistently about Ireland in the middle decades of the nineteenth century, a period in which the country's literature was reduced to a mere trickle of voices. He is almost unique in bearing witness, over a period of almost fifty years, both to everyday life as he perceived it was lived by various social classes in Ireland, and also to the great historical issues that were at stake in the country as a whole. He may, to our eyes and with the considerable benefit of hindsight, have misread some or perhaps even most of the important figures (O'Connell, Isaac Butt, Parnell) and inevitably have been on the wrong side of many important political, social, and historical questions (agrarian agitation, Ribbonism, the Famine, the campaigns for land reform and Home Rule), but that should not cause us to categorically dismiss his Irish novels as failures that cannot teach us about Ireland in mid-century. While politically we will undoubtedly have reservations, this fact should not negate their aesthetic affective, or moral worth. At a time when the Irish novel often understandably avoided dealing directly with traumatic realities such as the Famine, or took refuge in anachronistic humour, Trollope's voice, for all its limits, emerges as an unusually dogged, courageous, and constant one, offering a series of fascinating (if often flawed) attempts to render the complex Irish realities as he came to understand them.

For all this, Trollope is, quite simply, a vital presence in the literary canon of the Irish nineteenth-century novel and a key voice in the long and complicated Irish-English cultural and political conversation. Not only did Trollope succeed in his mediating role of helping his English readers to understand Ireland and to question their own assumptions about the country, but his works also lead today's readers to better comprehend the complexities of Victorian Ireland and to a richer grasp of English attitudes towards the country and its people. His Irish fiction, fruit of a sense of belonging and of gratitude towards Ireland as well as of his indelible belief in the Union between the two islands, forms a unique and substantial body of work in itself, but also signals an Irish stratum within his writing as a whole and bears witness to the acquired and nurtured Irishness of this most English of English novelists.

Bibliography

TROLLOPE WORKS WHOSE TITLES ARE NOT ABBREVIATED IN THIS VOLUME

Trollope, Anthony. *Clergymen of the Church*, with an introduction by Ruth Roberts. Leicester: Leicester University Press, 1974.

Trollope, Anthony. *Four Lectures*, ed. Morris L. Parrish. London: Constable, 1938.

Trollope, Anthony. 'The Genius of Nathaniel Hawthorne,' *The North American Review*, 129/274 (September 1879), 203–22.

Trollope, Anthony. *Miscellaneous Essays and Reviews*, ed. Michael Mason. New York: Arno Press, 1981.

Trollope, Anthony. *The Three Clerks*. New York: Dover, 1981.

Trollope, Anthony. 'Whom Shall We Make Leader of the New House of Commons?' *Saint Pauls Magazine*, 1 (1867–8).

NINETEENTH-CENTURY JOURNALS AND NEWSPAPERS

Academy
Anglo-Celt
Athenaeum
Blackwood's Edinburgh Magazine
Douglas Jerrold's Shilling Magazine
Dublin Review
Dublin University Magazine
Edinburgh Review
Fraser's Magazine
Hewitt's Journal of Literature and Popular Progress
Illustrated London News
Irish Times
The Nation
New York Times
Saint Pauls Magazine
Saturday Review
Spectator
The Times
Westminster Review

SECONDARY READING

Akenson, Donald Harman. *Small Differences: Irish Catholics and Irish Protestants, 1815–1922: An International Perspective*. Kingston and Montreal: McGill-Queen's University Press, 1988.

Anderson, Amanda. 'Trollope's Modernity', *ELH*, 74/3 (Fall 2007), 509–34.

Archdeacon, Matthew. *Everard: An Irish Tale of the Nineteenth Century*. Dublin: Taaffe, 1835.

Archdeacon, Matthew. *Legends of Connaught*. Dublin: J. Cumming, 1829.

Baker, Ernest A. *The History of the English Novel*, vol. 8. New York: Barnes and Noble, 1950.

Banim, John and Michael. *Canvassing, A Tale*. Philadelphia: Carey, Lea & Blanchard, 1835.

Bareham, Tony, ed. *Anthony Trollope*. London: Vision Press, 1980.

Bareham, Tony. 'First and Last: Towards a Re-Appraisal of Trollope's *The Macdermots of Ballycloran* and *The Landleaguers*', *Durham University Journal*, 47 (1986), 311–17.

Bareham, Tony, ed. *Trollope, The Barsetshire Novels: A Casebook*. London: Macmillan, 1983.

Barrell, John. *English Literature in History, 1730–80: An Equal, Wide Survey*. New York: St. Martin's Press, 1983.

Belanger, Jacqueline, ed. *The Irish Novel in the Nineteenth Century: Facts and Fictions*. Dublin: Four Courts Press, 2005.

Berol, Laura M. 'The Anglo-Irish threat in Thackeray's and Trollope's writings of the 1840's', *Victorian Literature and Culture*, 32/1 (2004), 103–16.

Bigelow, Gordon. *Fiction, Famine and the Rise of Economics in Victorian Britain and Ireland*. Cambridge: Cambridge University Press, 2003.

Bigelow, Gordon. 'Form and Violence in Trollope's *The Macdermots of Ballycloran*', *Novel*, 46/3 (2013), 386–405.

Birch, Dinah. 'A note on the manuscript', in Anthony Trollope, *The Duke's Children*. London: Penguin, 1995.

Blair, Frederick G. 'Trollope on Education: An Unpublished Address', *Trollopian*, 1/4 (March 1947), 1–9.

Blake, Andrew. 'Writing from the Outside In: Charles Lever', in Neil McCaw, ed. *Writing Irishness in Nineteenth Century British Culture*. Aldershot: Ashgate, 2007, 116–27.

Bliss, A. J., 'English in the South of Ireland', in P. Trudgill, ed. *Language in the British Isles*. Cambridge: Cambridge University Press, 1984, 135–51.

Booth, Bradford A. *Anthony Trollope: Aspects of his Life and Art*. London: Edward Hulton, 1958.

Booth, Bradford A., ed. *The Letters of Anthony Trollope*. Oxford: Oxford University Press, 1951.

Bowen, Desmond. *Paul Cardinal Cullen and the Shaping of Modern Irish Catholicism*. Waterloo, Ontario: Wilfrid Laurier University Press, 1983.

Bowen, Elizabeth. *Collected Impressions*. New York: Knopf, 1950.

Bowen, John. 'Introduction' to Anthony Trollope, *Phineas Redux*. Oxford: Oxford University Press, 2011.

Brantlinger, Patrick. 'The Famine', *Victorian Literature and Culture*, 32/1 (March 2004), 193–207.

Breathnach, Teresa. 'For health and pleasure: the Turkish Bath in Victorian Ireland', *Victorian Literature and Culture*, 32/1 (2004), 159–75.

Brent, Richard. *Liberal Anglican Politics: Whiggery, Religion, and Reform, 1830–1841*. Oxford: Oxford University Press, 1987.

Brown, Beatrice Curtis. *Anthony Trollope*. London: Arthur Barker, 1950.

Brown, Stephen James Meredith. *Ireland in Fiction: A Guide to Irish Novels, Tales, Romances, and Folk-Lore*, new edition. New York: Burt Franklin, 1919 & 1970.

Butler, Marilyn. *Maria Edgeworth: A Literary Biography*. Oxford: Oxford University Press, 1972.

Byrne, Patricia. 'Anthony Trollope's Ireland (Nineteenth-Century Ireland in the Life and Work of an English Novelist)'. MA degree thesis, University College Dublin, Autumn 1972.

Campbell, M. *Lady Morgan. The Life and Times of Sydney Owenson*. London: Pandora, 1988.

Carleton, William. *The Black Prophet. A Tale of Irish Famine*. London: Simms and M'Intyre, 1847.

Carleton, William. *The Squanders of Castle Squander*. London: Office of the Illustrated London Library, 1852.

Carleton, William. *Traits and Stories of the Irish Peasantry*, 2 vols. Dublin: Curry, 1834.

Carleton, William. *Traits and Stories of the Irish Peasantry*. Gerrards Cross: Colin Smythe, 1990 (reprint of 1842–3 edition containing Carleton's 'General Introduction').

Carlyle, Thomas. *Memoirs of the Life and Writings of Thomas Carlyle: With Personal Reminiscences and Selections from His Private Letters to Numerous Correspondents*. New York: Adegi Graphics LLC, 2001.

Carr, Ellis. *An Eviction in Ireland, and Its Sequel*. Dublin: M.H. Gill & Son, 1881.

Chadwick, Owen. *The Victorian Church*, vol. 1 (1966). London: SCM, 1987.

Cobbett, William. *Cobbett's Advice to Young Men, and (Incidentally) to Young Women, in the Middle and Higher Ranks of Life. In a series of letters, addressed to a youth, a bachelor, a lover, a husband, a father, a citizen, or a subject*. London: Henry Frowde, 1906.

Cockshut, A. O. J. *Anthony Trollope: A Critical Study*. London: Collins, 1955.

Cohen, William A. and Ryan Johnson, eds., *Filth: Dirt, Disgust, and Modern Life*. Minneapolis and London: University of Minnesota Press, 2005.

Colby, Robert A. *Thackeray's Canvass of Humanity: An Author and his Public*. Columbus: Ohio State University Press, 1979.

Connelly, Pierce. *Domestic Emancipation from Roman Rule in England*. London: T. Hatchard, 1852.

Connolly, Claire. *A Cultural History of the Irish Novel, 1790–1829*. Cambridge: Cambridge University Press, 2012.

Connolly, Claire. 'Irish Romanticism, 1800–1829', in Margaret Kelleher and Philip O'Leary, eds. *Cambridge History of Irish Literature*. Cambridge: Cambridge University Press, 2006, I, 407–48.

Connolly, Claire. 'The National Tale', in James H. Murphy, ed. *The Oxford History of the Irish Book, Volume IV: The Irish Book in English, 1800–1891*. Oxford: Oxford University Press, 2012, 399–410.

Corbett, Mary Jean. *Allegories of Union in Irish and English Writing*. Cambridge: Cambridge University Press, 2000.

Craig, David. 'Advanced conservative liberalism: party and principle in Trollope's parliamentary novels', *Victorian Literature and Culture*, 38/2 (2010), 355–71.

Cronin, John. 'Trollope and the Matter of Ireland', in Tony Bareham, ed. *Anthony Trollope*. London: Vision Press, 1980, 13–35.

Crowley, John, William J. Smyth, and Mike Murphy, eds. *Atlas of the Great Irish Famine*. Cork: Cork University Press, 2012.

Cullingford, Elizabeth Butler. *Ireland's Others: Gender and Ethnicity in Irish Literature and Popular Culture*. Notre Dame: University of Notre Dame Press/Field Day, 2001.

Curran, Henry Grattan. *Confessions of a Whitefoot*. London: Bentley, 1846.

Curtis, Jr, L. Perry. *Anglo-Saxons and Celts: A Study of Anti-Irish Prejudice in Victorian England*. Bridgeport: University of Bridgeport Press, 1968.

Cusack, George and Goss, Sarah, eds. *Hungry Words: Images of the Famine in the Irish Canon*. Dublin: Irish Academic Press, 2006.

Dames, Nicholas. 'Trollope and the Career: Vocational Trajectories and the Management of Ambition', *Victorian Studies*, 45/2 (Winter 2003), 247–78.

Davies, Hugh Sykes. *Trollope*. London: Longmans Green, 1960.

Deane, Seamus. 'The Production of Cultural Space in Irish Writing', in *Boundary 2, An International Journal of Literature and Culture*, 21/3 (Fall 1994), 117–44.

Deane, Seamus. *A Short History of Irish Literature*. London: Hutchinson, 1986.

Delaney, Frank. 'Introduction' to Anthony Trollope, *The Landleaguers*. London: Trollope Society Edition, 1995.

Dever, Carolyn and Lisa Niles, eds. *The Cambridge Companion to Anthony Trollope*. Cambridge: Cambridge University Press, 2011.

De Vere, Aubrey. *English Misrule and Irish Misdeed. Four Letters from Ireland, addressed to an English Member of Parliament*. London: John Murray, 1848.

Dolan, T. P. *A Dictionary of Hiberno-English*. Dublin: Gill and MacMillan, 1998.

Dolan, T. P., ed. *Irish University Review, The English of the Irish: Special Issue*, 20/1 (Spring 1990).

Dolin, Kieran. *Fiction and the Law: Legal Discourse in Victorian and Modernist Literature*. Cambridge: Cambridge University Press, 1999.

Donnelly, James. *The Great Irish Potato Famine*. London: Sutton Publishing, 2001.

Donovan, Robert A. 'Trollope's Prentice Work', *Modern Philology*, 53/3 (1956), 179–86.

Dougherty, Jane Elizabeth. 'An Angel in the House: The Act of Union and Anthony Trollope's Irish Hero', *Victorian Literature and Culture*, 32/1 (2004), 133–45.

Dowden, Edward, ed. *Correspondence of Henry Taylor*. London: Longmans, 1888.

Downey, Edmund. *Charles Lever: His Life in His Letters*, 2 vols. Edinburgh: William Blackwood and Sons, 1906.

Duffy, Charles Gavan. *Conversations with Carlyle*. New York: Scribner, 1892.

Duffy, Charles Gavan. *My Life in Two Hemispheres*. New York: Macmillan, 1898.

Duncan, Ian. *Scott's Shadow: The Novel in Romantic Edinburgh*. Princeton, NJ: Princeton University Press, 2007.

Dunleavy, Janet Egleson. 'Trollope and Ireland', in *Trollope: Centenary Essays*, ed., introd. John Halperin. New York: St. Martin's Press, 1982, 53–69.

Durey, Jill Felicity. '*Eye for An Eye*: Trollope's Warning for Future Relations between England and Ireland', *Victorian Review*, 32/2 (2006), 26–39.

Eagleton, Terry. *Heathcliff and the Great Hunger: Studies in Irish Culture*. London and New York: Verso, 1995.

Earls, Brian. 'Oral Culture and Popular Autonomy', *Dublin Review of Books*, 4 (Winter 2007–8). http://www.drb.ie/essays/oral-culture-and-popular-autonomy.

Edgeworth, Maria. *Castle Rackrent and Ennui*, ed. Marilyn Butler. New York: Penguin, 1992.

Edgeworth, Maria. *Harry and Lucy Concluded: Being the Last Part of Early Lessons*. London: R. Hunter, Baldwin, Cradock, and Joyce, 1825.

Edwards, Owen Dudley. 'Anthony Trollope, Irish Writer', *Nineteenth-Century Fiction*, 38/1 (June 1983), 1–42.

Edwards, Owen Dudley. 'Introduction' to Anthony Trollope, *The Macdermots of Ballycloran*. London: Trollope Society Edition, 1991.

Edwards, Owen Dudley. 'Trollope and the Reviewers: Three Notes', *Notes and Queries*, 15/11 (November 1968), 418–20.

Edwards, R. Dudley and T. Desmond Williams. *The Great Famine: Studies in Irish History, 1845–1852*. Dublin: Lilliput, 1994.

Egan, Maurice Francis. 'On Irish Novels', *Catholic University Bulletin*, 10/3 (1904), 31.

Emerson, Ralph Waldo. *The Early Lectures of Ralph Waldo Emerson, Volume III: 1838–1842*, eds. Robert E. Spiller and Wallace E. Williams. Cambridge: Harvard University Press, 1972.

Engels, Friedrich. *The Condition of the Working-Class in England: From Personal Observation and Authentic Sources*, ed. David McLellan. Oxford: Oxford University Press, 1993.

Epperly, Elizabeth R. 'From the Borderlands of Decency: Madame Max Goesler', *Victorians Institute Journal*, 15 (1987), 25–35.

Ervine, St John. *Some Impressions of My Elders*. London: Allen & Unwin, 1923.

Escott, T. H. S. *Anthony Trollope. His Work, Associates and Literary Originals*. London: John Lane/The Bodley Head, 1913.

Fallon, Peter and Derek Mahon, eds. *The Penguin Book of Contemporary Irish Poetry*. New York: Penguin, 1990, xviii.

Farrell, James Michael. '"This Horrible Spectacle": Visual and Verbal Sketches of the Famine in Skibereen', in Lawrence J. Prelli, ed. *Rhetorics of Display*. Columbia: University of South Carolina Press, 2006, 66–89.

Faulkner, Karen. 'Anthony Trollope's Apprenticeship', *Nineteenth-Century Fiction*, 38/2 (September 1983), 161–88.

Fegan, Melissa. *Literature and the Irish Famine, 1845–1919*. Oxford: Clarendon Press, 2002.

Ferris, Ina. *The Romantic National Tale and the Question of Ireland*. Cambridge: Cambridge University Press, 2002.

Filppula, Markku. *The Grammar of Irish English. Language in Hibernian Style*. London: Routledge, 1999.

Filppula, Markku. 'Subordinating *and* in Hiberno-English Syntax: Irish or English Origin?', in Ureland & Broderick, eds., *Language Contact in the British Isles*. Tübingen: Niemeyer, 1991, 617–31.

FitzGerald, Garrett. 'Estimates for Baronies of Minimum Level of Irish-speaking among Successive Decennial Cohorts: 1771–1781 to 1861–1871', *Proceedings of the Royal Irish Academy*, 84/3 (1984).

Fitzpatrick, William J. *The Life of Charles Lever*. London: Chapman and Hall, 1873, 269–70.

Flanagan, Thomas. *The Irish Novelists, 1800–1850*. New York: Columbia University Press, 1959.

Flint, Kate. 'Queer Trollope' in Carolyn Dever and Lisa Niles, eds., *The Cambridge Companion to Anthony Trollope*. Cambridge: Cambridge University Press, 2011, 99–112.

Foster, R. F. 'Adopting Ireland', *Trollopiana: The Journal of the Trollope Society*, 28 (1995).

Foster, R. F. *The Irish Story: Telling Tales and Making It Up in Ireland*. London: Penguin, 2001.

Foster, R. F. *Modern Ireland: 1600–1972*. New York: Penguin, 1988.

Foster, R. F. *Paddy & Mr Punch: Connections in Irish and English History*. London: Penguin, 1995.

Foster, R. F. *The Oxford History of Ireland*. Oxford: Oxford University Press, 2001.

Frank, Cathrine O. 'Trial Separations: Divorce, Disestablishment, and Home Rule in *Phineas Redux*', *College Literature*, 35/3 (Summer 2008), 30–56.

Friel, Brian. *Translations*. London: Faber and Faber, 1981.

Ganzel, Carol H. '*The Times* Correspondent and *The Warden*', *Nineteenth-Century Fiction*, 21/4 (March 1967), 325–36.

Garvin, Tom. 'Defenders, Ribbonmen and Others: Underground Political Networks in Pre-Famine Ireland', in C. H. E. Philpin, ed. *Nationalism and Popular Protest in Ireland*. Cambridge: Cambridge University Press, 1987, 219–44.

Garvin, Tom. *The Evolution of Irish Nationalist Politics*. Dublin: Gill and Macmillan, 2005.

Gikandi, Simon. *Maps of Englishness: Writing Identity in the Culture of Colonialism*. New York: Columbia University Press, 1996.

Gilead, Sarah. 'Trollope's Ground of Meaning: *The Macdermots of Ballycloran*', *The Victorian Newsletter*, 69 (1986), 23–6.

Gilmour, Robin. 'A Lesser Thackeray? Trollope and the Victorian Novel', in Tony Bareham, ed. *Anthony Trollope*. London: Vision Press, 1980, 182–203.

Glendinning, Victoria. *Trollope*. London: Hutchinson, 1992.

Golden, Catherine J. *Posting It: The Victorian Revolution in Letter Writing*. Gainesville: University of Florida Press, 2009.

Goodlad, Lauren M. E. 'Trollopian Form: An Introduction', *Literature Compass*, 7/9 (2010), 851–4.

Gray, Peter. *Famine, Land and Politics: British Government and Irish Society, 1843–50*. Dublin: Irish Academic Press, 1999.

Gray, Peter. *The Irish Famine*. New York: Dimensions/Abrams Discoveries, 1995.

Gray, Peter. 'The Triumph of Dogma: Ideology and Famine Relief', *History Ireland*, 3/2 (1995), 26–34.

Gray, Peter and Sarah Burns, eds. *Victoria's Ireland? Irishness and Britishness, 1837–1901*. Dublin: Four Courts Press, 2004.

Griffin, Gerald. *The Collegians, or The Colleen Bawn: A Tale of Garryowen*. London: Frederick Warne, 1887.

Griffin, Michael. *Enlightenment in Ruins: The Geographies of Oliver Goldsmith*. Lewisburg, PA: Bucknell University Press, 2013.

Griffin, Susan M. *Anti-Catholicism and Nineteenth-Century Fiction*. Cambridge: Cambridge University Press, 2004.

Gwynn, Stephen. *Irish Books and Irish People*. Dublin: Talbot Press, 1919.

Gwynn, Stephen. 'Trollope and Ireland', *Contemporary Review*, 129 (Jan./June 1926), 72–9.

Hadley, Elaine. *Living Liberalism: Practical Citizenship in Mid-Victorian Britain*. Chicago: University of Chicago Press, 2010.

Hagan, John. 'The Divided Mind of Anthony Trollope', *Nineteenth-Century Fiction*, 13/1 (1959), 1–26.

Hall, Anna Maria. *The Whiteboy*, 2 vols, 1845. New York: Garland Press, 1979.

Hall, Catherine. *Civilising Subjects: Metropole and Colony in the English Imagination, 1830–1867*. Chicago: University of Chicago Press, 2002.

Hall, N. John. 'Introduction' to Anthony Trollope, *The Macdermots of Ballycloran*. New York: Arno Press, 1981.

Hall, N. John. 'Introduction' to Anthony Trollope, *The Struggles of Brown, Jones, and Robinson*. Oxford: Oxford University Press, 1993.

Hall, N. John. *Trollope: A Biography*. Oxford: Oxford University Press, 1993.

Hall, N. John and Donald D. Stone, eds. 'Anthony Trollope (1882–1982) Special Issue', *Nineteenth-Century Fiction*, 37/3 (December 1982).

Halperin, John. *Trollope and Politics. A Study of the Pallisers and Others*. London, Macmillan, 1977.

Hamer, Mary. 'Introduction' to Anthony Trollope, *Castle Richmond*. New York: Oxford University Press, 1989.

Harris, Elizabeth Furlong Shipton. *From Oxford to Rome; Rest in the Church*, 1847. New York: Garland, 1975.

Harvey, Geoffrey. *The Art of Anthony Trollope*. New York: St Martin's Press, 1980.

Hastings, Max. 'Introduction' to Anthony Trollope, *Castle Richmond*. London: The Folio Society, 1994.

Hawes, Derek. 'Was Trollope a Freemason?', *Trollopiana*, 47 (1999), 14–22.

H. B. H. *Holiday Haunts on the West Coast of Clare*. Limerick: McKern & Sons, 1891. http://www.clarelibrary.ie/eolas/coclare/history/holiday_haunts/liscannor.htm.

Hennedy, Hugh L. 'Love and Famine, Family and Country in Trollope's *Castle Richmond*', *Éire-Ireland*, 7/4 (1972), 48–66.

Henry, P. L. *An Anglo-Irish Dialect of North Roscommon: Phonology, Accidence, Syntax*. Dublin: University College Dublin, 1957.

Hickey, Raymond. *Irish English: History and Present-Day Forms*. Cambridge: Cambridge University Press, 2007.

Hickey, Raymond. 'Models for describing aspect in Irish English', in Hildegard Tristram, ed. *The Celtic Englishes II*. Heidelberg: Carl Winter, 2000, 97–116.

Hilton, Boyd. *The Age of Atonement: The Influence of Evangelicalism on Social and Economic Thought, 1795–1865*. Oxford: Clarendon Press, 1988.

Hooper, Glenn, ed. *Letters from Ireland*. Dublin: Irish Academic Press, 2001.

Hurst, Michael. *Maria Edgeworth and the Public Scene*. Coral Gables: University of Miami Press, 1969.

Hylson-Smith, Kenneth. *Evangelicals in the Church of England, 1734–1984*. Edinburgh: T&T Clark International, 1989.

Hynes, John. 'Anthony Trollope's Creative "Culture-Shock": Banagher, 1841,' *Éire-Ireland*, 21 (Fall 1986), 124–31.

Hynes, John. 'Anthony Trollope and the "Irish Question"', *Études Irlandaises*, 8 (1983), 212–28.

Hynes, John. '*An Eye for An Eye*: Anthony Trollope's Irish Masterpiece', *Journal of Irish Literature*, 16/2 (May 1987), 54–8.

Hynes, John. 'A Note on Trollope's *Landleaguers*', *Études Irlandaises*, 11 (1986), 65–70.

Ingelbien, Raphael. 'Elizabeth Gaskell's "The Poor Clare" and the Irish Famine', *Irish University Review*, 40/2 (2010), 1–19.

Jackson, Alvin. *Home Rule: An Irish History, 1800–2000*. Oxford: Oxford University Press, 2003.

James, Henry. 'Anthony Trollope', in Donald Smalley, ed. *Trollope: The Critical Heritage*. London: Routledge and Kegan Paul, 1969, 525–45.

Jeffares, A. Norman. *Images of Invention. Essays on Irish Writing*. Gerrards Cross: Colin Smythe, 1996.

Jenkins, Brian. *Irish Nationalism and the British State: From Repeal to Revolutionary Nationalism*. Montréal: McGill-Queen's Press, 2006.

Johnston, Conor. '*The Macdermots of Ballycloran*: Trollope as Conservative-Liberal', *Éire-Ireland: A Journal of Irish Studies*, 16/2 (1981), 71–92.

Johnston, Conor. 'Parsons, Priests, and Politics: Anthony Trollope's Irish Clergy', *Éire-Ireland*, 25/1 (1990), 80–97.

Joyce, P. W. *English As It Is Spoken in Ireland* (1910). Dublin: Wolfhound Press, 1997.

Keen, Suzanne. *Victorian Renovations of the Novel. Narrative Annexes and the Boundaries of Representation.* Cambridge: Cambridge University Press, 1998.

Kelleher, Margaret. '*Castle Richmond:* Famine Narrative and Horrid Novel', *Irish University Review*, 25/2 (1995), 242–62.

Kelleher, Margaret. *The Feminization of Famine: Expressions of the Inexpressible?* Cork: Cork University Press, 1997.

Kelleher, Margaret. 'Prose Writing and Drama in English, 1830–1890: From Catholic Emancipation to the Fall of Parnell', in Margaret Kelleher and Philip O'Leary, eds., *The Cambridge History of Irish Literature*, 2 vols. Cambridge: Cambridge University Press, 2006, 1, 449–99.

Kelleher, Margaret and James H. Murphy, eds. *Gender Perspectives in Nineteenth-Century Ireland.* Dublin: Irish Academic Press, 1997.

Kelleher, Margaret and Philip O'Leary, eds. *The Cambridge History of Irish Literature*, 2 vols. Cambridge: Cambridge University Press, 2006.

Kelly, Jennifer. 'A Study of Ribbonism in County Leitrim in 1841', in Joost Augusteijn and Mary Ann Lyons, eds., *Irish History: A Research Yearbook 2.* Dublin: Four Courts Press, 2003, 42–52.

Kelly, R. J. 'Anthony Trollope and Ireland', *The Irish Book Lover*, 18/2 (March and April 1930).

Kerr, D. A. *A Nation of Beggars: Priests, People & Politics in Famine Ireland 1846–1852.* Oxford: Clarendon Press, 1994.

Kiberd, Declan. *Inventing Ireland, the Literature of the Modern Nation.* London: Vintage, 1996.

Kiberd, Declan. *Irish Classics.* London: Granta, 2000.

Kiberd, Declan. 'The War against the Past', in Audrey S. Eyler and Robert Garratt, eds., *The Uses of the Past: Essays on Irish Culture.* Newark, NJ: University of Delaware Press, 1988, 24–53.

Kinealy, Christine. *This Great Calamity: The Irish Famine, 1845–1852.* Dublin: Gill & MacMillan, 1994.

Kinealy, Christine and G. MacAtasney. *The Hidden Famine: Hunger, Poverty & Sectarianism in Belfast, 1840–1850.* London: Pluto, 2000.

Kingsley, Charles. *Alton Locke, Tailor and Poet*, ed. Elizabeth A. Cripps. Oxford and New York: Oxford University Press, 1983.

Kingsley, Charles. *His Letters and Memories of His Life*, vol. 2, Edited By His Wife. London: C. Kegan Paul, 1877.

Kinser, Brent E., ed. *The Carlyle Letters Online.* Baltimore: Duke University Press, 2007. http://carlyleletters.dukejournals.org/.

Knelman, Judith. 'Anthony Trollope, English Journalist and Novelist, Writing About the Famine', *Éire-Ireland*, 23/3 (1988), 57–67.

Knox, Robert. *The Races of Men: A Philosophical Inquiry into the Influence of Race over the Destinies of Nations,* 2nd edn, London: Henry Renshaw, 1862.

Kreilkamp, Vera. *The Anglo-Irish Novel and the Big House.* New York: Syracuse University Press, 1998.

Lansbury, Coral. *The Reasonable Man: Trollope's Legal Fiction.* Princeton, NJ: Princeton University Press, 1981.

Lasselle, S. C. 'Morality in Authorship', *The Author: A Monthly Magazine to Interest and Help All Literary Workers,* 6 (15 June 1889), 82.

Leerson, Joep. *Mere Irish and Fior-Ghael. Studies in the Idea of Irish Nationality, Its Development and Literary Expression Prior to the Nineteenth Century.* Cork: Cork University Press, 1995.

Leerson, Joep. *Remembrance and Imagination: Patterns in the Historical and Literary Representation of Ireland in the Nineteenth Century.* Cork: Cork University Press, 1996.

Lengel, Edward G. *The Irish Through British Eyes: Perceptions of Ireland in the Famine Era.* Westport, CT: Praeger, 2002.

Leslie, Shane. 'Introduction' to Anthony Trollope, *The Kellys and the O'Kellys,* ed. Shane Leslie. New York: Random House, 1937.

Leslie, Shane. 'Preface' to Anthony Trollope, *Phineas Finn.* Oxford: Oxford University Press, 1973, v–x.

Lever, Charles. *Charles O'Malley.* Dublin: William Curry, Jun. and Co., 1841.

Lever, Charles. *The Confessions of Harry Lorrequer.* Dublin: William Curry, 1839.

Lever, Charles. *The Daltons.* London: Chapman and Hall, 1852.

Lever, Charles. *The Knight of Gwynne, A Tale of the Time of the Union.* Boston: Little, Brown, and Company, 1899.

Lever, Charles. *Lord Kilgobbin.* New York: Harper & Bros., 1872.

Lever, Charles. *St Patrick's Eve.* London: Chapman and Hall, 1845.

Lever, Charles. *Sir Brook Fossbrooke.* Boston: Little, Brown & Co., 1917.

Lever, Charles. *Tom Burke of "Ours".* Boston: Little, Brown & Co. 1913.

Levine, George. 'Can You Forgive Him? Trollope's *Can You Forgive Her?* and the Myth of Realism', *Victorian Studies,* 18 (1974), 5–30.

Levine, George. *The Realistic Imagination: English Fiction from Frankenstein to Lady Chatterley.* Chicago and London: University of Chicago Press, 1981.

Lewis, Samuel. *Topographical Dictionary of Ireland.* London: Lewis and Co., 1837.

Lloyd, Clifford. *Ireland under the Land League: A Narrative of Personal Experience.* Edinburgh: Blackwood, 1892.

Lloyd, David. 'The Indigent Sublime: Specters of Irish Hunger', *Representations,* 92 (Fall 2005), 152–85.

Lloyd, David. *Nationalism and Minor Literature: James Clarence Mangan and the Emergence of Irish Cultural Nationalism.* Berkeley: University of California Press, 1987.

Loeber, Rolf and Magda Stouthamer-Loeber, with Anne M. Burnham. *A Guide to Irish Fiction, 1650–1900.* Dublin: Four Courts Press, 2006.

Lonergan, Patrick. 'Anthony Trollope's Palliser Novels and Anti-Irish Prejudice', *New Hibernia Review/Iris Eireannach nua,* 11/2 (2007), 116–29.

Lonergan, Patrick. 'The Representation of Phineas Finn: Anthony Trollope's Palliser Series and Victorian Ireland', *Victorian Literature and Culture,* 32/1 (2004), 147–58.

Longford, Christine. 'Trollope in Ireland', *The Bell*, 5/3 (1942), 183–90.

Lund, Michael. 'Literary Pieces and Whole Audiences: *Denis Duval, Edwin Drood*, and *The Landleaguers*', *Criticism*, 28 (1986), 27–49.

McCarthy, Justin Huntly. *England under Gladstone, 1880–1884*. London: Chatto & Windus, 1884.

McCarthy, Justin Huntly. *Reminiscences*. New York: Harper, 1899.

McCaw, Neil, ed. *Writing Irishness in Nineteenth-Century British Culture*. Aldershot: Ashgate, 2004.

McClintock, Letitia. *A Boycotted Household*. London: Smith and Elder, 1881.

McConnel, James. 'The Irish Parliamentary Party in Victorian and Edwardian London', in Peter Gray, ed. *Victoria's Ireland? Irishness and Britishness, 1837–1901*. Dublin: Four Courts Press, 2004, 37–50.

McCormack, W. J. *Ascendancy and Tradition in Anglo-Irish Literary History from 1789 to 1939*. Oxford: Oxford University Press, 1985.

McCormack, W. J. *Sheridan Le Fanu and Victorian Ireland*. Oxford: Clarendon Press, 1980.

MacCurtain, Margaret. 'Pre-Famine Peasantry in Ireland: Definition and Theme', *Irish University Review*, 4/2 (Autumn 1974), 188–98.

MacDonagh, Oliver. 'The Nineteenth Century Novel and Irish Social History: Some Aspects', O'Donnell Lecture, National University of Ireland. Delivered at University College Cork on 21 April 1970.

McLoughlin, Timothy. 'An Irish Reaction to English Domination: Swift's *The Story of an Injured Lady*', *Cycnos*, 6 (June 2008). http://revel.unice.fr/cycnos/ index.html?id=1140.

McMaster, R. D. *Trollope and the Law*. London: Macmillan, 1986.

MacRaild, Donald M. *The Irish Diaspora in Britain, 1750–1939*. London: Palgrave Macmillan, 2010.

Mandler, Peter. *The English National Character*. New Haven and London: Yale, 2006.

Markwick, Margaret, Deborah Denenholz Morse, and Regenia Gagnier, eds. *The Politics of Gender in Anthony Trollope's Novels*. London: Ashgate, 2009.

Martin, Berenice. *A Sociology of Contemporary Cultural Change*. Oxford: Blackwell, 1981.

Matthews, Brander. *The Philosophy of the Short-Story*. New York: Peter Smith, 1931.

Matthews-Kane, Bridget. 'Love's Labor Lost: Romantic Allegory in Trollope's *Castle Richmond*', *Victorian Literature and Culture*, 32 (2004), 117–31.

Maurer, Sara L. *The Dispossessed State: Narratives of Ownership in 19th-Century Britain and Ireland*. Baltimore: Johns Hopkins University Press, 2012.

Maxwell, Constantia. 'Anthony Trollope and Ireland', *Dublin Magazine*, 21 (1955), 6–16.

Maxwell, William Hamilton. *Wild Sports of the West*. Dublin: Talbot Press, 1910.

May, Charles E. *The Short Story: The Reality of Artifice*. New York: Twayne Publishers, 1995.

Melchiori, Barbara Arnett. *Terrorism in the Late Victorian Novel*. London: Croom Helm, 1985.

Michie, Elsie B. *Outside the Pale: Cultural Exclusion, Gender Difference, and the Victorian Woman Writer*. Ithaca: Cornell University Press, 1993.

Miller. J. Hillis. *Boustrophedonic Reading. Cultural Memory in the Present*. Stanford: Stanford University Press, 1999.

Mitchel, John. *The Last Conquest of Ireland (Perhaps)*. Glasgow: Cameron, Ferguson & Co., 1876.

Mokyr, Joel. *Why Ireland Starved: A Quantitative and Analytical History of the Irish Economy, 1800–1850*. London: George Allen and Unwin, 1985.

Monacelli, Martine. 'England's re-imagining of Ireland in the nineteenth century', *Études irlandaises*, 35/1 (2010), 9–20.

Moody, Ellen. *Trollope on the Net*. London: Hambledon Press and the Trollope Society, 1999.

Moore, W. S. 'Trollope and Ireland', *The Irish Monthly*, 56/656 (February 1928), 74–9.

Morash, Christopher. *Writing the Irish Famine*. Oxford: Clarendon Press, 1995.

Morash, Christopher and Richard Hayes, eds. *Fearful Realities. New Perspectives on the Famine*. Dublin: Irish Academic Press, 1996.

Morgan, J. H. *The New Irish Constitution*. London: Hodder and Stoughton, 1912.

Morgan, Lady. 'Mount Sackville', in *Dramatic Scenes from Real Life*, 1833. New York: Garland, 1979, 53–5.

Morse, Deborah Denenholz. *Reforming Trollope: Race, Gender, and Englishness in the Novels of Anthony Trollope*. London: Ashgate, 2013.

Mullen, Richard. *Anthony Trollope: A Victorian in His World*. Savannah: Frederic D. Beil, 1990.

Mullen, Richard and James Munson. *The Penguin Companion to Trollope*. New York: Trollope Society, 1996.

Murphy, James, ed. *Irish Novelists and the Victorian Age*. Oxford: Oxford University Press, 2011.

Nardin, Jane. '*Castle Richmond*, the Famine, and the Critics', *Cahiers Victoriens et Édouardiens*, 58, 'Studies in Anthony Trollope' (October 2003), 81–90.

Navakas, Francine. 'The Case for Trollope's Short Stories', *Modern Philology*, 83/2 (1985), 172–8. Review of *Anthony Trollope: The Complete Short Stories*, ed. Betty Jane Slemp Breyer.

Niles, Lisa. 'Trollope's Short Fiction', in Carolyn Dever and Lisa Niles, eds., *The Cambridge Companion to Anthony Trollope*. Cambridge: Cambridge University Press, 2011, 71–84.

Nolan, Emer. *Catholic Emancipations: Irish Fiction from Thomas Moore to James Joyce*. Syracuse: Syracuse University Press, 2007.

Nussbaum, Martha C. and Alison L. LaCroix, eds. *Subversion and Sympathy: Gender, Law, and the British Novel*. Oxford: Oxford University Press, 2013.

O'Beirne, Eugene Francis. *A Succinct Account and Accurate Account of the System of Discipline, Education, and Theology, Adopted and pursued in The Popish College of Maynooth.* Hereford: W. H. Vale, 1840.

O'Brien, William. *When We Were Boys.* London: 1890.

O'Connell, Daniel and Richard Lalor Sheil. *A collection of speeches spoken by Daniel O'Connell, esq. and Richard Sheil, esq. on subjects connected with the Catholic question.* Dublin: John Cumming, 1828.

O'Connell, Mrs Morgan John. *Charles Bianconi: A Biography.* London: Chapman and Hall, 1878.

O'Connor, Frank. *The Lonely Voice: A Study of the Short Story.* Cleveland: The World Publishing Co., 1963.

O'Connor, T. P. *Gladstone-Parnell and the Great Irish Struggle. A Complete and Thrilling History of the Fearful Injustice and Oppression inflicted upon the Irish tenants by Landlordism supported by coercive legislation.* Toronto: J. S. Robertson & Bros., 1886.

O'Donoghue, David J. *The Life of William Carleton: being his autobiography and letters, and an account of his life and writings, from the point at which the autobiography breaks off* . . . with an introduction by Mrs Cashel Hoey, 2 vols. London: Downey & Co., 1896.

O'Donovan, John. *The Tribes and Customs of Hy-Many, commonly called O'Kelly's Country,* first published from the Book of Lecan, a manuscript in the library of the Royal Irish Academy, with a translation and notes, and a map of Hy-many. Dublin: Irish Archaeological Society, 1843.

Ó Faoláin, Seán. 'An Autobiography for Authors', *Irish Times* (13 November 1943), 3.

Ó Faoláin, Seán. *The Short Story.* London: Collins, 1948.

Ó Gráda, Cormac. *Black '47 and Beyond: The Great Irish Famine in History, Economy, and Memory.* Princeton, NJ: Princeton University Press, 1999.

Ó Gráda, Cormac. 'Famine, trauma, and memory', *Bealoideas*, 69. Dublin: Folklore of Ireland Society, 2001, 121–43.

Ó Gráda, Cormac. *Ireland: A New Economic History, 1780–1939.* Oxford: Clarendon Press, 1994.

Ó Gráda, Cormac. *Ireland Before and After the Famine*, 2nd edn. Manchester: Manchester University Press, 1993.

O'Maolain, S. 'Alan Bliss, *Spoken English in Ireland, 1600–1740*. Representative texts assembled and analysed,' *English World-Wide*, 1 (1980), 139–40.

Ó Murchadha, Ciarán. *The Great Famine: Ireland's Agony, 1845–1852.* London: Continuum, 2011.

Ó Néill, Pádraig. 'The Fortescues of County Louth', *Journal of the County Louth Archaeological and Historical Society*, 24/1 (1997), 5–20.

O'Toole, Fintan. 'Writing the Boom', *Irish Times* (6 April 2002), 10.

Olmsted, John, ed. *The Victorian Art of Fiction: Essays on the Novel in British Periodicals*, vol. 2. New York: Garland, 1979.

Orel, Harold. *The Victorian Short Story: Development and Triumph of a Literary Genre.* New York: Cambridge University Press, 1986.

Otway, Caesar. *A Tour in Connaught, Comprising Sketches of Clonmacnoise, Joyce Country and Achill*. Dublin: William Curry, 1839.

Overton, Bill. *The Unofficial Trollope*. Sussex/New York: Harvester Press/Barnes & Noble, 1982.

Owenson, Sydney. *Dramatic scenes from real life*. New York: Garland, 1979.

Owenson, Sydney (Lady Morgan). *The Wild Irish Girl, a National Tale*, ed. Kathryn Kirkpatrick. Oxford: Oxford University Press, 1999.

Peel, Sir Robert. *Memoirs by the Right Honourable Sir Robert Peel*. London: Adamant Media Corporation, 2005.

Polhemus, Robert M. 'Being in Love in *Phineas Finn/Phineas Redux*: Desire, Devotion, Consolation', *Nineteenth-Century Literature*, 37/3 (1982), 383–95.

Polhemus, Robert M. *The Changing World of Anthony Trollope*. Berkeley and Los Angeles: University of California Press, 1968.

Poovey, Mary. *Making a Social Body: British Cultural Formation, 1830–1864*. Chicago: University of Chicago Press, 1995.

Pope-Hennessy, James. *Anthony Trollope*. London: Phoenix Press, 1971.

Potvin, John. *Material and Visual Cultures Beyond Male Bonding, 1870–1914: Bodies, Boundaries and Intimacy*. London: Ashgate, 2007.

Potvin, John. 'The Victorian Turkish Bath, Homosocial Health, and Male Bodies on Display', *Journal of Design History*, 18/4 (2005), 319–33.

Pratt, Mary Louise. 'The Short Story. The Long and the Short of It', in Charles E. May, ed. *The New Short Story Theories*. Athens: Ohio University Press, 1994, 91–113.

Quinn, D. B. *The Elizabethans and the Irish*. Ithaca: Cornell University Press, 1966.

Ray, Gordon N., ed. *Thackeray, William Makepeace. Contributions to the Morning Chronicle*. Urbana: University of Illinois Press, 1955.

Renan, Ernest. *The Poetry of the Celtic Races, and Other Essays*. Translated and with an introduction by William Hutchinson. London: Walter Scott, 1896.

Ridden, Jennifer. 'Britishness as an imperial and diasporic identity: Irish elite perspectives, c.1820–1870s', in Peter Gray, ed. *Victoria's Ireland? Irishness and Britishness, 1837–1901*. Dublin: Four Courts Press, 2004, 88–105.

Ridden, Jennifer. *Making Good Citizens: National Identity, Religion and Liberalism among the Irish Elite c.1800–1850*. PhD thesis, University of London, 1998.

Robinson, Lennox. 'Trollope in Ireland: An Open Letter to Winifred Letts', *Irish Times* (17 February 1945), 2.

Robson, Ann and John, eds. *John Stuart Mill, Collected Works*, vol. 25. *Newspaper Writings, December 1847–June 1873*. Toronto: University of Toronto Press, 1986.

Rotunno, Laura. *Postal Plots in British Fiction, 1840–1898: Readdressing Correspondence in Victorian Culture*. London: Palgrave, 2013.

Sadleir, Michael. *Trollope: A Commentary*. London: Oxford University Press, 1961.

Said, Edward. *Orientalism*. New York: Vintage Books, 1979.

Scanlan, Margaret. 'The Limits of Empathy: Trollope's *Castle Richmond*', in George Cusack and Sarah Judieth Goss, eds. *Hungry Words: Images of Famine in the Irish Canon*. Dublin: Irish Academic Press, 2006, 66–76.

Scarpato, Francesca. *Women Writing Ireland, 1798–1921: il popular novel tra identità nazionale e immaginario religioso nelle autrici cattoliche e protestanti*. Unpublished doctoral thesis, University of Bologna, 2012.

Scott, Walter. *The Journal of Sir Walter Scott*, ed. W. E. K. Anderson. Oxford: Clarendon, 1972.

Scott, Sir Walter. *Waverly; or, 'Tis Sixty Years Since*, ed. Claire Lamont. Oxford: Oxford World's Classics, 2008.

Scrope, George Poulett. *How is Ireland to be Governed?* London: James Ridgway, 1846.

Scrope, George Poulett. *How to Make Ireland Self-Supporting; or, Irish Clearances, and Improvement of Waste Lands*. London: James Ridgway, 1848.

Scudder, Horace Elisha. *James Russell Lowell: A Biography*. Boston: Houghton, Mifflin, 1901.

Siddle, Yvonne. 'Anthony Trollope's Representation of the Great Famine', in Peter Gray, ed. *Victoria's Ireland? Irishness and Britishness, 1837–1901*. Dublin: Four Courts Press, 2004, 141–50.

Smalley, Donald, ed. *Trollope: The Critical Heritage*. London: Routledge and Kegan Paul, 1969.

Smith, Adam. *Theory of Moral Sentiments* (1759). Indianapolis: Liberty Classics, 1982.

Smith, Cecil Woodham. *The Great Hunger*. London: Penguin, 1991.

Snell, K. D. M. *The Regional Novel in Britain and Ireland*. Cambridge: Cambridge University Press, 1998.

Snow, C. P. *Anthony Trollope, An Illustrated Biography*. London: Macmillan, 1975.

Somerville, Alexander. *Letters from Ireland during the Famine of 1847*, ed. K. D. M. Snell. Dublin: Irish Academic Press, 1994.

Stebbins, Lucy Poate and Richard Poate. *The Trollopes: The Chronicle of a Writing Family*. New York: Columbia University Press, 1945.

Stevenson, Lionel. 'Trollope As a Recorder of Verbal Usage', *Trollopian*, 3/2 (September 1948), 119–25.

Stone Donald, D. 'Trollope as a Short Story Writer', *Nineteenth-Century Fiction*, 31/1 (June 1976), 26–47.

Super, R. H. *The Chronicler of Barsetshire: A Life of Anthony Trollope*. Ann Arbor: University of Michigan Press, 1988, 62.

Sutherland, John. 'Introduction' to Anthony Trollope, *An Eye for An Eye*, ed. John Sutherland. New York: Oxford University Press, 1992.

Sutherland, John. 'Introduction' to *Early Short Stories by Anthony Trollope*, ed. John Sutherland. Oxford: Oxford University Press, 1994.

Sutherland, John. *The Stanford Companion to Victorian Fiction*. Stanford: Stanford University Press, 1990.

Swift, Jonathan. *The Prose Works of Jonathan Swift,* ed. Temple Scott, 12 vols. London: Bell, 1903.

Swift, Jonathan. 'The Story of the Injured Lady', *The Prose Works of Jonathan Swift,* ed. Temple Scott, 12 vols. London: Bell, 1903.

Swift, Roger and Sheridan Gilley, eds. *The Irish in the Victorian City.* London: Routledge, Kegan & Paul, 1985.

Terry, R. C. *Anthony Trollope: The Artist in Hiding.* Basingstoke: Macmillan, 1977.

Terry, R. C. *Oxford Reader's Companion to Trollope.* Oxford: Oxford University Press, 1999.

Terry, R. C. 'Three Lost Chapters of Trollope's First Novel', *Nineteenth-Century Fiction,* 27 (1972), 74–8.

Thackeray, William Makepeace. *Critical Reviews, Tales, Various Essays, Letters, Sketches, Etc. with A Life of the Author* by Leslie Stephen and a Bibliography. New York and London: Harper & Brothers Publishers, 1899.

Thackeray, William Makepeace. *The Irish Sketchbook.* New York: Scribner, 1911.

Thelwall, A. S., ed. *Proceedings of the Anti-Maynooth Conference of 1845: With an Historical Introduction, and an Appendix.* London: Seeley, Burnside, 1845. http://www.archive.org/stream/a609499200antiuoft/a609499200antiuoft_djvu.txt.

Tingay, Lance O. 'The Reception of Trollope's First Novel', *Nineteenth-Century Fiction,* 6 (1951), 195–200.

Tingay, Lance O. 'Trollope and the Beverley Election', *Nineteenth-Century Fiction,* 5 (1950), 23–37.

Tóibín, Colm. *The Penguin Book of Irish Fiction.* London: Viking, 1999.

Tomaiuolo, Saverio. *Victorian Unfinished Novels: The Imperfect Page.* Houndmills, Basingstoke: Palgrave Macmillan, 2012.

Tonna, Charlotte Elizabeth. *Irish Recollections.* Dublin: University College Dublin Press, 2004.

Tosh, John. *A Man's Place: Masculinity and the Middle-Class Home in Victorian England.* New Haven: Yale, 2007.

Tracy, Robert. 'Instant Replay: Trollope's *The Landleaguers,* 1883', *Éire-Ireland,* 15 (1980), 30–46.

Tracy, Robert. 'Introduction' to Anthony Trollope, *The Macdermots of Ballycloran.* New York: Oxford University Press, 1989.

Tracy, Robert. 'Trollope redux: the later novels', in Carolyn Dever and Lisa Niles, eds. *The Cambridge Companion to Anthony Trollope.* Cambridge: Cambridge University Press, 2011, 58–70.

Tracy, Robert. *Trollope's Later Novels.* Berkeley and Los Angeles: University of California Press, 1978.

Tracy, Robert. '"The Unnatural Ruin": Trollope and Nineteenth-Century Fiction', *Nineteenth-Century Fiction,* 37 (1982), 358–82.

Tracy, Thomas. *Irishness and Womanhood in Nineteenth-Century British Writing.* London: Ashgate, 2009.

Trevor, William. 'Introduction' to Anthony Trollope, *The Kellys and the O'Kellys*, ed. W. J. McCormack. New York: Oxford University Press, 1982.

Trollope, Thomas Adolphus. *What I Remember*. London: Richard Bentley, 1887.

Trumpener, Katie. *Bardic Nationalism: The Romantic Novel and the British Empire*. Princeton, NJ: Princeton University Press, 1997.

Turner, Mark W. *Trollope and the Magazines: Gendered Issues in Mid-Victorian Britain*. London: Macmillan, 2000.

Ua Broin, Liam. 'A south-west Dublin glossary. A selection of south-west county Dublin words, idioms and phrases', *Béaloideas*, 14 (1944), 162–86.

Van Dam, F. 'Character and the Career: Anthony Trollope's *Phineas Finn* and the Rhetoric of the Victorian State', *English Text Construction*, 2/1 (2009), 91–110.

Walpole, Hugh. *Anthony Trollope*. London: Macmillan, 1928.

Watt, George. *The Fallen Woman in the Nineteenth-Century English Novel*. London and Canberra: Croom Helm, 1984, 41–96.

Weber, Max. *The Vocation Lectures: Science As a Vocation, Politics As a Vocation*, ed. David S. Owen, Tracy B. Strong, and Rodney Livingstone. Indianapolis: Hackett, 2004.

Welch, Robert. *Changing States: Transformation in Modern Irish Writing*. London: Routledge, 1993.

Welch, Robert, ed. *The Oxford Companion to Irish Literature*. Oxford: Clarendon Press, 1996.

Whelan, Kevin. 'Writing Ireland: Reading England', in Leon Litvack and Glenn Hooper, eds., *Ireland in the Nineteenth Century: Regional Identity*. Dublin: Four Courts Press, 2000, 185–98.

White, Arnold, ed. *The Letters of S.G.O.;* a series of letters on public affairs written by the Rev. Lord Sidney Godolphin Osborne and published in *The Times,* 1844–1888. London: Griffith, Farran, Okeden & Welsh, 1890.

White, Gertrude M. 'Truth or Consequences: the Real World of Trollope's Melodrama', *English Studies*, 64/6 (December 1983), 491–502.

White, Terence de Vere. 'Introduction' to Anthony Trollope, *The Kellys and O'Kellys*. London: Trollope Society edition, 1992.

White, Timothy J. 'Modeling the Origins and Evolution of Postcolonial Politics: The Case of Ireland', *Postcolonial Text*, 3/3 (2007), 1–13.

Whitty, E. M. *History of the Session 1852–3: A Parliamentary Retrospect*. London: 1853.

Wilson, Ben. *The Making of Victorian Values: Decency & Dissent in Britain: 1789–1837*. New York: Penguin Press, 2007.

Wittig, E. W. 'Significant revisions in Trollope's *The Macdermots of Ballycloran*', *Notes and Queries*, 218 (1972), 90–1.

Wittig, E. W. 'Trollope's Irish Fiction', *Éire-Ireland*, 9/3 (Fall 1974), 97–118.

Wolff, Robert Lee. 'Introduction' to Anthony Trollope, *An Eye for an Eye*, 2 vols. New York: Garland, 1979.

Yeats, W. B. *Uncollected Prose by W.B. Yeats*, vol. 1, ed. John P. Frayne. London: Macmillan, 1970.

Young, Robert. *Colonial Desire: Hybridity in Theory, Culture and Race*. New York: Routledge, 1995.

Index